P9-AFI-142

Sea Struck

Sea Struck

W. H. Bunting

Martha's Vineyard Historical Society
Edgartown, Massachusetts

New Bedford Whaling Museum
New Bedford, Massachusetts

Published and Distributed by
Tilbury House, Publishers
Gardiner, Maine

Tilbury House, Publishers
2 Mechanic Street
Gardiner, Maine 04345
800–582–1899 • www.tilburyhouse.com

Martha's Vineyard Historical Society
Po Box 1310, 59 School Street
Edgartown, Massachusetts 02539
508-627-4441 • www.marthasvineyardhistory.org

New Bedford Whaling Museum
18 Johnny Cake Hill
New Bedford, Massachusetts 02740
508–997–0046 • www.whalingmuseum.org

First Printing: September 2004

Cataloging-in-Publication Data
Bunting, William Henry, 1945-
Sea struck / W.H. Bunting.— 1st ed.
p. cm.
Includes bibliographical references and index.
ISBN 0-88448-265-0 (hardcover : alk. paper)
1. Merchant marine—Massachusetts—biography. 2. Swift, Rodman, 1880- 3. Besse, Frank. 4. Allen, Carleton, 1880- 5. Square-riggers—Massachusetts—History—19th century. I. Title.
VK139.B86 2004
387.5'092'2744—dc22 2004009109

Jacket and text designed on Crummett Mountain by Edith Allard, Somerville, Maine
Layout by Nina DeGraff, Basil Hill Graphics, Somerville, Maine
Editing and production by Jennifer Bunting and Barbara Diamond
Scanning services by Integrated Composition Systems, Spokane, Washington
Printing and binding by Maple Vail, Kirkwood, New York
Jackets printed by the John P. Pow Company, South Boston, Massachusetts

10 9 8 7 6 5 4 3 2

For Agnes and Sally Swift

patient teachers, loyal sisters, devoted daughters.

Contents

PART *Four*

TOD SWIFT

FOREWORD

SOME THREE DECADES AGO, William H. Bunting, a young commercial fisherman just out of college, published his first book. The book's title was *Portrait of a Port,* and the book was then and remains today the best photographic history of maritime Boston in the period from the early 1850s to the eve of World War I.

The images reproduced in *Portrait of a Port,* many by such nineteenth-century masters as Henry Peabody, Baldwin Coolidge, and N. L. Stebbins, give the book distinction in visual terms. The extended captions are no less valuable and remarkable. They reveal an intimate knowledge of seafaring and of Boston's maritime past that seems almost uncanny coming from a writer born so long after the events he describes. As well as being wide-ranging and authoritative, Bunting's text is witty and beautifully written. It is the work of a sailor-scholar for whom the sea is a source of perpetual wonder and historical research a perpetual delight.

Although Bunting has Nantucket (as well as Maine) maritime roots and has sailed the waters of Vineyard Sound and Buzzards Bay, he never met Captain Rodman Swift (1880–1959), whose journal of a hard voyage before the mast in the Standard Oil Company four-masted bark *Astral* in 1904–05 is the inspiration for *Sea Struck*. For that matter he never met Frank Besse or Carleton Allen, whose shipboard journals add so richly to this evocation of turn-of-the-century American commercial sail. But Bunting understands, it seems instinctively, the character traits, the familial and geographic influences, and the alchemy of wind, water, and tide that produce the compulsion to seek a life at sea. Just as important, at the age of twenty Bunting made a world voyage as first mate of a barkentine and knows something of the rewards and penalties such a life entails.

All this Bunting does in *Sea Struck* without in any way slighting the story of New Bedford in the afterglow of its fabulous whaling prosperity; or Maine in its last years as a prodigious builder of wooden (and then of steel) sailing ships; or the complex and arcane (and baroquely intertwined) traditions and techniques by which large sailing vessels are managed under way and in port, fully laden and in ballast, in storm and in calm. As for the account of the destruction by volcano and tidal wave of the East Indian port of Anjer in 1883, it may be merely a footnote to the later shipboard experiences of three sea-struck young men from Massachusetts, but it will, I promise, leave the reader stunned and shaken.

At the heart of *Sea Struck* are, of course, the journals kept by Frank Besse, Carleton Allen, and Rodman Swift—and the extraordinary photographs taken by Allen. Given the closeness in age and experience of the three men, it should follow that their narratives would be similar, even repetitive. They are not. Each writer responded very differently to his shipboard situation, just as each sailed with very different masters and mates and crewmen. Yet for all these differences, the three left their ships nearly as sea struck as when they first set sail. One, Rodman Swift, later retired from a business career as a relatively young man and spent the balance of his days on or near his little schooner yacht *Tyche* and the island of Martha's Vineyard.

I first encountered Captain Swift and *Tyche* (and *Tyche*'s even more diminutive dory) in the spring of 1948 or 1949, when they were outfitting at my family's boatyard in Padanaram for the summer at Menemsha on Martha's Vineyard. There, clad in his trademark dungarees, blue work shirt, wool watch cap, and moccasins, Swift would be at work on *Tyche* or talking with Uncle Waldo Howland or one of the yard crew—or simply taking in the scene as he smoked his ever-present briar pipe. When Captain Swift was having a smoke, I could generally prevail on him to spin a yarn. Sometimes, though not often, the yarn concerned an incident aboard the bark *Astral*.

Although Captain Swift was a near New Bedford contemporary of my Grandfather Howland, and shared with Grandpa a virtually identical social, educational, and economic background, the resemblance ended there. Where Grandpa was outspoken, mercurial, quick to anger (and to laugh), ever restless, a martinet, and a firm believer in shined brass, Swift was gentle and deliberate in speech, steady and moderate in manner and habits, slow to anger, unassertive, and a devotee of linseed oil and galvanized hardware. Where Grandpa cultivated acquaintance among the high and mighty, Swift shunned it.

Grandpa did his yachting in style in a Concordia yawl with the help of a professional skipper. He flew the burgees of the New Bedford and New York Yacht Clubs. Captain Swift sailed mostly alone or with his daughters, on a tiny baldheaded schooner from which the only pennant that flew was a blue nighthawk, or night pennant.

Yet these two major role models of my boyhood were lifelong friends. Theirs was a kinship based on a frank recognition of how greatly their paths had diverged—and on a mutual recognition of their love of the sea. Their bond, symbolized by the fading tattoos that both men carried to their graves, is a bond that Bill Bunting shares with them and with who knows how many tens of thousands of sea-struck souls. It is an affliction from which the sufferer may try, but never truly wishes, to recover.

Sea Struck is a sweeping narrative of adventure afloat. It offers an exciting and exacting new perspective on the twilight of American commercial sail. It includes a gallery of powerful, unforgettable images of life before the mast.

Jointly published by the Martha's Vineyard Historical Society, the New Bedford Whaling Museum, and Tilbury House, *Sea Struck* is a splendid new chapter in the history of American seafaring. It will take a place of honor next to William H. Bunting's pioneering *Portrait of a Port* in maritime libraries throughout the English-speaking world.

Llewellyn Howland III

INTRODUCTION

The Journey Ahead Into Voyages Past.

ALL THE WORLD'S A STAGE, yet most of the world is awash in water. While humans are normally terrestrial by nature, some are sea struck—possessed from an early age by a fascination with ships, boats, and maritime affairs in general that is, in the severest cases, so ingrained that it surely must be genetic.

Rodman Swift, born in 1880 in the great whaling town New Bedford, Massachusetts, was one such hopeless case. Although "Captain" Swift did not make the sea a career, he surely would have excelled had he chosen that path. A sailor of great ability and a recognized maritime authority, he was also a most singular individual who all of his life placed conviction above convention.

This book had its beginnings when Sally Swift, Rodman Swift's younger daughter, broached the idea of publishing the diary kept by her father in 1904–05 when serving as ordinary seaman aboard the steel American four-masted bark *Astral.* The diary, or personal log, was to be accompanied by a brief biography. However, in often unexpected and even wonderful ways, one link led to another until at last this book emerged. In it, Swift's account is joined by those of two other genteel, sea-struck young Bay Staters, Frank Besse and Carleton Allen, who also sailed aboard latter-day American square-riggers. And, truth be told, we will board some other ships along with some other observers for briefer passages as well.

In the decade before the Civil War the American deep-water, square-rigged merchant marine was the world's finest, representing a triumph of enterprise, ability, and daring. The zenith of its glory is often held to be the era of the California clipper, from 1850 to 1860. The full-blown California clipper evolved from decades of American supremacy in the rugged North Atlantic packet trade, and from the smaller, swift clippers of the China trade. The California clippers, and even more impressive clippers built for trade with Australia, marked a major advance over ships that had come before and left a strong stamp on the ships that followed.

The builders, owners, and commanders of this great fleet—most were New Englanders—emerged from a remarkable geographic, economic, and cultural confluence originating in the colonial era and coming to flower with the new republic. Captain Arthur Clark, a clipper captain and historian whose distinguished seafaring career began when he was a boy sailing toy boats on the Frog Pond in Boston's Public Garden, wrote:

> TAKEN AS A CLASS, American sea captains and mates were perhaps the finest body of real sailors that the world has ever seen.... They were the first to establish discipline in the merchant service, and their ships were the envy and despair of merchants and captains of other nations.[1]

The strict discipline lauded by Clark, oftentimes absolutely necessary, also led to instances of outrageous abuse and criminal brutality. Some of the most notorious instances—surely involving criminal, certifiable psychopaths—occurred in the final decades of the American square-rigged marine. The first task of the historian is to identify the commonplace, and how commonplace the use of brutality or even hazing was aboard American ships is one reason why fresh, firsthand accounts of life aboard these ships are of special interest.[2]

The decline of the American deep-water fleet began shortly before the Civil War and was very much exacerbated by the war. After the war, British steamships and sailing ships of iron and steel—almost all American sailing ships were of wood—and America's preoccupation with westward expansion, combined to finish off the American square-rigger. It is noteworthy, however, that even during the half century of the fleet's demise the lofty ships of the American marine were yet considered to be the finest of their type ever built, and to be among the best kept and smartest-handled ships on the seas.

Our fascination with the ancient and once-routine business of global wind-powered transport—among the most important endeavors of man—only grows with the passage of time. For many boys and young men from coastal New England (and also the Maritime Provinces), going to sea was long a common response to social and economic circumstances. While firsthand accounts of going to sea comprise a large genre of nautical literature, the vast majority were written long after the fact. Our three diarists, on the other hand, were writing in the moment, allowing us to eavesdrop as a storied way of life drew to a close far faster than many participants realized.

All of our diarists were financially well off, well educated, and well connected. Two sailed aft as cabin passengers, rather than as sailors before the mast. While none aspired to a seafaring career, their experiences at sea marked them for life, ranking among their very proudest achievements.

History—or at least history that is worth pursuing—is rarely a simple tale easily told. This book is a construction of connections, some more obvious than others. The successful reader will have remembered who was who, minded well the sailing directions, and kept an eye on the compass.

Frank Besse, the oldest of the three diarists, voyaged from 1881 to 1883 aboard the full-rigged ship *William J. Rotch* of New Bedford, a ship named for Rodman Swift's grandfather. Carleton Allen—like Swift, he was born in 1880—in 1898 sailed aboard the bark *Guy C. Goss* of Wareham, Massachusetts; Wareham, located near New Bedford, was Frank Besse's hometown, and the *Goss*, like the *Rotch*, belonged to the fleet of fine ships built for the order of Wareham native Captain William Besse. William Besse—Frank Besse's second cousin—was an important American maritime figure whose story has heretofore never been told.

Most of Besse's fleet was built at the great Kennebec River shipbuilding town of Bath, Maine, also the builder of *Astral*. *Astral* and her sisters were the final American square-riggers of consequence to be built.

Captain Walter Mallett, with whom Carleton Allen went to sea aboard the *Guy C. Goss* in 1898, was a Kennebecker who had himself first gone to sea as a sea-struck lad in a Besse bark. Allen, equipped with a camera, rejoined Mallett in 1904 aboard the steel, British-built American four-masted bark (or barque) *Hawaiian Isles*.[3] Supplementing Allen's fine photographs are the outstanding images made in 1905 aboard the very similar British-flag four-masted barque *Queen Margaret* by Fred H. Taylor, a New Jersey high school boy.

Captain Francis Stone—Rodman Swift's Uncle Frank—who also went to sea in a Besse bark and later commanded two fine members of the Besse fleet, provides a further tie with Besse and also New Bedford. Frank Stone was Rodman Swift's lifelong friend and mentor, and it was Stone who pulled the strings that placed Swift aboard *Astral*. (Captain Jonathan Dunham, *Astral*'s master, emerges as an intriguing character as well.)

Only Rodman Swift's diary appears in full. Only Swift sailed before the mast. To Swift is given the starring role, and his story opens and also closes the book.

A housekeeping matter: A "ship" can be either a vessel of not inconsiderable size—particularly if oceangoing—or else a "full-rigged ship," i.e., a sailing vessel with at least three masts all of which are fully rigged with square sails. Sailors freely use "ship" in both senses, even in the same sentence, with no apology or explanation.

And one more thing. Whatever else this book is or is not, it isn't exactly a conventional book. For one thing, the notes for some chapters all but outweigh the text—the other choices were either to annoy and discourage the casual reader with speed bumps or else cast away into the dark abyss material believed to be worthy of repetition or preservation. Readers are free to delve deeper or not as they wish.

1. Arthur H. Clark, *The Clipper Ship Era* (New York: G. P. Putnam & Sons, 1910), pp. 123–24.

2. Admittedly the examination of the commonplace inspires little enthusiasm among trade publishers of maritime history, who are much more interested in the rare voyages in which, perhaps, a ship's company ate one another.

3. "Bark" was the more common American spelling; "barque" the British.

Acknowledgments

Agnes Swift wanted Tod Swift's log be published; Sally Swift made that happen, and a good deal more as well. I am grateful to both for providing me with this opportunity.

Louie Howland, good and steady friend of so many, got me together with Sally, and then fashioned our happy alliance with Matthew Stackpole of the Martha's Vineyard Historical Society, Michael Jehle of the New Bedford Whaling Museum, and Jennifer Bunting of Tilbury House, Publishers. My thanks to all.

Leonard Bachelder, Bruce Besse, James Jung, Richard Mallett, Anne Mallett, and Harry Stone all provided important family journals, letters, photos, and stories and information. Bob Birely's generous and ingenious assistance in locating certain key information was also critical.

For various and sundry deeds—not a few of them of great importance to this effort—my sincere thanks to Edith Allard, John Arrison, Lisbet Bailey, Charlie Burden, Edward Coffin, Knight Coolidge, Diane Cooper, Lorna Condon, George Decas, Catherine DeTaub, Barb Diamond, Joan Druett, Michael Dyer, Paul Edgerly, Thornton Gibbs, Captain Harold Huycke, Paula Johnson, Paul Johnston, William Lafferty, Lydia Lauderdale, Captains Doug and Linda Lee, Tad Lhamon, Tad Lyford, Cathy Matteo, Ted Miles, Rob Napier, Andrew Nesdall, Nicholas North, Ann Pappi, Captain Lew Parker, Everett Poole, Laura Saunders, Earle G. Shettleworth, Jr., Captain Norman Smith, Renny Stackpole, Doug Stover, Paul Stubing, David Warr, members of the Marhst-L maritime history group, and surely others whose names have slipped my mind.

Institutional sources of images and information included the Admiral Digby Library and Historical Society, Penobscot Marine Museum, the San Francisco Maritime National Historic Park, the Wareham Historical Society, the Peabody-Essex Museum, the Harvard University Archives, the Maine Historic Preservation Commission, and the Smithsonian Institution, along with the New Bedford Whaling Museum and the Martha's Vineyard Historical Society. Particular thanks are due the Maine Maritime Museum for use of the resources of the library, and for Librarian Nathan Lipfert's many favors. Also due special note are the unflappable Jill Bouck of the Martha's Vineyard Historical Society, Susan Pizzolato of the Wareham Free Library, and Valerie Scholey of the Admiral Digby Library and Historical Society.

W. H. Bunting

Part One

The Setting and the Ships

Chapter 1

New Bedford, and the Swifts, Rotches, Rodmans, Etc.

Introducing Rodman Swift's Hometown and His Illustrious and Thoroughly Entangled Family Tree.

New Bedford, Massachusetts, and neighboring Fairhaven, together straddling the mouth of the brief Acushnet River on the western shore of Massachusetts's Buzzard's Bay, arose on land purchased in the late 1700s by foresighted Nantucket whalers who realized that their island port was inadequate. During the whaling industry's period of great expansion following the War of 1812, New Bedford's fleet far outstripped that of Mother Nantucket, peaking, in 1857, at 324 vessels. The American whale fishery of the early 1800s was of global economic, diplomatic, cultural, scientific, and ecological importance, and encompassed, in ample measure, all the best and the worst aspects of human nature.

Herman Melville's description of New Bedford in *Moby Dick* is readily available; those of Charles Nordoff and George Brown Goode are less so. About 1850, young Nordhoff, newly arrived and seeking a berth on a New Bedford whaler, took the measure of the town:

> For a place in which so large a business is carried on as here, "Bedford" is remarkably still. At the distance of three squares from the water side, one would never guess that he stood within the bounds of a city which ranks in commercial importance the seventh seaport in the Union, and whose ships float upon every ocean. A more quiet and rural looking place than that portion of the city beyond the immediate business limits, it would be difficult to imagine. And a more beautifully laid out or better kept city I never saw. It was now mid-summer, and the spacious mansions, embowered in green foliage, which border the principal streets, looked really enchanting to my eyes, long wearied with monotonous salt water views; while a walk up the well-shaded streets was like a trip into the country. New Bedford well deserves the name of one of the most beautiful cities in New England.

The business portion of the town is confined within a comparatively limited space. One long street, running parallel with wharves, is almost exclusively devoted to the shops of the outfitters, who play a far from unimportant part in the drama of whaling....

Passing by the boarding houses, we come to the wharves, along which, fronting the water side, are the warehouses and counting rooms of various ship owners and dealers in oil, bone, and spermaceti. These are scattered along, without regular connection, the scene varied here and there by a blacksmith's or cooper's shop, which two branches of industry seem to be in a peculiarly flourishing condition hereabouts.

Looking down to the water now, we see a few straggling wharves, between which lie numerous vessels in various states of readiness and unreadiness for departure on their long voyages.

Here lies a huge hull, careened over on the flat, her exposed side and bottom being thoroughly resheathed and new coppered, dozens of men crawling all over her vast bilge, sawing, fitting, and hammering. Yonder is an old hulk, whose topsides have been torn away, to make room for new ones, by which she will become almost as strong as a new vessel. Here, at the wharf, is a craft in a more forward state; her masts are now being put in, and as we are looking at her, a general shout proclaims that the main-mast has just been stepped. And a little farther on we see a rusty-looking old tub, just being converted into a saucy clipper by the aid of a plentiful application of paint.

All is life, and wherever the eye rests the scene is one of ceaseless activity. Yet there appears none of the hurrying, bustle, and in particular, none of the noise which is a disagreeable attendant on all business about the wharves of other large cities. In this, more than aught else, New Bedford differs from any other American seaport....

At every few steps, all locomotion is hindered or obstructed by long tiers of huge, dirty casks, redolent of train oil, while ever and anon, one stumbles over a bundle of whalebone, or brings up against a pile of harpoons, boat spades, and other implements for dealing death to leviathan—all of which proclaim the calling of the place. With here and there a patched, weather-beaten whaleboat, turned bottom up upon the shore, and occasional pile of oars, the view is tolerably complete.[1]

Thirty-odd years later, Special Agent Goode reported in the 1880 *Census*:

New Bedford is built on high ground, and the cross streets, running east and west, have an easy slope, affording a fine view of the Acushnet River and the harbor with its forest of masts of whaling vessels. Fairhaven on the east and Buzzard's Bay in the distance on

> the south, make the view complete. New Bedford…in proportion to its population of 26,845…is said to be the richest city in the United States.… Various causes have led to a decline in [the whaling] industry, among them were the panic of 1857, the destruction of thirty vessels by Confederate cruisers during the late war, and the loss, in 1871, of twenty-four vessels in the Arctic Ocean. Another and perhaps the chief cause of a decline was the substitution of cotton-seed oil and petroleum for whale oil.… The whaling fleet of New Bedford at present numbers 123 vessels, aggregating 31,568.83 tons, valued, with outfits, at $2,414,000, and manned by 3,336 men.[2]

It would take more than forty years to fully extinguish New Bedford whaling. Meanwhile, wealthy New Bedforders, taking advantage of local atmospheric conditions conducive to the weaving of cotton, to the availability of cheap waterborne coal from mid-Atlantic ports, and to a ready supply of immigrant (mostly French-Canadian) labor, built miles of textile mills at New Bedford and neighboring Fall River. Soot from mill stacks settled alike on the flowered gardens of mansions and threadbare washing hung from tenements, and the once beautiful harbor grew rank with pollution, but the old order held.[3]

Rodman Swift, known all his life as "Tod," was a son of two prominent New Bedford families, the Swifts and the Rotches, and a cousin to several others, including the Rodmans. Tod's mother, Sarah, was a Rotch, pronounced "Roach," and in New Bedford, that said it all. No family was more closely associated with—or had profited more handsomely from—the rise of the Nantucket and New Bedford whaling fisheries and from the growth of New Bedford. Theirs is one of the great American family sagas.

Swifts had been settled in Dartmouth long before the arrival of Rotches. Tod's grandfather, William Cole Nye Swift, beginning in the 1850s, became a leading agent of whaleships and was senior member of the firms Swift & Perry and, later, Swift & Akin. He had also been interested in the "live oaking" business, providing southern live oak ship timber to northern shipbuilders, in which the Swift family was prominent.[4]

New Bedford's whaleship agents, who managed the great fleet, were masters of practical and pecuniary detail. As a group they have stood accused of habitually taking advantage of persons—especially green recruits—less well informed than they. Clifford Ashley's description of them was more charitable:

> THE WHALESHIP "AGENT" of New Bedford combined the offices of shipping-master, outfitter, and owner. In this way he was obligated to himself to fill each office fairly, since the skimping of one job resulted

in injury to himself in one of his other capacities. He shipped the best men and officers he could obtain, and bought the most suitable provisions, since this was the best insurance for an economical and successful voyage.... Many New Bedford agents maintained their own stores and outfitting establishments. Outfitters were always referred to locally as "sharks." In spite of this name, they conducted the cheapest shops at which to buy their own sort of goods. Their range of stock was not wide, and their turnover was tremendous.... Without doubt the sailor sometimes paid dearly for his outfit, when the outfitter was at the same time the agent, and thrift got the better of him.[5]

Frederick Swift, Tod's father, after graduating from Harvard in 1874, joined William Swift's business. For several years in the mid-eighties, just as young Tod was at the age when the foundation relationship between a father and son is formed, Frederick was absent much of the time, working in San Francisco (then the center of American whaling) at the firm of Wright & Bowne.[6] When Swift returned to New Bedford he became associated with American Car & Foundry, and later, a Boston rail car wheel manufacturer. At the time of his death in 1915 at the age of sixty-three, he had been appointed deputy collector for the IRS.[7] An expert yachtsman and the consummate clubman, Frederick was a commodore of the New Bedford Yacht Club and held other social memberships commensurate with being a hail-fellow-well-met of New Bedford's ruling class. He also drank too much.

Sarah Rotch, the daughter of the richest man in a town of very rich men, grew up in the largest mansion in a town of large mansions. Her ancestor Joseph Rotch, a cordwainer, or leatherworker, moved to Nantucket about 1725, soon becoming a prosperous ship owner. In 1765 he purchased a large portion of the districts of the town of Dartmouth which would become New Bedford and Fairhaven, naming the village which sprang up "Bedford." There he built the ship *Dartmouth,* of Boston Tea Party fame. Also at the Tea Party was the brig *Beaver*, owned by his son William, who had by then become the richest man on Nantucket and would be the most famous member of the family.

In 1775, at the outbreak of the Revolution, Nantucket's whale fleet numbered 150 vessels. The isolated island's pacifist Quaker plea for neutral status—William Rotch was chief spokesman—brought grief from both sides, as the islanders, caught "between the upper and nether millstones of war...were quite ground to powder."[8] At least 134 Nantucket vessels were lost to the British, with 1,200 men lost or captured. There were 202 widows in 800 families.[9] The whaling industry was all but ruined. William Rotch himself lost over $60,000, yet the first vessel to fly the American flag in English waters after peace was declared was his brig *Bedford,* loaded with 487 butts of whale oil.

Before the war London's streets had been illuminated with American sperm oil, but afterwards this vital market was closed by high tariffs. John Adams observed to William Pitt that it was surprising that the English would prefer "darkness, and consequent robberies, burglaries, and murders in your streets.... The lamps around Grosvenor Square [burning vegetable oil]...are dim by midnight, whereas our oil would burn bright till 9 o'clock in the morning...."[10]

Domestic markets having been disrupted as well, Rotch, an internationalist far in advance of his time, attempted to relocate the business to England. Thwarted by political opposition, in 1787 he moved operations instead to Dunkirk, France, a decision credited with preserving Nantucket's whaling industry.

Despite the oddness of a colony of drably cloaked Quakers coexisting in colorful, dissolute Catholic France, the expatriate Nantucketers prospered until the onset of the French Revolution. During the Reign of Terror the outspoken William did well just to keep his head; in 1793, two days before the king lost *his* head, William and the remaining Americans escaped to England aboard a Rotch ship.[11] Son Benjamin would remain in Britain, establishing a whale oil business at Milford Haven, Wales, on the estate of Sir William Hamilton, husband of Lady Hamilton, Nelson's mistress.[12]

Old William Rotch retired to New Bedford, living until 1828 and age ninety-four. An 1825 portrait shows a square-shouldered, straight-backed man looking much younger than his years, with all-encompassing eyes, dark eyebrows, a long nose, and firm mouth apparently still containing real teeth. His high, broad dome of a forehead is yet evident in some descendants. At New Bedford, William's sons, sons-in-law, nephews, and grandsons would carry on the family tradition of doing very well, thank you, by doing business shrewdly and—reportedly—honestly. Community pillardom came as part of the package.

The relationship between morality and the business of whaling was complex. In 1770 William Rotch emancipated the slaves on Nantucket and few industries became more thoroughly integrated, notwithstanding charges in later years that black and also Native Americam whalemen (Wampanoag Indians from Martha's Vineyard were skilled whalers, much sought-after) were swindled worse even than were white greenhorns.[13] During boom times from the 1830s to 1860, few industries more systematically exploited its workers or, indeed, its basic resource, the hapless whale. At the same time, business dealings between the industry plutocrats were dependent on personal honor and credit, underscored by a heritage of religious probity, and backed by strong family ties and standards.[14]

While there can be no denying the considerable financial risks taken by owners—although usually risks were spread out through partial ownership of multiple vessels—these investments often paid off most handsomely. Melville described the great houses built along New Bedford's County Street—which runs imperiously atop and athwart the lesser streets running down to the wharves—as having been "harpooned and dragged up hither from the bottom of the sea." Quakers, for all their rejection of extravagant dress and unseemly conduct, offered no apologies for making lots of money or for spending it on trophy houses—indeed, who else could afford to illuminate mansions so economically? Yet the fireplace mantels in the great houses were spare and of wood—showy, polished marble replacements would be added by a generation to come.

The age of extravagance began after 1821, when a great schism resulted in the expulsion of a number of leading and theologically liberal members of the congregation, including Rotches, from the New Bedford Society of Friends. Ill blows the wind which profits no one, and the Quakers' loss was the Unitarians' gain. Coats of gray gave way to coats of blue with gilt buttons, music and dancing were rampant, "thee" and "thy" became "you" and "your."[15] The young, however, would continue to be educated at the old Friends School, one of whose founders was William Rotch, Jr., and certain identifiable vestiges of Quaker values persist to this day in descendants many generations removed from any formal association with the religion.

The sole remaining intact example of New Bedford's grand whaling mansions is the stately, Italianate-style "Rotch-Duff," i.e., William Rotch, Jr., house, built on County Street in 1834. Its neighbor, the pillared William Rotch Rodman house, is now a den of lawyers. Also on County Street, the Wamsutta Club occupies the much reduced remains, on the drastically reduced grounds, of the William J. Rotch mansion. "William J." (1819–93)—a great-grandson of old William, and Tod Swift's grandfather—inherited this house from his very rich uncle, James Arnold, who had built on a vast lot inherited from William Rotch, his wife's grandfather. William J. enlarged Arnold's house upwards and outwards and filled it with nine children and "all the home treasures that wealth can procure."[16]

William J. had grown up in the great ark of a Federal mansion which, with its gardens, occupied a full city block next door to the aforementioned mansion of William Rotch Rodman. There was also at least one William Rodman Rotch—the intermingling of Rotches and Rodmans in business, fortunes, matrimony, and neighborhoods began back on Nantucket, with three Rotches marrying three Rodmans in one generation.

Other great houses belonging to members of this inbred clan included the pillared temple of Charles W. Morgan, iron founder and whaling merchant (the last surviving whale ship is named for him). One of three Morgan siblings to marry Rodmans (a sister married a Rotch), several of their children married Rotches as well. In due course, Rotches would marry Rotches as cousins married cousins, double cousins married double cousins, and cousins married cousins' children. Further confusing the issue (no pun intended) was the practice of continuing certain surnames—by 1900 there had been christened, among the Rotches, more than a dozen Williams, five Elizabeths, seven Francises, six Josephs, and so on. The Rodman clan included five Samuels.[17]

William J.—Tod's grandfather, it may be recalled—married two of Charles W. Morgan's daughters (he married the second after the death of the first). A man of culture and the richest man in town, he was New Bedford's second mayor, founder and president of the New Bedford Cordage Company, a banker, president of a large textile mill, the owner of considerable real estate and "vessel property," a director of nearly every New Bedford business of consequence, and an amply rewarded backer of the revolutionary McKay shoe machine.[18] His estate was substantially reduced by a combination of financial panic and the tragic and costly failure of a trusted associate in the textile industry, its remains being divided nine ways.[19]

Young Tod Swift was well familiar with his grandfather's mansion, as with other great houses of the family. However, not only would he not have the means to live in such grand style, he never wished to and had no intention of spending his life trying to do so.

The William J. Rotch mansion, County Street, New Bedford, circa 1900.
RODMAN SWIFT COLLECTION.

1. Charles Nordhoff, *Whaling and Fishing* (New York: Dodd, Mead & Co., 1855), pp. 23–25. Nordhoff, being an experienced sailor, had difficulty signing aboard a whaler, since wide-eyed farm boys, easily cowed, molded, and defrauded, were the preferred recruits.

2. George Brown Goode, *The Fisheries and Fishery Industries of the United States, Section II* (Washington, D.C.: U.S. Government Printing Office, 1887), pp. 270–72. In 1877 valuation in real estate was $12,609,200, and in personal property $10,854,900, or a total of $23,464,100. Hartford, Connecticut, is said to have also been a contender for the title.

3. Visitors to New Bedford today hoping to experience firsthand something of the town's old sense of self and wealth are advised to visit, in addition to the Whaling Museum and the Rotch-Duff House, the Free Public Library. A magnificent edifice, it was built as a town hall in 1838 and '39. After 1847 it served as the city hall until a fire in 1906. Disassembled, rebuilt, and enlarged, it has housed the library ever since.

4. This business, which peaked between the end of the American Revolution and the outbreak of the Civil War, involved the annual winter migration of hundreds of "live oakers"—choppers, hewers, and ox-drovers (and oxen)—by schooner from southeastern Massachusetts to the coastal forests of South Carolina, Georgia, and Florida, to "get out"—fell, hew, and haul—live oak ship frame timber. This heavy, rot resistant timber, hewed to patterns, was carried by schooner to northern shipyards. Much went into the construction of whaleships which, despite their often work-worn appearance, were among the most expensively constructed of all merchant vessels. See Virginia Steele Wood, *Live Oaking* (Boston: Northeastern University Press, 1981), pp. 69–87. Northerners were also active getting out white oak frame timber, primarily from the forests of coastal Virginia. This business lasted into the early 1900s, by then having for some time been led by Mainers.

5. Clifford W. Ashley, *The Yankee Whaler* (Boston: Houghton Mifflin Company, 1938), pp. 107–08. New Bedford's best known agent in later years was John Wing of the firm of J. and W. R. Wing, who entered the business in 1856 and decades later was described as yet flapping about the wharves like a crow with a broken wing. In the 1880s George Fred Tilton, a seasoned whaler from Martha's Vineyard, discovered too late that Wing had charged his account $3 for every sewing needle and spool of thread in his kit. The cost of his outfit was $183.15 with the $.15 "added for appearances." Not a single article of clothing fit, aside from an Ulster coat which held too much wind to be worn aloft. When Tilton was paid off in San Francisco—the Wings were by then bi-coastal—he owed for three outfits, surpassing his earnings, which were figured on San Francisco prices, not the higher East Coast prices. Tilton concluded, "It ought to be clear how these old-time ship owners made their fortunes." Captain George Fred Tilton, *"Cap'n George Fred" Himself* (Garden City: Doubleday, Doran, 1929), pp. 96–97.

6. In October 1887 Frederick Swift wrote his wife, "One str. has come in 'full' and a ship has arrived from Ochoitsk. By both of them we have good news from our ships. My two Arctic ships I expect will get very good catches as they were in exactly the right place when the *Orca* left and whales were plenty and the weather fine.... Of course the large catch will make bone very much cheaper but that will be for the good of the biz. as it will bring bone into more general use." Even after whale oil had been largely supplanted by petroleum—although it still held value as a lubricant and as the preferred fuel for railroad lanterns, since it didn't blow out; "whalebone," the springy plankton-filtering slats from the mouths of certain species of whales, remained highly valuable until its market utterly collapsed at

the turn of the century. Its uses were many, including being woven into fine French silk dresses. *San Francisco Examiner*, 12 Nov. 1893. All quoted correspondence here and hereafter from members of Tod's immediate family is from the Captain Rodman Swift Collection, Martha's Vineyard Historical Society, Edgartown, Massachusetts.

7. Zephaniah W. Pease, *History of New Bedford*, Vol. III (New York: Lewis Historical Publishing Co., 1918), pp. 415–17; *Taunton Gazette*, 17 Dec. 1915.

8. Alexander Starbuck, *History of the American Whale Fishery* (Secaucus, N.J.: Castle Books, reprint of 1878 edition, 1989), p. 72.

9. Ibid., p. 77. Rotch put the loss at 200 vessels.

10. Ibid., p. 85.

11. John M. Bullard, *The Rotches* (privately published, New Bedford, 1947), pp. 37, 320. A number of fugitives having stowed away aboard his ship, Rotch distracted suspicious port officials with a lavish spread of food and wine.

12. At Milford Haven the Rotches joined a small colony of Nantucket whalers who had recently relocated from Dartmouth, Nova Scotia, where they had first removed in order to escape the ruinous duty on American sperm oil. About Emma Hamilton, Benjamin Rotch's daughter Eliza recalled, "The weather was very warm when Lady Hamilton was in Milford, and she walked about the town in two garments only, showing her shape most indecently. [She was then pregnant by Nelson]. My mother had resolved to take no notice of Lady Hamilton.... But that bold woman was resolved that it should not be said that Mrs. Rotch would not receive her; so one very warm day...she walked into our drawing-room, where my mother and I were sitting, and greeted us very familiarly. Though I was but a child, I was struck with the coldness of my mother's reception, and wondered that she was not more cordial to such a lovely and fascinating guest." Bullard, *The Rotches,* p. 326. Nantucket, which had supplied 83 captains for the French fishery, supplied 149 captains for the English fishery. Starbuck, *Whale Fishery*, p. 82.

13. Elmo Paul Hohman, *The American Whaleman* (New York: Longmans, Green & Co., 1928), pp. 50–51.

14. A notably jaundiced and dismissive view of the whaling industry, which was then in its final years, is presented in Samuel Eliot Morison's *The Maritime History of Massachusetts* (Cambridge: Houghton Mifflin, 1921). While surely a classic work of wonderfully "wet" history, it would have been greater yet had not Morison inexplicably neglected to mention the Rotches in general, or William Rotch, in particular. It was left to Edouard A. Stackpole in *The Sea-Hunters* (Philadelphia: J. B. Lippencott, 1953), to restore Rotch to his proper place in history. One wonders if Morison was under the sway of Captain Arthur Clark, who wrote: "Whaling is one of the least hazardous, the most commonplace, and, taken altogether about the laziest occupation that human beings have ever been engaged in upon the sea...a 'spouter' was generally regarded among seamen as one of the biggest jokes afloat." Arthur H. Clark, *The Clipper Ship Era* (New York: G. P. Putnam & Sons, 1910), p. 78. On the other hand, whaling captains, as a group, were the best of navigators, for whom the demanding lunar sight was common practice. Their ranks also included highly observant naturalists, pioneering oceanographers, and bold explorers.

15. Daniel Ricketson, *New Bedford of the Past* (Boston: Houghton Mifflin, 1903), p. 53. Mary Rotch (a daughter of William) who became a Unitarian convert, was credited by Ralph Waldo Emerson with having guided the formation of his religious beliefs. She was also a good friend of writer Margaret Fuller, but one of an army of famous people whom various Rotches were associated with or related to.

16. *New Bedford Sunday Standard Times*, 30 May 1937. After Mrs. Rotch's

death in 1917 the estate's vast gardens were subdivided into building lots. The 265-acre Arnold Arboretum, although located in Boston's Jamaica Plain, is yet a manifestation of Arnold's fortune and also the garden envy that once was rampant along County Street.

17. Another town noted for the marriage of cousins was Searsport, Maine, famed for its many captains. Thus was the ownership of vessels kept within the family.

18. Selling rope to whalers was like selling dope to addicts! Whaleships, it might be noted, never switched to wire shrouds, preferring the equalizing stretch of hemp rigging when subjected to the great loads of "cutting in" a whale. The amount of cordage required to outfit a single whale ship—the standing rigging alone of a ship-rigged merchant ship required some 2,000 fathoms of large-circumference rope—was staggering. The McKay shoe machine played an important—and profitable—role in putting the Union army in shoes.

19. Bullard, *The Rotches,* pp. 105–10.

Chapter 2

Young Tod the Sailor

We View Young Tod Growing Up on His Home Waters.

RODMAN "TOD" SWIFT was the youngest of three children, the eldest being Helen, followed by Frederick. At a young age Tod was well familiar with the New Bedford waterfront, yet redolent with whale oil seeping from row upon row of seaweed-covered barrels awaiting a rise in price that never came. Ancient rigged-down hulks and spruced-up active whaleships floated alike in the dirty Acushnet. (Coasting schooners, coastal steamers, tugs, and various small craft patronized the harbor as well.)

Veteran shipwrights of deliberate step, stoop-shouldered sailmakers, tarry-handed riggers, sooty-browed smiths, shifty-eyed outfitters, and ink-stained clerks still manned their respective posts in the famous old waterfront, over whose wharf caplogs untold thousands of men had gone a-whaling. Marine artist Clifford Ashley, a New Bedford boy the same age as Tod but from a different neighborhood (and who, like Tod, also went to sea in 1904, shipping aboard the whaling bark *Sunbeam* to record the fishery's final era) recalled:

> FOR THE FORTUNATE youth of that day the unpoliced ships and grass-grown wharves made a marvelous playground. We learned to swim from the bob-stays of old hulks. We contrived to paddle and row on rafts fashioned of hatch-covers, and used in boarding parties overside. We swarmed over the rigging and slid down the backstays, spun the wheels, and on rainy days gathered in the cabins and played games and pretended one thing and another; and always it was something that smacked of the sea.... There were whole wharves along New Bedford's waterfront that served no purpose save that of a playground, and there was never another like it.[1]

Tod was not a member of Clifford's crew of young cutthroats; the two became good friends only many years later. An undated letter from young Tod to his traveling mother (he was staying with his Grandmother Rotch in the Rotch mansion) suggests that Tod and Clifford would have been fast friends as boys as well:

Old whalers laid up at New Bedford, likely around 1890. At far left, rigged down, is the bark Kathleen, *built at Philadelphia in 1844. The three-masted schooner* Lottie Beard, *center left, built at Fairhaven in 1866, traded to the Azores, carrying supplies out and whale oil back. At right foreground lies the ship* Eliza Adams, *built at Fairhaven in 1835. Astern of her lies the ship* Niger, *built at Rochester, Massachusetts, in 1844. The ancient little schooner* United, *a local maid of all work, lies at the outer wharf. A small coaster, loaded with firewood, is anchored in the stream. Whale oil barrels lie in the foreground; more barrels, covered with seaweed, are fenced in beyond a brick pitch oven.*

RODMAN SWIFT COLLECTION

> THE ACUSHNET MILLS burnt down yesterday...one of the boilers exploded and knocked tar out of everything and set the mill on fire. Two alarms were rung and we hustled down but had hard work getting inside the ropes on account of the cops but we got by them and had fine sport. Two men were killed by the explosion and many injured. We were on hand when they found them and they were fine looking sights (one without a head) and they were buried under about four feet of brick...a piece of the boiler six feet square weighing half a ton was sent a quarter of a mile and landed on the roof of the police station and went right through it.... O! but it was a dandy fire. You ought to have been here.[2]

Instead of swimming in the dirty harbor, Tod was privileged to learn to dog-paddle along a sandy beach in the clean, warm waters of Nonquitt, a small, exclusive summer resort in South Dartmouth. Located several miles to windward of New Bedford, Nonquitt was founded in the 1870s on pastureland by members of New Bedford's upper crust, including Rotches.

Nonquitt's summer residences quickly advanced from tents and small, board-sheathed camps to shingled "cottages," some of large proportions indeed, which rose up from the barren moor like great gray puff balls. (One of the largest was that of Tod's mentor and uncle, Captain Frank Stone.) Their broad piazzas gloried in jute, wicker, and ease; upstairs rooms were furnished with simple iron beds, painted bureaus, and sandy scatter rugs. In the evenings the sou'west wind, blowing briskly up the bay, sang seductively through the window screening, making mischief with the scandalized curtains.[3]

Nonquitt's crescent-shaped beach, bounded to the north by the old stone post office wharf and to the south by a great granite ledge topped by a large boulder, was a perfect saltwater nursery. On a clear day, with a northwest breeze blowing off the land, the Elizabeth Islands lay boldly at the horizon, beckoning the young sailor-to-be. Here Tod enjoyed his first command, a five-foot by thirty-inch by eighteen-inch square-ended, pine-planked punt, outfitted with tholepins, two ash oars, seven fathoms of anchor rode, and an iron grapnel. No millionaire yachtsman can purchase pleasure afloat surpassing that enjoyed by a small child set loose in even a five-foot boat. During golden days of watery play Tod absorbed that intuitive feel for boats that is difficult if not impossible to obtain as an adult.

As a teenager Tod shifted his flag to a lapstraked, gaff-rigged, cat-ketch "smack boat" named *Jag*—not the usual choice for a scion of a prominent yachtsman. *Jag*'s broad beam, raked transom, and outboard rudder were characteristic of traditional Narragansett Bay boats commonly used for fishing. Sixteen feet long—her broad beam effectively made her much

Rodman Swift, circa 1890.
RODMAN SWIFT COLLECTION.

bigger—*Jag* was robust enough to handle Buzzard Bay's infamous chop yet light enough to be rowed by boys and landed on a beach. Despite having neither a centerboard nor a deep keel, Narragansett Bay boats were said to be able, stable sailors. Their simple, divided rig, with loose-footed mainsail, was easily handled. Had Winslow Homer spied *Jag* he surely would have wished to paint her and her tanned and barefoot crew with cheek.

Cheek Tod had, and in spades, and after a season or two spent sailing close to home, he began to make longer cruises accompanied by a pal. The waters and shorelines of Buzzard's Bay and adjacent Vineyard Sound formed perhaps the most perfect cruising grounds on the seaboard.[4] The bay, about thirty miles long by, at most, ten miles wide, lay south-west by north-east. The mainland shore was deeply serrated by harbors, the quaintest lined with tall elms and the big, white-fenced houses of retired sea captains. The bay's eastern border was the sheep-grazed Elizabeth Islands—Naushon, Pasque, Nashawena, little Penikese—not yet cursed with its leper colony—and Cuttyhunk, to seaward. Naushon was the summer headquarters of the Forbes clan, well known to Tod, whose fortune was founded in the China Trade. In the summer, the shallow bay's famous "smoky sou'wester," when opposed by an ebbing tide, created short, steep waves which have surprised many a visiting boater. Spray that would be a cold annoyance in Maine waters was here but a relatively tepid nuisance.

Vineyard Sound, twenty-odd miles by five, lies between the Elizabeth Islands and Martha's Vineyard. The Sound is entered from Buzzard's Bay through passages between the islands—Wood's, Quick's, and Robinson's Holes, and Canapitsit Channel. The six-foot tidal range of Buzzard's Bay is twice that of the sound, periodically turning some of these passages into virtual sluiceways, pulling buoys under and teaching the unwary a crash course in watery reality. The Sound's southern portal was Gay Head—Indian country—with its famous lighthouse standing boldly atop high cliffs of reddish clay that were vividly illuminated in the low rays of the setting sun. A most welcome sight to many a storm-tossed and disoriented sailor, it was one of the notable sea-marks of the coast.

Vineyard Sound, with adjoining Nantucket Sound, was one of the great thorofares on the coast, providing shipping with a passage—although by no means peril free—inside of dangerous, offshore Nantucket Shoals. The tide ruled navigation in the Sounds as well, and coasting schooners, ranging from small Down East two-masters loaded with lime casks, lumber, shingles, and spiling to huge, multi-masted coal carriers, were often grouped in motley fleets formed by wind and tide. Anchorages such as Naushon Island's Tarpaulin Cove, Menemsha Bight, and, especially, Vineyard Haven, on Martha's Vineyard, were often crowded with schooners and also barges.

Long tows of coal barges—many barges were old, cut-down, square-riggers, their counters still adorned with gold-leafed carvings—towed by big, smoking, coastal tugs, drifted across the channel with the tide. Fast coastal express steamers which slowed for no fog were dangerous passers-by. Surely the most fascinating transients were lofty square-riggers returned from long voyages, their sailors tanned to a turn.

The waters of bay and sound were then also alive with a variety of watermen—weirmen, market hunters, boat fishermen, quahoggers, and various small schooner, sloop, catboat, and scow men—men who recognized, respected, and kept a watchful eye on *Jag* and her dauntless crew.

Tod's doting mother Sarah, bravely permissive, set a ten-day limit for *Jag*'s absences. Before a long cruise she prepared a dozen pots of baked beans—as Tod once explained, " When the beans have gone rotten, a pot pops, and then I know its time to go home." Sarah's other rule was that the boys had to sleep ashore every night.

For stowage aboard *Jag*, Tod rolled up his two wool blankets in a water-

Cat-ketch Jag, *shown (above and below) at Nonquitt, 1890s. The long building—actually it is an assembly of smaller buildings under one roof—is the bathhouse, where bathers changed clothes. Swimsuits were to be worn only when the wearer was in the water or alongside it.*
RODMAN SWIFT COLLECTION.

proof ground cloth. An oilskin bag contained a ditty bag, a pair of woolen socks, a Guernsey frock, a pair of warm pants, a roll of local Eldredge charts, parallel rulers, and a divider. An old boat compass was hung in a box-drawer on the underside of the after thwart. Oilskins, boots, black sou'wester, shoes for shore, a tin fish horn, a couple of hurricane lanterns, lamp oil, matches, a canvas bucket, a pump, sponge, oars, and two anchors—a light "short stay" and a heavier bower—with rodes, completed the outfit.[5]

Provisions also included sliced jerked beef, apple turnovers deep fried in fat, a small bag of hardtack, and a well-secured stone jug of fresh water. Driftwood, which burned blue and orange from the salt, lay readily at hand. The boys could dig clams and pick beach plums; eggs fresh from the nest, milk fresh from the cow, and fruits of the garden were easily come by at saltwater farms where weathered barns were yet fitted with alert weathercocks and the doorway trellises of ancient capes were draped with shawls of long-prickered pink roses. At night, we may imagine the friendly glow of lamplight behind a small farmhouse window being early extinguished, leaving the sound of the turning tide lapping at the nearby beach (and faithful *Jag*'s lapped strakes) as two tired boys rolled up in blankets against the dew.

The following is an undated letter from Tod to Sarah (who was presumably visiting in New York) regarding a cruise in *Jag* to the westward to Narragansett Bay. (The catboat *Push* belonged to Tod's sister Helen.)

> DEAR MAMMA, I have just got back from a cruise to Bristol where I took the *Push*. I had Charles Rotch with me.... I in the *Jag* and C. in the *Push*. On Saturday we got underway [from Newport] about eleven and headed north for Bristol.... We got there and found the man after a good deal of hunting and then we handed over the *Push* and he handed over $30. He has taken her at $5 a week.... His name is Robert P. Bass and he...is a Harvard man.... There is a good harbor there so the *Push* is all right. I will go and get her when he is done with her. Well, on Sunday we started back to Newport and had to beat all the way. On Sunday we stayed in Newport for it rained with an easterly wind nearly all day. We were very comfortable for we just got out the blankets and lay down and slept for we were perfectly dry for the awning did not leak a bit. I told you I bought one for $3.00 and sewed myself didn't I? I sewed some and Mrs. Stone sewed some. Well on Tuesday up to Cormorant rocks then we found our compass was affected by our ballast so we headed SE by E and struck the right place. Then by heading E by S we picked up Hen

and Chickens [lightship] and from there Dumpling and we got in about eight o'clock.... In all we sailed about 130 miles in the *Jag*.... Sorry this did not get on today's steamer, Your loving son, Rodman

A blurry snapshot shows Tod sailing as mate for the day aboard the small and ancient schooner *United* (among *United*'s usual tasks was setting and hauling moorings for yachtsmen at $1.50 apiece).[6] *United*'s master, Captain James A. Stubbs, was an old China clipper hand who shared his tiny cabin with seven or eight cats and many more cockroaches, the latter signed aboard for flea control. Captain Stubbs, despite appearances, was no fool and shared with rapt boys spellbinding yarns and shrewd social commentary not heard on the piazzas of Nonquitt or in the parlors of County Road.[7] Evidently Tod was one of Captain Stubbs's protégés. It was on the water aboard *Jag* and perhaps *United* that Tod early entered a double life, thereafter simultaneously living at ease in two very different worlds.

But Tod was always a reluctant and restless scholastic inmate, suffering successively through New Bedford's Friends School, Milton Academy in Milton, and finally Harvard College. Unlike some puritanical private schools, where education was employed in the manner of a perpetual youthful punishment, Milton espoused a more humane and affirming philosophy, reflecting the influence of the founding Forbes family. Tod did at least enjoy gymnastics, and being light, tough, and fearless of heights, he always topped the human pyramids.

Tod's boyhood dream had been to make a long voyage with his Uncle Frank—Captain Francis Stone—aboard the splendid 2,077-ton full-rigged merchant ship *Francis*, and in March of 1897 it appeared quite possible that this would come to pass. The bubble burst with the news that May that the *Francis* had burned and was a total loss off the New Jersey shore, only hours short of completing her passage from San Francisco to New York.

Encouraged by another seafaring uncle, Franklin Swift, who appears to have been captain of the U.S. Fish Commission steamer *Fish Hawk*, Tod then applied, unsuccessfully, for one of the few remaining openings, via political appointment, to Annapolis. He then entered Harvard with the class of '03, having made a pact with his family to stay and graduate in return for their dropping any opposition to his making a voyage in a square-rigger afterwards.

Otherwise we know little of Tod's college career. Following in the wake of his father and Uncle Frank, he became a member of the A. D. Club, a favored resort for Old Colony sons from south of Boston. An undated letter to Sarah during Tod's college years indicates that a sail around Cape Cod with Uncle Frank in a small yacht was of far more interest than academics:

THANK YOU FOR THE CHECK.... I am having a hard time with chemistry and German and I think I may drop Engg.1d...my instructor says I can't pass Engg.1d anyway.... Tell Papa that Uncle F. and I left Gloucester at 8 A.M., wind NW good breeze. After we had got about 15 miles the wind left us and later came out about SSE which was ahead. We got to Highland Light just after dark about 8 P.M. wind SW strong whole sail breeze; about 10 P.M. we put in one reef and about 11 P.M. we put in another and took the jib in for it blew hard SW. Got to Pollock Rip 4:30 A.M. put whole sail on her but owing to light winds SW and head tide did not get through. Tide turned about 10 A.M. and we went through. Off Handkerchief wind freshened SW. Off Cross Rip wind strong SW. Got to Vineyard 4 P.M. Strong SW wind. Had fair tide through Wood's Hole but were too lazy to go home that day so we spent night at V[ineyard] H[aven]. Under way at 5 A.M. wind light SW through Quick's, head tide, wind SW just strong enough to send us through. Butler's Flats wind NW very strong, boat on her beam ends but wind did not extend out of harbor. Almost calm in bay. Dropped anchor about 12 A.M. and went ashore to breakfast. Must go to a lecture now.

Tod often enjoyed sailing with his sister Helen, a young woman of great beauty and charm who was three years older and a skilled sailor, unlike brother Fred, two years older. Helen's life in later years would not be all that it might have been, and Tod has been described as being one of but very few men she ever fully trusted.

In August 1900, two months before Helen's marriage to William Scudder (one of Teddy Roosevelt's well-bred Rough Riders), which would produce two lovely daughters and a divorce, Helen and Tod—then age twenty—made a cruise to Long Island Sound in a buoyant little sloop named *Alcedo*. After calling at sweltering Greenport, Long Island, to replace the main sheet, take on more pipe tobacco—Tod's pipe had already become a natural appendage, and when cruising, Helen smoked one also—and to search in vain for a tide book, they headed for home, but ended up putting in to Duck Island Roads on the Connecticut shore. Helen wrote:

ANCHORED IN DUCK ISLAND Roads about 11:30. Went in swimming and had lunch. Wind came around to E. and squalls seemed to come up from all directions. We spent the afternoon reading and watching a small tub about 15 ft. with five men on board come in and anchor. Two coasters and a knockabout also came in. Wind increased, cloudiness increased. We warped in nearer breakwater, put out two anchors and turned in about 9:30 after a good supper and

Captain and crew—Tod and Helen Swift—
aboard the sloop Alcedo, *August 1900.*
RODMAN SWIFT COLLECTION.

some ale as conducive to sleepiness. About 11 both awoke to find it raining. Peered out, wind seemed flatter so we dashed back to our downy cots and slept.

AUGUST 13TH. Wind still East. Put in a reef and after a fast breakfast got under way at 7 thinking to beat to New London in spite of a head tide, but two hours later found us back anchored behind the breakwater once more, where we furled, put down a second anchor and retired below to keep warm. The Tub, the Knockabout and one coaster went to the westward early. The Capt. raided the other coaster *Andrew Burton* and returned laden with a jug of water and a loaf of bread.[8] By close calculation we have concluded our provisions will last us until Thursday, then we must live on oatmeal.... The day was spent in reading, the Capt. leaping up to view the weather every two minutes and the crew casting curious glances to windward in the intervals. The sun appearing once caused hopes to go up 100 percent but this boom in the market lasted but a moment as the clouds returned and there was a drop. Hope is now extremely cheap....

ABOUT 3:50 P.M. a hard-pressed young sloop came around the breakwater, did a few queer things, was treated badly by the tide, but finally got safely anchored. Wind was blowing a gale from E. At half hour intervals about there followed another smaller sloop, a big sloop, the *Regina*, and a cat boat. All had difficulties except the *Regina*. The blowing increased and we were unhappy. Finally about 6 the Capt. had an idea which saved us many hours' sleep. He went to the *Regina* and asked for an extra anchor. They had one and lent it willingly. We then with three anchors down were happy (comparatively) and after a good supper of soup and coffee we dropped asleep. Woke and turned in properly about 10:30. Blowing a gale still and raining perfect St. Bernards and tiger pussies....

Difficulties with differential calculus required Tod to repeat his entire senior year, as was then proscribed, and he finally graduated in 1904 with a degree in Mining and Metallurgical Engineering. His choice of concentration, influenced by a roommate, was, in fact, a sound one, calculus notwithstanding, for Tod had a mathematical mind, a penchant for order, a gift for problem solving, and no desire for work in an office. Additionally, the mining engineer—particularly the mining engineer who struck it rich in the far west—had become a popular romantic figure.

1. Ashley, *Yankee Whaler*, p. 118.

2. From his cocky writing style, one suspects that Tod had been reading boys' red-blooded adventure novels.

3. When, several times a summer, separate dances were held in the barn-like Casino social hall for the help, cottagers were "requested to instruct their servants at the close of the dance to promptly and quietly return to their houses." Anne Morse Lyell, *Nonquitt, A Summer Album, 1872–1985* (South Dartmouth, MA: Barekneed Publishers, 1987), p. 241.

4. Of course, this claim could then also have been made for many other regions from the Maritime Provinces to Key West, including once unspoiled Long Island Sound and Chesapeake Bay. Today, all along the seaboard what were once quiet, rural coves are now lined with cottages, condominiums, marinas, or worse, and are choked with plastic boats and copious regulations. Any shoreland yet free from development is usually posted. Campers are not welcomed.

5. Llewellyn Howland, "Captain Swift and the Schooner *Tyche*," *Yachting* (May 1954), p. 49.

6. *United* may have pre-dated the ark, as no age is found for her in the *List of Merchant Vessels.*

7. Llewellyn Howland, *The Middle Road* (South Dartmouth, MA: Concordia Company, 1961), pp. 46–50; Captain William Hawes, *New Bedford in the China Trade* (New Bedford, MA, 1940), n.p.; statement for $1.50 for "hauling out buoy at Nonquitt" from Frederick Swift to Captain James A. Stubbs, "master of the sch. *United*," 7 Nov. 1894.

8. Presumably this was the schooner *Andrew Burnham*, of Boston, built at Essex, Massachusetts, in 1865, and soon to vanish from the *List of Merchant Vessels*

Chapter 3

When Uncle Frank First Went to Sea

We Learn How Tod Swift's Mentor and Uncle, Francis Stone, Went to Sea, Helped by His Family's China Trade Connections.

HAD TOD AND HIS Uncle Frank been born in each other's shoes, each very well might have followed paths similar to those the other chose. Uncle Frank—Francis Hathaway Stone—was born into the lap of the old China Trade and would later be said to be New Bedford's last China Trade captain. His mother Elizabeth was a Hathaway and the Hathaways were New Bedford's China Trade grandees. Elizabeth was one of the four orphaned children of China merchant Nathaniel Hathaway; Elizabeth and her sister Caroline, like their brothers Francis and Horatio, invested their inheritances in their uncles' Far East mercantile adventures, and were well rewarded.

Frank's father, Joshua, a distinguished New Bedford lawyer who at one time was a partner with the famous William W. Crapo, was a Forbes cousin. Frank's brother Nathaniel became a senior partner in the firm of J. M. Forbes & Co., "Asiatic shipping merchants," and a prominent financier active in Chicago-area railroad development.[1]

Although never a major cargo-handling port, New Bedford's merchant shipping activities and connections were, in fact, quite considerable, although greatly overshadowed by the far larger whaling industry. Early whaleships were commonly also employed as freighters. Rotch ships carrying oil and candles to London frequently returned with Russian goods—especially hemp, for cordage—from the Baltic. (The Rotch ship *Dartmouth,* after playing a central role in the Boston Tea Party, was outfitted for a whaling voyage to the Brazil Banks.)[2] During the Napoleonic Wars, New Bedford shipowners, as others, did well by neutral trading—in 1805 the *Ann Alexander*, sailing as a merchantman—she would gain lasting fame after being sunk by a whale in 1851—nearly blundered into the Battle of Trafalgar.

For the better part of a century New Bedford merchants and mariners were engaged in trade with China and the Far East, although their ships sailed primarily from New York.[3] Indeed, in 1786, two years before the Boston ship *Columbia*—commanded by Wareham's Captain John Kendrick—brought her celebrated cargo of Pacific Northwest sea otter pelts to Canton as barter, a cargo of seal skins, skinned from their original Falkland Island owners by the crew of Francis Rotch's ship *United States*, had found its way to Canton. Thus began another "fishery," with its own epics of enterprise, bravery, fortitude, greed, gore, and tedium.[4] In 1805 American ships at Canton landed 140,297 seal skins as compared with 17,445 sea otter skins.[4]

The key to trade with China was having something which the Chinese wished to acquire—no easy task! By introducing opium—most came from British India—into China, Westerners created a new market which would eventually grow to such importance that it would play a central role in the financing of world trade. When the Chinese government outlawed opium imports, suppliers became smugglers. The British East India Company was by far the largest player, but American participants held their own, the most famous being Milton's dynamic Forbes brothers, John Murray and Robert Bennet. "J. M." went on to become a great financier and railroad builder and owner of Naushon Island; "Bennet" became a Boston maritime institution, inventing a lifesaving double-topsail rig, helping to establish the lifesaving Massachusetts Humane Society, helping to combat famine in Ireland, and penning pithy letters to the newspapers.

The China Trade fostered the development of fast, small, clipper brigs and schooners for smuggling as well as larger clipper ships whose fast passages between the United States and China enabled their owners to profit from the eighteen-month float allowed before high import duties had to be paid.

The California gold rush fostered more, bigger, and better clippers, some of which sailed to the Far East by first sailing west around Cape Horn with high-priced goods—including preserved Maine eggs—for San Francisco, there earning specie with which to purchase goods in China.

The trade functioned with bills of credit rather than with long-distance transfers of specie. Honesty and reliability were basic requirements for traders, typically young men from good families. At Canton, long the only port open to foreigners, the traders were largely restricted to a riverside compound, keeping "bachelors' hall" in the upper floors of their "factories," or "hongs." In 1835 J. M. Forbes shared living quarters with Francis S. Hathaway, whose family's China Trading may have begun as early as 1817. In 1834 Forbes married Sarah Hathaway, Francis's cousin (Hathaways also married Rotches, Rodmans, and Morgans).[5]

Three sons of shipowner Humphrey Hathaway—Francis (Forbes's roommate in Hong Kong), Thomas, and Nathaniel—founded a prosperous ship-owning, tea-importing, China Trade firm, with "counting houses" at New Bedford and New York. After the untimely deaths of Nathaniel and his wife, their two boys and two girls (one being Uncle Frank Stone's mother, Elizabeth, of course) were raised by bachelors Francis and Thomas. Nephews Francis and Horatio would later join the family firm.

The Hathaway ship *Oneida* was employed primarily in the China Trade from 1832 until 1863, when she was burned west of Anjer by the Confederate "pirate" *Florida*.[6] The famous ship *Horatio* sailed under the Hathaway's house flag for forty-two years before burning at Shanghai in 1874; during her career $500,000 was paid in insurance premiums on the ship and her cargoes. The last ship built for the firm was the clipper *Hotspur* of 1857; when she was lost on a Chinese reef in 1862, her cargo was valued at $1,000,000.

Thomas Hathaway died in 1878, at which time the firm was replacing its own ships with chartered tonnage. The last of the family's fleet were likely several whalers—the Hathaways dabbled in whaling as well—and small schooners; one schooner regularly freighted home whale oil left for her at various South Atlantic points. And, last but not least, the Hathaways were major investors in vessels built in the 1870s and '80s for the fleet managed by Captain William Besse, of New Bedford.

The Hathaways' New York tea business ended in the mid-1890s, although for many years afterwards family members received annual gifts of tea from old suppliers (in that vein, the Hathaways carried on as suppliers of wine, whiskey, and also cigars to fellow members of New Bedford's maritime gentry). The family invested heavily in New Bedford's textile industry, and although this business, too, would eventually die, the Hathaway name yet survives, if only as a relic, in the Berkshire-Hathaway Corporation, a holding company whose spectacular and legendary rise on Wall Street under financier Warren Buffet was staked by the liquidation of Hathaway textile properties.

* * *

BUT BACK TO young Francis Hathaway Stone. After graduating from Friends Academy, Frank entered Harvard with the Class of 1879. Handsome, charming, and a member of several clubs, in the middle of his junior year he nevertheless left school, sailing a few days later for the Azores as a passenger aboard the Boston bark *Azorean*.[7]

The Azores, or Western Islands, and New Bedford were closely linked. The islands provided crew members and served as a convenient mid-Atlantic base for whaleships to reprovision and offload. New Bedford (along with Boston) provided the islands with a doorway to America,

Francis H. Stone, Harvard Class of 1879.
HARVARD COLLEGE CLASS OF 1879, FIFTIETH ANNIVERSARY, NINTH REPORT, 1929.

which explains, in part, the large "Portuguese" population of southeastern Massachusetts. Ships in the trade returned with whale oil, fruit (especially oranges), pottery, large complements of passengers, and cheap "Pico Madeira" wine, much of which, at Boston, was granted a new identity as a choicer vintage.[8]

Frank returned home from his cruise two months later, but, still restless, soon sailed for the Azores again aboard the bark *Veronica*, of New Bedford, owned by the Snows. This time he sailed "before the mast" as an ordinary seaman. Horatio Hathaway—Frank's cousin—wrote of the activities at New Bedford's Rotch Wharf when the *Veronica* was in port:

> ON THE OPPOSITE corner of Rodman and Front Streets was the four-story stone building occupied by Loum Snow & Son, whose business was largely in the trade with the Azores; and the loft, filled with casks of Madeira wine and Fayal pottery, was always a place of absorbing interest to us boys, especially when the ship *Veronica* came into port and the wine was transferred from the hold to the loft by means of a heavy tackle and a barrel sling.
>
> My cousin, the late Richard H. Morgan, worked for a short time in this office, and being entrusted with directing the hoisting of some wine to the loft, dropped a cask three stories, causing a flooded office, and a near riot in the street, as the gutter flowed with good Fayal Madeira. This mishap lost him his job with the firm.[9]

Frank, home once again, then took the first steps towards entering a management career in textiles, a commonly trod path taken by sons of New Bedford's elite:

I GOT HOME FROM that trip early in the following December, and having had enough of the sea for awhile, determined to try my hand at a little shore work. Accordingly, the first of February, 1879, I entered the office of the Potomska Cotton Mill in New Bedford. My hardest work was to go to the post office. Unfortunately my salary was in proportion to my duties. I stood this two months, and then came to the conclusion that even going to sea was better than life in an office. I left the office early in April 1879, and went to England, to join the barque *Jonathan Bourne* (1,500 tons) at Cardiff, Wales, for Yokohama, Japan.[10]

The bark *Jonathan Bourne*, of New Bedford, was built at Bath, Maine, in 1877 by the firm of Goss & Sawyer for a group of New Bedford-area owners, including Jonathan Bourne, a leading whaleship owner and agent. Other owners of shares—ships were traditionally divided into 64ths—included Thomas Hathaway and Captains Alden and William Besse. Captain William Besse was the bark's managing owner.

Her master, Captain Alfred Doane, was a Cape Codder hailing from Orleans. Doane had served the Hathaways most ably for many years, coming into their employment with the purchase of the medium clipper *Endeavor*, which Doane had commanded since her launching at East Boston in 1856. In 1868 he moved to the command of the Hathaway's new medium clipper *Cleopatra,* making many fast passages in her, primarily voyaging between the East Coast and the Far East. In 1876, after *Cleopatra*—like so many American square-riggers at the time—was sold under the German flag, Captain Doane took command of the new bark *Jonathan Bourne.*[11]

Of good model, well-sparred, and with an old-time clipper captain in the cabin, the *Bourne* made good passages. After calls at Melbourne, Sydney, Honolulu, and London, she shifted to Cardiff, where Frank joined her. Bound for Yokohama she no doubt loaded coal; from Yokohama she sailed for San Francisco to load grain for Hull, England. Returning to San Francisco from Newcastle (doubtless with coal), she sailed to Havre (doubtless with grain). In July of 1881 she sailed from Havre to New York, there to load a cargo—doubtless case oil—for Yokohama. From Yokohama she sailed to Hong Kong.

The *Bourne,* of 1,472 tons and measuring not much over 200 feet in length, sailed from Hong Kong in May of 1882 with a cargo of 650 "Chinese passengers"—popularly called "coolies"—bound for Victoria, British Columbia, and (surely) the pleasure of helping to build the Canadian Pacific Railway.[12] During this passage the *Bourne* ran into a typhoon, losing nearly all of her sails, yet made port after a fast passage of but thirty-four days.[13] During the storm the Chinese were shut away in the dark, crowded, reeking hold under the most frightful circumstances. The strain on the master, officers, and crew—Frank, having rapidly risen through the ranks, was now chief mate—was also beyond easy imagining.

While family connections surely did Frank's career no harm—and in Captain Doane Frank had the best of teachers—Doane would not have promoted any man in whom he did not have confidence, no matter who his family was. That his judgment was well-founded was demonstrated not only by Frank's subsequent career in command, but by the lasting relationship between the two men.

---

1. Frank was the third of five children. Henry, the eldest, a practical engineer, advanced from foreman of the locomotive shop to general manager and second vice president of the Chicago, Burlington & Quincy Railroad. His deft handling of strikes in the late '80s was said to have postponed union dictation for thirty years. He then became very successful in the telephone business. On July 4, 1897, he accidentally blew his head off at the Independence Day Celebration at Nonquitt. Frank's younger brother Frederick was a Boston lawyer; kid sister Caroline married J. Delano Wood.

2. Bullard, *The Rotches*, p. 50-51.

3. In the early 1800s, New Bedford candle and whale oil merchant Cornelius Grinnell moved his business to New York; in 1815 he formed a partnership with his cousin, Preserved Fish, a New Bedford whaling captain, and the two founded the Swallowtail Line of Liverpool packets. Grinnell's son Joseph became a member of the firm, while son Moses began his career working for William J. Rotch. Soon, desiring wider horizons, Moses shipped as supercargo on a vessel bound for Brazil. His subsequent speculation in a cargo of coffee for a European port proved most fortunate. Moses and brother Henry, along with brother-in-law Robert Minturn, eventually took the firm over, forming Grinnell, Minturn & Company. Grinnell, Minturn & Company—the Hathaways may have been the "Company"—became one of the great shipowning firms in an era of extraordinary maritime expansion. Operating packet lines to Liverpool and London, they owned some fifty ships employed in various trades, and played a large role in the development of the port of New York. (A Delano would also become a partner.) The Hathaways owned one-eighth of the firm's famous clipper *Flying Cloud*, whose master, Captain Josiah Perkins Cressy, had earlier distinguished himself while commanding the Hathaway's old ship *Oneida*.

4. Stackpole, *The Sea-Hunters*, p. 188.

5. Questions regarding the morality of the trade have vexed the often still well-fixed descendants of opium smugglers ever since. (Quaker merchants shunned the business, but then, Quakers shunned dancing.) Opium was then legal in the United States, and while R. B. Forbes suggested in his autobiography that the drug's effect was less harmful than that of the "vile" Chinese rice wine, in a letter to his wife he recognized the drug's effect in "demoralizing the minds, destroying the bodies, & draining the country of money." Robert B. Forbes, *Personal Remi-*

niscences (Boston, 1882), p. 144; Phyllis Forbes, ed., *Letters from China* (Mystic, CT: Mystic Seaport, 1996), p. 101. Some Bostonians, using fast steamers, persisted in smuggling opium via Formosa as late as the 1870s.

6. Anjer is often spelled Angers, or by our intrepid diarists later in the book, Anjers, Angier, and Angiers.

7. *Azorean* was owned by the Dabneys, a Boston family long prominent in trade with the islands.

8. Samuel Eliot Morison, *The Maritime History of Massachusetts* (Boston: Houghton, Mifflin Company, 1921), pp. 293–94.

9. Horatio Hathaway, *A New Bedford Merchant* (privately published, n.d.), pp. 5–6

10. *Harvard College Class of 1879, Fiftieth Anniversary Report* (1929), p. 501–02.

11. Frederick C. Matthews, *American Merchant Ships*, Series I (Salem, MA: Marine Research Society, 1930), pp. 77–78.

12. As will be discussed in more detail in a later chapter, the distinction between "Chinese passengers" and "coolies" was an important one to shippers, and was also a matter of law.

13. *New York Maritime Register*; Frederick C. Matthews, *American Merchant Ships 1850–1900,* Series II (Salem, MA: Marine Research Society, 1931), p. 204. Matthews reported the passage as 38 days.

Chapter 4

Captain Besse and His Fleet

Several of Captain Besse's Fine Ships Will Figure Large in Our Unfolding Story.

Captain William H. Besse succeeded the Hathaways as New Bedford's leading merchant shipowner. However, unlike the old merchant princes who owned ships and cargoes outright, Besse was a "managing" owner, owning but a portion of each ship under his house flag, and collecting commissions for his services on their behalf. Attracting buyers of shares in new ships was a critical part of his business, and the mine he worked most successfully was that of wealthy, ship-minded New Bedford, where he established his office. Able and innovative, Besse continued building new ships even as many other American square-rigger owners were disposing of tonnage wholesale.[1]

William Besse was born in 1828 in Wareham, a Buzzard's Bay town northeast of Fairhaven and New Bedford. He died in New Bedford in 1900.[2] The year after William's birth his father, also named William, age twenty-five, was lost at sea.[3] At age ten, following the common practice, Besse joined the crew of a small coaster. As was also common, Besse attended his district school during the winter term when his schooner was laid up. After a few years he joined a larger schooner and acquired a thorough knowledge of the coast from the Bay of Fundy to the Mississippi. At age nineteen he became captain.

With the onset of the California gold rush Besse joined a party of Forty-Niners bound for San Francisco from nearby Mattapoisett in the ship *Mount Vernon*. December of 1849 found Besse working an open boat on the Sacramento River, carrying mail and passengers, trading with Indians, and socializing with the famous Captain Sutter, at whose mill gold was first discovered. The following year he bought a string of mules, packed them with provisions, and headed for the gold mines on the Yuba River. Besse spent the next four years working in mines on the Yuba, American, Feather, and other rivers, returning home with his earnings in 1855.

In 1856 Besse went to Cleveland, Ohio, and bought two large "laker" schooners, loading one with black walnut lumber, the other with a cargo of flour. He brought the schooners down Lake Erie, through the Welland Canal, down Lake Ontario, through the Lachine Canal, past Montreal, down the St. Lawrence, and out around to Boston, thus beginning his career as a shipowner.[4] From 1862 to 1866 Besse is listed as owner and master of the ancient full-rigged ship *Uncas*, 412 tons, built at Falmouth, Massachusetts, in 1828, in which he evidently engaged in Northern Pacific trades.

In 1868 Besse purchased from the navy the surplus steam sidewheel gunboat *Genesee*, which had been built at Boston in 1862, and converted her for the Hong Kong–Portland, Oregon, "coolie" trade.[5] After removing her machinery he rigged her as a "four-masted bark."[6] Just as *Genesee* had been very successful as a steamer, so the re-named *Hattie C. Besse*—evidently Mrs. Besse preferred Hattie to Harriet—proved very successful as a sailer. She also made money, and when she was lost (under another captain) on the Washington Coast in 1871, Besse had already moved on to command the fine new 842-ton bark *Alden Besse,* built for his order earlier that year (the bark was named for Captain Alden Besse, William's first-cousin-once-removed). The *Alden Besse* was the first of a notable fleet of barks and ships built for Besse by the firm Goss & Sawyer (and successors) of Bath, Maine.

> FROM TIME TO TIME there comes into New York Harbor, says the [*New York*] *Sun*, first-class wooden ships in ballast, flying the American flag and new from the shipyards of Maine.... They are the elite of the sea. In point of aesthetic interest, at least, there is no comparison between the full-rigged American-built wooden ship of from fifteen to twenty-two hundred tons and anything else that floats on the ocean. The greater part of the surviving fleet of American [full-rigged] ships was built in Maine, where the industry is still active despite discouraging conditions. The yards of Bath and neighboring towns on the Kennebec are foremost in the world of wooden shipbuilding.
>
> —*Bangor Industrial Journal*, 24 January 1884.

These ships have since become known as "Down Easters" In their day the best were commonly called "clippers," in part because many were legitimately "medium clippers" in model, and because the term had arguably evolved to encompass the best, largest, and loftiest ships of the day, including even some relatively blunt bulk carriers.[7]

About 1880 Henry Hall, special agent of the United States Census, wrote of Bath:

It is a remarkable fact that while Bath builds the cheapest wooden vessels in the United States at present, nearly every ton of timber, iron, pitch, hemp, salt, canvas, etc.…is imported into the town.… As the cost of material is two-thirds the cost of the ship, the state of Maine has a smaller interest in her own vessel building than the rest of the country.… The cost of building vessels at Bath is kept low on account of the system of operation, the low rate of wages, and the great efficiency of the men.[8]

Whereas pre-Civil War Bath had been dominated by proprietary yards building square-riggers for their owners' fleets, the leading postwar firm, Goss & Sawyer, sought outside customers.[9] Among the earliest of many vessels built by Goss & Sawyer for Southern New Englanders was the schooner *John H. Perry,* built for New Bedford owners in 1867. Favorably impressed Cape Cod parties placed an order for the bark *Xenia*, and William Besse, visiting the yard to order the schooner *Jesse Murdock* for Captain Alden Besse, so greatly admired *Xenia* that he later had the bark *Alden Besse* built there.[10] And the rest is history.

The 1871 bark *Alden Besse* was followed in 1873 by the 1,027-ton bark *William H. Besse*, initially commanded by Captain William Besse himself—how better to refine the design of the next ship? In 1876 the 1,135-ton bark *Western Belle* and her near sister, the 1,169-ton bark *Belle of Oregon* were added to the fleet. Owned largely in Portland, Oregon, both were intended for employment in the West Coast-to-Europe grain trade and the flour and "Chinese passenger trade" between Portland and Hong Kong. For the latter they were fitted with extra long poops and large cabins and featured superior ventilation in the hold. They were adorned with spectacular figureheads by Bath's Colonel Sampson. Of *Western Belle*'s figurehead an enraptured reporter gushed:

Like Venus, who is fabled to have risen from the foam of the sea, and Minerva, who sprung forth from the immortal head of Jupiter, so the Western Belle sprung forth from the forests of Maine, and while Michael Angelo could see an imprisoned angel in the block of marble by the wayside in the City of Florence, so a Sampson saw the beautiful creature, constituting his beau-ideal, in the shapeless log lying before him.…[11]

William Besse took *Western Belle* on her maiden passage to Cardiff, there turning her over to the first mate. Besse's son William, age eighteen, who had been second mate, became first mate. Described as an exceptionally bright officer, off the Cape of Good Hope young William was washed off the cabin top and lost.

The 1,296-ton bark *Forest Belle*—also largely owned by Portland, Oregon, parties—and the 1,472-ton bark *Jonathan Bourne* were both launched in 1877.[12] Both were wrecked on uncharted reefs while yet new, *Forest Belle* being lost off Formosa on her maiden voyage. The 1,459-ton bark *Gerard C. Tobey*, launched in 1878, was named for Alden Besse's next-door Wareham neighbor.[13] She was followed into the Kennebec in 1879 by her near sister, the 1,572-ton bark *Guy C. Goss*—the hundredth ship built by (Guy C.) Goss & Sawyer, and the largest wooden bark then afloat.[14] The 648-ton bark *William W. Crapo,* named for a prominent New Bedford lawyer and congressman, was built in 1880.[15]

In 1881 the 1,718-ton full-rigged ship *William J. Rotch*—Rotch, Tod Swift's grandfather, has already been introduced—followed. The 1,174-ton auxiliary steam bark *George S. Homer*, named for a prosperous New Bedforder, and the 1,976-ton ship *Henry Failing*, named for a wealthy

Bark Alden Besse, *at Goss & Sawyer's, Bath, 1871. Note the shipyard ox team. Oak timber in foreground was hewn to shape to form frame parts, or "futtocks."*
J. C. Higgins. Courtesy of Wareham Historical Society.

Portland, Oregon, dry-goods merchant, were launched in 1882. The 1,309-ton ship *Hotspur*, named for a clipper built for the Hathaways in 1857, was the first of two handsome, three-skysail ships built in 1885. *Hotspur* made her maiden passage to Melbourne in the clipper time of eighty-two days; on her second voyage she was lost in the Philippines, another victim of a previously unknown reef. The splendid 2,077-ton *Francis* was built for the command of Captain Francis Hathaway Stone—Tod Swift's Uncle Frank.

The 673-ton barkentine *Hustler*, launched in 1890, was lost in March 1891 on her maiden passage while bound from Philadelphia to Seattle. She sank after striking a rock in Nassau Bay, in Cape Horn waters.[16] The

1876. The new bark Western Belle, *"light" and floating high with an empty hold, on the Kennebec.* Western Belle *was said to be the first bark to cross a skysail yard. Reflecting Captain Besse's tastes, she crosses double-topgallant yards and is painted bronze green.*
J. C. Higgins. Courtesy of Wareham Historical Society.

final sailing vessel built for Besse's fleet was the 1,469-ton "bark" *Olympic*, launched in 1892 and rigged in the same novel manner as the *Hattie C. Besse*. Her combination of hard bilges and relatively light rig allowed her to be sailed—at least on short runs—without ballast. Reportedly she was to be the first of six similar vessels to be built for "line" service carrying spars and timber between Puget Sound and New York.[17]

Besse's Bath-built vessels were handsome and stylish, representative of the best of their type. All crossed at least a main-skysail yard, and many were rigged with double-topgallant sails, something of a Besse trademark. Having been very well built, those which did not come to a disastrous end by shipwreck were notably long-lived.

It is probably no coincidence that the four Bath-built full-rigged ships were associated with unusually wealthy owners, since "ships" always carried more prestige in New England (or likely anywhere) than did barks. Besse himself clearly understood that despite this bias, the bark was cheaper to rig, man, and maintain, and, other factors being equal, performed as well or even better than the ship.

Bath, June 1876. The bark Belle of Oregon *shortly before her launching. Note her celebrated figurehead. Beyond may be seen the rigging of Besse's bark* Western Belle. *The bark lying alongside the wharf at right is the whaler* John & Winthrop, *of New Bedford, also built that year by Goss & Sawyer. In 1876 the firm launched four full-rigged ships and four barks.*

J. C. Higgins. Courtesy of Maine Maritime Museum.

The celebrated figurehead of Belle of Oregon, *at the Bath shop of shipcarver Colonel Charles Sampson, 1876. The right arm was detachable and was removed at sea. Figureheads were carved from white pine. The contrast between the rough building and the finely made creation crafted within was typical of the waterfront.*
J. C. Higgins. Courtesy of Maine Historic Preservation Commission.

Other members of Besse's fleet included the ship *Syren*, a true clipper by anyone's definition, built at Medford in 1851, and the bark *Mary S. Ames*, built at East Boston in 1876. In 1884 Besse was listed, along with the whaling merchant Captain William Lewis, also of New Bedford, as the owner of the steamer *Al-Ki*, built at Bath for West Coast service. He owned shares in a number of New Bedford vessels, including coasters and whalers, managed by others.

Between 1896 and 1899 Besse was the managing owner of six large, coastal schooner-barges built for the coal trade at Bath. They included *Forest Belle* (son Walter was listed as co-managing owner), *Ocean Belle, Kentucky, Virginia, West Virginia*, and *New York*.

Opposite page top: June 23, 1892. The bark Olympic *on the ways at the New England Company. The (typically) spindly scaffolding is being detached from the ship and the christening party is gathered forward at the knightheads. Ships were christened aboard, saving expense and allowing the owner's party to ride into the river with the new ship.*
WILSON F. KLIPPEL. COURTESY OF MRS. CHARLES HEWITT.

Opposite page bottom: The bark Olympic *slides into the Kennebec. Designed to carry Puget Sound timber to the East Coast, she could load 1.5 million feet of sawn lumber, including a deckload carried on the 130 feet of clear space between the poop and the forward house. Spar timber was loaded into the hold by way of bow and stern ports*
WILSON F. KLIPPEL. COURTESY OF MRS. CHARLES HEWITT.

Below: 1885. The lofty three-skysail-yard full-rigged ship Hotspur, *of New Bedford, departs Boston for Melbourne on her maiden voyage. The sailors, hoisting the fore-topgallant yard, are likely singing a tipsy chantey.*
NATHANIEL L. STEBBINS. COURTESY OF SOCIETY FOR THE PRESERVATION OF NEW ENGLAND ANTIQUITIES.

The newly rigged bark Olympic *prepares to sail to New York, which she did with "swept holds," i.e., without ballast—a unique accomplishment for a big square-rigger—made possible by her model and rig. Her main skysail yard will be crossed at New York. Likely the only sailing vessel launched with this rig, some Bathites opined that she was a "four-masted bark." Captain Besse simply called her a bark. She sailed very well and for many years, being last under sail for a Hollywood movie in 1924 before being cut down for a fishing barge.*
WILSON F. KLIPPEL. COURTESY OF MRS. CHARLES HEWITT.

1. According to the *Bangor Industrial Journal*, 11 May 1888, within the past year 180 deep-water American ships, amounting to 270,000 tons, had been sold foreign or cut down for use as coastal coal barges. For some years the Germans had been major buyers of old American ships.

2. Florence Besse Ballantine, *Descendants of Anthony Besse 1609–1956* (privately printed, 1965). The grandsire of the Besse tribe, Anthony, arrived at Boston from London, aboard the ship *James* in 1635. He settled in Sandwich, at the base of Cape Cod, and is known to have expressed concerns regarding the welfare of Indians. By the early 1700s Besses had settled in neighboring Agawam—Wareham to be—where today (indeed, as also in Sandwich) some Besses yet reside. (After the Indian wars, several Besses removed to the District of Maine, establishing there a prominent branch of the family.) Farming, shipbuilding, shipping, small cotton mills, and iron-founding early became important Wareham industries. The cut-nail industry, which would grow to large proportions, began about 1820. By 1830 the Wareham Iron Company claimed one of the most advanced rolling mills in the country (in 1834 it came under New Bedford ownership—New Bedford's whale fishery consumed large quantities of rolled barrel hoops).

3. Like his father, Besse would marry into the Briggs family, another local seagoing clan. Captain Benjamin Briggs, of Wareham, famously and mysteriously disappeared with his family and crew from the half-brig *Mary Celeste* in 1872, in mid-Atlantic.

4. *New Bedford Evening Standard*, 10 April 1900.

5. Although commonly called the "coolie" trade, the Hong Kong–West Coast trade in "Chinese passengers" should not be confused with the earlier notorious trade carrying coolies to Cuba, Peru, and elsewhere. This will be addressed in greater detail further along.

6. Unlike later "four-masted barks," however, she carried the rig of a three-masted bark with a fourth mast, with spanker, stepped aft of her mizzen mast. This rig was clearly selected out of concern for the shoal-drafted former steamer's stability, as it put less weight aloft, yet with the square-sails placed forward, where they were most effective in downwind trade-wind sailing. With *Olympic,* it also satisfied Captain S. B. Gibbs's concern that command of a mere barkentine was unbecoming to a square-rigger captain. See *American Neptune,* vol. iv, p. 237.

7. The first use of the term "Down Easter" to differentiate a certain type of vessel, as opposed to its place of origin, may have been in the English historian Basil Lubbock's book *Before the Mast* (London: John Murray, 1902). Henry Hall in 1884, and historian Winthrop Marvin in 1902 called them "medium clippers," while their leading historian, Frederick C. Matthews—no fan of Lubbock's—called them simply "American merchant ships." Whether one is referring to the largest of ships or the smallest of watercraft, the classification of types of floating creations was evidently less a matter of concern to their contemporaries than to subsequent historians. Howe and Mathews—Octavious T. Howe, M.D., and Frederick C. Matthews, *American Clipper Ships 1833–1858* (Salem, MA: Marine Research Society, 1929), p. vi—defined a clipper ship (i.e., clipper full-rigged ship) as "a sailing vessel of peculiar construction, designed for great speed rather than for capacity." In their opinion the last American "extreme clipper" was laid down in 1854, to be followed until the late 1860s by "medium clippers." Yet even

the foremost chronicler of Boston's extreme clippers of the '50s, Duncan McLean, referred to "clippers" sailing in the late '90s which had to have been constructed in more recent decades. He also referred to McKay's 1869 ship *Glory of the Seas*—sometimes called the first Down Easter—as "a combination of the clipper and the New York Packet-ship, designed to carry a large cargo, to sail fast, and to work like a pilot-boat." (Duncan McLean, "The Old Days of Clipper Ships," *Harper's Young People,* 19 Jan. 1897.)

8. Hall reported that Virginia, Maryland, and Delaware white oak for frames, and southern longleaf pine for planking and keelsons, were the chief woods of choice. Some native hardwood (beech, birch, and maple) was used for floor timbers, along with hackmatack frame top timbers, and white pine and Oregon pine for decks. Oregon pine, i.e., Douglas fir—as it happens, delivered by Besse ships—was preferred for masts. Hall wrote: "Bath vessels are famous for their excellent models and their handsome appearance, and are popular with captains on account of the pains which have been taken to fit up the cabins in style and comfort. Nearly all the New Bedford vessels are now built in Bath." Henry Hall, "Report on the Shipbuilding Industry of the United States," *Tenth Census* (Washington, D.C.: U.S. Government Printing Office 1884), p. 102.

9. The firm began with the 1865 alliance of Captain Guy C. Goss and Master Builder Elijah F. Sawyer. In 1886 Goss, age sixty-two, was described as "Maine's foremost shipbuilder—no small title—with a sunshiny bronzed face crowned with snowy hair." At age thirty the master of a brig, two years later the master of a ship, Goss had retired from the sea in 1862. The firm was known successively as Goss & Sawyer, Goss, Sawyer & Packard (1873), the New England Shipbuilding Company (1884), and the New England Company (1888 to 1906). In 1880 Goss was a founder of the Goss Iron Works, an iron-working and engine-building company which became part of the shipbuilding firm in 1885. Along with five steam auxiliary schooners, the firm built seven steam auxiliary barks. Four of the barks were for New Bedford owners engaged in the San Francisco-based Arctic whaling fleet; one was a South Pacific missionary ship; and two were merchant carriers, including Besse's 1882 "yacht-like" *George S. Homer.* The *Homer* was intended to operate between the Atlantic and Pacific Coasts via the Strait of Magellan, but her engine was removed as uneconomical as soon as she reached Oregon on her maiden voyage. Thereafter, the fine-lined bark proved an excellent performer under sail. Losses incurred from the auxiliary merchant bark venture evidently caused the shipbuilding firm's failure and reorganization.

10. *Bangor Industrial Journal,* 15 April 1887.

11. *Bath American Sentinel,* 27 April 1876. Today *Western Belle's* figurehead resides at the Peabody Essex Museum at Salem, Massachusetts, and *Belle of Oregon*'s is at the Mariners' Museum, Newport News, Virginia. *Forest Belle*'s survived shipwreck to find her way home—one version has her taking passage aboard the *Alden Besse*—to Portland, Oregon, where she now resides at the Oregon Historical Society.

12. The three *Belles*' names may well have been inspired by the most celebrated clipper ship built on Cape Cod, the sharp, saucy, and lofty flyer *Belle of the West,* built at East Dennis in 1853.

13. When the *Tobey* arrived at Valpariso, Chile, in December 1892, young sailor Charles G. Davis, aboard the American bark *James A. Wright,* described her

in his journal as looking like a clipper. Charles G. Davis, *Around Cape Horn* (Camden, ME: Down East Books, 2004), page 100. Tobey was a lawyer, banker, industrialist, and most fortunate heir to a Wareham iron foundary fortune.

14. In 1879 Goss & Sawyer also launched ten three-masted schooners, a steam whaling bark for New Bedford, and a steamer. In all the firm would build just over 300 vessels, the majority being three-masted schooners but including more than 60 barks and ships.

15. Crapo, a lawyer in New Bedford and once partner with Frank Stone's father, was elected to Congress four times. He played a central role in the *Alabama* Claims settlement, by which terms Great Britain paid partial restitution to American shipowners—including many New Bedforders—whose vessels had been captured by English-built and sponsored Confederate commerce raiders. (Crapo also caused a claim to be filed against the Chinese government by the U. S. government for the burning of *Forest Belle*—in which he was an owner—by Formosans after the bark had been run ashore after striking an uncharted rock.) The brief contract—less than one thousand words—covering the design and construction of the *Crapo* reveals the level of trust between the builders and Besse, and the economical and practical approach to wooden shipbuilding. The "party of the first part" was obligated to build, launch, and "equip ready for sea" a bark of "Two hundred feet keel, Forty one and one half feet Beam, Twenty-four feet deep." The completed vessel was to qualify for a fourteen-year rating from French Lloyds, with "first class" windlass, pumps, boats, chains, workmanship, and so forth, to the satisfaction of the "party of the second part." Said vessel was to be completed between July and November. The cost of the vessel was set at $40 per ton per "old government tonnage," to be paid in several installments. The builder took a large 3/8 ownership. And that, in less than one thousand words, was about it. The final line, i.e., "The builders guarantee that the vessel will stand up with spars aloft and sails bent & without Ballast," is of particular interest, given that these ships were essentially designed by hunch, art, and experience, and not by computers, engineers, and a legal team. Over the course of a long life a vessel's ability to stand up in port "with swept hold" would save her owners a great deal of money and save her captains time, bother, and worry. *American Neptune,* vol. 8, pp. 152–53. The assumption by the builders of a substantial ownership in the new bark, in lieu of cash, was a strong vote of confidence in Besse's management. The hulls of wooden ships at Bath (and elsewhere in Maine) were designed by means of a wooden half model. The chief modeler at Bath (and surely the designer of Goss & Sawyer square-riggers) was the skilled and prolific native son William Pattee, who had apprenticed under Boston's great Dennison J. Lawlor.

16. *New York Maritime Register*, 10 June 1891.

17. *Bangor Industrial Journal*, 27 Nov. 1891.

Chapter 5

BESSE SHIPS AT SEA AND IN PORT, 1883

We Join the Barks William H. Besse *and* Jonathan Bourne *Working Through Perilous Waters; Catch a Glimpse of Uncle Frank Stone, First Mate of the* Bourne; *and Are Witness to the Great Eruption of Krakatoa.*

THE PICTURESQUE TABLEAU, described earlier, as the little Western Island packet *Veronica* lay at Rotch's Wharf discharging casks of wine under the windows of her owner's counting house, was a romantic throwback. By the late 1800s most deep-water sailing vessels were employed in a relatively limited number of long-distance trades. Most involved the carriage of bulk cargoes of relatively little value via tradewind routes and around Cape Horn or the Cape of Good Hope.

Some American ships sailed for years without returning to American waters and then largely confined their visits to a handful of major ports. Captain Besse, riding herd on his fleet from his New Bedford office by means of letters and cryptic telegrams generally only laid eyes on his ships on their occasional visits to East Coast ports.

During the week of April 11, 1883, as gathered from reports in the *New York Maritime Register*, the eleven members of Besse's fleet were well scattered about the globe. The bark *Alden Besse*, Captain Noyes, was sailing from Portland, Oregon, to Hong Kong, likely carrying flour and returning coolies, there to load more Chinese. The bark *Gerard C. Tobey*, Captain Baker, was bound from New York around Cape Horn to San Francisco, doubtless with a general cargo—this was legally a coastwise passage restricted to American ships. The ship *Henry Failing*, Captain Merriman, was lying at San Pedro, having arrived from Tacoma, likely with lumber, after a passage from Philadelphia. The bark *Guy C. Goss*, Captain Freeman, was en route from New York to Yokohama, doubtless with "case oil"—tins of kerosene in wooden cases. *Belle of Oregon*, Captain Mathews, was at Newcastle, New South Wales, surely loading coal. The new auxiliary bark *George S. Homer*, Captain Crowell, was somewhere between New York and Portland, Oregon, no doubt carrying a general cargo.

The bark *William W. Crapo*, Captain Hardy, was bound from Port Townsend, Washington, for Bath with a cargo of Oregon pine spars. She had returned to Port Townsend with a mutinous crew, shipped a new mate, and departed once again.

The ship *William J. Rotch*, Captain Bray, was en route from New York to Hiogo, Japan, doubtless with case oil. The old ship *Syren*, Captain Crocker, was sailing from New York to Anjer—the door to the Far East—for orders; perhaps she had case oil as well. The bark *Mary S. Ames*, Captain Elijah Crocker, was somewhere between San Francisco and New York.

The bark *Jonathan Bourne*, Captain Doane (with young Frank Stone—Tod Swift's uncle—serving as first mate), and the bark *William H. Besse*, Captain B. C. Baker, were en route from Hong Kong to Manila to load sugar. Both had brought coal to Hong Kong from Newcastle, New South Wales, and were sailing to Manila in ballast.

The *Besse* arrived first. Reports received at Hong Kong of a cholera epidemic at Manila had almost sent Mrs. Baker and their son home by steamer, but in the end, they had remained aboard. At Manila the epidemic was found to be running unchecked. Ships anchored far out in the bay, and were loaded from lighters, and contact with the shore was kept to a minimum. Anyone going ashore in a small boat had first to enter narrow Pasig River, lying under the guns of a mammoth sixteenth-century stone fort and filled with rotting refuse, dead animals, and filth of every description.[1]

Aboard the *Besse*, efforts at staving off the disease included keeping meals very simple—"gungy water," made from rice, toast water, and oatmeal gruel was standard fare.[2] To avoid chills, no one sat out on deck at night. Mrs. Baker later wrote: "The harbor was filled with the groans of the dying—like sheep they were falling right and left. Scarcely a *tobanger* passed us without its dead."[3]

When a sailor fell ill one day while Captain Baker happened to be ashore, Mrs. Baker sent a boat requesting help to the only other American vessel in the port, the handsome three-skysail-yard ship *Northern Light*, Captain Joshua Slocum.[4] Slocum promptly came on board, took off his coat, and entered the *Besse*'s fo'c's'l to nurse the sailor, who died that evening. Two more sailors sickened and were taken ashore for care, where they died.[5]

A day or so later the *Jonathan Bourne* arrived. As the *Bourne* was free of disease, Mrs. Baker and her son Sidney temporarily moved aboard—the Bakers and Captain Doane being fellow Cape Codders, this was just part of being neighborly. The *Bourne* departed Manila for New York on May 15; on the twenty-third, the *Besse* departed as well. "We never turned our backs upon land with more thankfulness than when the *Besse* took her anchors and sailed into purer air," Mrs. Baker recalled.

But ships, such as the *Jonathan Bourne, William H. Besse*, and *Northern Light*, which were headed home from the Far East by way of the Indian Ocean and the Cape of Good Hope, had first to pass through the treacherous blockade of the Indian Archipelago—the Dutch East Indies, now Indonesia—with its thousands of islands, myriad uncharted reefs, strong currents, and fickle winds. Routes were selected according to the seasonal monsoon winds. Findlay's 1889 *Directory for the Navigation of the Indian Archipelago*—a nearly six-pound, four-inch-thick tome first published in 1869—waxed poetic when advising shipmasters:

> IN THE NORTHERN WINTER, when the sun is *South* of the Equator, and the great Asiatic continent is cool, the regular N. E. trade wind prevails over the whole region North of the Equatorial Calms, and is generally known as the *North-east Monsoon*, which is only liable to local deflection.... To the South of the Equatorial Calms, the S. E. trade prevails throughout the season of October to April, when the sun is in the southern signs...and therefore, in the western portion of the area...the winds pursue their ordinary courses.
>
> But when the sun enters into North latitude...and...is vertical over an immense area of land South of the Himalaya Mountains, the desert regions of Arabia, the burning plains of Western India, countries where the earth is fire, and wind flame; and when this intense heat is extended to the southern portions of China, the S. E. trade wind, receiving a *northern* impulse, follows up the retreating N. E. trade to the foot of the Himalayas....
>
> The effects of this S.W. monsoon are felt very far beyond the coasts, upon which its first furies fall in the burst of its commencement.... While this deflected S. E. trade wind, in the form of the S. W. monsoon, North of the Equator, is blowing between May and October, the S. E. trade proper prevails over all that part of the Indian Ocean which is not skirted to the South by large tracts of land.....
>
> The Monsoons, therefore, of the Indian Archipelago are not *two* in number, but are *four*—the N. E. and S. W. to the north of the Equator, and the S. E. and N. W. to the South of the line.[6]

The *Bourne*, *Besse,* and *Northern Light,* sailing on the very tail end of the northeast monsoon, headed south, through Mindoro Strait into the Mindoro and Sulu Seas. Then they would head through the Sulu Archipelago and into the Celebes Sea for Macassar Strait, the great equatorial channel into the Java Sea east of Borneo. At the entrance of Macassar, the *Besse* came upon both the *Bourne* and *Northern Light*. Mrs. Baker, aboard the *Besse*, later recalled:

> WE MADE MERRY by signaling through the day and burning torches at night. Thus passed several days until one Sunday morning there came a dead calm, and from the *Bourne*'s signals we read, "I'll come on board." We watched the little dinghy skim under the *Bourne*'s bow, and rejoiced to meet our old friend where every breath was not a groan. That Sunday at sea was a benediction; it gave us rest and hope.

Back on May 30, while in the Sulu Sea, Captain Doane had written the Bakers a letter, which he now delivered in person. In it he had written:

> TWO LONG AND TEDIOUS WEEKS have elapsed since I bid you good night on the eve of leaving the port of desolation for our welcome homeward bound passage, and daily do I hold you in remembrance and long to know if all is well with you.... I find that at noon we are only 514 miles S. by East from Manila and that our log shows our sailing to have been 874. This leaves 360 miles that we may call yachting, although there has been no fun attached to it, but a full measure of care and anxiety.

Captain Doane then related a string of misfortunes, beginning with a near collision with a Quebec bark when "*Jonathan* performed an evolution on getting under weigh [*sic*] that has astonished my weak nerves ever since." The following morning, as Corregidor Island at the mouth of Manila Bay finally dropped astern, the weather began to look poorly. The next morning found the *Bourne* scudding before a typhoon under bare poles. That afternoon, in very violent wind and irregular seas, the bark broached to, i.e., turned broadside to sea and wind. Captain Doane wrote:

> THINGS WERE RATHER moist for a time. Got two canvas bags with oakum saturated with lamp oil, and put them over the side, but the wind blew the top of the water off so I fancy they did not much good.[7]

When the storm had passed, nineteen inches of molasses was sounded in the well, which took the steam pump eight hours to remove—"Thereby hangs a long yarn," wrote the captain. Finding himself blown to the southwest, into the South China Sea, Doane thought he might try to sail to the west of Borneo, then head south for the Strait of Sunda. But the arrival of strong headwinds forced a change of plans:

> NOW, FRIEND BAKER, you know my weakness for China Sea, having had such good luck on two former passages in May...as the wind

had got around to South I would still keep on, which I did for another day.... I was just congratulating myself on how I was going to astonish all you fellows that took Mendora Passage, when my attention was called to something coming up from the Gulf of Siam. Well to make a long story short it was an argument that proved most conclusively to my mind, as I saw topsail halyards going, and both leaches off our best mainsail...that China Sea was impracticable just at this time. So we up helm and run for poor despised Mendora.

When entering the Sulu Sea the *Bourne* kept company with a German barkentine and the ship *Belle of Bath*, of Bath, also built by Goss & Sawyer in 1877 and of nearly identical measurements to the *Bourne*, differing in her ship rig and lack of a main skysail.

ON THE 29TH the German and ourselves were over on the Basilan shore when we were favored with the first of a southeast breeze.... The *Belle of Bath* was nearly out of sight astern at sunset. After getting safe into the Sea with a moderate breeze from S.S.W. I lay down and had the first good sleep since we left port, and this morning...I saw neither land or the *B. of B.* I was ready to sing all the Sankey and Moody hymns in the double ender....[8] Mr. Stone is a genius. A few days after leaving Manila I passed his room, and there he sat in his bunk, a picture of patience and contentment. One leg was thrown promiscuous like over the edge of the berth showing the calf well tied up with the cholera band Mrs. Baker so kindly made. He explained that having worn the belt, and never feeling an ache or pain in the region of the diaphragm, and discovering a small boil on his leg he thought it advisable to move the band nearer the seat of disease, and was happy to say that the result was proving the wisdom of his judgment, and his gratitude to Mrs. Baker for her thoughtful favor will be everlasting.[9]

Nothing aged a captain faster than sailing through distant, poorly charted waters with numerous shoals and reefs, some named for the ships that had been their first recorded victims. Not only were there many more reefs awaiting rude discovery, but many of the dangers marked on the charts were inaccurately plotted or did not exist at all. Referring to the Palawan Passage, one of the several major routes to and from Manila, Findlay's cautioned:

IN FORMER TIMES, the imperfect observations of passing vessels, and the too frequent very desultory notices of presumed discovery of dangers, caused the charts to be embarrassed with a multitude of reefs which have no existence.

> But in the space between the two channels, as they may be termed, that along the Asiatic side, and that parallel with Palawan, there still remains an Archipelago of Reefs, a labyrinth of clusters, shoals and reefs, in many cases of doubtful existence, but in more of doubtful position...this area..."*ought to be avoided by all navigators.*" This truth cannot be too strongly impressed upon all, for although it is possible that a ship might pass unharmed through this region of dangers, coralline reefs, and sand-banks, of strong currents and irregular tides, yet the risk is very great, and the greatest caution will not be an excuse for venturing into such imminent danger.[10]

And of the Java Sea route, where the *Bourne,* the *Besse*, and *Northern Light* were carefully threading their ways to the south, Findlay cautioned:

> FOR THE GREAT PORTION of its area there is no proper survey, and therefore it should be navigated with more than ordinary caution, as defective charts are *stated* to have been one cause of disaster.

Mrs. Baker, sailing aboard the *Besse*, would recall their fateful passage south:

> JUNE 24TH, SHIP *NORTHERN LIGHT* ahead, we made the South Watcher, the first of the southern portion of the Thousand Islands. The day was beautiful; the Easterly Monsoon was gentle and soft as a zephyr; every sail was full, and our hearts were as light as the air we breathed. We passed one and another island until at 5 P.M. our captain judged we were clear of danger. The *Bourne* was near us, her white wings making a pretty picture which we never tired of watching. The second mate from aloft had just made his report of the position of Babia when the bell rang for dinner. As I arose from my chair I felt a terrible shock which threw me off my feet in an instant. We knew we were hard and fast on some coral reef which doubtless had been thrown up during some of Nature's numerous convulsions. Our first thought was to save the *Bourne* whose captain we knew was at dinner, and felt, like ourselves, that all danger had passed. We shouted, all to no purpose. On came the noble ship until it seemed that both would find a burial there. Our captain and men were using every means in their power to call attention to our position, when for the

---

Following pages: Sailing track chart for the Indian Archipelago for the south–west monsoon.
FINDLAY'S DIRECTORY, 1889.

THE
INDIAN ARCHIPELAGO
TRACK CHART
in the South-West Monsoon
(April to September)
Outward
Homeward
Telegraph Cables, thus
CHIN
CANTON
SIAM
CAMBODIA
BANG KOK
G. of Martaban
Mergui Arch.
GULF of SIAM
MALACCA STRAIT
SINGAPORE
SUMATRA
BORNEO
JAVA
SUNDA STRAIT
BATAVIA
INDIAN OCEAN
Equator
Natuna I.
Paracels I.
TONG KING GULF
COCHIN CHINA
Saigon
Hue
Apr. to Aug.
Sept. Oct.
Keeling I.
Christmas I.
95
100
105
110

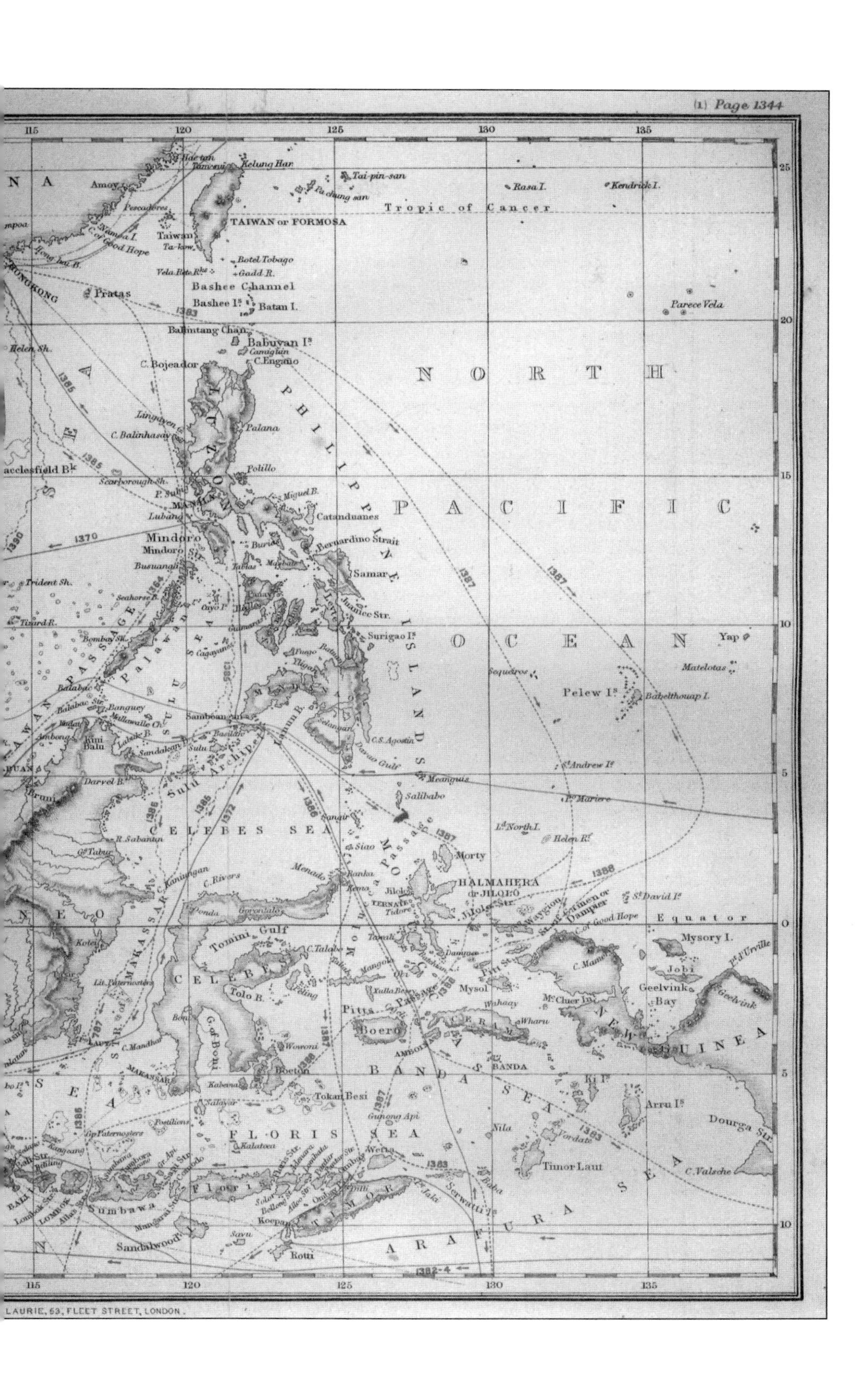

BESSE SHIPS AT SEA AND IN PORT, 1883

> first time in our lives our Stars and Stripes went up union down. T'was a hard pull, it meant so much.
>
> The *Bourne* was scarcely fifty yards from us when at the lee rail came the captain's head, just in time to hear our captain shout "For God's sake port your helm!" He sprang to the wheel, shouting "All hands aft!" He had heard the cry, seen the coral, felt it graze his ship's side, and sprang to save her. One moment longer and the two would have lain there with trembling hulls and flapping sails.
>
> As the *Bourne* dipped into deeper water our captain shouted "I'm ashore, come on board." The reply came across that sunlit water, "I will, as soon as I can deepen my water." Silently save for the dip, dip of the oars came the *Bourne*'s captain. Over our fallen ship's side he climbed and grasping our captain's hand said, "Baker, you've saved me." The reply came in low tones—"This is the last of the *W. H. Besse* and the last of me; take my wife and child to Angier with you; I must know they are safe, and I will come to them as soon as I can."[11]

Mrs. Baker and young Sidney remained onboard, however, and the *Bourne* sailed on to Anjer, the famous port of call in the Straits of Sunda, there to telegraph for assistance from Batavia. Victor Slocum, Joshua's son, had a different vantage point aboard *Northern Light*. He later wrote:

> IN SAILING FOR ANJER POINT, we were followed by two other American ships.... They were the *Wm. H. Besse* and the *Jonathan Bourne*. There was a light breeze, and all three ships in a line within easy signal distance of each other, when we observed the *Besse* to come up suddenly, all standing, and stop. She had grounded on a reef which had been cast up by sub-marine volcanic action in the very spot over which we had passed but a quarter of an hour before. The sea was trembling and in bubbles. A lead that was cast came up from the bottom so hot it melted out the tallow armor, showing that it was of a temperature higher than the boiling point.
>
> The *Northern Light* braced up her yards and came up into the wind, but as the *Bourne* came up astern of the *Besse* and hove to, to offer assistance, we kept off for Anjer, which was by this time but a few miles distant.... Before we left Anjer, the *Bourne* came in and reported that the *Besse* had grounded easily, was in no immediate danger, and that a tug was on the way from Batavia to her assistance.[12]

In fact, back at the reef, a heavy sea had arisen, and despite great efforts through the night to work her clear, the *Besse* bumped and thumped sickeningly, with water gaining on the pumps. The boats were readied for her abandonment. The following morning the bark was kedged clear of the reef, only to be swept back against it by the tide, broadside-to, leaving her pounding heavily, with the masts shaking like reeds. Further attempts to kedge her off and the jettisoning of some cargo were to no avail. But the *Besse* lived through the night, and the following day a steamer towed her to Batavia, there to become prey "for every land vulture that could in any capacity swoop down upon us." After the cargo of sugar was unloaded and warehoused the bark was put into a floating dry dock for extensive hull repairs. To escape the dreaded fever and cholera, Mrs. Baker and her young son were sent up to the mountains for the weeks that the ship was being repaired.[13]

When *Northern Light* departed narrow, busy Sunda Strait she passed by the island of Krakatoa, whose volcano, having reawakened in May, was in eruption. Bright fire created a column of black steam and ashes reaching an altitude of seventeen miles (as measured by sextant) escaping from a crater located at about 1,200 feet in the great depression created by an ancient explosion. The sea in the strait was white with pumice, created from falling ashes.

On August 26 the repaired *William H. Besse*'s sailors gratefully hove up her anchors and set sail for home. Meeting headwinds, however, in the evening the pilot elected to anchor. Just as the chains rattled overboard there commenced a fearful thundering and cannonading from the south, which the pilot identified as the volcano acting up, about forty miles distant. The thundering continued all through the night.

In the morning the pilot departed, and the bark proceeded on her way. But conditions rapidly deteriorated and when the barometer began rising and falling violently Captain Baker anchored and secured all sail. Then, "like a curtain fell a darkness so intense no human eye could penetrate it. Ashes were falling like snow. Lifelines were run for the safety of those who worked, for fingers and feet were eyes." Findlay's *Directory* later described this famous eruption:

> ON THE EVENING OF THE 26TH some violent explosions took place, audible at Batavia, 80 miles distant, and between 5 and 7 A.M. by a detonation so terrific, as to be heard even in India, Ceylon, Manila, and the West Coast of Australia, over 2,000 miles away. Following on these came a succession of enormous waves, which completely swept the shores of the strait, utterly destroying Anjer, Telok Batong, and numerous villages, the loss of life being officially estimated at over 36,000 souls. The coasts and islands in the vicinity were buried under a layer of mud and ashes....
>
> A wave of atmospheric disturbance was...generated, which has been traced three times completely round the world, traveling at the

> speed of sound. The height of the column of steam and smoke...is estimated at from 9 to 12 miles...large quantities of fine dust were discharged into the upper regions of the atmosphere, giving rise to those beautiful sunsets observed all over the world.... The amount of solid matter ejected has been computed at over 4 1/4 cubic miles.[14]

With the air thick with sulfur, the *Besse* was battened down and her people sought refuge inside. The wind howled fearfully, the sea rose, and the tide surged—nothing less than the Day of Judgment seemed to be at hand. Both anchors were down, with 720 feet of chain out on each, yet the *Besse* dragged for miles—a parted link would have sent her back on the coral and to her doom. When soundings were attempted, the thirty-pound deep-sea lead floated atop the thick layer of pumice.

> AT FIVE O'CLOCK OUR CAPTAIN opened the cabin door and beckoning to us said, "Come here."...Standing in the darkness he pointed to a little rim of light which seemed far, far on an unknown shore, and whispered "'tis a promise of another day.' That night was quiet, save for a troubled sea.... The 28th of August was nearly all spent in heaving short our anchor[s].... Our chains were so foul and the sun so hot that we did not make sail until six on the morning of the 29th, when it was thought best not to carry but little sail and to proceed cautiously, for with the exception of St. Nicholas Point neither land nor soundings were familiar or as they should be. Sight after sight was worked and every time the captain would say, "I don't understand it; according to my sights we are sailing over the top of Angier." And we have since learned it was indeed so....

Anjer, the most welcomed and welcoming port of call in the East Indies, was gone. Gone were the great banyan trees; the fort; the bum-boats offering fresh fruit and caged birds; old friends from past voyages; the precious packets of mail; the coded telegrams which directed ships hither and yon; and the treasured files of hometown newspapers, some but several months old, left by outward-bounders.[15]

Mrs. Baker continued:

> ON THE 30TH DURING THE MORNING we were startled by our captain's cry of 'Hard up! Hard down! Easy! Hard up! Hard up! Hard down!', each order following quick after the other...'twas a sight I shall never forget. Our way seemed blocked by every conceivable thing: human beings bloated beyond recognition, boats, trees, fruit, and animals. Should we ever be able to leave it all!
>
> Like all other days, that came to an end. We passed through the

gates out into the Indian Ocean without other stain than the clinging ashes which never entirely left the vessel as long as she floated.... At evening we passed Prince's Island, which thus far was the first land that we had passed as it should be. The [dry] dock in which we repaired pulled from its moorings on the 26th and floated by us that day.... For six hundred miles we sailed in the open sea ere we found blue water...a dire stillness fell among us. One and another was taken; even the mate yielded.... One evening just at nightfall we folded our flag over a box which held one of the crew. The captain read the burial service and into the ocean the box was lowered. Java fever or Beri beri as they called it lingered about us all the voyage, so that when off Hatteras we were ill prepared to battle with a hurricane.

However, when the three lights of Truro [on Cape Cod] were sighted, and later Highland light, the home hawser was pulling so strong that courage came to every heart but mine.

---

1. Mrs. B. C. Baker, "Reminiscences of a Voyage in the Bark William H. Besse," American Neptune 4, no. 2. Victor Slocum, Capt. Joshua Slocum (New York: Sheridan House, 1950), p. 80.

2. Toast water was drink made from burned toast used like tea leaves, taken cold for fevers, or as a hot drink by the poor.

3. Likely she meant *gobang*, or dugout canoe.

4. The *Northern Light* was of 1,795 tons, built at Quincy, Massachusetts, in 1872. William F. Weld & Co., of Boston, owned her for her first three years. In 1885 she was sold under the Norwegian flag.

5. Slocum's willingness to expose himself, and by extension, his family and crew, to the disease for the sake of a common sailor surely says a great deal about this controversial man, who was then in the midst of a most difficult voyage which ended with his being tried in federal court in New York on charges of cruelty. Shortly after leaving New York with case oil for Yokohama, *Northern Light* had put into New London, Connecticut, for rudder repairs. A mutiny among the crew while in port resulted in the stabbing death of the first mate. With the ringleaders removed and a new mate signed on, Slocum set sail with the same crew, who proved troublesome for the remainder of the voyage. When homeward bound, off the Cape of Good Hope, the ship's rudder head was twisted by heavy seas, causing the ship to broach to. A leak dissolved sugar in the lower hold, and the ship became crank, or top-heavy, forcing the jettisoning of part of the cargo of Manila hemp. Under jury steering gear the ship made Port Elizabeth, where the remaining cargo was discharged and the ship overhauled. A new third mate, named Slater, was signed on. Subsequently revealed to be a British ex-convict with forged discharges, Slater was disrated by Slocum for insolence, then put in irons for fifty-three days for fomenting mutiny. In court Slocum was fined $500. Slater recanted his charges, but, years later, when the two men met in Australia, recanted his recantation. See Slocum, pp. 149-75; also, Walter Magnus Teller, *The*

Search for Captain Slocum (New York: C. Scribner's Sons, 1956), pp. 27–31, 111–25.

Slocum was an old Philippine hand, having formerly been in the ship-timber trade from the islands to China, and having built a 150-ton steamer on the jungled shore of Subic Bay. In the 1890s he would rebuild the old sloop *Spray* on the Fairhaven shore of New Bedford Harbor, sail her alone around the world, and write one of the great books of the sea. In 1902 Slocum bought a farm on Martha's Vineyard and for several summers *Spray* was a common sight on Vineyard Sound and Buzzard's Bay. It is very likely indeed that Uncle Frank Stone (and Tod Swift), cruising about those waters as well, met up with him, and that Uncle Frank and Slocum reminisced about the time they crossed paths in Manila in 1883. Incidentally, Slocum had ancestral ties to southeastern Massachusetts; his great-grandfather, following his Quaker beliefs, joined the Tory diaspora, moving from Taunton, Massachusetts, to Digby, Nova Scotia, to start a frontier life anew.

6. Alexander George Findlay, *A Directory for the Navigation of the Indian Archipelago* (London, 1889), p. 1299. This volume was an outgrowth of the *Oriental Navigator*, first published in 1775.

7. An oil slick, by reducing the surface tension of the water, can greatly diminish the incidence of breaking seas. Turpentine and sperm oil are the most effective oils; petroleum, the least.

8. Dwight Moody and Ira Sankey were fundamentalist Protestant revivalists who attracted a large following in the U.S. and Great Britain. Sankey, singer and organist, composed hymns and created a popular hymnal, published in 1874. The "double-ender" is surely a reference to Captain Doane's dinghy, likely hoisted to davits and serving as a fine imaginary pulpit.

9. Flannel cholera bands, adopted from the Indian cumberbund and worn around the midriff, were thought to ward off the disease. Captains customarily addressed mates as "Mister." The immense social and legal chasm between the office of master and first mate was generally closely observed, however, the aforementioned to the contrary not withstanding, Captain Doane and Mr. Stone were clearly on the friendliest of terms.

10. Findlay, *Directory* p. 621–22.

11. Baker, "Reminiscences," p.1 26.

12. Slocum, *Capt. Joshua Slocum*, pp. 169-70.

13. Returning to Batavia, Mrs. Baker was surprised to find that staying in the hotel with them was an American circus company, whose members were continually crying out "Spider! Spider!," American for "Sparder," which was Malay for servant boy.

14. Findlay, *Directory for the Navigation,* p. 78.

15. Victor Slocum recalled that on *Northern Light*'s visit some weeks before the explosion the Dutch authorities were organizing a punitive expedition to put down a rebellion stewing in Sumatra, and native colonial troops "in gaudy trappings and with burnished arms" were filing aboard a gunboat to carry them across the strait. He later noted that the authorities might have saved themselves the trouble.

Chapter 6

CAPTAIN FRANK STONE

Frank Stone Assumes Command of the Bark Jonathan Bourne, *and Then a Splendid New Command, the* Francis.

HOMEWARD BOUND from Manila, the *Jonathan Bourne* passed Anjer on June 25th—two months before the eruption—and arrived at New York October 15, 1883. In November, while the bark was lying at New York, first mate Frank Stone, age twenty-six, Harvard dropout, was promoted to master—in but three and a half years Frank had progressed from ordinary seaman to captain.[1] Having had Captain Doane as a tutor was surely worth more than additional time spent under many lesser men.[2] There is no question that Frank was a fast learner and had the right stuff. Frank, of course, also had the all-important connections with the tight little community of the bark's owners, which included experienced mariners William and Alden Besse and Jonathan Bourne, and also China merchant (and Frank's uncle) Thomas Hathaway.

Family ties and money certainly helped put Frank in the captain's cabin and eased the heavy burden of the fledgling captain's large outlay for navigational supplies (including chronometer, charts, and directories), to say nothing of the traditional master's share ($^{1}/_{8}$, or, more precisely, $^{8}/_{64}$) of the ship. But these advantages would have been of no use whatsoever to young Frank once the pilot was dropped off Sandy Hook. There was a story told among knowing shipmasters of a young captain's first night of command, having been caught by an equinoctial gale in the dangerous, funnel-shaped Bight of New York. Seas were breaking over the deeply laden ship, which, with sails blowing away, was laboring under a heavy press of canvas while trying to keep off the Jersey Coast. The new crew was still drunk, and one man had been lost overboard. Lashed to the cabin skylight, the young captain cried out, "Oh!, but for one hour of my old captain!"

Captain Stone's opening passage from New York to Melbourne was no milk run. Taking his ship into the Great Southern Ocean's "Roaring Forties," he would enter the band of endless westerly gales and mountainous seas which formed the great globe-circling conveyor of commerce where the square-rigger made its final stand against steam. It was in these fierce latitudes that clipper captains, while "running their easting down," learned the trick of reducing the effect of a heavy gale to that of a strong breeze by boldly carrying sail and running at unheard-of speeds while making record runs.[3]

During the southern winter Great Southern Ocean passages were arguably the hardest of any on the planet, including "doubling" Cape Horn, exposing ships to thousands of miles, and week upon week, of relentless, sleet-filled gales with huge, dangerous following seas. Historian and square-rig sailor Carl Cutler wrote of the experience:

> ONE CANNOT DESCRIBE this sort of thing. Perhaps only those who have sought the infinitely grateful shelter of a freezing fo'csle with its sea chests bumping around in six inches of sloshing ice water; who have found in a sodden dripping bunk an all-too brief glimpse of heaven on earth, can appreciate it.[4]

Masters, for their part, worried about twisted rudder heads, being "pooped" by a rogue sea, broaching-to, being dismasted, springing a leak, and endless other dire possibilities. Some, overwhelmed, left orders to carry all possible sail and then vanished into their cabin to seek escape in the bottom of a bottle. While the *Bourne* would not be experiencing winter conditions, at no time was this a place for any but a well-found, well-manned, well-commanded ship, since the consequences of any serious mishap were likely to be fatal.

The *Bourne* departed New York on December 10, 1883, no doubt carrying a cargo of general merchandise—this was among the last general cargo trades dominated by sail. She arrived at Melbourne on March 15, 1884, after a very creditable run of ninety-five days, almost three weeks faster than her maiden passage under Captain Doane.[5]

The *Bourne* left Melbourne April 18, and ten days later arrived at Newcastle, New South Wales, to load coal for Manila. On May 21 she departed Newcastle. The July 23 *New York Maritime Register* reported:

> *JONATHAN BOURNE*, Stone, from Newcastle NSW, for Manila, has been abandoned at sea in a sinking condition. The passengers and crew landed at Apo, one of the Philippine Islands, prior to July 21.

On August 7 Frank wrote home from Hong Kong:

> WE STRUCK A REEF off Mendora Sts. in the China Sea, not laid down on my chart, which was an English Admiralty chart, and of

the latest date. We were two days and nights in the boats and finally landed at Manila, all well. The loss of the *Bourne* is hard to bear, but thank God, I cannot reproach myself with negligence.

Writing to her cousin Sarah Forbes, Frank's mother wrote:

THE THOUGHT OF HIS disappointment and regret for his employers' losses coming into his early career is saddening, but I know how much of good these experiences bring as well as suffering, and I am trying to hope patiently for further tidings.[6]

Years later Frank would dryly note in his Harvard class report that he "had the misfortune to discover a reef in the China Sea and knock [the bark's] bottom out on it. Vessel and cargo a total loss. Succeeded in landing all hands safely at Manila, in the boats. Arrived home in November 1884."[7] Frank's obituary many years later, written by a classmate, would note that the bark sank in less than fifteen minutes and that Frank single-handedly controlled a mutinous crew, who, "but for his determination and courage, would have sacrificed the lives of their companions."[8]

Finding himself rudely cast ashore, Frank returned home and attempted a career in the telephone business. But telephones didn't take with Frank, and by March 1885 it had been decided by friends and family in New Bedford that a new ship should be "got up" for him.

Given the shrinking opportunities for shipmasters under the American flag, having family and friends willing to finance a new ship was surely the only way that Frank could return to command. Fortunately, his friends and family not only had the required means, but because most of their fortunes stemmed from maritime enterprises they could appreciate both Frank's ability and his passion.

The state of the shipping business in 1885, suffering from a worldwide glut of tonnage, was hardly encouraging. That November in Britain—whose huge production of iron and steel tonnage was a major factor in the slump—eighty-nine steamers and twenty sailing vessels were reported laid up on the Tyne, and there were said to be "miles" of laid-up ships on the Thames, Mersey, and the Clyde.[9] On the Kennebec, at Bath, Maine, shipbuilders were hungry, and the $100,000 it would cost to build Frank's new ship at "Goss & Sawyer"—now doing business as the New England Shipbuilding Company—was said to have included but little profit.[10]

As was traditional, the ownership of Frank's ship was divided into 64ths. The "largest" owners, with ⅛ apiece, included the builders, "managing owner" Captain William Besse, Horatio Hathaway, Francis Hathaway, Captain Francis Stone, and John Murray Forbes.[11] Lesser owners included Edward Mandell (of a whaling family), William Crapo, William J. Rotch, Leander Plummer, and F. Francis Parker. (Besse, Rotch, and Crapo, of course, had been owners in Besse-managed vessels named for them.) Excepting Forbes and Parker, all were of New Bedford.[12] The quick assembly of this tight syndicate to build a costly ship for a worthy son of the clan is a striking example not only of New Bedford's wealth, but of its tribal loyalty. Of course it also represented a calculated investment.

The new ship was "laid down"—i.e., her keel was "stretched"—in April 1885. She would be a large vessel, with registered dimensions of 231 feet length by 43.4 feet beam by 17.7 feet depth of hold, measuring 2,077 gross tons.[13] A lofty three-skysail yarder, she would be among the best of the select fleet which constituted the final generation of big wooden American square-riggers.

With the builders' typical dispatch, Frank's ship was completed in about six months' time. She was launched on a chilly day early in October

October, 1885. The splendid 2,077-ton full-rigged ship Francis, *of New Bedford, ready for launching at the New England Shipbuilding Company, Bath. The hull is sheathed with copper alloy sheets to the load waterline for protection against shipworms and to reduce marine growth.*
J. C. HIGGINS. COURTESY OF HENRY B. STONE.

with the owners' party aboard. Horatio Hathaway's daughter Elizabeth, while holding Frank's hand, smashed a bottle of wine over the starboard bow, christening the good ship *Francis.* Obediently, the mammoth yet masterfully modeled hull promptly "shot" down the smoking, tallowed sliding ways to splash into the welcoming Kennebec in a thrilling and gratifying manner.[14]

From her launching in 1885 to her loss in 1897 the *Francis* would make nine round-trip voyages, five of them taking her around the globe. These multi-passage world voyages began with carrying case oil around the Cape of Good Hope to Japan, and sometimes included a cargo of sugar or even tea delivered to the West Coast. Each included delivery of a cargo of wheat around Cape Horn to Liverpool or Harve. For example, on her maiden voyage the *Francis* sailed from Philadelphia to Hiogo with case oil in 145 days, then sailed to British Columbia to load coal for San Francisco; at San Francisco she loaded wheat for Harve, returning from Harve

The ship Francis *at the fitting-out wharf. Robustly constructed and beautifully modeled, with graceful ends, a sweeping sheer, and a lofty rig, the* Francis *represented the epitome of the wooden American square-rigged merchant ship. She would also be one of the very last such built.*
J. C. Higgins. Courtesy Henry B. Stone.

to Philadelphia to once again load case oil for Hiogo. (In the course of the following voyage she delivered two cargoes of sugar from Manila to San Francisco.) And so on.

In the 1890s the *Francis* made four round-trip Cape Horn voyages between Atlantic ports and San Francisco in the trade made famous by the California clippers. In 1895 the *Francis* returned to Japan with case oil, loading sugar in Java for Philadelphia, where she arrived under jury rig after a very close call with an Indian Ocean cyclone. Her next voyage, also beginning, in 1895, with another case oil passage to Japan, would end with her loss when but hours away from New York.

Frank was not involved with the loss of his ship; indeed, he had not then commanded her for several years. In 1887 Frank married Anna Rotch—Tod Swift's Aunt Anna and the daughter of William J. Rotch, New Bedford's wealthiest man. Marriage put a crimp in Frank's career possibly due to the crimp Frank's career had put in the honeymoon. Initially Frank was spelled for a lengthy passage on long voyages by his old mentor, Captain Doane. In 1892, at the grand old age of thirty-six, Frank officially retired from seafaring, turning the *Francis* over to Captain Doane and taking over the management of the ship from Captain Besse, whose ownership interest Frank bought out.[15] So, where once upon a time Stone had replaced Doane as master of the *Jonathan Bourne*, now, nine years later, Doane replaced Stone as master of the *Francis*.

On her homeward passage in 1895 from Manila, the ship was severely battered by an Indian Ocean cyclone. From the South Atlantic Captain Doane wrote Captain Stone:

> Ship *Francis* Feb. 3rd., 1896
> 61 days out. Lat 30 30 South
> Long. 10 40 East
>
> MY DEAR CAPT. STONE,
> We left Probolinggo on the evening of Dec. 4th and proceeded through Lombok Straits on the 9th. Had light air and calm weather 'till the 17th, with the temp. above 90 in the shade. Dec. 20th Lat. 13 36' South. Long. 107 40' East, we had a violent tempest, probably the beginning of a cyclone. Lost and split several sails including topsails and mainsail. After this we made moderate progress to the westward—wind from SSW to SSE, with cloudy and unsettled weather. Dec. 26th Lat. 19 21' Long. 92 52', Bar. 29" 74', for the past 24 hours, the wind has been steadily increasing in force from SE, with dark gloomy weather. At 8 A.M. blowing a strong gale, put ship under bare poles, and hove to with a view of noting the veering of the wind. At 6 P.M. wind unsteady from the SE to ESE, set fore and main lower top-

sails and bore up WSW. Hard gale and strong squalls during the night. Friday 27th Dec. Lat. 19 57' S Long. 91 19' E. Bar. 29" 67'. At 3 P.M. blowing a full gale. Sea very large, and the weather indicating a cyclone in our vicinity, we again put the ship under bare poles, and hove to on the starboard tack, as the wind was very slowly veering to the southward.[16]

The ship lay very nicely bowing the easterly sea. At 6 P.M. wind SE by S. Bar. 29" 50'. At 8 P.M. 29 61', at 9 P.M. 29 57', at 10 pm wind SSE, Bar. 29" 50'. From this time on the wind increased to a frightful velocity, the Bar. fairly tumbling down $^{4}/_{10}$ of an inch during the next hour, as it stood 29" 10'at 11 P.M.

It is no exaggeration to say that the roar of the wind was equal to the heaviest artillery, while the commingled elements of wind, clouds, rain, and sea—in one continuous mass—swept over us with a force that nothing could resist. The ship lay very steadily heading E by S, with the rail submerged and the decks flooded, washing out galley, carpenter's shop, and filling forecastles with water. At 11:15 P.M. (Bar. 29" 05' velocity of wind 150 miles per hour) I heard a slight cracking sound and looking aloft saw the mizzen top gallant mast going over the side. The fore and main [topmasts] had already gone—no one saw or heard them when they fell. Providentially, none of the spars fell on deck, or was any of the crew injured. On examination later we found that the masts were blown over the side by the violence of the wind, as none of the rigging or lanyards carried away first. At midnight the Bar. stood 28" 98', the lowest point during the storm. Soon after the wind began to decrease in force. At 4 A.M. Bar. 29" 26', the wind moderating rapidly.

At daylight the ship presented a woeful condition—the combination of broken spars, tangled rigging, and torn canvas formed a picture beyond my power to describe. Most of the wreckage forward fell into the water. The starboard backstays fell over the topsail yards, breaking lifts, end of lower yard inside sheave hole, and tearing the sails from the yards, and cockbilling them, 'till they in turn fouled the fore yard, destroying lifts, sail, and braces. The upper portion of the main top gallant mast was lodged in the main rigging doing considerable damage to the shrouds. The lower part of the mast, together with the topmast head, royal and skysail yards, fell into the water. Both upper and lower top gallant yards were hanging from the topsail and main yards, which cockbilled them to an angle of 45 degrees with the lifts, braces, and sails torn and broken.

At the mizzen, only the skysail yard reached the water, the mast breaking above the cap left the top gallant yards aloft. The mizzen royal yard with mast attached was secured to the mizzen rigging. The cro'jack was the only square sail that escaped any serious injury. The jibs and staysails were but little injured. Fortunately all the lee backstays with gear attached fell into the water between the ship's side and the wreckage, which prevented serious injury to the bends.[17] During the storm the sugar settled to port a foot or more from the starboard side giving the ship a bad list, and causing her to roll very deeply in the confused sea that followed the decrease of wind.

As soon as possible all hands turned to to clear the wreck. We first secured the spars that were in the water, hoisting the sound ones on deck and cutting the broken ones adrift, after saving all the rigging and iron work we could. The fore topmast head broke off so close down into the eyes of the rigging that it required extra lashings to keep the backstays in place. At noon Sat. Dec. 28th '95, light air from NNE Bar. 29" 62' Lat. 20 13' S, Long 90 East. Thus ends the most furious and to me the most disastrous storm I ever witnessed during my forty years experience at sea.

Yours Truly,
A. Doane

MONDAY NOON DEC. 30TH—60 hours after the accident had everything secured—sails changed—and set including lower mizzen top gallant sail, and main top gallant staysail from topmast head. We find the ship quite badly strained about the decks, and forward house where it joins the top gallant forecastle. It worked so badly and let in so much water into the house, that we were obliged to mast coat it across the forward end.[18] Water seems to have got in through the decks and topsides fore and aft, although we had the main deck caulked in Singapore. We shall have some damaged sugar, although I have protected it all we can with old sails. I think the only way we can fix the forward house will be to cut away the beam about two inches so the house will stand free of the top gal. forecastle (unfortunately the carpenter lost nearly all his tools in the Cyclone, so he is badly handicapped in his work). The rudder head shows evidence of a very heavy strain on it, there are more rents and the bands and tiller got quite loose during the storm. It will be best to thoroughly examine it when the ship is repaired.

The following is a list of our losses. Three top gallant masts; fore and main topmast heads gone close to the eyes of the rigging; fore lower topsail yardarm inside sheave hole; fore upper top gallant; royal and skysail yards; all the jib stays and one boom guy broken; fore top gallant and royal brace pendants; fore upper topsail and fore lifts gone on port side; also upper topsail brace pendant; top gallant and royal chain and wire sheets. Also fore sheets together with all the topgallant, royal and skysail running gear. The hounds on the jibboom are crushed in a couple of inches showing the great strain on the guys; lost iron work on one side of the top gallant and royal yards. Main and mizzen skysail yards broken, all the rest in fair condition will do to use again. Will require about two dozen blocks, nearly all new lanyards, new jib stays and boom guy, lifts, pendants, and lots of running gear.

As it will require an *entire* new outfit of yards, sails and gear for the three skysails, I suggest that it will be a good plan to do away with them. The ship is ten years old, and very lofty as you know. The latest type of English ships only carry double topgallant sails above the topsails.

For another voyage the *Francis* will require a new fore sail and mainsail, lower main topsail, lower and upper topgallantsail, main royal, three skysails if rigged as before, lower mizzen topsail, lower and upper mizzen topgallant sails, and mizzen royal, main top mast staysail. For the mizzen royal and mizzen topgallant sails, the canvas could be taken [with us] and sails made on board.

At first I thought we should have to put into Mauritius, but as I got accustomed to our crippled condition and found we were making fairly good progress, I decided to keep on the voyage. We passed Cape Good Hope Feb. 1st, 59 days out. We had a strong NW gale for two days off Cape Agulhas. I find the ship labors heavily in a large sea since the loss of our masts.[19] If we succeed in arriving at D. B. [Delaware Breakwater] all right, I do not think it wise to proceed elsewhere if ordered, without the aid of a good tug. And this expense the merchants should bear. I am not quite certain how much of a claim we have on the cargo for general average.[20] We certainly have made *some* sacrifices for the general benefit. And could easily have made the question *sure* by cutting *everything* adrift as is too frequently done to prevent *foundering* on the wreckage, but *more* often to save the *labor* and *trouble* of securing it. I preferred to save everything I could for the benefit of all interested parties. I would call your attention to an article on maritime law and general average in the [*New York*] *Maritime Register* April 24th, May 1st and 8th, 1895.

Our prolonged passage—two very healthy Dutch passengers, and *two stowaways* that put in their appearance after a few days at sea, to my intense disgust—has made such an inroad on our stores that I propose to touch at St. Helena for a supply and forwarding this letter.

Yours very truly,
A. Doane[21]

Having delivered his crippled ship, under jury rig, from the Indian Ocean to Delaware Breakwater, and after more than forty years of seafaring, Captain Doane retired. He had never lost a vessel nor put into a port in distress. Only two seamen had been lost in ships he commanded.

After refitting, the *Francis* departed Philadelphia once again carrying case oil to Japan under her new master, Captain A. T. Smith, of New Bedford; Smith had reportedly been first mate under Doane, and was experiencing his first command. On the passage to San Francisco Mrs. Smith died. Captain Smith had the body shipped on ahead to Boston; last rites were to be held after his arrival at New York.

On May 8, 1897, after an uneventful passage of 120 days from the Golden Gate and but hours from New York, twenty-five miles to the southeast of Little Egg Harbor, New Jersey, the *Francis* caught fire under the cabin from spontaneous combustion possibly caused by a leak from 500 barrels of whale oil reacting with baled rags.[22]

The crew fought the flames with the pumps, but it was a lost cause. With a strong fair wind blowing, Captain Smith decided to try to make New York. Observers at Atlantic City saw the *Francis* passing up the coast, evidently in distress, with a tug following closely astern. When it became obvious that the race could not be won, Smith, at the urging of the frightened crew—and with the heroism of the helmsman, who stuck to his post when cut off from the rest of the ship by flames and smoke—grounded the ship on a bar off Little Egg Harbor. When the boat crew of the Little Egg Harbor Life-Saving Station boarded the ship they found the crew still working heroically to suppress the fire. When the hatches were removed flames enveloped the mizzen rigging, driving the men from the ship. Reboarding the ship from the windward side, working with hatchets and pikes, the men jettisoned burning cargo, to no avail. When the ship was finally abandoned the mizzen rigging was gone and the rest about to follow, with the after portion of the ship destroyed. His ship a total loss, Captain Smith was described as being "almost heartbroken by his great misfortune."[23] One man's misfortune is often another's gain, however, and a religious revival meeting underway on nearby Brigantine Island fell into disorder when casks of wine from the *Francis*'s cargo washed ashore.

Frank Stone had been considering resuming command of the *Francis* for her next voyage, one attraction surely being the prospect of being joined by his sea-struck nephew Tod Swift. In March Uncle Frank had written Tod at school at Milton:

> I HAVE NOT DECIDED yet about going to sea, but will let you know in time for you to make arrangements. Shall expect you to stand by for a call.

Upon learning that the *Francis* was grounded and afire, Tod sent a post card to his mother, then in Paris:

> DEAR MAMMA, The *Francis* is on fire on Jersey Beach and will probably be a total loss. She was only 12 hours out of N.Y. I will have to look around for some other ship to go on this summer. Terrible isn't it? Hard on Uncle Frank. R. S.

A few weeks later Uncle Frank wrote Tod:

> DEAR TOD,
> I am sorry I did not see you on Monday in Milton. I am sorry enough that your plans are so unsettled by the wreck of the *Francis*. I shall not go to sea at present, if ever. I feel there are too many things requiring attention here—broken fragments that must be gathered up and glued together. If I ever do go you shall go too, but when that time will be I cannot say.
>
> Sincerely yours,
> F. H. Stone

---

1. At this date there were no official licensing requirements for officers of American sailing vessels, although master and mates had to be citizens. While it was by no means unusual for men in their twenties to receive a command, in most instances these were men who had been at sea since boyhood, and their first command was generally a smaller, less valuable vessel employed in a less demanding service than a nearly new 1,472-ton bark trading to the Far East.

2. After leaving *Jonathan Bourne*, Captain Doane took a shipmaster's holiday by delivering the newly built 1,100-ton wooden steamer *Al-Ki*, built at Bath by Goss & Sawyer, to San Francisco. According to an article in the *Nautical Gazette*, the steamer was built for W. H. Besse and Captain William Lewis, of New Bedford, to run between San Francisco and Coos Bay (the owner of record was the Oregon South Improvement Company). Lewis, whose home office was located at New Bedford, operated a half dozen Bath-built, San Francisco-based steam auxiliary barks in the Arctic whale fishery. Captain Doane next made several voyages in the Besse bark *Guy C. Goss*.

3. Cutler, Carl C., *Five Hundred Records of American Built Ships* (Mystic, CT: Marine Historical Association, 1952), pp. 90-91. Cutler pointed out that while fine-lined British-built clippers made their best runs in the calmer North and South Atlantic, big, flat-floored American-built clippers—often sailing under the British flag—were at their best "running their easting down." p. 39.

4. Ibid., pp. 90–91.

5. While the old clippers made this passage many times in seventy-five days or less, the *Bourne* was no all-out, heavily manned flyer risking all to make a name for herself. A timely arrival with all in good order was what her owners desired.

6. From a letter by Mrs. J. Delano Wood—Frank's sister Carrie—quoting a

letter from her mother, courtesy of Henry B. Stone. Reports put the loss at either $50,000 or $90,000, uninsured. *Bath American Sentinel*, 31 July 1884.

7. *Harvard College Class of 1879*, Boston, 1929, p. 502.

8. Manuscript in Harvard Archives.

9. *Bangor Industrial Journal*, 27 Nov. 1885.

10. Interviewed early in 1886, when shipping prospects were no better, Captain Guy Goss predicted that not a single "ship,"—i.e., a full-rigged ship or large bark—would be built in Maine that year. He said that the two ships he had built in 1885—*Hotspur* and *Francis* —were built at a very low rate for old customers. Ibid., 26 Feb. 1886. Francis and Horatio Hathaway were the principle owners of *Hotspur*, whose construction preceded Frank's ship. Smaller, but lofty and handsome, the three-skysail-yarder *Hotspur* was named after the Hathaway's famous 1857 clipper. Also a member of William Besse's fleet, she was lost on a reef in the Philippines on but her second voyage.

11. Forbes's wife, Sarah Hathaway, was a cousin of Frank's. See Llewellyn Howland III, *The New Bedford Yacht Club, A History* (South Dartmouth, MA: New Bedford Yacht Club, 2002), pp. 30–31.

12. Plummer, with a finger in many pies, was a partner with Rotch in the New Bedford Cordage Company. He later came to financial grief. Plummer's son, Henry Merrihew Plummer wrote the classic yachting tale, *The Boy, Me, and the Cat.*

13. Measured tonnage reflected capacity, not weight.

14. *Bath Daily Times*, 8 October 1885. A description of the *Francis* appeared several years later in a London paper, as reprinted in the *Bath Daily Times*, 19 July 1889:

> In our column yesterday we made a brief reference to the fine American ship *Francis* as being one of those which distinguished itself on "Independence Day" by its tasteful display of bunting. We yesterday had an opportunity of closely inspecting this vessel, and it seems to us that in spite of the suppression of wood by iron and steel, our American friends have by no means lost the art of turning out specimens of naval architecture which are even improvements on those beautiful clippers which, under a more favorable fiscal policy, would have contested with our own ships in the carrying trade of the world.
>
> The *Francis* is a large wooden ship.... Owing to the excellent system adapted of strengthening by means of iron diagonal ties, intercostals, etc., she is structurally as strong as an iron or steel vessel of the same tonnage. She has most beautiful lines, and an amount of sheer such as the sailor loves to see.... She is, as will be seen, a very large carrier, and owing to her good proportions a perfect "demon" to sail. In fact, her officers speak of her as being more like a yacht as regards sailing powers. She is full-ship rigged, with double topsail and topgallant yards. Her [lower] masts (which are iron), spars, yards, etc., present that graceful appearance which distinguishes American clippers. All the standing and most of the running rigging is of wire [this was a reporting error]. She is fitted with a powerful steam donkey engine for loading, discharging, hoisting, and pumping purposes. She possesses all the latest improvements for quick working and handling.
>
> One very noticeable feature on board is the cleanness and neatness of every part, and the evident pride there must be taken by officers and men in keeping everything in the best of order. The houses on deck, cabin, forecastle, lockers,

bulwarks, etc., are all painted pure white, and internally there is a corresponding brightness. The captain's cabin and the dining saloon—though of small dimensions compared to those on steamers carrying passengers—are beautifully decorated with seven kinds of wood. The panels of the doors and partitions, etc., are made up and divided by finely polished Honduras baywood, bird's eye maple, mahogany, red cedar, French burl, Hungarian ash, and cherry wood. The cabin is fitted up with a handsome dispensary or medicine cabinet, containing bottles specially made for it. The adjoining apartments are all furnished in a neat and comfortable way. The *Francis* is commanded by Captain Doane, and his chief officer is Mr. Sweeny. She has just completed her maiden voyage [in the grain trade] from San Francisco with 3,000 tons of grain. Her builders are the New England Shipbuilding Company, Me., U.S., and we congratulate [her builders] on building such a fine ship.

15. About 1890 Frank and Anna constructed a large Italianate house at 35 Arnold Street, on a lot subdivided from the spacious grounds of the estate of Anna's father, William J. Rotch. They would also build an outsized cedar-shingled "cottage" at the summer resort of Nonquitt.

16. Wind "veers" to the right, or clockwise, and "backs" to the left, or counterclockwise, in both hemispheres. By observing the direction of the shifting wind, Doane was ascertaining his position relative to the cyclone's center. In the southern hemisphere—where cyclones rotate clockwise, opposite to storms in the northern hemisphere—the left-hand semi-circle of a cyclone (as determined by facing the track of the storm) is considered the most dangerous sector. By heaving-to on the starboard tack Doane hoped the ship would work away from the left-hand sector.

17. "Bends" in this instance refers to the hull planking; the backstay rigging, having fallen between the broken spars and the hull, prevented the former from damaging or puncturing the latter.

18. A mastcoat was the tacked and sewn-in-place waterproof canvas cover affixed around a mast and the mast wedges at the deck. Thus, to have mastcoated a leak was to have covered it with canvas, likely fastened by nailing through battens.

19. A vessel is said to labor heavily when she works heavily, with severe or irregular motion, in a seaway. In this instance, due to the loss of counterbalancing weight aloft, the moment, or frequency of the ship's roll has been quickened.

20. General average is a matter of liability based on the theory that a loss incurred as the result of actions taken by the master to preserve the ship and the cargo should be borne, proportionately, by all the parties involved in the venture. In other words, had Doane ordered the spars to be cut adrift so as to prevent them from imperiling hull and cargo, the owners of the cargo—in practice, through their insurance underwriters—would be liable to pay an appropriate share of the loss.

21. Courtesy of Mr. Henry B. Stone.

22. Japanese rags were then in great demand for papermaking. The greatest part of her cargo was either 4,000 or else 10,000 barrels of wine, along with canned fruit.

23. The sailors, as was typical aboard American ships, were all foreigners with northern European names. *New York Evening Telegram*, 10 May 1897. See also *New York Maritime Register*, 12 May 1897.

Part Two

Frank Besse

Chapter Seven

FRANK BESSE GOES TO SEA

We Learn About the Case Oil Trade and Frank Besse Begins a Long Voyage Aboard the Ship William J. Rotch.

WHEN YOUNG FRANK BESSE set out on his long sea voyage on July 2, 1881, it was atop a cargo of 58,500 cases of case oil. The shipping of case oil, in large part to the Far East—"case oil" cargoes were of (generally) five-gallon tins of kerosene, packed two to a wooden case—originated at New York and Philadelphia. Beginning about 1870 and peaking shortly before World War I, the trade was a major employer of sailing vessels. It was long monopolized by the Standard Oil Company.

Hunter's Point juts into the East River just north of the mouth of Newtown Creek, which separates Long Island City and Brooklyn. Once the site of John Jacob Astor's country estate, later the center of New York's once great shipbuilding industry, by the 1880s the creek's banks were lined with at least fifty oil refineries and other industrial works. Raw sewage, packing plant trimmings, other industrial wastes, and large quantities of refinery effluent—gasoline was a refinery waste product—were heedlessly dumped into the creek, which remains to this day one of the nation's most polluted waterways.[1]

The first coal oil "kerosene" refinery in the United States was built on Newtown Creek in 1854; the first modern petroleum kerosene refinery in 1867. Kerosene refined from Pennsylvania and Ohio crude oil was an effective, clean, safe, and inexpensive illuminant, a catalyst for vast social and economic changes, and the foundation for Rockefeller's vast wealth.

Kerosene pioneer Charles Pratt, of Brooklyn, quietly folded his Astral Oil Company into Rockefeller's Standard Oil in the 1870s. Pratt's right-hand man in his refinery was Henry H. Rogers, of Mattapoisett and Fairhaven, Massachusetts. Son of a one-time whaler, by 1888 the courtly, handsome, and forceful Rogers, one of the "great men" of his era, all but ran the operations of Standard Oil.[2]

Over half of American kerosene production in the late 1800s was exported as case oil. In 1886 the 12,244,300 cases shipped to the "East" were carried by nearly 300 sailing vessels—nearly 100 were American—as compared with but 27 steamers.[3] By 1889 the oil trade was the leading trade for American deep-water sailing vessels.[4]

Beginning in the late 1870s larger and more convenient New York Harbor refineries were built at Bayonne, New Jersey. At Philadelphia, oil exports departed from the large Atlantic Refining Company facility—Atlantic Refining was a part of Standard Oil, of course—at Point Breeze, on the Schuylkill River.

The rapid growth of the trade was made possible by the development of more efficient means of manufacturing nonleaking cans. Cans had been used for coal oil since the 1850s; in 1865 Charles Pratt hired Herman Miller, a German inventor whose advances in design allowed a man and a boy to solder-up 850 five-gallon cans a day.[5] Mechanized can-making followed, and by the late 1880s Standard Oil's Devoe plant alone produced 60,000 tins a day. In the Far East emptied oil tins were fashioned into numerous products, becoming an export item of no small social importance in themselves.[6] Case oil shipped to Asia and the Orient replaced plant-derived oils, freeing up vast areas of cropland for food crops, and thereby opened the way for a population explosion.[7] The case oil trade was controlled by Standard Oil until the monopoly's forced breakup in 1910.

Now back to our young sailor. In January 1883 Frank Alden Besse departed the ship *William J. Rotch* at Dublin after having enjoyed an eighteen-month grand ocean tour. On March 27, in a Paris hotel while preparing for a packaged Thomas Cook & Co. tour of Italy, Frank wrote in his journal:

> ANOTHER COLD STORMY DAY.... Went to my banker's and drew the remainder of my money, 1,200 francs, then went to my room and packed my things, also wrote a letter to mother. Went to the reading room again at 5 o'clock and saw the arrival of the ship *Wm. J. Rotch*, March 25, 50 days from Dublin to New York. Rather a long passage but presume she went the southern route. I also noted the arrival of the *Low Wood* in New York on the same day.[8] She sailed from Dublin about two weeks ahead of the *Rotch*. Saw the report of the arrival of the barks *Wm. H. Besse* and *Jonathan Bourne* at Hong Kong, March 10. This evening Bodfish, Santry, Morse, and I played billiards for two hours....[9]

As we already know, the *Besse* and the *Bourne* (with our other Frank—Frank Stone—as mate) would depart Hong Kong for cholera-ridden

Manila. The *Rotch,* meanwhile, made a rapid turnaround at New York, and was soon on her way towards Hiogo, Japan, with case oil. This passage was a reprise of her maiden passage, made two years earlier, with Frank Besse aboard as a paying passenger/supercargo of sorts.[10]

When Frank Besse was four his two-year-old brother Isaac Henry had died, leaving Frank to grow up as a spoiled only child in the stately Greek Revival mansion his father, Captain Alden Besse, had built for his wife in 1847 overlooking the river at Wareham's "Narrows Village." At age twenty-five Frank was adrift, clerking in a Wareham store, when Father Alden, an owner in the *Rotch*, is believed to have decided that a sea voyage—even in

Portrait of the ship William J. Rotch *by Charles Sidney Raleigh. Raleigh, born in England in 1830, thirty years a sailor, arrived in New Bedford seriously ill. He recuperated at the home of his ship's cook, at nearby Bourne. Settling in New Bedford, Raleigh began a second career as an artist, painting ship portraits and marine scenes, signs, and decorating houses and carriages. His masterwork was a great panorama of whaling scenes depicting a voyage aboard the ship* Niger. *He died at Bourne in 1925. This painting was presented to the Wareham Historical Society by Harry Besse.*
COURTESY OF WAREHAM HISTORICAL SOCIETY.

the comfort of the cabin—might help give Frank direction. While it might seem a stretch to include Frank among such hands-on, sea struck young men as Frank Stone and Tod Swift, he was well informed in nautical matters, and took a lively interest in ships, shipping, and shipping people.[11]

Captain Alden Besse had been born in Wareham in 1821, the son of a noted pilot, and at age twelve, after a firm grounding in education, succumbed to the "strong predilection for the sea" then common among coastal boys. Shipping as cook aboard the coasting sloop *Gypsy,* he remained in her for six years. At age eighteen, he made the first of four cruises in the Wareham whaling brig *Inga*, a phenomenally successful ship which in seven years of relatively short cruises landed 5,000 barrels of sperm oil.

Leaving *Inga* as first mate, from 1846 Alden successively commanded the New Bedford whalers *Charleston Packet*, *Hecla*, and *John Wells* of the Knowles fleet. He then made a four-year voyage in command of Jonathan Bourne's ship *Hunter*, sperm whaling in New Zealand waters, followed by two years of cruising in the North and South Atlantic. It was said that no ships in the whale fishery were more certain to return full of oil and with the crew in good health than were Alden's, and that he never had a serious misfortune at sea.[12]

Besse was equally fortunate in his investments. At the outset of one voyage he handed Jonathan Bourne $10,000 to invest in stock of the Boston & Worcester Railroad, which grew into the Boston & Albany, one of the best-paying roads in the country.[13] He owned shares in coasting schooners, whalers, and in many of the ships managed by his kinsman, Captain William H. Besse. One of those ships was the *William J. Rotch.*

So on July 2, 1881, Frank, his father, and others in their party joined the loaded *Rotch* at her East 31st Street berth, on New York's East River. She had there completed her cargo by loading 200 tons of merchandise atop the 58,500 cases of case oil loaded across the river at a Standard Oil subsidiary, the Devoe Manufacturing Company's refinery at Hunter's Point, Long Island City. Beneath the case oil she carried 101 tons of coal as "stiffening" ballast.[14] All told she loaded 2,350 tons of cargo.[15]

The *Rotch*'s master, George L. Bray, of Newburyport, Massachusetts, of a prominent maritime family, was to be accompanied for the voyage by Mrs. Bray. The first mate, a Mr. Delano, was likely a New Bedforder, as was Second Mate Frank Shurtleff, and also the ship's "boy," a young man named Samuel Loring, who had traveled from New Bedford with Frank, his father, Dr. H. M. Knowles, a Mr. Chipman, and with Shurtleff and Loring.[16] (The total ship's company, with crew signed aboard and guests departed, would number twenty-six.) Frank wrote in his journal on July 2, 1881:

Captain Alden Besse and his wife Betsy, circa 1900, enjoy the Greek revival mansion Alden built at Wareham for his bride in 1847. Murals, including a whaling scene painted on the ceiling of the room behind the first floor windows at right, were painted by Raleigh. Betsy Besse was the widow of Alden's brother Isaac, who was lost at sea. Other family members lost at sea included Alden's brother Sam, his Uncle Elisha, and cousins Seth and William (William was Captain William Besse's father). Another uncle was killed by an exploding boiler on the Mississippi. Shipmasters retired to Buzzards Bay towns took great pride in their homestead fences.
COURTESY OF BRUCE BESSE.

A different perspective on the Alden Besse house, taken in the later 1900s.
COURTESY OF BRUCE BESSE.

AFTER EATING BREAKFAST at the Astor House, we went up to the ship which was all ready for sea, the crew having just come on board. The tugs *Vim* and *J. Jewett* came alongside at half past 12 o'clock and towed us down to Throg's Point, where they left off, and the *Narragansett,* one of the most powerful tugs on the Sound, took hold and is to tow us outside of Block Island.[17] The wind is about S. by E. very moderate and smooth. We have nearly all sails set and going along nicely. The ship is drawing 22 feet of water forward and 22 $^1/_2$ feet aft, and is in good sailing trim. This evening the mates chose their watches.... We have a good crew to all appearances, they being nearly all young Germans.[18]

The report was circulated about the city this morning that President Garfield had been shot. I should like very much to know whether it is true or not, but don't suppose I shall until we arrive in Japan.

I became a little better acquainted with the Capt. and his wife, and know I shall like them very much.

Ship William J. Rotch, *of New Bedford, June 1893, evidently at Long Island City loading case oil for Hong Kong. Her topgallant masts have been "housed" to afford passage under the Brooklyn Bridge.*

THOMAS A. LUKE. COURTESY OF PEABODY-ESSEX MUSEUM.

Ship William J. Rotch, *of New Bedford, at New York, early 1890s. Wooden fenders hang alongside.*
THOMAS A. LUKE. COURTESY OF PEABODY-ESSEX MUSEUM.

JULY 3RD. Father, Dr. Knowles, and Mr. Chipman left the ship this morning at half past 7 o'clock in the tug boat which is going to New Bedford. She towed us about ten miles to the eastward of Block Island; then we set all sails and with a fair wind started our journey.... There was quite a heavy swell on.... It did not seem like Sunday, as the men were obliged to work all day taking the anchors on deck and lashing boats and other things.[19]

---

1. Greenpoint, Brooklyn, on Newtown Creek, is the site of the nation's largest underground oil spill—17 million gallons, twice the *Exxon Valdez* spill, resulting from explosions and leaks at a Mobil tank farm in the 1950s. Having migrated underground, this oil creates a constant sheen on the surface of the creek.

2. Elbert Hubbard, *Little Journeys to the Homes of Great Businessmen* (East Aurora, 1909); *Dictionary of American Biography.*

3. Ninety-eight sailers were American, eighty-six British, forty-five Italian, nineteen Norwegian, nine German, five Austrian, three Dutch, and two Swedish. *Bangor Industrial Journal*, 23 January 1887.

4. Ibid., 15 February 1889. The separate North Atlantic "barreled oil" trade, carrying barreled crude oil to Europe and returning with empty barrels, gave a second life to many older American-built square-riggers, called "Petroleum Klippers" by their proud German owners.

5. Yacht designer Ralph M. Munroe wrote of perfecting a machine circa 1875 which made seamless wooden kegs for kerosene exports. Charles Pratt secured the patent without realizing that cylindrical kegs wasted too much space in the hold. Although there were other viable uses for the kegs, Pratt, "in accordance with what came to be known as Standard Oil tactics, did not propose that the patents should benefit anybody but himself" and locked them up. Ralph M. Munroe and Vincent Gilpin, *The Commodore's Story* (Narberth, PA: Livingston Publishing, 1966 reprint), pp. 64–65. Two monuments to Pratt that remain in Brooklyn are the famous Pratt Institute in Bedford-Stuyresant, and in gritty Greenpoint, the Astral Apartments, a magnificent brownstone edifice built in 1885 as refinery workers' residence. Fittingly, it sits between Java and India Streets.

6. See Robert Lloyd Webb, "Tinned Light: The Case-Oil Trade to Meiji Japan," in *Meiji Japan* (Bath, ME: Maine Maritime Museum, 1996); W. H. Mitchell and L. A. Sawyer, *Sailing Ship to Supertanker* (Lavenham: Terrence Dalton, 1987); Basil Lubbock, *Coolie Ships and Oil Sailers* (Glasgow: Brown, Ferguson, 1956).

7. An observation made by the late Dr. John Lyman.

8. The barque *Low Wood*, of St. John, N.B., 1,091 tons, was built at Portland, N.B., in 1878, for Troop & Son.

9. From a journal kept by Frank A. Besse from June 30, 1881, through June 9, 1883, and distributed in typescript to several Cape Cod-area libraries and institutions by his son, Harry W. Besse. A microfilm copy of the journal in the Kendall Institute of the New Bedford Whaling Museum is listed as PMB film 294, Doc. 1054, Reg. #694.

10. Construction of the ship *William J. Rotch* for Wlliam Besse by Goss & Sawyer at Bath, Maine, commenced in November 1880. Despite having been built outdoors in winter, the ship was launched on April 26, 1881. Her registered dimensions were 218 feet long by 42 feet beam and 24 feet depth of hold, measuring 1,718 tons. She was fitted with a 15-horsepower steam donkey engine, and was classified, for insurance purposes, as A1 for fourteen years, indicating a very high level of construction typical of her builders. She was rigged with double topgallant yards on fore and main mast, and crossed a main skysail yard. Her cost, when ready to sail from New York, including copper sheathing, all "outfits," and even the sailors' advances on wages, was $96,000.

11. There is an indication that Frank might have made the maiden transatlantic passage in the bark *Western Belle* with Captain William Besse in 1876. Also, a small photo was discovered in the Alden Besse mansion of a man named Diaz who had once "saved Frank from drowning."

12. In one close call Alden and his boat crew were lost from the *Inga* for three days in the South Atlantic.

13. *Wareham Courier*, 3, 10 July 1903.

14. A homogenous and relatively light cargo, case oil was liable to make a ship "crank" or insufficiently stiff unless some heavier "stiffening" was carried beneath it. Oil shippers were notorious for trying to overload ships, and for objecting to the carriage of ballast.

15. The *Rotch* had been sailed to New York from Bath in nine days with a crew of "runners," i.e., sailors hired for the "run." At New York she was drydocked for copper sheathing. The new ship was inspected by members of the press and the maritime community, receiving highest praise from the *Journal of Commerce*, which noted her graceful and easy lines, and reported that she was much admired by the underwriters; *Bath American Sentinal*, 7 July 1881. Some owners preferred to copper-sheathe new ships after the hull had had a chance to settle after being afloat, rather than when on the building stocks.

16. Knowles, wealthy from whaling, invested in a number of ships of the Besse fleet.

17. The *Rotch* departed via Long Island Sound, the long tow evidently being deemed preferable to having to house and then re-rig her upper masts to go under the Brooklyn Bridge.

18. By the mid- to late-1800s Northern Europeans composed the bulk of the crews of American (and also Canadian and British) deep-water ships. Although it is true that America never possessed a true deep-sea proletariat such as Europe did, many ships in the early to mid-1800s sailed with predominately native-born crews. In 1834, when Dana left Boston bound for California in the brig *Alert,* nine of the thirteen sailors were native-born Americans, seven of those being New Englanders. When he transferred to the ship *Alert,* he found all thirteen sailors to be native-born Americans, mostly New Englanders.

19. Anchors were not literally hoisted "on deck." Rather—after the ship had made a good and safe offing from the land, and was well and fairly departed on her passage—the flukes were hoisted inboard and secured on the topgallant forecastle deck, with the stocks left outboard. The anchor chains were unshackled and the hawsepipes plugged.

Chapter 8

PASSAGE TO JAPAN, 1881

We Join Frank at Sea Aboard the Ship William J. Rotch, *New York to Yokohama, Followed by a Bit of Sightseeing, Court Testimony, and Socializing.*

THE *ROTCH* MADE A FAST and largely uneventful passage. Frank suffered no real seasickness nor, to his surprise, homesickness. Journal snippets follow:

JULY 6TH,1881. Helped the Capt. knot his log-line this morning....[1] Had quite a long talk with Loring this evening and judge by what he said that he was a little sick of his bargain and wished he had stayed at home.... He gets six dollars a month wages, with a promise of more as soon as he becomes better acquainted with the ropes. Shurtleff does very well as second mate and I guess gives satisfaction. His wages are $35.00 per month.

JULY 7TH. We have 25 hens and a rooster, three small pigs, two canary birds, and two cats on board.... The ship seems to be very stiff and sails a little better than average, I think. She does not leak much if any....

JULY 8TH. This evening, which was very pleasant and bright moonlight, I had quite a talk with the 3rd mate, Mr. Ferrin, who is also engineer, and the steward, a colored man named Brown. They were both up in the Arctic Ocean last summer; the 3rd mate as 2nd engineer of the steam whaler, *Mary and Helen*, and the steward as cook of the bark *Legal Tender*.[2] They described the habits of the natives, the method of going through the ice, and the taking of whales.

JULY 11TH. Perfectly calm. Made 3 miles during the last 24 hours by drifting. The men worked all day setting up the rigging and I helped them a little by holding turn on capstan.[3]

JULY 14TH. The men were this morning put on an allowance of one gallon of water each per day. Out of that they are obliged to give the cook enough to make their tea and coffee with and to cook their victuals, besides what they drink.... The [American barks] *Oneida* and *Penobscot* are this evening about twelve miles to leeward of us, the *Rotch* having gone ahead as fast as they, and to windward much better.[4] Spent most of the day in working on a beef barrel; scraping it and taking the bark off the shooks, to catch water in. Shurtleff struck a man in his watch this afternoon for not knowing the ropes; did not hurt him much.

JULY 17TH. At 6 o'clock this evening, a bark signaled us that she was on short allowance of provisions. We hauled aback the main yard and the Capt. came on board. We found she was the English bark *Lugar* of Ayr, Capt. Arrowsmith, 500 tons measurement, 115 days from Fanning Island for Hamburg, with 800 tons guano.[5] We let him have two barrels of bread, one barrel of flour and 87 lbs. of sugar for which he seemed to be very thankful.... The bark was loaded deep, leaking badly and altogether was in a bad predicament.... The Capt. said he had just left the Trade Winds and we may expect to fall in with them tomorrow.

JULY 18TH. We are in the beginning of the trades, which although they are called the North-East Trades, do not always blow from that direction. They took up the after-cabin carpet today and stowed it away in the lazerette...then they holystoned the floor and made it very smooth and white. I stood some time this evening looking over the stern of the ship at the phosphorescence which extended for some distance in the wake.

JULY 19TH. Shurtleff unmercifully pounded a poor German for nothing at all except that he did not move quite quick enough to suit him. I pitied him but did not say anything about it.

JULY 20TH. Wind very strong from E. to E. S. E. Have been going along most all day, ten knots with the yards braced sharp up and the spanker and stay-sails furled. Made 200 miles S. by E. The ship throws some water and heels over considerably, so that it makes walking very difficult and a number of the sailors had falls.

JULY 21ST. Capt. Bray was taken quite sick last night with a severe attack of vomiting and has been up but very little all day. He feels a little more comfortable this evening.

JULY 22ND. Shurtleff had a fight with one of the sailors this morning; but you could not exactly call it a fight for it was all one-sided. The man was sent up aloft to reeve off some gear and did not do it quite right and when he came down, Shurtleff struck him with his fist; when the man drew his sheath knife and started for him, he grabbed a belaying pin and hit him on the head, knocking him down and cutting a very deep gash, which may lay him up for a day or two.

Capt. Bray called Shurtleff aft and talked with him some time about the matter and that will probably end it. I do not approve of such actions for they were wholly uncalled for and neither of the other officers have had any trouble with the crew.

JULY 23RD. Got the fore-studding sail out and set it this forenoon for the first time....[6] Capt. Bray gave me about one hundred Manila cigars this morning as he had a lot of them and wanted the box they were in for some other purpose. I commenced reading today the *History of Our Times* by Justin McCarthy.

JULY 25TH. The little pig that was taken sick yesterday died this morning and the cook held a post mortem examination...but was not skilled enough in the business to discover anything. Mrs. Bray and myself planted some lettuce and radishes in the garden, which consists of two boxes filled with earth.... This evening Capt. and Mrs. Bray, Mr. Delano, and myself figured a long time on an example given by Delano. It was to multiply 19L 19s 11d 3f by itself. I obtained an answer 399L 19s 2d 1/960f.

JULY 26TH. This evening we took in staysails, fore and mizzen royal, sky-sail and spanker, as it looked as if we might get some wind in the night. I think Capt. Bray is a very cautious man and does not want to run any risk or be taken unawares.

JULY 27TH. Commenced holystoning the poop deck today. First the sailors scrape it with their sheath-knives, then put on fine sand and water and scour it, smoothing with holystones. It is very slow work and tiresome, and six men working all day only finished one half the poop as far as the forward part of the cabin.

JULY 29TH. Our little kitten had so many fleas that she was quite sick and Capt. Bray and myself washed her and combed out, I should think, over 100. She took it very quietly and seemed to know we were doing her a kindness.

AUGUST 7TH. As I may wish to know at some future time what our regular sea diet consisted of, I will set down each day this week the principal articles for each meal. Breakfast: fried ham, boiled potatoes, and onions, muffins and hominy. Dinner: roast chicken and potatoes, canned fresh beef and tomatoes, plum duff.[7]

AUGUST 8TH. This evening at quarter of 7 o'clock while sitting on deck and talking with the officers, we felt the ship tremble all over. We all jumped to our feet and thought that she had struck something but finally came to the conclusion that it was a shock of an earthquake for they are sometimes felt when crossing the Equator, but not very frequently. Capt. Bray had never experienced any before.

We are about thirty miles North of the Equator and will probably cross it during the night. The three mates held a consultation to see what should be done with those on board who have never crossed the line before as they said Old Neptune always demanded an initiation fee for the first time crossing. They took my case into consideration first and decided that I must give them ten cigars each or Neptune would make his appearance and shave me. I concluded to let them have the cigars....

Bill of fare.... Breakfast: Rice and curry. boiled potatoes and onions, salt beef and buckwheat cakes. Dinner: Pea soup, salt beef, potatoes, and pudding. Supper: Beef and potatoes, apple sauce and cake.

AUGUST 9TH. This evening Neptune made his appearance on deck again, this time in company with his wife and after going aft and presenting the Capt. with a letter and collecting postage, which in this case consisted of some tobacco, went forward and took one of the men whom they had overlooked last night and shaved him. Then they came up to see me and said I had not paid my footing. I told them I had and would not go with them for I did not wish to go through the ceremony, so after a few words they left.

AUGUST 12TH. The ship is very easy in a sea-way and you can carry sail on her long after most vessels would be obliged to take it in.... This afternoon we sighted a bark ahead and by dark were up abreast of her. She was steering the same course that we were, and was running under topsails with a reef in her fore while we were carrying main royal at the same time.

AUGUST 13TH. Bill of fare for Saturday. Breakfast: Sausage, salt beef, boiled potatoes and oat meal. Dinner: Codfish, salt beef, potatoes, onions, buckwheat cakes. Supper: fish balls, beef, apple sauce and cake.

In addition to the above we have tea, coffee, lime juice or water, pickles, canned fruit of various kinds, sardines, lambs tongues, etc. I think we live very well indeed.

AUGUST 14TH. The wind has been so far to the S. since we crossed the Equator that we have been driven pretty well in towards the coast of Brazil.[8]

AUGUST 17TH. A large whale came within fifty yards of the ship and spouted four or five times. Capt. Bray said he read New Bedford on the stern of the vessel and then started off as fast as he could go.

AUGUST 18TH. Have been in company all day with the English ship *Anglo America* of St. John, N.B., from Liverpool for Calcutta.[9] We have carried more sail than she has and have gained about four miles on her in the day's run. This is the heaviest head sea we have experienced...and the ship goes into it very easily.

AUGUST 23RD. We have two men laid up in the forecastle; one with a very sore throat and the other with a bad cold. In fact, we have had quite a hospital on board ever since we left New York, one or more being laid up all the time.

AUGUST 24TH. Made 240 miles S. E. by E. a good day's work. There is quite a heavy sea running and the ship occasionally takes a sea over her quarter, but steers easily and seems to be very easy in a sea-way.

AUGUST 25TH. As [the wind] is directly aft, we cannot get much sail to draw.... The ship rolls considerably when running before the wind, and the woodwork in the cabin creaks very much, making it unpleasant while below.

AUGUST 27TH. Sighted the island of Tristan [da Cunha] this morning.... Took several sights to set our chronometer, and then kept off on our course again S. E. by E. ½ E., the wind blowing too hard for any of the inhabitants to come off to the ship in boats.... Saw one vessel.... We signaled her as she went by and found she was the English iron ship *Ben Nevis* 49 days from London for Sidney, Australia.[10] As she sailed after we did, we asked him if the President was still alive. He answered yes.... We asked him who shot him and he said Guiteau.

SEPT. 5TH. Passed Cape of Good Hope last night.[11]

SEPTEMBER 6TH. Put a reef in the mainsail and furled all but topsails, lower main topgallant sail, foresail, fore and main topmast-staysails, and she is going along nicely. Made 245 miles. E. I have had the toothache for several days and this morning Mr. Delano pulled it out for me. It came quite hard, he having to pull twice before it came out.

SEPTEMBER 7TH. We had a very disagreeable night last night. This has been the heaviest blow and the worst sea we have experienced since leaving port, and the ship works fully as well as we expected she would. She steers easily; and does not take in much water when kept steadily. Pleasant.

SEPTEMBER 13TH. Had the fore topmast studding sail set all day; but took it in this evening, it looked rather squally.[12]

SEPTEMBER 14TH. The sailors discovered a keg of tripe in the midship house that had just been opened and during the night stole and ate nearly all of it, but of course, no one knew who did it.

SEPTEMBER 15TH. Very strong breeze from the N. all day. Had all sail set this morning including studding sail. From 8 o'clock A.M. to 4 P.M. she made 12 knots an hour. She seems to go 11 or 12 knots very easily but it is almost impossible to get any more than that rate.

SEPTEMBER 25TH. Since crossing the equator and all of the time running our easting down, we have had unusual light winds. After leaving Tristan, we caulked all the hatches and windows and prepared for bad weather, and were agreeably surprised at not having any. Capt. Bray said that he never came around the Cape before without experiencing some gales.

SEPTEMBER 26TH. This afternoon I found a number of books which had been given to Capt. Bray by a relative who works in Rand Avery & Co.'s printing office, Boston, Mass. They were sample copies with some defect.

SEPTEMBER 30TH. My 23rd year which ended today passed very quickly and pleasantly to me, and I have not had one day of sickness during the time.

OCTOBER 2ND. The cat which the sailors had favored came into the cabin last night and caught and ate one of Mrs. Bray's canaries, and this morning Mr. Delano knocked her [the cat] in the head and threw her overboard.

OCTOBER 8TH. Got the anchors over the bow this afternoon, and the awning out for use in calm, hot weather, and unbent the main spencer which we did not have any occasion to use while rounding the Cape. Took in studding sail and got out deep sea lead, for we shall probably sight land before morning and we could not have a better night for it as it is bright moonlight.[13]

OCTOBER 9TH. Made the island of Lombok at 5:30 o'clock this morning and entered Alas Strait at 9 and passing out at 5 o'clock P.M.…[14] On the west the strait is bounded by Lombok Island, which contains several high mountains, the highest of which, Lombok, is over 10,000 feet above the level of the sea, and from its top, we could see smoke issuing. There are numerous villages along the coast, situated in very large coconut groves.

OCTOBER 10TH. After passing through Alas Strait, we entered the Java Sea, about 250 miles wide, with a fine breeze from the East. Captain Bray was taken quite sick to his stomach this evening. We keep a man on the foreyard all of the time on account of shoals, land, and vessels.[15]

OCTOBER 14TH. [in the Celebes Sea] Saw three vessels bound to the South one of which, a Dutch bark, came so near us that Mr. Delano, Sam Loring, one of the sailors, and myself boarded her to see if we could procure some fruit and vegetables. We succeeded in getting a sack of rice, four squashes, about fifty bananas, and some dried fish, but they had no potatoes or yams. She was loaded with gutta-percha and rattan and bound from one of the ports on Celebes to Singapore.[16] She was three days out and had an ugly looking crew of natives. The Capt. treated us very kindly and would take no pay for the provision.

OCTOBER 21ST. The light which we saw last evening proved to be a volcano.… It answered the purpose of a guide as well as a lighthouse.… We went through [the channel in the night] and entered the Pacific Ocean this morning having made the run through the straits and seas in eleven days and a few hours…a very good passage.

NOVEMBER 12TH. The Capt. and 1st and 3rd mates got into a row with one of the sailors for being saucy, and gave him a pretty good beating.

NOVEMBER 15TH. At the time I am writing this (10 o'clock P.M.) we are having a very heavy squall from the North and are under three lower topsails.… Discovered bedbugs in the cabin and gave all the staterooms a thorough overhauling, finding quite a number. They probably came from forward [that is, from the sailors' fo'c's'le].

NOVEMBER 17TH. Our cook has been sick for a week or more, and the Captain decided today that he had Bright's disease of the kidneys which is very dangerous and may prove fatal. Sam has been acting cook and does very well. One of the sailors has a touch of scurvy.

NOVEMBER 21ST. The wind commenced to increase rapidly...last night until it reached a heavy gale, or young hurricane, with a terrible sea.... We were all rather uneasy this morning for we did not know exactly where we were [while] scudding before the wind.... At noon we sighted Rock Island lighthouse.... Signaled for a pilot this evening by flash-light and saw an answering light to the leeward. We ran for it as long as we dared to then stood off-shore.... We did not know whether it was really a pilot or some natives trying to allure us on shore....

This morning I saw Fuji Yama [Mount Fujiyama]...the top was covered with snow which looked very pretty in the rays of the sun.

I did not sleep a particle last night on account of the glass being so low, and a gale coming on. Capt. Bray said he never saw it blow harder and was considerably worried, but the vessel acted splendidly and he said she is a remarkably good sea boat. She took considerable water on board but no where near as much as I expected she would.

NOVEMBER 22ND. We tacked off and on at the entrance of the channel leading to Yokohama all night, and took a pilot on board at 7 o'clock this morning. His name is Mr. Hodnette, a Scotchman who has been here for 16 years and I think understands his business.... We arrived at Yokohama and dropped anchor a short distance from our berth at 7 o'clock P.M. We made the passage from Block Island in 142 days having sailed 19,305 miles, an average of 135 miles per day. Our smallest day's work was...only 3 miles; our biggest...245 miles. It seemed good to be at anchor once more after being in perpetual motion for so long a time.

The sailors and officers are pretty nearly played out having had no sleep for 48 hours. The pilot brought off some papers, and then for the first time I learned for certain that President Garfield was dead.... We have beaten the ship *Cora*, which sailed from New York 18 days before us, and they thought we must surely be her.[17]

NOVEMBER 23RD. This morning a tugboat took us in tow, and put us in our berth about one mile from shore. We hoisted a signal for a doctor and he soon came off to see the cook, who for the last few days has been suffering very much. He was removed to the hospital and the doctor said he could live but a very short time, as he had a cancer in his stomach. We had another cook come off this morning.

We have been without potatoes and fresh meat for 3 months, and this a.m. for breakfast we had beefsteak and vegetables which I enjoyed very much.... We are chartered for $20,000 to take passengers from Hong Kong to Portland, Ore., or Victoria, B.C., which I like very much....

We took dinner at the Windsor House, an American hotel, and after dinner I took a little ride in a jinrikisha.... There are very few horses here and rikishas are the only means of getting around the city. The men can run for hours without stopping and do not seem to get out of wind at all.

There are several men-of-war of all nations in the harbor and only one American bark, the *Annie W. Weston*, whose captain we met on shore at the stevedores. We met Capt. Sawyer of the ship *New Era* on shore and he is a friend of the captain's, he came off on board with us. He lost his ship a few weeks ago and is on his way to San Francisco.[18]

NOVEMBER 24TH. The old cook died last night in the hospital.

The ship *William J. Rotch* lay at anchor at Yokohama from November 22 to December 27, discharging her cargo and taking on sufficient ballast to make the passage to Hong Kong. Cargo and ballast were transported from and to the ship by lighters, subject to weather conditions. The stevedore, a Westerner named Collyer, with 350 full-time workers on his payroll, handled all cargo operations, extended assistance and courtesies to members of the cabin, and sold the ship provisions.

In 1881 Japan was well embarked on its transition from feudalism to the modernization of the Meiji Era, and anti-Western elements had been disarmed and eclipsed. Frank saw the local sights, accompanied variously by Mr. Delano, the Brays together or singly, an Episcopalian missionary from Captain Bray's home town, and a Mr. Cabot. Mr. Cabot, a man of "considerable property," arrived aboard the ship *Cora* intending to make a tour of Japan, China, India, and Europe. Frank also played a good deal of billiards and cards and went to church (Congregational, he thought) with Captain and Mrs. Bray.

NOVEMBER 25TH. An English bark arrived yesterday from England. She had 162 days passage and during the gale that we had, she lost most of her sails and topgallant mast. We did not part a rope yarn.

NOVEMBER 26TH. The old carpenter deserted the ship last night and today the Capt. had a letter from the consul ordering him to appear before him with the 1st and 2nd mates on a charge of ill treatment. Discharged 2,300 cases of oil.

NOVEMBER 28TH. Discharged 3,000 cases of oil this afternoon...went to the Consulate with the Capt., 1st mate, and three of the sailors to testify on the complaint made by the carpenter. He complained of ill treatment and insufficiency of food, but did not prove his claim satisfactorily.... He has another hearing tomorrow. I was put on the witness stand for the first time in my life to testify to his inability to do his work and as to the quantity and quality of his food. As I passed considerable time in the carpenter shop on the passage, I had a good opportunity of judging as to both.

Old Bill, a sailor, deserted night before last.

NOVEMBER 29TH. The captain and 2nd mate went on shore to answer a complaint made by several of the sailors of ill treatment by the second mate. Part of evidence heard and case adjourned.... One of the sailors...came on board drunk and was unruly and saucy, and finally put him under arrest and locked him up.

NOVEMBER 30TH. Fourteen caulkers came on board this morning and commenced to caulk the decks.... Went into a large tea-refining establishment and saw the process.... After once seeing it prepared, a good many people would stop drinking it...have had one man in irons all day for refusing to go to work. He said he was sick, but the doctor said there was nothing the matter with him.

DECEMBER 1ST. Discharged and paid off the carpenter and hired another one. The consul refusing to give any decision in his complaint against the officers. Discharged 3,000 cases of oil.

DECEMBER 3RD. [During sightseeing] The distance from the temple to the minister's house is three miles which we passed over in 23 minutes. We had two men to a rikisha and they ran every step of the way, as fast as they could go.

DECEMBER 8TH. Captain Talpey of the *Wandering Jew*, his wife, and lady passenger came on board today and took dinner.[19]

DECEMBER 9TH. Quite a frost on deck last night. Discharged 3,100 cases of oil. The ship *Cora,* [Captain] Combs, arrived this morning 177 days from New York.... Capt. Reynolds of the ship *Humbolt* arrived on the *City of Tokyo* and has been spending the day on board the *Rotch*. He lost his ship in the China Sea on Lincoln Island during a cyclone a short time ago.[20]

DECEMBER 13TH. Took dinner at the Windsor House with Capt. Bray and met Mr. D. Henshaw Ward, who is the charterer of the *Rotch* from Hong Kong to Victoria.... He seems to be a very pleasant man. He is on his way to Hong Kong from California on the steamship *City of Rio Janeiro*.[21]

DECEMBER 21ST. Finished discharging coal.... Took in about 40 tons ballast.[22] Paid off and discharged six of the men who had entered complaints against the officers.

DECEMBER 23RD. Capt. went on shore this morning and got his papers and cleared at the custom house. Settled for the [30] missing cases at invoice price of $1.90 per case. Six Japanese sailors came on board.

DECEMBER 24TH. Mr. Cabot has given up his proposed trip...and starts for San Francisco tomorrow on steamer *Belgic*.

DECEMBER 25TH. Have in 415 tons ballast...and are drawing 12½ ft. forward and 13 ft. aft. It being Christmas Day, Mrs. Bray made me a present of a very pretty cup and saucer.

DECEMBER 26TH. Got up steam and hoisted anchors and were towed down below the lightship and anchored as there was no wind. Capt. Bray and myself went back to the city in the tugboat. Took dinner and tea with Mr. Collyer [and] met Capt. Call of the ship *Adam W. Simpson* who had just arrived below 152 days from Cardiff, Wales.[23] I bought a canary and gave it to Mrs. Bray for a present.

My sightseeing in Japan is over with. I have enjoyed it very much and have become quite attached to the place.

---

1. The captain was making up the traditional "chip" log outfit, consisting of a wooden "chip," a 150-fathom-long line of "halyard stuff" on a hand-held reel, divided every forty-seven feet, three inches with a knot, or, more properly, with a short length of fishline with a knot for every division.

2. The *Mary & Helen* was a steam auxiliary whaler built by Goss & Sawyer at Bath in 1882 for William Lewis. The bark *Legal Tender*, of San Francisco, was built at Port Madison, Washington Territory, in 1863.

3. The *Rotch*'s new iron-wire rigging (and also the hemp lanyards that secured the lower ends of the stays) had stretched and had to be properly set up, or tightened.

4. The ship *Oneida*, of Searsport, Maine, was built at Searsport in 1866; the bark *Penobscot*, of Bucksport, Maine, was built at Bucksport in 1878.

5. Fanning Island, a small island in the North Pacific Ocean just north of the equator, about 1,200 miles south of Hawaii, was uninhabited when discovered in 1798 by sealing brig captain Edward Fanning, of Stonington, Connecticut. With the exhaustion of the guano fertilizer on Peru's Chincha Islands in the 1870s, the search for new deposits of valuable tropical bird dung brought a short-lived boom to Fanning.

6. References to studding sails on merchant ships in the late 1800s are always of interest, there being a mistaken notion that the use of these sails ended with the passing of the clipper.

7. The sailors forward ate a far simpler diet. The scale of provisions for seamen on American ships at this date only specified (along with water and ascorbics) the amounts of the basics—bread, beef, pork, flour, peas, tea, coffee, sugar, and so on, with allowable substitutes. Although some captains claimed that their sailors were also fed canned vegetables and such, it was also claimed that sailors, being habitual complainers, when treated to a more varied diet, demanded a return to their standard salt beef and pork.

8. Ships were also set into the bulge of Brazil by the Equatorial Current.

9. The ship *Anglo-American*, of St. John, N.B., was built at Portland, New Brunswick, in 1876. Ships from the Maritime Provinces flew the British flag and were typically termed "English."

10. The high island was an important ocean way point for the checking of chronometers. The ship *Ben Nevis*, of Glasgow, was built at Glasgow in 1868.

11. While running her "easting down" the *Rotch* experienced unusually moderate conditions. She following a route that passed within sight of the lonely island of St. Paul, 38° 47' south latitude, 77° 51' east longitude.

12. Studding sails are often thought of as strictly fair weather sails, but Victor Slocum, writing of his boyhood voyage in the *Northern Light* in 1882, recalled that while running their easting down from the Cape to the coast of Tasmania, running before a moderate gale, "It was weather for low sails as we bowled along under stowed royals, but with the tops'l stunsails set out to windward during the first section of the passage." Slocum, *Captain Joshua Slocum*, p. 161.

13. After heading north off the west coast of Australia, Captain Bray elected to pass through the blockade of the Indian Archipelago by way of Alas Strait (east of Sunda Strait, and just to the east of the more heavily traveled Lombok Strait; spelled "Allas" in Findlay).

14. Aided by fair tide and wind, the *Rotch* transited Alas in one day—a most fortunate circumstance given the narrow confines, poor charting, and many hidden reefs of the passage.

15. After crossing the Java Sea the *Rotch* transited the Strait of Macassar into the Celebes Sea, the fine breeze continuing.

16. Gutta-percha is a valuable rubber-like substance obtained from the milky sap of the *percha* tree, with many uses.

17. The *Cora*, of Belfast, Maine, built at Belfast in 1869, would prove to be the last full-rigged ship from Belfast. Although a maiden passage invariably revealed certain shortcomings and deficiencies needing correction, Frank only mentioned leaks in the poop deck which defied all attempts at recaulking, and oversized sails, which had had to be reduced.

18. The bark *Annie W. Weston,* of Boston, was built at East Boston in 1867. The bark *New Era*, of Boston, was built at East Boston in 1870.

19. The ship *Wandering Jew*, of Camden, Maine, was built at Camden (in the village now in the town of Rockport) in 1877. She had arrived on the 7th, 148 days from Cardiff.

20. The ship *Humbolt,* of Bremerhaven, was built at St. John, New Brunswick, in 1863.

21. The 18 May 1899, *San Francisco Examiner* reports that D. Henshaw Ward had contributed seventy-four rare English volumes from the 1700s to the library of the University of California. A genealogist informs me that Ward was a Bostonian, descended from Artemus Ward, famed Revolutionary War general. He was evidently not related to John E. Ward, the American diplomat who, after arriving in Hong Kong in 1859, worked to end the horrors of the coolie trade to Cuba and Peru.

22. With but very few exceptions, cargo-carrying square-riggers could not safely sail with "swept" or empty holds—indeed, some ships could not even safely lie empty in a harbor.

23. The steam was gotten up in the donkey engine boiler. The ship *Adam M. Simpson*, of Philadelphia, was built at Bath, Maine, in 1876 by Goss & Sawyer.

Chapter 9

ON TO HONG KONG

Frank Besse Helps Sail the Ship, Espies the Bark Alden Besse, *then Socializes Among the Large Fleet of American Ships at Hong Kong. The* Besse *Loads Her Cargo of Chinese Passengers, and We Learn About the Infamous "Coolie" Trade.*

DECEMBER 27TH. Mr. Hodnette, pilot, came on board this morning and we got underway at 7 o'clock, and with a moderate, fair breeze started down the Channel. Discharged the pilot at 10 A.M. Sent down the skysail yard and lashed things, expecting to get bad weather....[1] Towards evening it became very puffy and squally, and we took in topgallant sails and mainsail. Heavy swell heaving in from the S. W. which makes the vessel rather uneasy.

DECEMBER 29TH. At 8 P.M. we reefed topsails and mainsail.... Must have passed very near the Bayonesse, a dangerous clump of rocks, during the night. I stopped on deck nearly all day and helped work the ship as we are rather shorthanded and the Japs we shipped know very little.

DECEMBER 30TH. Wind continued very strong from W. N. W. with quite heavy sea. The ship seems to be very stiff, and holds on pretty well considering the amount of ballast we have in.

JANUARY 4th, 1882. After the wind hauled to the West, we gave up the idea of trying to go down the Formosa Channel and kept away South for the Bashee [Bashi] Channel.... Wrote a copy of the Hong Kong Charter Party for the Captain. We are to take merchandise and passengers from Hong Kong to either Victoria, British Columbia, or Portland, Oregon. If we go to Victoria we get $20,000; if to Portland, $21,500. Lay days to commence 24 hours after the ship is ready to receive cargo and to continue 40 days. After that demurrage at the rate of $100 per day.[2]

JANUARY 6TH. Passed through the Bashee Channel and entered the China Sea.... In coming through the channel we gave Gad Rock (a very dangerous rock nearly in the middle of the passage, on which there is 9 feet of water) and the Forest Belle rock (on which the bark *Forest Belle* was wrecked in 1877) a wide berth....[3] Navigating the China Sea is very dangerous during the typhoon season from July to November. Last season they had 19, a much larger number than usual.

JANUARY 7TH. Passed quite a number of junks hove-to and saw one bark bound east.... At 8 P.M. heavy gale from N.... Just at sunset we caught a glimpse of the mountains on the coast of China about 40 miles distant.

JANUARY 8TH. Very strong breeze from the north. Have had topgallant sails furled nearly all day.... Sighted Lamma Islands, situated to the south of Hong Kong, at 12 o'clock M. Took a pilot at 2 o'clock and commenced to beat up to the island of Hong Kong.... We made the passage from Yokohama to Hong Kong in twelve days having sailed 1,944 miles, an average of 162 miles per day. Our...largest [work] was 235 miles.

As we entered the channel, we saw a bark just ahead of us beating up; as we got nearer we saw it was the *Alden Besse* from Portland with a load of [returning Chinese] passengers. We gained on her some in going up as we had more sails set. Our pilot is a Chinaman who talks considerable English. In the boat that he came off was his wife and five children, the wife taking charge after he came on board. He worked the ship splendidly and did not miss-stay once all the way up. We pay him $15 for bringing us in. He asked $40.[4]

JANUARY 9TH. Towed up to our anchorage in the roads this morning and unbent all sail. There is quite a large fleet of vessels in the harbor, fifteen American vessels, among them the *Syren*, *A. Besse*, *Coloma*, *Panay*, *Ringleader*, and *Blue Jacket*.[5] Capt. [Stephen P.] Bray of the *Panay* and [Captain William Bray] of the *Ringleader*, came on board this morning, and soon after Capt. M. Noyes, Brown, and several others.[6]

JANUARY 10TH. Went on board the *Panay* this morning with Capt. Bray. She is very nice and kept in first class order. After looking at her, went to the *Syren* [a Besse ship, an old clipper built in 1851] and was agreeably surprised to see her looking as well. I think she will compare favorably with any ship in the harbor, and looks a great deal better than many comparatively new ships. Had quite a long talk with

Capt. Brown about the vessel.... Mr. Ward (the charterer) and wife were on the *Rotch* to dinner.

JANUARY 11TH. Went to Hong Kong Hotel where most of the captains meet. Saw Capt. Noyes of the *Alden Besse* and had quite a talk with him. Capt. Bray of the *Panay* is spending the evening on board.

JANUARY 12TH. Capt. Bray, wife, and myself took tea on board the *Ringleader* (Bray). He has his wife with him. She is a very pleasant lady and agreeable company. After supper Capt. Bray of the *Panay* came on board and we had a six-handed game of cards.

JANUARY 13TH. Capt. B. and myself went on board *Coloma* and *Red Cross*.[7] Capt. Wm. Bray and wife of the *Ringleader*, Capt. Bray of the *Panay*, and Capt. [James E.] Howland of the *Red Cross* were on board for supper. After supper Capt. and Mrs. Brown of the *Syren* came and we passed the evening in playing games. Mrs. Brown played on the piano considerable.

Commenced to paint the ship. Have contracted with a Chinaman to paint all of the white work and yards.

JANUARY 14TH. There has been a difference of opinion between Mr. Ward and the captains of the vessels that he has chartered in regard to who should furnish extra boats and numerous other articles required for carrying passengers. The charter party does not state that they shall be furnished by the ship and today Mr. Ward acknowledged that he was caught and offered to find them if, after arriving in Victoria, the owners of the ship would not pay for them, he would do so himself.[8]

We are to take 553 passengers which is 150 less than Mr. W. expected. He says he will lose $11,000 on the three vessels now here and feels quite badly about it. Our lay days would commence next Monday, but we cannot possibly get away until after the first of March, and as he has acted very fair with us, we have agreed to give him until March 1st before we come on demurrage to oblige him.

JANUARY 19TH. [Returned from Canton and] went to the Hong Kong Hotel intending to stop there until they had finished painting the cabin of the *Rotch*, but Capt. Brown of the *Syren* said I must come off to his ship and stop, so I consented....[9] This evening went on board the *Ringleader*. They had a kind of party. There were twelve captains (American) and seven ladies there. Had a pleasant time and played games.

JANUARY 21ST. Went to a picnic today.... There were about 25 captains with their wives.... Went back to the *Rotch* after taking supper on the *Syren*. We have taken in 425 chests of tea. We had to take out our mud ballast and take in stone, lest we should damage the tea.[10] The charterers furnish the ballast.

JANUARY 23RD. Quite a number of American ships sailed today.... Capts. Horton, Sherbon, William Bray and wife spent the evening on board the *Rotch*.

JANUARY 24TH. Colonel Mosby (consul) and all of the Bray family took tea on board this evening.[11]

JANUARY 27TH. The English man-of-war *Inconstant* in beating into the harbor came in collision with the *Alden Besse* and carried away the *Besse*'s mainyard, two of her chain plates and backstays, and chafed her side quite badly.[12] It was a piece of carelessness on the part of the Man-of-War. She undertook to come about just ahead of the *A.B.*, got stern way on and drifted broadside into her.[13] Called on the *Tecumseh* [arrived 180 days from Cardiff with coal] with Mr. D.

JANUARY 28TH. Capt. Bray and his wife went on board the *Twilight* to spend the evening, and Mr. Luscomb, mate of the *Panay*, Mr. Nye of the *Syren*, and the mate of the *Twilight*, came on board the *Rotch* and stopped until 10 o'clock.[14]

JANUARY 29TH. Mr. Delano and myself went on shore and met several mates. All took rikishas and went to Wanchi and Happy Valley.... The *Importer* arrived today. 199 days—Cardiff.[15]

JANUARY 30TH. One of my wisdom teeth has been troubling me.... The carpenters have commenced to put in berths for the passengers. Capt. and Mrs. Bray took tea on the *Coloma*.

JANUARY 31ST. Took in 100 tons ballast.... Capt. Brown, wife, and child have been spending the day here. Capt. C. M. Noyes of the *Coloma* came on board and we played cards.

FEBRUARY 2ND. Took in some nut oil and rice this afternoon. This evening Capt. C. M. Noyes and wife, Capt. A. Noyes, and Capt. S. P. Bray came on board.

Following Pages: Magnetic variation chart for China and Japan.
FINDLAY'S DIRECTORY, 1889.

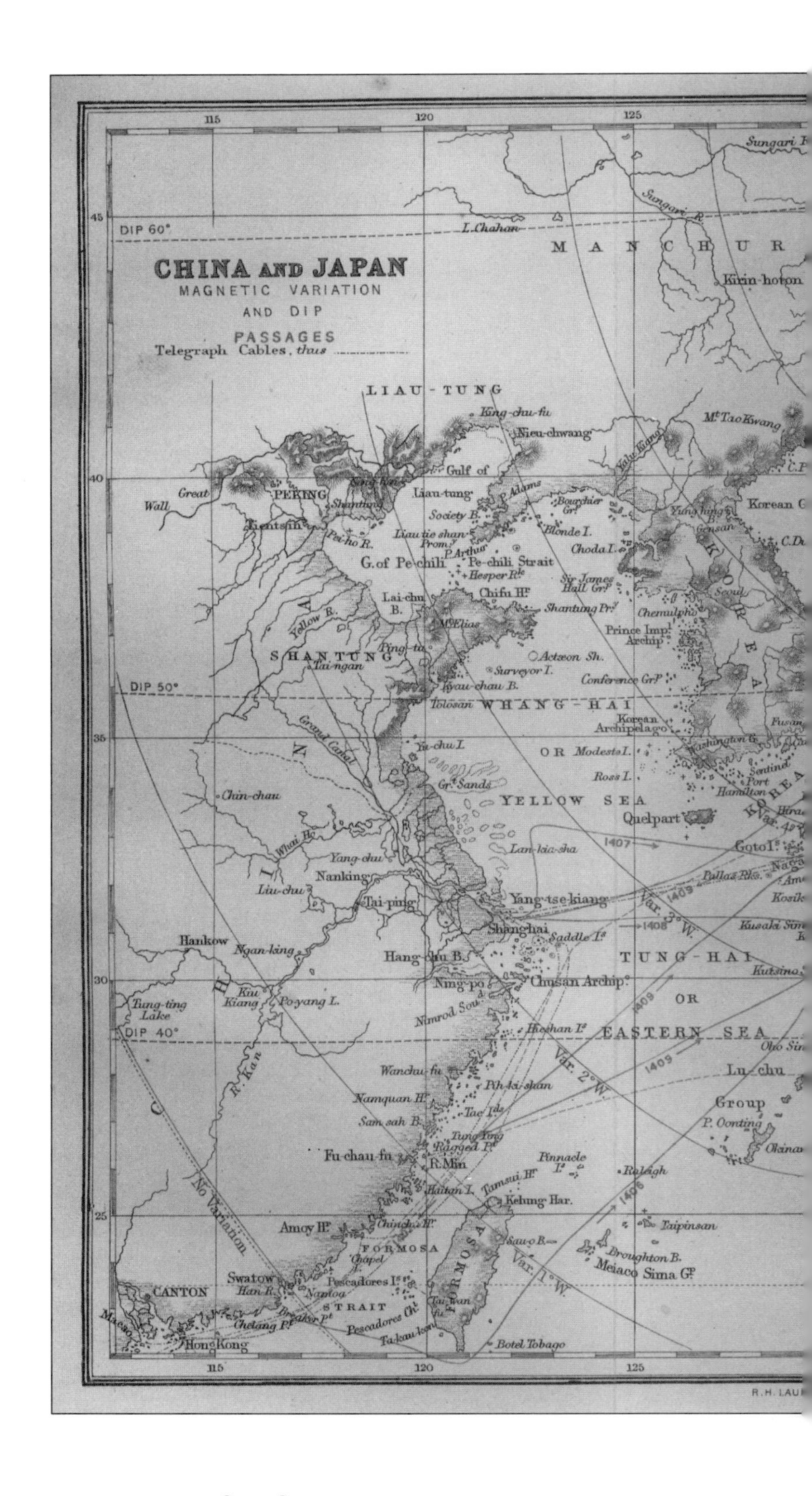
CHINA AND JAPAN
MAGNETIC VARIATION
AND DIP
PASSAGES
Telegraph Cables, thus
DIP 60°
DIP 50°
DIP 40°
L. Chahan
MANCHUR
Kirin-hoton
Sungari R.
LIAU-TUNG
King-chu-fu
Nieu-chwang
Mt. Tao Kwang
Yalu Kiang
Gulf of
Liau-tung
Great
Wall
PEKING
Tientsin
Pei-ho R.
Society B.
P. Adams
Bourchier Gr.
Blonde I.
Liau tie shan Prom.
P. Arthur
Choda I.
G. of Pe-chili
Pe-chili Strait
Hesper Rk.
Sir James Hall Gr.
Chifu Hr.
Lai-chu B.
Shantung Pr.
Chemulpho
Prince Impl. Archip.
Mt. Elias
Yellow R.
Ping-tu
SHANTUNG
Tai-ngan
Actæon Sh.
Surveyor I.
Conference Gr.
Kyau-chau B.
Tolosan
WHANG-HAI
Korean Archipelago
Korean G.
Yung hing B.
Gensan
Seoul
KOREA
Fusan
Port Hamilton
Grand Canal
Yu-chu I.
OR
Modeste I.
Ross I.
Gr. Sands
YELLOW SEA
Quelpart
Chin-chau
Whai R.
Lan-kia-sha
Goto I.
Pallas Rks.
Yang-chau
Nanking
Liu-chu
Tai-ping
Yang-tse-kiang
Var. 3° W.
Shanghai
Saddle Is.
Hankow
Ngan-king
Hang-chu B.
TUNG-HAI
Ning-po
Chusan Archip.
OR
Tung-ting Lake
Kiu Kiang
Po-yang L.
Nimrod Sound
Heshan Is.
EASTERN SEA
Var. 2° W.
R. Kan
Wanchu-fu
Pih-ki-shan
Lu-chu
Group
P. Oonting
Namquan Hr.
Tae Is.
Sam sah B.
Tung Yung
Ragged Pt.
Fu-chau-fu
R. Min
Pinnacle Is.
Raleigh
Haitan I.
Tamsui Hr.
Kelung Har.
No Variation
Amoy Hr.
FORMOSA
Taipinsan
Chapel
Sau-o B.
Broughton B.
Meiaco Sima Gp.
Var. 1° W.
Swatow
Han R.
Pescadores Is.
Namoa
CANTON
STRAIT
Macao
Chelang Pt.
Pescadores Ch.
Tai-wan fu
Hong Kong
Ta-kau-kon
Botel Tobago
R.H. LAU

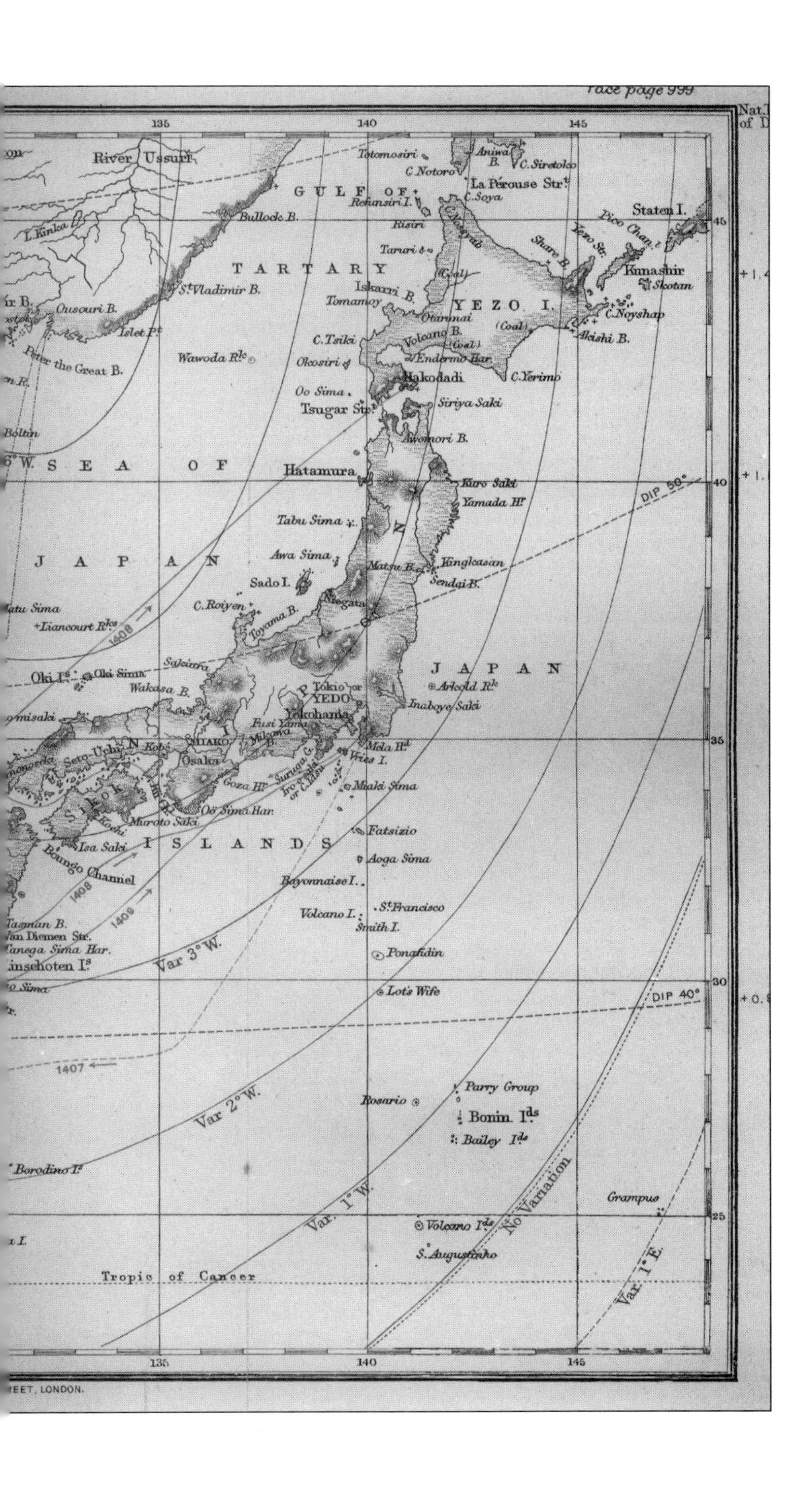

Face page 99
GULF OF
TARTARY
SEA OF JAPAN
JAPAN
YEZO I.
ISLANDS
Hakodadi
Tsugar Str.
Hatamura
Sado I.
Tokio or YEDO
Yokohama
Osaka
Kobe
Bonin Ids
Tropic of Cancer
No Variation
Var. 1° W.
Var. 2° W.
Var. 3° W.
Var. 1° E.
DIP 50°
DIP 40°

FEBRUARY 8TH. Started at 10 o'clock this morning with all except two or three of the American captains and their wives to make a circuit of the island of Hong Kong.... There were twenty-eight chairs each having four coolies, and three extra coolies carried the provisions, making 115 Chinese. We went around the island, stopping about half way round to eat dinner, which they had carried with them, and arrived back to the ship at 7 P.M.

The coolies were pretty tired by the time we reached the city having carried us fully twenty miles, and nearly half of that uphill. They complained considerably of the long distance, and had one fight amongst themselves which alarmed the ladies.... A large junk came alongside this morning with a miscellaneous lot of articles for us to take to Victoria. She was a very large coasting junk and carried eight cannons.

FEBRUARY 10TH. Capt. Call and wife of the *Adam M. Simpson* have been spending the day on the *Rotch*. In the evening Capt. Allyn of the *Importer* and Capt. S. P. Pray came on board and had a sing.[16]

FEBRUARY 11TH. Nearly all of the Americans in port including Mr. Mosby...hired a large steam launch and went about fifteen miles up the Canton River and had a picnic. Capt. Lincoln of the *Tecumseh* made an excellent fish chowder....[17] Took in 4,000 mats of rice.[18] The A[merican] bark *Cashmere* arrived this morning.[19]

FEBRUARY 13TH. This afternoon I took a sampan and visited nearly all of the American ships up at Wanchai to see what each would furnish for the social party to be holden on board the *Panay* next Thursday evening. I am on the decoration committee, also one of the floor managers of the ball. Took tea on board the *Adam M. Simpson* in company with Capt. Bray and wife, and Capt. S. P. Bray. Nearly all of the evening was passed in talking about and making arrangements for the ball.

FEBRUARY 14TH. Took dinner on the bark *Pearl* with Capt. Howes after which we went around to some of the ships and collected their flags to decorate the ballroom with.[20]

FEBRUARY 15TH. Went on shore this forenoon and the *Panay* this afternoon. Her between decks are trimmed up very prettily with flags and Japanese lanterns. We took in some tea and empty water casks.

FEBRUARY 16TH. At 7:30 o'clock P.M. went over to the *Panay*. Shortly after that time the company commenced to arrive and by 9 o'clock there were about fifty ladies and gentlemen present. Nearly all of the

American shipmasters and their wives, and also quite a number of people from shore.... The ship looked very pretty indeed. One hundred tropical plants and orange trees in pots were arranged very tastefully around her sides, making, in connection with the flags and lanterns, a sight well worth seeing.

The dancing commenced at 9 and continued until 12 when we adjourned to the supper room, where we partook of oyster stew, meats of many kinds, cake, piers of fruit and nuts The table, which was in the forward part of the between decks, separated from the ballroom by flags, was decorated very nicely with flowers and waited upon by the Chinese stewards of the fleet. I took a Miss Williams of the bark *Brazos* to supper.[21] She is a very pretty young lady of about fifteen, but does not dance. After supper we again commenced dancing and continued until 4 o'clock when the party broke up.... For music, we had two violins, a bass viol, and a piano.... The party was an entire success.

FEBRUARY 17TH. The China New Year commences tonight. All of the sampans and houses are covered with Joss paper and there is one continual war of fire crackers which cost $2.00 per 10,000.

FEBRUARY 18TH. Went on shore with Capt. Bray and met quite a number of captains and commenced to make New Year calls upon our compradores [agents] and other Chinese acquaintances.... This is the only holiday the Chinese have during the whole year.... It is one continual roar of fire crackers.... The English authorities do not interfere with them for 48 hours. They may use as many fireworks as they please during that time; but they are not allowed afterwards.

FEBRUARY 19TH. At 12 o'clock went over to the *Panay* and took dinner with Mr. Luscomb and Capt. LaFavor of the *White Cloud*.[22] Returned to the *Rotch* at 4, Mr. LaFavor coming and stopping to supper. After tea, Capt. S. P. Bray and myself went down to the *Simpson*; there was quite a company of ladies and gentlemen there, and we passed the evening very pleasantly in singing.... Mrs. Call is one of the pleasantest ladies that I have ever met.

The bark *Wm. H. Besse* arrived late this p.m. from Australia. She came up in ballast as coal freights from Newcastle were only 12s per ton, which would hardly pay; and then, he was in somewhat of a hurry to get here before the last of April as his charter would expire then. She had a very good passage of 43 days, and is looking nicely as she had been painted on the way up.

FEBRUARY 20TH. Went over with Capt. Bray and called upon Capt. Baker of the *WHB* this morning. He has his wife and son about ten years old with him.... Mrs. Bray has not been feeling very well for the last few days and has gone over to the *Simpson* to spend the day and escape from the noise here. We found that the between decks leaked and have forty Chinamen at work caulking.

Capt. and Mrs. Bray took tea on the *Simpson*. I had an invitation but did not go until after supper. Capt. S. P Bray and Mr. Mosby were there and we passed the evening in singing and talking.

FEBRUARY 21ST. Went around to all the American ships and invited the captains to a picnic and ball to be holden at Mr. Rozario's place in Kowloon tomorrow.... Took dinner on the *Panay*.... Capt. Call and wife and S. P. Bray took tea and spent the eveining on board the *Rotch*.

Capt. Baker, wife, and son called on the *Syren* this morning and the boy fell through a scuttle in the pantry and struck his head, hurting him badly. He did not break any bones, but this afternoon has been out of his head and the doctor is fearful that he has concussion of the brain and will not live. Twenty-four hours will decide it. The *Twilight* (Warland) sailed for New York.[23]

FEBRUARY 22ND. I went on board the *Wm. H. Besse* this A.M. to see how his son was getting along, and found he was much better and considered out of danger. Then went on board the *Panay* where we were all to meet. Only about thirty came. We hired a steam launch to tow our sampans to Mr. Rozario's summerhouse, where we spent the day in dancing. The party was in honor of Capt. Allen Noyes's birthday—also Washington's. The Capt. enjoyed himself very much and although he is 60 years old, danced nearly every set.

Went on shore this evening and played billiards with Mr. Delano and Mr. Luscomb. Took in over 1,000 bags of sugar.

FEBRUARY 23RD. Met Capt. LaFavor and Mr. Luscomb, and we went down to the races which commenced today.... This evening took tea on board the *Panay* with Capt. and Mrs. Call, Capt. and Mrs. Bray, and Mr. Mosby. Took in some cargo, also firewood and medicines for the passengers. Four American ships arrived today: three from Australia and one from Cardiff.

FEBRUARY 24TH. Capt. Bray and wife and myself each took a chair and four coolies and started at 2 o'clock [to climb 1,800-foot Victoria Peak].

FEBRUARY 25TH. Called on *Simpson* and *Blue Jacket*.... We are to have a European doctor for the passengers. He is a young man about my age (23) and is not a regular practicing physician but still I think will be better than the Chinese doctors. Finished bending sails and took in nearly all of the Chinese stores. We have 82,590 lbs. of rice, 36,000 lbs. of salted eggs, and many other articles of Chinese chow. Capt. and Mrs. Call and Capt. S. P. Bray spent the evening on board.

FEBRUARY 28TH. Met on board the *Panay* at 10 o'clock and from there went to Mr. Rozario's...where nearly all the ladies and gentlemen of the fleet had assembled to have a dance and good time generally. Stopped there until 6 o'clock.... I think that will conclude the pleasure-making here this season as many of the vessels sail soon.[24] Took in the last of the stores, caulked ports and hatches, and are all ready to receive passengers

An English man-of-war, while beating up the harbor, ran into the *Panay* carrying away her fashion piece and damaging her stern a little. The damage to the steamer was more extensive as she smashed one of her boats and bent her davits and broke her anchor stock. This is the second accident that has occurred and both were occasioned I think by foolishness. The English men-of-war in port are ordered by the Admiral to go out and return under sail for practice, and as they do not work quickly, it is difficult to avoid collision where there are so many vessels.

MARCH 2ND. The Chinese passengers commenced to come on board this morning and by night were all vaccinated, examined, and passed. As fast as they came over the rail, two doctors stood ready to vaccinate them, then they were questioned by the American Consul's interpreter as to their name, destination, and if they went of their own free will.

Each man had a ticket which the Vice Consul stamped as they passed him. They were then examined by another doctor after which they were allowed to take their goods and go below. Each man has a large basket which contains his personal effects and a straw mat for a bed. Nearly all talk at the same time making a perfect babel of voices.

The captain cleared at the Consul's and harbormaster's and received one day's demurrage $100. Capt. Call and wife, Capts. Baker and S. F. Bray, Capt. Crowell, and wife and Mr. Mosby spent the evening on board and bid us good-by.

Went over to Kowloon to see the bark *Alden Besse*. She was in dry dock being remetalled.... She looks very well but Capt. N. says she has got considerable soft wood about her in places and will require a good deal of money laid out on her soon.

Went on a tour of inspection this evening between decks. It was very warm and close down there and already smells quite disagreeable,

> but the passengers did not seem to mind it any. I believe there are but 539. We were to take 553 and I do not understand why they did not all come. They are a fine looking lot of fellows and come from the interior. Most of them have been farmers.

Although Frank Besse wrote of "coolies" in China—a coolie was but a laborer—it was no accident that he referred to the men coming aboard the *Rotch* as "passengers." Even the term "coolie trade" was legally distinct from the trade engaged in by the ships of the Besse fleet, and carried with it terrible baggage.

Both the Indian coolie trade—a trade which existed within the British Empire from the 1830s to the early 1900s, and which was well regulated—and the notorious Chinese coolie trade were responses to the ending of black slavery within the British Empire in 1838, and to the increased international naval efforts to suppress the African slave trade beginning in 1841. This was a period of great population growth in China, particularly in the south, where, coincidentally, opium imports, tea cultivation, and cheap Western cotton goods were depressing the rural economy.

The trade in Chinese coolies, ostensibly contracted to work for a fixed term, may have begun with the departure in 1844 of a shipload of coolies bound for British Guinea.[25] In 1847 the Portuguese ship *Don Pedro* departed Macao with three hundred coolies who thought they were headed for Java, but instead were delivered to a Spanish planter in Peru. Almost half died on the passage and the survivors were treated as virtual slaves. Word spread to the Spanish planters of Cuba, who ordered cargoes of their own. Coolies were subsequently sent all over the Portuguese and Spanish dominions, and to Peru, Australia, Surinam, and the Indian Archipelago.[26]

A dwindling supply of volunteering coolies led to a twenty-year period of kidnapping, buying and selling, shipboard shackling, and starvation. Parents sold their children, night-raiders stole fathers, sons, and whole families. Portuguese ships called "Lorches"—veritable men-of-war—prowled bays and rivers, raiding villages. Wars between rival clans, and the complicity of mandarins who sold their own subjects, fueled the trade. Out of 150,000 Chinese taken "under contract" to the Spanish colonies and South America before 1856, it was estimated that fewer than five hundred ever returned to China.[27]

While plantation coolies were commonly treated worse than black slaves—black slaves, after all, represented significant capital investment—far worse was the fate of those coolies sent to work the guano deposits on Peru's Chincha Islands. Suicide was a major cause of death among the guano workers—in 1856, three hundred coolies drowned themselves in a single day.[28]

Although captains received a bonus for every coolie landed, the history of the trade nevertheless included torture, disease, mutinies, murder, starvation, cannibalization, drowning, suicide, mass asphyxiation (aboard ships battened down in typhoons), and mass incineration.

In 1856 Bostonian George Francis Train wrote home from China:

> THE *WESTWARD HO*, Boston clipper, has just passed Anjer with 800 Coolies from Swatow to Callao, and others have and are continually passing with their living freights. The days of the African slave trade are of the past, save what the Brazilian, and Cuban traders may be engaged in, but the traffic in human life is not wholly abolished when we see English coal ships, Peruvian convict hulks, and American clippers, all heading towards the west coast of South America, every square foot of space occupied by a poor devil of a Chinaman, who thinks...he is leaving purgatory for paradise.[29]

Captain Hays of the ship *Otranto*, of San Francisco—a ship engaged carrying "Chinamen," i.e., Chinese passengers, not "coolies," to California—described to Train, with disgust, the terrible conditions in the port of Swatow [Shantou], from whence coolies were shipped to Peru. The business there was run by a young American named Bradley, in association with the Peruvian consul. Coolies who were brought from the distant interior by Chinese "crimps," and who failed medical inspection, were turned ashore to die of starvation or exposure, and great numbers were to be seen along the beach in this state. They were, Captain Hays believed, far better off than the wretches who supposed they were bound for California or Australia but who, once they had crossed the Rubicon, were headed for the "iron bondage" of Cuba or South America.[30]

In 1855 British ships were forbidden to engage in the trade to other than British colonies, serving to drive the worst elements of the trade to other flags; in 1862 the United States at long last prohibited the transport of Chinese contract laborers in American ships. Several American clippers were sold under the Peruvian flag, including the Kennebec-built clipper *White Falcon*, which became the *Napoleon Canavero*. In 1866, on a passage from China to Callao, the *Canavero*'s coolies became rebellious and were secured below decks under battened hatches. Suffocating, the desperate men set fire to the ship. The officers and crew put off in boats, and were rescued, while the 650 coolies died most horribly.

A different sort of trade in Chinese passengers also developed. Twenty-odd fugitive coolies from Peru arrived at San Francisco in 1848 or '49. Upon returning to China, their stories of gold and freedom touched off an exodus, and by the end of 1851 it was estimated that 25,000 Chinese were in California, largely engaged in placer mining and manual labor.[31] A distinction was made between the trade in contract coolies to Cuba and Peru and those who paid their own expenses to California.[32] After 1855 Hong Kong became the sole port for emigration for San Francisco, and both the American consul and British authorities theoretically exercised governmental oversight.[33] (Meanwhile, the really bad old coolie trade continued at Portuguese Macao, and at Whampoa.)

As in the forced coolie trade, instances of mass death by asphyxiation, disease, and so on, occurred, although surely far less often. The passage was relatively short, and the weather—except when typhoons were encountered—was relatively temperate and benign.[34]

Very large numbers of Chinese were also carried by the "palace" steamships of the Pacific Mail Line, whose Chinese sailors were an attraction to prospective passengers. In 1876 Captain J. H. Drew, of the new Boston ship *Sea Witch*, just arrived at San Francisco from Boston, wrote of newly arrived Chinese disembarking from a steamer, and the welcome accorded them by his ship's dog, Blanco:

> IT IS ACTUALLY TRUE that a dog will immediately grapple a Chinaman the moment he lands in San Francisco, and Blanco, no exception to the rule, for he joined the other dogs in a jiffy. It was with the utmost difficulty that I could get him away from the poor Celestial. Nobody seemed to care, but thought it was good fun.[35]

Initially the Chinese were hailed as a great asset, but it didn't take long for opposition to develop, led in California by Irish immigrants and Southerners. In 1868 and 1869 the "contract coolie" charge was leveled at the importation of several thousand workers required for the completion of the Pacific railroads who had signed promissory notes for their fares.[36] Reflecting a political alliance of the South and the West against the East, the Chinese Exclusion Act of 1882 was part of the political fallout following Garfield's assassination, and ended the United States-bound branch of the Chinese passenger trade, as such.[37]

The traffic in Chinese between Hong Kong and Portland, Oregon, began in 1867. Besse's converted steamer *Hattie C. Besse*, making her first such voyage in 1869, was the fourth vessel to join the trade.[38] The four ships employed in the trade in 1872 included the American bark *Garibaldi*, Captain Cyrus M. Noyes (whom we met in Hong Kong), and the new bark *Alden Besse*. Besse's new ships built in the 1870s specifically for the trade were surely the best ships in the service.

The building of the Canadian Pacific Railway, an engineering marvel, between 1881 and 1884, attracted 17,000 Chinese laborers, with over half—including those who boarded the *William J. Rotch*—coming directly from China. About 1,500 coolies died on the job of injury and disease; in 1885, with the road completed, about 1,000 returned home. Rising political opposition to continued Chinese immigration to British Columbia after the completion of the railroad culminated in 1886 with a $50 head tax, which effectively ended the Chinese passenger trade to Victoria.[398]

---

1. Ships sailing "in ballast" commonly sent down their skysail yard(s), primarily to reduce the buoyant vessel's enhanced tendency to roll, and also to help prevent the capsizing of a too-tender vessel under extreme circumstances.

2. This meant that Mr. Ward, the charterer, had forty days after the ship was ready to receive its cargo to complete loading without paying a daily penalty, or demurrage.

3. This was, of course, William Besse's bark *Forest Belle*, lost on the rock on her maiden voyage.

4. To "miss stays" is to fail in an attempt to tack, or turn, the ship through the eye of the wind. Successfully tacking a full-rigged ship, especially in close quarters, required a nicety of judgment. That the pilot did so well on a strange ship speaks well of both the pilot and the ship.

5. Captain George Bray and Captain Stephen Bray both came from Newburyport, Massachusetts, and likely William did as well. The bark *Coloma*, of Portland, Oregon, was built at Warren, Rhode Island, in 1869; the ship *Panay*, of Salem, Massachusetts, was built at East Boston, in 1877; the ship *Ringleader*, of Boston, was built at Chelsea, Massachusetts, in 1868; and the ship *Blue Jacket*, of San Francisco, was built at Greenport, Long Island, in 1865.

6. "Captain M. Noyes" was presumably Captain Cyrus Noyes, of Searsport, Maine, of the bark *Coloma*. He was the elder brother of Captain Allen Noyes, the master of the Besse bark *Forest Belle*, lost on her maiden voyage off Formosa (Taiwan).

7. The ship *Red Cross*, of Richmond, was built at Richmond, Maine, in 1877.

8. Extra boats provided greater means for transferring passengers from a wrecked or sinking ship to another ship or to shore. Their capacity did not begin to accommodate all who were on board.

9. Frank spent several days in Canton, taking in all the usual points of interest to tourists, including a visit to the court to see flogging and finger and toe stretching. No executions having been scheduled that day, Frank had to settle for seeing clotted blood at the execution ground. At the "temple of horrors"—no further explanation is given—he saw cats, dogs, and rats being prepared for eating.

10. The foul odor of mud ballast could damage the flavor of the tea. The carriage of chests of tea was a very specialized business, and utmost cleanliness was demanded by the shippers. A ship that leaked a little was considered preferable to a tight ship since the bilge water would not be so stale—considering that the bilge water of a coolie ship was unlikely to be very sweet, one wonders where exactly the tea was stowed. One aspect of the stowing of tea is worth repeating: "When stowing the last chest in an early tier, a Chinaman, rather than strike it with any

hard instrument, walks off to a distance, and running back jumps into the air and falls in a sitting posture on the chest, which is thus sent uninjured into its place." Charles H. Hillcoat, *Notes on the Stowage of Ships* (New York: Colonial, 1919), pp. 223–24. The motherlode of tea stowage lore is found in Robert White Stevens, *On the Stowage of Ships* (London: Longmans, Green, Reader, & Dyer, var. editions).

11. This was none other than Colonel John Singleton Mosby, Confederate cavalry hero, leader of "Mosby's Guerrillas," who, after the war, became a great friend of Grant's, and a rabid Republican. A tall, angular man, he was said to bear so many scars that he couldn't walk straight. As consul in Hong Kong he was notorious among sailors for giving their complaints short shrift, particularly if they were black Americans. Among captains he was well known for eagerly accepting shipboard hospitality, especially for breakfast, where he was served his favorite highly spiced Spanish omelet. On Inauguration Day—4 March 1881—he persuaded Captain and Mrs. Joshua Slocum to name their new son Garfield. Slocum, *Captain Joshua Slocum*, p. 135. See also James H. Williams, *Blow the Man Down* (New York: Dutton, 1959), p. 54.

12. Beating was working to windward by successively "tacking" across the wind. When tacking, a vessel turns to bring the wind to its opposite side.

13. HMS *Inconstant* was a ship-rigged iron screw frigate of 5,780 tons, recognized as the fastest ship of the fleet when under sail. In 1881/82 she was the flagship of the Flying Squadron under Rear Admiral the Earl of Clanwilliam, a devotee of sail. There have been a half-dozen HMS *Inconstants*, a most curious name whose derivation has evidently been lost to history. My thanks to Peter Beeston.

14. The ship *Twilight*, of Mystic, was built at Mystic, Connecticut, in 1866. Joseph W. Luscomb, of Salem, and Captain Stephen Bray, Jr., of Newburyport, are pictured standing on the poop deck of the splendid ship *Panay* in my book *Portrait of a Port, Boston 1852–1914* (Cambridge, MA: Harvard University Press, 1971), p. 347.

15. The ship *Importer*, of Boston, was built at Newburyport, Massachusetts, in 1870.

16. With the failure of *Importer*'s owners, Howes & Crowell, in 1883, Allyn, a Cape Codder from Hyannis, lost most of his means. He swore off the sea but was later persuaded by shipowner J. Henry Sears to put what funds he had left into the ship *Titan*, which he commanded until 1894, when she was lost, taking Allyn's remaining funds with her. Matthews, *American Merchant Ships*, Series II, pp. 185–86.

17. The ship *Tecumseh* of Boston was built at East Boston in 1866.

18. Perhaps something was lost in the transcription. Rice was a most problematical cargo, and mats were laid beneath the bagged rice and the bottom of the hold to entrap grains from broken bags.

19. The bark *Cashmere*, of Boston, was built at Medford, Massachusetts, in 1862.

20. The bark *Pearl*, of Boston, was built at Medford, Massachusetts, in 1862.

21. The bark *Brazos*, of New York, built at Portland, Connecticut, in 1870.

22. The bark *White Cloud*, of Boston, was built at Boston, Massachusetts in 1874.

23. Captain William C. Warland would later command the ill-fated Besse ship

Hotspur, in which he was a substantial owner.

24. For brevity, not all mention of picnics, ship visits, shoreside socializing, churchgoing (by the Brays), and billiard playing (by Besse and various mates) have been included. With the anchorage transformed momentarily into a floating New England community, one senses an almost frantic compulsion for rampant socializing, suggesting how lonely life in the cabin of a ship at sea often was. For wives, in particular, who were long separated from the company of other women, such gatherings were of special importance. It was at Hong Kong that Captain Robert Tapley, of West Brooksville, Maine, met and wooed his future wife Agnes, who was there aboard the ship commanded by her father, Captain William H. Gould, of Kennebunk, Maine. Surely there were many other such stories.

25. Mary Roberts Coolidge. *Chinese Immigration* (New York: Henry Holt, 1909), p. 44.

26. Russell H. Conwell, *Why and How: Why the Chinese Emigrate, and the Means They Adopt for the Purpose of Reaching America* (Boston: Lee and Shepard, 1871), p. 83.

27. Ibid., p. 93. The estimated totals to 1870 included 130,900 coolies to Cuba, 197,000 to Peru and elsewhere in South America, 7,000 to Java, and 35,000 to Australia.

28. Ibid., p. 87. Guano, seabird dung that had accumulated over centuries in the rain-free environment, was nasty stuff which wonderfully reinvigorated worn-out farmland. The carriage of guano, primarily to Europe, provided critical employment, especially during the Civil War, for many American ships.

29. George Francis Train, *An American Merchant in Europe, Asia, and Australia* (New York: G. P. Putnam, 1857), p. 76. The orders from *Westward Ho*'s owners not to carry coolies had reached China too late.

30. Ibid., p. 79. W. A. Fairburn, *Merchant Sail*; Fairburn Marine Educational Foundation, Center Lovell, 1945–55, p. 2258-59; Basil Lubbock, *Coolie Ships and Oil Sailers* (Glasgow: Brown, Ferguson, 1955), p. 43.

31. The estimated numbers of Chinese resident in California grew from 25,000 in 1852 to 35,000 in 1860, 50,000 in 1870, and 75,218 as enumerated by the 1880 census. Many others had arrived, worked, and then returned to China.

32. Coolidge, *Chinese Immigration*, p. 46; Conwell, *Why and How*, p.156; M. F. Farley, "John E. Ward and the Chinese Coolie Trade," *American Neptune*, vol. 20, p. 209.

33. However, American regulations limiting passenger numbers on ships leaving Hong Kong were "wonderfully abused during the excessive immigration of Chinese into California from China in the years 1850, 51, 52." Stevens, *On the Stowage of Ships*, p. 480. Also, some departing ships took on additional passengers in outer Hong Kong Harbor, and disembarked excess passengers in outer San Francisco Harbor. It is a pity that Besse does not tell us of the sanitary arrangementes provided for the passengers aboard the *Rotch.* A law passed later in 1882 (Chapter 374, Section 3) required all American vessels to be fitted with a privy for every 100 male passengers or for every 50 female passengers or young children. These were to be constructed "on each side of the vessel." A good description of the latrines fitted aboard a British coolie ship (carrying Indian coolies) may be found in H. C. DeMierre, *The Long Voyage* (New York: Walker and Co.), 1963, pp. 25–26.

34. San Francisco merchant Nicholas Largo was the agent who arranged the re-flagging of American clippers as Peruvian ships. One would suspect that he was also involved in the Hong Kong–San Francisco coolie trade.

35. Clipping from the *Boston Record.*

36. Ironically, although California-bound passengers were not, as a rule, slaves in China, many had sold family members into bondage for passage money, intending to buy them back from the money lenders with their earnings. Conwell, *Why and How,* p. 191.

37. Coolidge, *Chinese Immigration,* p. 168.

38. E. W. Wright. *Lewis & Dryden's Marine History of the Pacific Northwest* (Seattle, 1967), p. 199. She was lost in November 1871, under Captain James Gragg, near Cape Flattery, having parted her cables after having fallen in too close to the coast in fog. She had been headed to Burrard's Inlet from San Francisco to load lumber for Shanghai.

39. Patricia E. Tan and Roy Jin, *The Chinese in Canada* (St. John), pp. 5, 7.

Chapter 10
Hong Kong to Victoria

The William J. Rotch *Carries Chinese Passengers Across the North Pacific.*

We will now rejoin young Frank Besse aboard the ship *William J. Rotch* as she departs Hong Kong for Victoria, British Columbia, with 575-odd persons on board. Since even a day when "nothing of importance" occurred aboard a 218-foot-long, 1,700-ton ship with 575-odd persons in residence might be considered important in and of itself—and in light of the rarity of this account—we will take some note of every day of the passage.

> March 3rd, 1882. Got up steam and hoisted anchor at 7 o'clock and taking two tug boats and the same pilot that we had when we went in we towed out of the Lymoon pass. The tugs left us at 10 o'clock and with a fine breeze from the N. E. we set all sail and headed her for America.[1]
>
> The captain has appointed me as kind of overseer of the passengers, and I am to keep account of all of the provisions they use on the passage. This morning I got out 800 lbs. of rice and 1,500 salted eggs, and 11 lbs. of tea, and their cooking and eating utensils. There have been but very few on deck today, most of them lying in their berths and sleeping or playing dominoes. There is a little swell on, and some feel a little uncomfortable, but none are real sick. Mrs. Bray is quite sea sick and did not come out to dinner. Towards evening the wind increased and many of the passengers were sick.
>
> March 4th. Strong breeze from the N. E.... There has been quite a chop of a sea on all day and nearly all of the passengers have been sick and but very few came on deck. I got up this morning and dealt out the provisions to the cooks at 6 o'clock. Gave them 800 lbs. rice, [believed to be 1 bbl.] salt beef, 304 lbs. turnips and cabbage, 11 ½ lb. tea, and 300 gal. water. That is not their allowance, but so many are sick that they would not eat at all. Made several trips between decks

but did not stop long, as it smelled rather disagreeable. Have been a little sick all day, and lost my dinner.

MARCH 5TH. Quite a heavy gale from the N. E. all day with a rough sea. Stood to the S. E. until 5 o'clock when Luzon, one of the Philippines bore east about 15 miles, then wore ship and stood to the N. W. Have reefed topsails and furled mainsail and am going under easy sail but do not make much headway.... Have not got over my seasickness yet, and the passengers have been worse today and have eaten very little.

MARCH 6TH. Wind continued to blow a gale from the N. E.... Stood off shore until 5 o'clock this morning, then tacked and ran within 10 miles of Cape Bojeador (Luzon) when we tacked again.... Cape Bojeador is where the American ship *New Era*, Capt. Sawyer, was lost last October during a typhoon.... I am nearly over my seasickness and many of the passengers are getting better and came on deck. While on deck, they employ themselves in searching for lice, of which they all have an abundance. If we arrive in Victoria without getting covered with insects ourselves, we shall be very fortunate. I have to go down amongst them several times a day. In the morning at 6 o'clock to get out their provisions for the day and afternoon to see that everything is all right.

MARCH 7TH. Strong N. E. monsoon continued all day with cloudy weather and frequent rain squalls...it blows so hard that we lose as much on leeway as we make in beating.[2] It is rather discouraging.... The passengers continue to improve and I think will soon be able to eat their allowance.

MARCH 8TH. Shook our reef from main sail at noon and set topgallant sails and crossjack during the afternoon but took them in again at night.... Had all of the passengers on deck this p.m. for one hour, and gave the between decks a good cleaning out and airing; then sprinkled sand and plenty of carbolic acid about as there was a very disagreeable odor down there. Today is the first time since leaving port that we have had them all on deck and some did not want to come up now as they had not recovered from their seasickness. They are divided off into messes of ten men each, and at meal time one man from each mess goes forward and gets a bucket of rice and pan of fish, or whatever they may have; then they form in groups about the deck, or below, and eat and talk.

MARCH 9TH. Gale of wind again from the N. E., ship under reefed topsails and main sail...we made the Batan or Bashi Islands; then tacked to the N. W.... Nothing of importance occurred among the passengers.

MARCH 10TH. At night down to topsails again.... Had all the passengers on deck again today and cleaned out below. The sea has gone down very much and the Chinamen are happy. They are singing and playing dominoes and cards between decks and they keep it up nearly all night.

MARCH 11TH. All sail set this afternoon.... Sighted the South Cape of Formosa this A. M. and headed through the Bashi Channel..... Saw Botel Tobago and Little Botel Tobago [Islands], six miles from which the bark *Forest Belle* was lost in 1877. The rock upon which she struck has been recently found....[3] It seems nice to have the ship more steady and the passengers seem to appreciate it also, as they come on deck in larger numbers and I had to give them their full allowance of provisions this morning. Capt. Bray turned his ankle over this a.m. and hurt it quite badly.

MARCH 12TH. Passed out of the China Sea this morning into the Pacific Ocean...we are tumbling and rolling about under reefed topsails and spanker...but very few passengers ventured on deck today.

MARCH 13TH. Wind a little more moderate.... Nothing of importance occurred. Every day I go through the same maneuvers. I get up at 6 o'clock, drink a cup of coffee and eat a couple of crackers, then take three or four men and go down in the hold and get out the passengers' provisions for the day—that takes about one hour. Then I have a good wash with carbolic soap and by that time breakfast is ready.... In the evening I usually sit in the after cabin reading or talking...and set down an account of the Chinese provisions, then retire.

MARCH 14TH. One of the passengers was found dead this morning between decks. He had been seasick ever since we left Hong Kong, but we thought it nothing serious. The doctor said he died of exhaustion, or a kind of starvation, as he could keep nothing down. We sewed him up in his blanket and tied a bag of sand to his feet and placed him on a plank and launched him overboard. The Chinamen did not want him buried, but put in a box and carried to Victoria, but that would have been impractical. They did not make near as much fuss as I expected they would and most of them did not seem to care anything about it. As he went over the rail, they threw a bunch of joss sticks after him to carry him to China heaven. It made me feel a little bad to see a man buried at sea, although he was a Chinaman.

MARCH 15TH. It was almost uncomfortably warm and nearly all of the passengers were on deck sunning themselves and busily employed searching for lice.

MARCH 16TH. Moderate breeze from the N. E. with pleasant weather.... The passengers have all come up to their appetites and this morning asked for more than their allowance, but I did not give it to them and they were going to have satisfaction by licking the interpreter and we had to protect him for a few minutes. It is quite amusing to watch them in the morning when they are pumping up their fresh water; they come on deck with little tin pails and stand near the couplings of the hose, and the minute your back is turned they will unscrew them a little, so they will leak and they catch the water. They are very saving of water and do not waste any by washing themselves.

MARCH 17TH. Very pleasant and warm.... Saw a school of porpoises this afternoon. The Chinamen all rushed to the side and shouted for they had never seen that kind of a fish before. They have been barbering today and many had their heads shaved and hair combed and queues braided. Some of them had splendid heads of hair; black as coal, thick, and reaching below their waist.

MARCH 18TH. Very pleasant and warm.... All the passengers have been on deck today and it has been so smooth that there were no sick ones. They seem to be very happy and sing and laugh most of the time, as they have nothing to do, but eat and sleep. Probably they never had so long a time of loafing before.

MARCH 19TH. Passed the south end of the Lov Chov Islands, but did not see them. Gave the passengers an extra bag of rice and they felt pretty good natured. We have to pump up their water during the night as they unscrewed the couplings of the hose so they would leak and they could catch water.

MARCH 20TH. These pleasant days the passengers eat their chow on deck. They have two meals a day, one at 10 o'clock, and the other at 4. They always have a great deal to say about meal time and take good care that the cooks do not show any partiality in filling up each squad's rice basket.

MARCH 21st. Had to keep off our course about a half-hour this morning to avoid a large water spout.

MARCH 22ND. Gale of wind from the S. W. all day with heavy sea on.... The passengers have been on deck but very little today, but they do not seem to be frightened any at a gale and whenever a sea comes on board and happens to wet somebody, they all laugh. While writing this, she is doing some pretty heavy rolling.

MARCH 23RD. Sighted Aoga Shima and Fatsizio Islands this afternoon and passed between them...the latter...at one time was used as a penal settlement for Japanese convicts. It has been quite cool today and the passengers did not care about coming on deck as they have very few clothes to wear.

MARCH 24TH. Strong breeze from the N. W. all day with some spiteful rain and wind squalls.... It is a real pleasure to stand on deck and see her go during some of the squalls when she is making twelve knots but never since she was built have we had a strong breeze on her quarter for twenty-four hours, so have made no very large day's run. Very few passengers on deck as it is quite cold.

MARCH 25TH. Nothing of any importance transpired.

MARCH 26TH. At 8 o'clock P.M. it was blowing a heavy gale, and the ship down to reefed topsails, and whole foresail and fore topmast staysail, and making twelve knots at that.

MARCH 27TH. The wind blew very hard during the night and there was a bad sea running. The ship rolled heavily and everything that was not firmly lashed or wedged was on the move.... The wind died out this morning but the sea continued running high, making it, if possible, more uncomfortable.... Some of the berths carried away during the night in the hold, and the Chinamen had to sleep on the deck.

MARCH 28TH. Fine breeze from the S. W.... I have been nearly sick all day.... Nearly all hands have colds.... Have all the passengers on deck for an hour this afternoon, and gave the between decks a good cleaning out and sprinkled plenty of chloride of lime down there, as it was smelling very disagreeable.

MARCH 29TH. Moderate breeze from the S. W.... Quite a number of passengers have been on deck all day playing dominoes. This is the only game I have seen them play.... This evening I played cribbage with Mrs. Bray.

MARCH 30TH. There was quite a fight among the Chinese this P.M. but nobody hurt. One mess got two baskets of rice and did not want to give up the one that did not belong to them.

MARCH 31ST. Had the passengers all on deck this afternoon for about an hour. There are a few who like to stay on deck, but the larger part stop below nearly all the time and only come on deck when they are driven up. Nearly all are barelegged and wear short pants, but have plenty of clothes around their body.

APRIL 1ST. All Fools' Day. Not much notice taken of it as regards fooling each other, but still a little fun amongst the officers.... During one of the squalls it snowed and the passengers looked at it in astonishment as many of them had never seen snow before.

APRIL 2ND. During the night there were several snow squalls and considerable snow collected on deck. The passengers came up and asked if it was good to eat, and on being told that it was filled up their pails and carried it below.[4]

APRIL 3RD. Fine breeze.... Sailed 260 miles E. N. E. with the main sky sail set. That is the largest day's work the ship ever made. Crossed the meridian of 180 at half past 12 this noon, and we are now in West longitude once more.

APRIL 3RD. Since leaving New York we have gained one day, and it is usually customary to change the day when you cross the meridian of 180...we decided to call this day Monday, the 3rd of April, the same as yesterday.... All passengers on deck for short time.

APRIL 4TH. Reefed topsails and mainsail. Played cribbage this evening with Mrs. B.

APRIL 5TH. Half a gale of wind from the N. E. with a heavy sea on.

APRIL 6TH. Had all the passengers on deck and cleaned out below.

APRIL 7TH. Nothing of importance occurred.

APRIL 8TH. The passengers seem to be unusually happy tonight, and are singing and making a great noise between decks.

APRIL 9TH. Quite a number of passengers on deck today busily engaged in killing livestock on their bodies. They run the seams of their clothes through their teeth as a quick and easy way of disposing of the inhabitants. They have had several rows amongst themselves this afternoon and on this evening; but there is more noise and running about than fighting and nobody hurt. The fuss commenced by one of the cooks thrashing one of the passengers for stealing water. After that the friends of that fellow caught the cook alone and commenced to pound him, but the officers soon separated them.

APRIL 10TH. Took all the tickets from the passengers this noon and have been all the afternoon counting them, and setting down their numbers. I had them all come on deck and took their tickets as they came up. We found we had 546 which with the one that died makes ten more than we thought we had, but there can be no trouble as we are allowed to carry 553.

APRIL 11TH. Sailed 198 miles E. N. E., and at noon were 1,200 miles from our port of destination.... Arranged the tickets in the order of their numbers and checked them off on the list.

APRIL 12TH. Light breeze from S. E....veering to N. E. with rain towards evening.... Reefed topsails, and fore and mainsails, although it does not blow very hard, and we could easily carry topgallant sails. Capt. Bray is very cautious about carrying sail, and said he never carried away a sail in his life, and I don't think he ever will. All the officers and crew laugh to see him shorten sail when a cloud makes its appearance.

APRIL 13TH. Played cards this evening with Mrs. B. The wind backed into N. N. W. during the night and blew a stiff breeze from that quarter until 10 P.M., when it commenced to hawl back to N. E.... Very few passengers on deck except the cooks.

APRIL 15TH. Commenced to write letters home.

APRIL 16TH. Thick weather and rain so could get no sights all day.... Barometer 29.08 in a great fall since yesterday.

APRIL 17TH. Thick fog and rain. Have had the fog horn going all day and tonight the dismal noise is heard every few minutes. We are getting near the coast and shall go into the straits tomorrow if the fog will lift up.... I made a bet with Mr. Delano that the ship would not make 1,200 miles in six days, and today I received fifty cigars as payment as he did not accomplish it.

APRIL 18TH. Sighted land at 3 P.M. and entered the Strait of Juan de Fuca at 8 P.M. in a heavy squall from the South during which we put her under lower topsails.... Have had a signal for a pilot flying for a number of hours, but did not succeed in getting one. The Strait of

Juan de Fuca is about 60 miles long and from 13 miles, at the entrance, to 9 miles in width with no anchorage. The Capt. had never been here before, and did not wish to enter the straits without a pilot, especially on a dark night, but circumstances compelled him to. The Chinese stared at the land but did not seem particularly pleased to know that they were so near the place of destination. They have had nothing to do but eat and sleep and I think have rather enjoyed the passage. Both watches on deck all night.

APRIL 19TH. The wind hauled to East at 12 o'clock last night and from that time until 3 o'clock this afternoon we beat back and forth across the channel, sometimes with a heavy squall and soon after nearly a calm. At that time the wind came out of the West and with a light breeze we ran up to Royal Roads and dropped anchor at 8 P.M. At 12 o'clock M. the squalls were coming so heavy from the East and the barometer was so low, that both Capt. Bray and Mr. Delano thought we were going to have a gale, and concluded it would be best to put out to sea again. So we put her before the wind and headed out the channel, but had not run far before the wind hauled a little and we put her about again and were thankful when we let go anchor.

A U.S. Revenue Cutter came down to see us this morning and hailed us, but when she found we were bound to an English port left us a small bundle of papers and went back. We had the jack flying for 24 hours for a pilot but did not see a sign of one until after we had dropped anchor when one came on board and then of course we did not want him.... We would have given a good price for a big [tug]boat when we squared away to run out.... Saw two barks this a. m. bound down.... On the south the Olympian Range of Mountains in Washington Territory runs parallel with the coast. The tops were covered with snow at which the Chinese stared with astonishment.... We were 48 days on the passage during which we sailed 7,584 miles, an average of 158 miles daily. Largest day's work 260 miles, smallest 92 miles. Officers and crew are nearly played out as they had no sleep last night.

APRIL 20TH. The Capt. went on shore this morning...and returned at 2 P.M. with a tugboat, two customhouse officers, the mayor of Victoria, a doctor, and an agent of Mr. Ward to look after the passengers. After the doctor had examined the passengers, we hoisted anchor with the engine, and were towed into Esquimalt Harbor. There are but three ships in the harbor besides ourselves.... It is closely landlocked and has deep water close to the shore.

Mr. Reed, the overseer of the Chinamen, remained on board all night and the passengers leave in the morning on a river boat.... It will be a long time before they will have as easy a time as they have passed for the last fifty days. And I pity the poor fellows when I hear of the hardships they have got to pass through and think the man who died on the passage was the most fortunate of them.... The Olympic Mountains looked very pretty this morning with the snow shining on their snowcapped summits.

APRIL 21ST. The steamer *Princess Louise* came alongside this morning early, and the passengers with their baggage were soon transferred to her decks and packed away like cattle. On a lot of straw hats that they had worth about $20, they had to pay $36 duty and the officers were going to charge duty on the rice I put on the boat for their chow this morning, but the overseer growled at that and said before he would pay, they might go on board the ship again and cook their breakfast, finally they allowed it to pass free. The steamer...will take them as far as Westminster, where they will take another boat and go to Yale and from there go in flatboats as far as they can up the Fraser River, then walk about 20 miles to the camp. As soon as they had gone, we commenced to take down berths, hospital, etc., and by night had them all down and washed off.

APRIL 22ND. Went on shore this morning with Capt. B. Took a buggy and drove over to Victoria, a distance of about four miles.... First went to Stahlschimidts & Ward [presumably the ship's agents].... Next we went to the American Consul's. The Consul is an old man of 70 years, and he is as smart as a boy of 12.... [Victoria] is a city, but a small one, and very quiet. Every other building seems to be a liquor saloon with the usual number of loafers and deadbeats.

The ship *Blue Jacket* arrived today, 45 days from Hong Kong. She made a little quicker passage than we did, but had bad weather and a great deal of trouble with the Chinamen. Capt. Percival looked pretty well played out as his mate had been laid up all the passage, which made more work for him. He lost four Chinamen on the passage (died) and also his cook.[5]

There are ten vessels in the harbor and roads, among them the *Germania*, *John Worster*, and *John Trahey*.[6] They are all light and came here for orders, and will take coal or lumber. We are chartered to load coal at Nanaimo, Departure Bay, for San Francisco, at $2.50 per ton of 2,240 lbs., a fair freight although expenses are very high there.

APRIL 24TH. The steamer *Enterprise* came alongside and took about 50 tons of cargo this A.M. The Chinamen left the *Blue Jacket* this A.M....had a nice time talking with the old gentleman [Allen Frances, the American consul] while the Capt. was transacting business with Mr. Ward. He gave me some account of his acquaintance with President Lincoln and how he came to have his position here. Spent the evening on board *Blue Jacket* and listened to Capt. Percival's account of the passage.... The Am[erican] ship *Belvedere* put in here for a harbor this morning as the wind blew a gale from the east.[7]

APRIL 29TH. Drove into town this morning with Mr. Shurtleff to show him the way. He intended to have a tooth extracted.... Finished discharging stores with the exception of the wood and cleared the ship at the Custom House. The wood the Capt. bought for $15 to save time and get ahead of the *Blue Jacket* and the *Queenstown*, both of which are bound to Departure Bay for coal.

SUNDAY, APRIL 30TH. Rowed to the head of the harbor in a boat, and walked from there with Mr. Delano to a trout brook, where we fished for two or three hours and caught eleven fish.

---

1. The N. E. wind was a headwind.

2. A ship "beating" is attempting to work to windward by successive "tacks," or legs sailed with the wind on alternate sides of the vessel.

3. The bark *Forest Belle*, you'll remember, was a member of Besse's fleet, lost on her maiden voyage.

4. Evidently April Fools' Day came a day early.

5. The *Blue Jacket* was a bad-luck ship. Her first captain, James S. Dillingham, had been master of the clipper *Snow Squall*. See Nicholas Dean, *Snow Squall* (Gardiner, ME: Tilbury House, 2001).

6. The bark *Germania*, of Breman, ex-*Coringa*, was built at Bath, Maine, in 1858. The bark *John Worster*, of Boston, was built at Medford, Massachusetts, in 1867.

7. The ship *Belevedere*, of San Francisco, was built at East Boston, in 1857.

Chapter 11

Frank's West Coast Tour

Frank Besse Travels Overland from Departure Bay to San Francisco.

May 1st. The steam tug *Alexander* took us at half past 7 o'clock and towed us up to Departure Bay, a distance of 74 miles, where we…dropped anchor in twenty fathoms…. The tug is a very large and powerful one, and belongs to the coal company.

Six of the men we shipped in Hong Kong ran away last night. The officer in charge of the deck (the carpenter) was asleep and they got away with all of their dunnage…. Just as we hoisted anchor, they came out of the woods and gave three cheers. I think they were assisted by the crew of a man-of-war lying in Esquimalt Harbor, as a number of them were on board yesterday. They had about $10 apiece coming to them, which of course they lose.

Joining the *Rotch* in the anchorage was the old Besse clipper *Syren*, and the ships *Adam M. Simpson* and *Ericsson*, the latter a famous old ship owned and commanded by Captain Plummer, "a rough old fellow [who] has trouble in nearly every port he enters."[1]

Frank was recovering from an accidental bullet wound—he had dropped the loaded cylinder of his revolver, causing a cartridge to go off, striking a knee bone. From May 19 to June 14 Frank traveled from the important but small coal-mining settlement of Nanaimo—Mr. Delano and four men rowed him up to catch the steamer for Victoria—to San Francisco. At Victoria Frank took a room in the best hotel, met Captain Waterhouse of the bark *Escort*, and took in two plays, *The Banker's Daughter* and *East Lynn*.[2] On the steamer to Seattle (by way of the lumber ports of Port Townsend—the sound's port of entry—Port Gamble, and Port Madison), he met a sound pilot, Captain Oliver, who was from New Bedford.[3]

Upon arrival at Seattle, population 6,000, Frank took a room in the Arlington House, "the best hotel in the place." Setting off on a tour of the town, he visited a sawmill, a turning mill, and eventually gained entrance into a closely guarded barrel factory with a wonderful machine that turned out one thousand barrels a day. While Frank was dressing the next morning, Captain Brown of the *Syren*, just arrived from Port Townsend, knocked on his door, and Frank went aboard the ship for breakfast:

> THE SHIP WAS LOOKING nicely on deck but her copper is entirely off her bows and she will have to have some put on.... It has been on but one year and must have been a poor quality. She loads spars and deck planks here for Bath and gets $15,000 freight. Her crew are discharged and I am afraid he will have trouble to get another one, as men are scarce and wages from $40 to $50 per month.[4]

Frank, never missing a chance to accept the hospitality of the cabin, made the acquaintance of Captain Killam of the bark *Amethyst*, of San Francisco. Built at Boston in 1822, *Amethyst* was said to be the oldest bark under the American flag.[5] When walking down to *Syren* later, Frank passed a scaffolding where vigilantes had hanged three hoodlums the previous January, as a warning to "hoodlums and black legs" to clear out of town. Frank inspected the new ship *Iroquois*, of Bath, 2,120 tons, built and managed by the Sewalls—without donkey engine or long poop, she was not as much to his liking as the *William J. Rotch*.

On May 24 Frank took passage aboard the stern-wheel steamer *Zephyr* for Olympia, becoming friendly with the captain, who would introduce Frank to his two daughters. Frank escaped from the daughters by catching a train to the bank of the mighty Columbia, where he boarded the powerful sternwheeler *Bonita* for Portland. At Portland, population 20,000, he checked into the St. Charles, then had supper aboard the ship *Importer* with his Hong Kong friend, Captain Allyn, and Captain Shearbourn, the *Importer*'s, long-time commander.

Frank was "much pleased" with Portland, where he sought out various owners in ships of the Besse fleet, including Henry Failing and a U.S. senator-to-be, Jonathan Bourne, Jr., son of the great New Bedford whaling merchant of the same name.[6]

> THIS AFTERNOON walked through the principal streets in the city. On the top of one of the buildings, The Mariners Home, I saw a figurehead of a vessel which struck me at once as the one that was on the *Forest Belle* when she was lost, and on making inquiries, I found such was the case.[7]

Frank took note of Sunday picnics "up the river" and bands in the streets—with no blue laws, saloons and theaters were doing a good business. Hearing that the *Alden Besse*, *Coloma*, the Searsport bark *Wakefield*, and the Bath bark *Edwin Reed* were at Astoria, at the river's mouth, he postponed his departure to San Francisco to await their arrival at Portland.[8] Frank eventually took the train for Roseburg, up the fertile, cultivated Willamette and Umpgua Valleys. From Roseburg he continued by stage over rough roads—"not the easiest thing in the worlds to ride in"—at one point passing by hundreds of Chinese grading the Northern Pacific Railroad.

At the mining town of Jacksonville Frank got off to visit a gold mine—a placer mine where water from a ditch twenty-five miles long was forced by gravity through a six-inch nozzle, producing a stream that could shoot 450 feet, and washed the bank away rapidly. The twelve workers were Chinese. Frank pocketed one dollar's worth of gold for a keepsake.

Three more adventurous days of stages—the driver pointed out where the stage had been robbed two weeks earlier, and where stages had tipped down precipices and killed people and horses—brought Frank over the 4,000-foot Klamath Hills, down the Strawberry Valley, over the Sacramento Mountains, to Redding and a train. Drivers were changed every forty miles, the horses, every fifteen.

> JUNE 13TH. Was called at half past 3 o'clock this morning and took the train…arrived at Sacramento a distance of 170 miles. The road runs through the Sacramento Valley which is perfectly level and nearly all under wheat cultivation. One man, Dr. Glen, has a farm of 75,000 acres.
>
> JUNE 14TH. At 4 P.M. took the train for San Francisco. Passed through many wheat farms and vineyards and over the river at Benicia in a monster ferry boat which took two trains of cars. Arrived at Oakland at 7 and crossed to San Francisco in the ferry. Went to the Palace Hotel and engaged a room…. The Palace is the largest and finest hotel in the world and cost $8,000,000. It has all the modern improvements and is lighted by electricity as are many of the streets in the city.
>
> JUNE 15TH. After breakfast found Mr. J. N. Knowles' office and got my letters there….[9] While reading them Capt. Bray came in and was pleased to see me. After stopping there a while, I went down to the *Rotch*. All hands had left with the exception of Mr. Delano, Shurtleff, the carpenter, and Sam Loring. They were discharging coal and everything was covered with dust, I did not stop long…went down on board the bark *Amethyst*…. This evening called on Capt. and Mrs. Bray who are boarding on shore and had a very pleasant talk.

June 17th. All the ships in port have their flags up as it is the anniversary of the Battle of Bunker Hill.... Went to Mr. Knowles's office and got $100.

June 18th. Mr. Delano and myself hired a...team and went out to the Cliff House, a kind of summer resort which looks out on the ocean.... Sunday is a great holiday here. There were thousands of people in the park and gardens and the theaters were all in full blast.

June 19th. Went into Handly & Snow's ship chandlers, where nearly all the captains congregate and was introduced to several by Capt. Bray.

June 20th. The steamer *Escambia* which was in D. Bay with us... discharged [coal] at the same dock here that the *Rotch* is laying at and after loading with wheat went out yesterday. She was not loaded properly and became very crank and after going about five miles rolled over on her beam ends and sank, the Capt. and two men swam ashore; the remainder of the crew were drowned.

June 21st. Went down to the ship.... Mr. Delano and myself went to Taber's photograph rooms and had our pictures taken, after that played a few games of billiards.... After supper went to the California theatre and saw *Fritz*.

June 25th. Mr. Delano and myself went up to Fairfax Park to a picnic of the riggers and stevedores of the city. We took the boat and went to San Quentin then got on flat cars and went up to the park, passing through San Rafael, a very pretty little town. The amusements on the grounds consisted of foot races for men and women, jumping matches, dancing, etc. There were thousands of people there, among them a good supply of hoodlums, who toward the last part got pretty full, and there were quite a number of fights and when we got on the boat there was one continual row all the way to the city. The police did the best they could but there were too many for them.

For the next nine days Frank toured Yellowstone and the San Joaquin Valley. On July 2 he wrote:

Just one year today since the ship sailed from New York. It has been a prosperous year for her and she has sent home and divided amongst her owners a little over $25,000, which is much better than she will do during the coming year, at the present rate of freights in San Francisco.

Returned to San Francisco, Frank was offered positions both in J. N. Knowles's office, and in the office of Richard S. Howland. Howland, a New Bedforder, was the West Coast agent for his family's whaling enterprises and may also have acted as agent for New Bedford whaling merchant Jonathan Bourne, Jr. (the elder).

JULY 6TH. Called on Mr. Howland this morning and took lunch with him, and talked about stopping here in his office. He said he should be pleased to have me here and if I concluded to stop, he would discharge the boy they now have and give me the position.... I did not decide, but do not like the idea of being the means of discharging the other young man for he might have some difficulty in getting another position, and is really in more need of it than I am.

On the seventh Frank went to Oakland to visit Captain J. C. Ainsworth, who owned the controlling interest in the *Alden Besse*, in Ainsworth's "elegant" house, equipped with a "splendid billiard room, which, with the ornaments, cost several thousand dollars."[10]

JULY 8TH. Met Capt. Lucas of the new ship *Charmer* this morning in the office, and on getting into conversation with him found he was a brother to Aunt Mary Besse; also was introduced to Capt. Ross of the new ship *William H. Lincoln* just arrived from New York.[11] Saw Capt. Call of the *Adam M. Simpson* who had just come down from Departure Bay.

Frank did more sightseeing—took in the massive unfinished city hall, its funds stolen by contractors; and saw more plays, *Streets of New York, American Born.*

JULY 12TH. The *Rotch* towed down from Port Costa this afternoon and anchored just above the ferry. I went off to her and stopped about an hour. The crew are all shipped.... They were pretty full and will not be fit for much tomorrow.[12] Capt. Bray and wife, Capt. Call and wife, Mrs. Nelson and myself went to...hear Haverly's Minstrels.

JULY 13TH. I have finally decided to continue on the ship to Europe. I suppose I am acting against my own interest, and know I shall wish, after we get to sea, that I had decided to stop.... I paid my bill at the hotel and went off aboard the ship intending to stop there tonight, but Mr. Delano wanted me to go...to the theatre for the last time... and so I consented and we stopped at the Occidental Hotel.

JULY 14TH. After bidding farewell to my friends, I went off to the ship.

1. Captain George Plummer was a Kennebecker, possibly from Dresden, Maine. Over at least the previous twenty years he had assembled, as captain and managing owner, a large fleet of older square-riggers, mostly Maine-built, which he employed in the West Coast lumber trade. The *Ericsson* was built at New York in 1852 as a transatlantic liner powered by an enormous but low horsepower Ericsson hot air engine. In 1867 the engine was removed and she was rigged as a ship. Long of hull, with a clipper model, and very well built, she was a great success as a sailing ship. Captain Plummer commanded her for many yeas. She was lost in 1892, going ashore while bound for Nanaimo. See Cedric Ridgely-Nevitt, *American Steamships on the Atlantic* (Newark: University of Delaware Press, 1981).

2. The bark *Escort,* of Boston, was built at Newburyport, Massachusetts, in 1870.

3. The sawmilling towns of Port Gamble and Port Ludlow were developed by the great lumbering firm of Pope & Talbot, of East Machias, Maine, origin. Port Gamble was a Down East village, complete with picket fences, rock maples, and a copy of the East Machias "Congo" church.

4. The first cargo of Oregon (i.e., Douglas) fir spars and shiptimber to arrive at Bath—and presumably, the first to reach the East Coast—arrived in November 1877 aboard the bark *William H. Besse*, inaugurating a trade which William Besse would make a specialty. Bath shipbuilder Guy C. Goss is credited with having come up with the idea after making a West Coast tour in 1876. William Baker, *Maritime History of Bath, Maine* (Bath, ME: Marine Research Society of Bath, 1975), p. 534.

5. The whaling bark *True Love*, of London, was built at Philadelphia in 1764. The New Bedford whaling bark *Tamerlane* was built at Wiscasset, Maine, in 1824.

6. A native of New York, Failing moved to Oregon with his father, who founded a dry goods business which Henry later turned into a large wholesale operation. He and a partner bought all the stock of Portland's First National Bank, for many years the only national bank west of the Rockies. He served as Portland's mayor and in many other civic and charitable positions. Jonathan Bourne, Jr., the second would become a congressman and senator, and had extensive interests in mining, farming, cotton mills, and other enterprises.

7. This figurehead is still in Portland. See Mary Ann Amacker, *The Forest Belle and Its Figurehead*, Oregon Maritime Center and Museum, May 1969.

8. The mouth of the Columbia was among the most dangerous in the world, and in July 1887 would claim the bark *William H. Besse*, Captain Gibbs, loaded with railroad iron, while she was attempting to enter without a pilot.

9. Captain Josiah N. Knowles, a Cape Codder, was one of San Francisco's leading shipping agents. Son of a shipmaster and brother to three others, Josiah's last command was the McKay medium-clipper *Glory of the Seas*. Knowles had earlier commanded the Richmond, Maine, clipper *Wild Wave,* whose life ended one night in 1858 on the reef of the uninhabited South Pacific isle of Oeno due to a faulty chart. All hands (and ten passengers) were landed safely. Knowles, the mate, and five men, taking two chests containing $18,000 in gold coin, rowed a boat to Pitcairn Island in three days. Discovering that the inhabitants had recently been removed, the men built a small schooner in which they sailed 1,150

miles to the Marquesas Islands. Knowles was the West Coast agent for New Bedford whaling merchant William Lewis—Knowles's wife was a New Bedforder—and in 1883 he became general superintendent of the Pacific Stream Whaling Company. His large house and fine grounds in Oakland became a local landmark. Matthews, *American Merchant Ships,* Series II, pp. 154–55; Michael Jay Mjelde, *Glory of the Seas* (Middletown: Wesleyan University Press, 1970), pp. 32–37, 90, 124.

10. Ainsworth, an Ohio native, cut his teeth as a steamboat man on the Mississippi, rising to pilot. Removing to California in 1850, he soon found himself steamboating on Oregon's Willamette River. The guiding spirit of the Oregon Steam Navigation Company, he was also a remarkably successful financier known coast to coast. He was instrumental in the construction of the Northern Pacific Railroad between Puget Sound and the Columbia, having invested heavily in Tacoma real estate. In 1880 he moved to Oakland, spending $3,000,000 developing the resort of Redondo Beach. Wright, *Lewis & Dryden's Marine History*, p. 91.

11. The ship *W. H. Lincoln*, of Boston, was built at Newburyport, Massachusetts, in 1881.

12. Sailors were not delivered to a ship (especially if lying at a wharf, and especially at San Francisco, notorious for its unscrupulous treatment of sailors) until shortly before the tug made fast, lest some escape, costing the shipping masters their advance upon the sailors' wages, and "bonus blood" money, paid by the captain to obtain a crew. Shipped sailors were kept drunk—dead drunk if possible—by the shipping masters to make them easier to control. Also, it made the odd genuine corpse more likely to escape detection by the mates.

Chapter 12
To Ireland with Wheat

Frank Travels from San Francisco to Dublin, Where He Leaves the Rotch.

JULY 15TH, 1882. The tug and the pilot came off at 4 o'clock this morning and we got under way and were towed out through the Golden Gate and across the bar, where they left us. We set all sail, and with a light breeze from the South stood over for the Farallons. We made two tacks, and passed about one mile to the South of S. Farallon...a barren rocky place...a great place for seals and birds, and thousands of the latter could be seen in the water....[1] There is a lighthouse situated on the highest point...a steam fog whistle and two or three houses. Saw a large English iron ship bound in.

The *Rotch* has in, according to her bill of lading, 2,379 tons of wheat and draws 22 ft., 6 in. strong on even keel. She is bound for Queenstown for orders, and gets 50s if ordered to Bristol Channel, Dublin, or Liverpool and 51s-6 if to Havre. Her expenses have been very heavy in San Francisco, $12,531, and we drew on the outward freight for $6,000. We have a fine crew I think. Part of them belonged to the English ship *Lammarmoor* which was wrecked a short time ago, off the entrance of San Francisco by the carelessness of the captain. We have no 3rd mate but carry two boatswains.

We have three dogs, two sheep, two pigs, two dozen hens, and two canaries, so shall not want for pets, such as they are. I feel very sorry to leave San Francisco, and already begin to wish I had decided to stop there. I...have enjoyed myself there, better than in any other port I have been in.

JULY 18TH. Moved about 200 sacks of wheat from forward and stowed it aft, to put ship in better sailing trim.

The California-to-Europe (primarily Liverpool) trade in wheat began in the late 1860s in response to European drought. California's great Sacramento and San Joaquin Valleys produced a hard, dry white wheat quickly prized by British and Irish millers, and although it was the last of the crops to arrive at market, brought premium prices at the Liverpool Corn Exchange.[2]

Grain was a hull-straining, perishable cargo, and at 14,000 miles the California grain trade was among the longest and most demanding, crossing the equator twice and rounding Cape Horn. It employed only the world's best square-riggers. In the peak 1881–82 season, 560 ships—154 of them American, including the *William J. Rotch*—were employed in the trade.

Early high shipping rates—for the 1872–73 season San Francisco rates averaged 85s per gross ton—spurred both British iron and American wooden shipbuilding. Having lost the North Atlantic to steam and foreign sail (much of it old American tonnage), the California trade gave hope to American (primarily Maine) shipbuilders and owners.[3] From 1881 to 1885, an average fleet of over one hundred American wooden ships sailed in the grain fleet, as compared with 170 British ships, primarily of iron (fifty were of wood). Plummeting rates in the mid-1880s—in 1886, rates offered to American wooden ships fell to 25s—effectively ended the building of wooden American square-riggers.[4]

Britannia ruled the golden waves of grain, the crop and its shipping and insurance being controlled in England. When the British grain fleet crowded the bay, San Francisco was effectively an outpost of the Empire.

By 1889 only thirty American ships remained in the trade—although they arrived at Cork, on average, nineteen days ahead of British ships, they received 30 percent less per ton, and paid from 15 to 30 percent more in discriminatory insurance rates to English underwriters on account of being wooden. However, a detailed study by Captain W. W. Bates, United States Commissioner of Shipping, demonstrated that wooden American ships in the grain trade delivered more tons per ship, faster, cheaper, and in better condition, with less wear and tear and loss of life, than did the British ships of metal or of wood.[5]

But back to the *Rotch* and her cargo of grain. The *Rotch* crossed the equator on August 8, after three weeks of light to moderate N. E. and S. E. trade winds. This was not considered a good run.

> AUGUST 3RD. We have a number of quite good singers among the crew, and one musician, and during the dog watches the sailors sing and play and dance, and that part of the day passes off quite pleasantly.[6] The remainder of the time I pass in reading.
>
> AUGUST 18TH. Quite a brisk breeze from the North, but as it is right aft and we have a head sea to climb over, do not go ahead very fast.... The steward and a Chilean (one of the crew) had a fight this after-

noon in which the Chilean came off second best with a bad cut over the eye. That is the first row that we have had since leaving port and I do not know what occasioned that. We have a first-rate crew who do their duty well, and so far have found no fault with their provisions or anything.

AUGUST 19TH. Crossed the Tropic of Capricorn.... Discovered where some rats had been in the lazarette and eaten some of the bags, so this forenoon I made a box trap to catch some.

AUGUST 20TH. It was our intention to have stopped at Pitcairn Island and perhaps replenish our stock of vegetables, but the wind enabled us to go about 300 miles to the Eastward.

SEPTEMBER 3RD. The wind kept increasing until afternoon when it blew a heavy gale from S. S. W. with a very rough sea running which continued all night. The ship rolled badly and shipped large quantities of water, the most she has taken on board since she was launched. Several rain and hail squalls throughout the day.

SEPTEMBER 8TH. A tremendous swell set in towards night from the North and the ship rolled terribly, keeping the deck full of water and making sleep impossible.

SEPTEMBER 9TH. Last night was the most uncomfortable one that I have passed since leaving New York on account of the heavy rolling of the ship, and I doubt if she will ever roll worse than she has for the past 24 hours.[7]

SEPTEMBER 10TH. Gale of wind all day from the N. W. Passed quite near a vessel last night, and this afternoon the bark *Euclid* of Dundee came within signal distance. She was the first vessel I have seen since the second day out from San Francisco. She was under lower topsails and was bound to the Westward.... While reefing topsails, last night, the main one was torn quite badly, and had to be unbent and sent down.

SEPTEMBER 11TH. Moderate breeze from the North with fine weather, altogether too pleasant to last long. Have had all sails below the skysail set, except crossjack and mizzen royal. Passed Cape Horn this afternoon 58 days from port, which I believe is about the average from San Francisco. We could just make out the loom of the mountains.... Saw two barks this morning bound to the Westward.... All of the window shutters are closed and caulked and I have to burn a light in my stateroom.

SEPTEMBER 12TH. Read the history of George the Fourth.

SEPTEMBER 13TH. A finer day I don't believe was ever seen off Cape Horn. Had all sail set.

SEPTEMBER 21ST. It has been much warmer in rounding Cape Horn in the winter than I had supposed it would be, and with the exception of one night, no ice has been formed. Icebergs are sometimes seen, but...we saw no signs of any.

SEPTEMBER 22ND. Mr. Shurtleff and one of the men had a fight this morning in which the sailor came out second best, with a black eye, and face badly scratched.... My face has been swollen and pained me for several days, occasioned by the growing of one of my wisdom teeth. This forenoon I painted the inside of the wheelhouse.

SEPTEMBER 26TH. It looks as if we might have a gale from [the S. E.] and I shall not be very sorry to see it, we have had so much moderate weather.

SEPTEMBER 27TH. Moderate gale from the S. E. during the night.

SEPTEMBER 28TH. Continued to blow a gale from the North all day.... Think this will have to pass for the equinoctial gale.... We are now in the latitude of the River Plata, 36 South, but about 800 miles to the Eastward of it. It is good whaling grounds around here, and most every day we see some blows.

SEPTEMBER 30TH. This is my 25th birthday.... I shall ever look back upon [the past year] with pleasure.

OCTOBER 2ND. Crossed our track in Lat. 30 30' S., Lon. 28 37' that we made on the 23rd of August 1881 on the way to Yokohama. I have thus circumnavigated the earth and sailed, according to the account I have kept, 39,017 miles in doing so. We are now in the track of vessels bound to Africa and around the Cape of Good Hope, but have seen none yet.

OCTOBER 4TH. Overhauled and spoke to the English bark *Mary Blundell* of Liverpool, from Valparaiso, this forenoon and this afternoon the bark *Silurian* of London, 59 days from Chili for Swansea, both loaded with copper ore.[8] At sunset they were both out of sight astern. This p.m. Mr. Delano and the steward had a short fight. The dispute arose about a dog belonging to Mr. Delano which the steward had abused. The Capt. soon separated them but not until Mr. D. had got his face quite badly bruised and scratched. Played cards this evening with Mrs. Bray.

OCTOBER 5TH. Came up with and passed the ship *India*, 1,295 tons register, Capt. Rich, 95 days from San Francisco for Antwerp. She is an American ship and hails from Bath.[9] Exchanged longitudes with her and wished her a pleasant passage, and at sunset she was about 10 miles astern.

OCTOBER 6TH. Two vessels in sight, one a long distance astern, the other within speaking distance...found she was the *Adolph Obrig* bark, Capt. Staples, from Portland to Liverpool, about 100 days out. She is a new vessel and was built in Camden, Maine.... Whether she came up on us during the night or we have been gaining on her I cannot tell yet, as we have not had wind enough today to determine her sailing qualities.

OCTOBER 8TH. Both vessels still in sight.

OCTOBER 9TH. All hands hard at work, sewing sails, rattling down, or painting and making the best of the pleasant weather.[10]

OCTOBER 11TH. Unbent the mainsail and all hands have been at work repairing it. Finished it at 4 o'clock and bent it again and trimmed all sail as nice as we could, for there is a large American ship a long distance to windward which we want to catch up with, for the Capt. thinks it is the *St. John* which sailed from San Francisco two days before we did.[11] The bark, which is English, is about ten miles to windward of us, and I think we have not gained much on him today.

OCTOBER 12TH. Passed the English bark.... The other vessel has disappeared ahead.

OCTOBER 13TH. Saw a Swedish bark bound to the S. E. which we signaled. She was loaded with deals and was 76 days out from some port in Sweden, for South Africa.[12]

OCTOBER 14TH. Passed three vessels during the night, all bound to the S. E.

OCTOBER 18TH. Mr. Delano's dog, Tobey, has been acting very queerly for the last few days, and has had several fits this evening.[13]

OCTOBER 19TH. Tobey died this morning in a fit. He was a Japanese dog, very intelligent and playful, and could perform quite a number of tricks. We had all become very much attached to him, and feel sorry to lose him.

From the nineteenth of October through the first week of November the *Rotch* experienced mostly light and moderate winds from various points, including what passed for the S. E. and N. E. Trades. Vessels sighted included the London bark *Trowbridge*, an Austro-Hungarian brig, a small brigantine; the American bark *Silas Fish* and ship *Belle Morse*; a brig (which the *Rotch* nearly collided with in the dark—had that occurred either Frank's account would have been more eventful or would possibly not exist); a Norwegian bark; and a Nova Scotian bark, laden with deals and so "crank" that she was sailing nearly on her beam ends in but a moderate breeze with royals and mainsail furled. All hands aboard the *Rotch* were busily employed painting the ship, oiling the poop deck, and scraping down the masts.

> NOVEMBER 9TH. Strong breeze from the South...at noon were 200 miles from Fayal, one of the Azores Islands. If pleasant tomorrow, we may make that island, and I hope it will be for I have not seen any land for 117 days.
>
> NOVEMBER 9TH. Half a gale of wind from the S. W. with a bad sea. During the night the ship did some pretty heavy rolling and filled her decks full of water quite often.... Passed between the islands of Flores and Faial this P.M., but it being cloudy and quite hazy we could not see the land.... We have had a splendid run since crossing the equator, and were but twenty days to the Azores.
>
> NOVEMBER 10TH. We were but 950 miles from Queenstown this noon, and I am impatiently looking forward for letters.
>
> NOVEMBER 12TH. Heavy gale of wind from the North.... A bad sea is running which makes the ship very uneasy and stops her headway. Saw a small Danish brig this forenoon. She ran to us and we exchanged longitudes. Her name was *Thora* and she was bound for Genoa, Italy. The longitude she placed upon her black board was 16 10' W. which was 250 miles to the Eastward of ours. Whether they reckoned from the meridian of Cadiz, had been running by dead reckoning, or made a mistake, I do not know.
>
> NOVEMBER 14TH. A small steamer named *Hugewden* passed us this afternoon bound to the S. W. We undertook to signalize with her, but they were so slow about answering that we made out nothing.
>
> NOVEMBER 15TH. This evening split the fore-topmast staysail, but that was owing to its having been sewed with poor twine. Capt. Bray has found considerable fault with the twine that was used in making most all of our sails.... Sent down the skysail yard and put it away as we shall not probably have much need of it the remainder of the passage.

NOVEMBER 16TH. Signaled the ship *Henry* of St. John, N. B., and exchanged longitudes with her. She was bound to the Westward, and only differed three miles from us.... The ship is fairly overrun with cockroaches, and today we had a fire in the cabin stove, and they seemed to come from all directions attracted by the heat. The cabin is swarming with them and we have killed hundreds of them this evening. They are harmless but it is very disagreeable having so many around.

NOVEMBER 17TH. Did not get an observation of the sun and so do not know our exact position but by dead reckoning we were but 175 miles from Cork Harbor this noon.... Got the anchors and chains ready, and the deep-sea lead up, handy for use.

NOVEMBER 18TH. Moderate breeze from the Westward with foggy weather. Have been on soundings all day and heave the lead about every hour in fifty fathoms of water. Shortened sail and stood in for the land...we ran until three o'clock and then it shut in so thick that we wore ship and stood out again, but had not gone far before it let up and commenced to break away.[14] Put the ship about and at 5 o'clock P.M. made Kinsale Head Light and shortly after Danuta Rock Light Ship, and then Ballycotton Light. From those we found our exact position and felt greatly relieved, for we had no observation of the sun for two days and the current had set us about 30 miles to the S. E. of our position by dead reckoning and we were fairly lost in the fog. If we had not seen the lights, we should have passed a very anxious night. Reefed topsails and put the ship under snug sail and shall stand off and on until morning.

NOVEMBER 19TH. Stood in for the land this morning and after taking a pilot on board, headed towards the harbor. Just as we were going in through the passage a squall drew out and we were obliged to let go the anchor, and afterwards...towed inside. Since leaving San Francisco we have sailed 16,002 miles and were 127 days on the passage, an average of 126 miles per day. Our largest day's work...was 258 miles, our smallest...8 miles.

The *Big Bonanza*, Capt. Jones, which sailed from San Francisco a week before we did arrived last night.[15] None of the other vessels that sailed about the same time we did have arrived yet, with the exception of the *G. C. Trufant,* who beat us a few days.[16] Capt. Bray and wife and myself went on shore soon after the ship was anchored and got our letters; then went to the Robinson Hotel and had a nice time reading them. Met Capt. Jones there and after a nice dinner of fresh beef and turkey which tasted first rate after twenty-two consecutive meals of fresh pork....[17] Tonight it is blowing a gale of wind from the N. W. with very heavy rain squalls.

NOVEMBER 20TH. I met and was introduced to Capt. Mills of the ship *Harvey Mills*. He ran into a vessel in a thick fog about six months ago and was sued for the cost of vessel and cargo, and the case was decided against him. He sold his vessel and has been here a long time settling it.[18]

Queenstown—formerly and now once again Cobh—was located in the great harbor of Cork, one of the most perfectly formed and—in the age of sail—most strategically located havens in the world. Since a cargo of grain might have been sold several times after it left San Francisco, ships called at Queenstown (or failing that, Falmouth) for telegraphed orders as to where to proceed.

The *Rotch* was ordered to Dublin, 170 miles to the north, through St. George's Channel and into the Irish Sea. These were dangerous waters, and for £65 the powerful tug *Mount Etna* took her there and docked her. Grain ships discharged right in the heart of the city, lying at stone quays lining the narrow River Liffey below the Carlisle bridge. In port were the ships *Willie Reed*, Captain Yates; *Great Admiral*, Captain Thompson; *G. C. Trufant*, Capt. Thomas; *Annie H. Smith*, Captain Bartlett; and *Importer*, with Frank's old friend Captain Allyn. Frank directly commenced to socialize, see the sights, and go to theaters. He became quite chummy with Mr. Blanchard, mate of the *Willie Reed*. [19]

NOVEMBER 24TH. All the men who had money in the Captain's hands received it this morning and went on shore for two weeks' liberty, which is equivalent to discharging them. One of the men had his money stolen from him on the passage. He still remains on the ship, also one of the boatswains and two boys and Sam Loring.

NOVEMBER 25TH. One of our sailors who had a good chest of clothes and over $60 came on board this morning, having lost all his clothes and every cent of money. I pity the poor fellow for he is an old man, has a family in England, and has been away fifteen months, and now has not enough to get home. Bad company and too much liquor is the secret of his misfortunes.

The ship *Great Admiral* started this morning for Cardiff in tow of a tug, but had only gone a short distance when she came in collision with the ship *Annie H. Smith* and considerable damage was done to both ships. The *Smith* had her windlass injured, anchor stock broken, and her bow stove in. The *Admiral* carried away her cat head, main and mizzen channels, bumpkin, scratched her side badly, and broke foreyard, studding sail booms and injured her rig considerably. It was entirely the fault of the tugboat but it is doubtful whether she can be made to pay damages.

The *Admiral* hauled in alongside of the *Rotch* and will be delayed about two weeks.... Shall commence to discharge tomorrow.

NOVEMBER 28TH. Took out 58 tons. There were a few bags that were damaged on top, but most of it has come out in excellent condition. They work very slowly and will take fully a month in taking it all out. Another man was murdered last night.[20]

NOVEMBER 29TH. A proclamation called the Curfew Act was issued this morning by the Lord Lieutenant.... It is really not safe to be out late nights.... Four old women had a great row on the dock this afternoon.... Nobody killed but several black eyes given and considerable profane language used.

NOVEMBER 30TH. Thanksgiving day. We had a nice turkey on board the *Rotch* for dinner and Capt. Thompson, wife, and little boy dined with us. All of the American captains with their wives and myself were invited on board the *Importer* to a dinner at 6 o'clock.

DECEMBER 1ST. A fine drizzle of rain all day.... Discharged a little over 100 tons. They work very slow here...and do not seem to want any improvement on the old-fashioned way. The wheat is first emptied into the hatchway, then sacks which hold 240 lbs. are filled, and hoisted out with a common winch. It is then weighed and a man takes it on his back and walks onto the dock and loads it onto drays. Rather a heavy backload, but they do not seem to mind it.

Albert Lockhardt, a boy whom we shipped in San Francisco, ran away from the ship about a week ago and has been stopping at one of the principal hotels in the city. Capt. Bray went up and brought him back this afternoon and gave orders not to allow him to go on shore again. He is a young fellow about eighteen years whose parents are quite well off and live in San Francisco. He was getting a little wild at home and they thought by sending him to sea before the mast might make a change for him.... When Capt. Bray went for him he was lying back reading a paper, and had a new beaver hat on. He had $40 that his mother gave him...and had spent all of that and his hotel bill is still unpaid.

DECEMBER 2ND. Mr. Delano saw a man walking off with a sack of wheat from the ship that he had stolen, and took chase after him. He tried to drag him back to the ship, when several of his companions came to his assistance and he escaped.... The police here are afraid of their lives and do not dare to make an arrest.

This evening Mr. Delano and I went to the Gaiety Theater and saw the *Lady of Lyons* played. I liked it very much....[21] The hoodlums take charge of the gallery and the police have no control over them.

DECEMBER 3rd. A dark, rainy, disagreeable day.... Capt. Bray started for Liverpool this evening to purchase an extra anchor and chain ... and to see if he can get some freight for New York.

DECEMBER 5TH. Capt. Bray returned.... He saw an account of the arrival of the [Besse bark] *Mary S. Ames* at San Francisco, 176 days from New Bedford. Long passage.

DECEMBER 6TH. Snow storm all day. Rather unexpected and unusual ... this storm seems to paralyze the inhabitants.

DECEMBER 8TH. The *Annie H. Smith* sailed for New York in ballast this morning, and the ship *Great Admiral* started for Cardiff in tow... she is to load coal for Hong Kong...ship *Fiona* [lost] with all hands. She loaded near the *Rotch* at Port Costa and sailed from San Francisco the day we did. She was lost during the heavy gale Wednesday night in the English Channel bound for Hull.[22]

DECEMBER 11TH. Capt. Bray received a letter from Capt. William H. Besse containing the charter party of the *Rotch* from New York...to load case oil at N. Y. for Yokohama or Hiogo, Japan, and gets 33½ cents per case, if ordered to one port, and 35 cents if ordered to both. That is some better than last voyage, when she had 25 cents and I think better than she could do by loading [coal] in Cardiff for Hong Kong at 26s a ton.

DECEMBER 14TH. There is a great deal of business carried out along the dock we are lying at, and hundreds of teams are employed making it difficult to get to and from the ship in a cab.

DECEMBER 15TH. Our steward struck a man who was working on the ship and was arrested and fined 1£. Albert Lockhardt, the boy who came from San Francisco with us, and who ran away ten days ago from the ship, stole a watch and chain from the steward of the *G. C. Trufant* and disappeared taking a 5£ overcoat that he had not paid for and leaving two weeks' hotel bill unpaid.

DECEMBER 18TH. Rain nearly all day. The *Willie Reed* started in tow this morning for Cardiff. She has in 1,000 tons of [iron] blooms, and is to take the balance of her cargo (about 1,000 tons of coke) there. She gets 1,750£ ($8,750) nearly and goes to San Francisco. Very poor freight. A fine iron ship of a little over 1,300 tons register was lost, with twenty-four of her crew, during the gale of Friday night, on Tuskar Rock.

DECEMBER 19TH. Discharged 235 tons of wheat, the largest day's work we have accomplished since arriving at Dublin.

DECEMBER 20TH. Thick weather, with rain towards evening. Went to the dentist's at 12 o'clock and had two more teeth filled with gold.... The stores are all trimmed up, and they are making great preparations for Christmas. The show windows look very pretty and the streets are crowded most all day with people shopping or buying presents.

DECEMBER 23RD. Have taken out 2,233 tons, and according to the bills of lading ought to have 137 tons in her now. Took in 40 tons of sand ballast. Went up town this afternoon and bought some presents for Christmas. Shall give Mrs. Bray a pair of opera glasses, 3£ 5s; Capt. Bray a meerschaum pipe and a cigar case, 2£; Mr. Delano a photograph album, 1£.

DECEMBER 25TH. Christmas Day. At the breakfast table there was an exchange of presents. Mrs. Bray gave me a nice Russian pocket book. They all seemed very much pleased with the presents I gave them. The ship is on demurrage and this morning Mr. McGaw, our consignee, knowing that we could not get men to work today, sent down some teams after wheat. He...could then claim that he was not liable for demurrage; but the mates, carpenter, Sam Loring, and I went to work and loaded one team and were then stopped by the Custom House authorities as it is against the law to work on Christmas. Mr. McGaw says he will not pay us for the loss of time, but if we can get it by suing him shall do so.[23]

DECEMBER 26TH. We had a few men at work on the ship, but they were a sorry looking lot after the dissipation of yesterday and did not accomplish much.

DECEMBER 29TH. Took a walk through some of the poorest streets in the city. The Irish in America complain of the filth of the Chinese, but I did not see any more filth or signs of poverty in Canton, China, than I have seen here.

DECEMBER 31ST. Mr. Delano and I went uptown at 12 o'clock and took the McCudden girls to the exhibition building where there was a sacred concert.[24] After that...we passed a very pleasant evening and watched the old year out and the new one in. At a little before 12 o'clock the church bells commenced ringing and continued about a half hour.

[American evangelists] Moody and Sankey are here.... They held their first service this afternoon.

JANUARY 2ND, 1883. Heavy gale of wind from the westward.... Finished taking in ballast, and put out the lumber used for sealing the ship [that is, lining the sides of the hold]. This evening...Mr. Delano and I went uptown to hear Moody and Sankey.... I liked the speaking and singing very much.

JANUARY 4TH. Went uptown with Capt. Bray. Took tea and spent the evening at Mr. McCudden's with Mr. Delano and Capt. Saunders of the bark *Low Wood*.[25] Have taken in 300 bbls. of ginger ale today.

JANUARY 5TH. Have taken in 300 bbls. of porter today. The lawyer into whose hands Capt. Bray had placed his demurrage claim settled with Mr. McGaw today. The claim was for 200£ but he settled for 60£ and the lawyer's fee, rather than go to court.

JANUARY 8TH. Have had fine weather and taken in [today] 600 bbl. of porter. One of the teamers came on board the ship this morning and kicked Mr. Shurtleff's dog. Mr. S. knocked him down and gave him a black eye and he went away "a sadder and wiser man." Soon afterwards he came back with a policeman who took Mr. Shurtleff's name and I suppose tomorrow he will have a warrant and be fined.

JANUARY 10TH. Several police came down to the ship this evening with a warrant for the arrest of Mr. Shurtleff.... Capt. Bray went to the police station with him and tried to bail him out but could not do it, so Mr. Shurtleff has to remain there all night.

JANUARY 11TH. We now have 3,000 bbls. of porter and ginger ale, equal to 300 tons at 9s per ton. It is consigned to E. & J. Burke, New York. Capt. Bray and I went to the police station this A. M. to see Mr. Shurtleff and from there to the court...he was discharged on payment of a fine of 10s. He gave the sergeant of police10s for testifying in his behalf and cab hire amounted to 7s, so it cost him altogether 27s and he was lucky to get off for that amount.

I finished packing my things and obtained a draft on Paris for 75£ (1,875 francs) and took 25£ in Bank of England notes. Gave Capt. Bray a draft on father for 140£ in favor of Capt. William Besse.

The *Rotch*'s departure being delayed by weather, Frank postponed his own departure as well.

> THE *ELIZA KENNEY* has been lying in the harbor a month waiting for a chance to get down the channel. She was all ready when the *Annie H. Smith* left but did not think it best to start, and has not had a chance since, so is still here and the *Smith* has arrived in New York.
>
> JANUARY 18TH. The wind still continues S. W. but not very strong, so the captain determined to start. Got all the lines singled and everything in readiness to start at a moment's notice. The captain went uptown for the remainder of his crew, and the tugboat, and found to his dismay that the boat had gone out of the harbor.... Mr. Delano and I passed the evening at Mr. McCudden's very pleasantly. Felt quite sorry to say good-bye to Annie Laura, as I have been in her company a good deal...and think she is a nice girl.
>
> JANUARY 19TH. Heavy gale of wind from the South with rain, which will detain the *Rotch* still longer. I had made up my mind to start for Liverpool.... Got up a little earlier than usual and ate breakfast with the officers, then bid Capt. and Mrs. Bray good-bye, also the other members of the ship, and went up to the steamer *Lily*, which started for Holy Head at 9.30. It seemed almost like leaving home to leave the ship. I have been on board of her most of the time the past eighteen months, and Capt. and Mrs. Bray have been as kind to me as if I were their own son. I have also been on the best of terms with the officers and crew, and they all seemed about as sorry to have me go as I was myself.

Aboard the channel steamer Frank was dismayed to be seasick, but had plenty of company. At Liverpool he stayed in the North Western Hotel, where, he noted, he had stayed in 1876 with Captain William Besse and family—this suggests that Frank may have sailed on the transatlantic passage of *Western Belle*'s sad maiden voyage, after which mate William Besse, Jr., was lost. Of course Frank found more American ships to visit before departing for London, on his way to Paris. March 27—which is where we began his account—found him in Paris, reading of the arrival of the *Rotch* at New York on March 25.

On May 30, returned from Italy, Frank was back in Liverpool, boarding the Cunarder *Cephalonia* for Boston via Queenstown.[26] Aboard ship Frank became friendly with Captain Nichols and his daughter, of the Searsport ship *Lucy A. Nickles*.[27] On June 9, Frank wrote:

WHEN I WENT ON DECK this morning the shores of Cape Cod were in sight in the distance. Everything was bustle and excitement and the passengers were dressed in their best.... The view in going up the harbor was very fine. We had to wait outside about a half hour for the tide, enough to pass through the Narrows, and after arriving at Deer Island we were detained nearly an hour to pass quarantine, after which we proceeded up to the city, and went to the Cunard wharf.... The customshouse officers came on board and took our depositions of dutiable articles and we were then allowed to land...hired a team and by hurrying, succeeded in getting to the Old Colony station in time to catch the 4:10 train for home.... On the train I met several Wareham men and found my parents were in good health. They were not expecting me tonight, and when I went to the house even my father did not recognize me at first. There have been but a few changes in the town and it seems very quiet to me after passing through so much bustle and excitement. It has been nearly two years since I commenced this journal and as I shall remain at home some time now and have nothing particularly interesting to write, I will not continue it at present.

Frank A. Besse, at center with mustache, amidst a greed of bankers at a meeting of the Massachusetts Savings Banks Officers Club, Young's Hotel, Boston, January 27, 1922.
COURTESY OF GEORGE DECAS, ESQ.

Frank Besse never went to sea again. In 1890 he married Mary Gammon, a Wareham banker's daughter; father-in-law Edward Gammon was president of the National Bank of Wareham, known as the "Tobey Bank" after Wareham's leading family. With Captain Alden's death Frank succeeded his father as lord of the Besse manor, and after Edward Gammon's death he became president of the bank.

Frank and his wife had four sons and one daughter. The young wife of son Gerard C.—named for neighbor Gerard C. Tobey—lived in the Besse mansion during World War I and later recalled Frank as a gruff figure sitting at the head of the long dining room table straining chowder through his enormous walrus mustache.

Frank died in 1924; his widow Mary lived until 1961, spending summers in the Wareham mansion and winters in the Bellevue Hotel, Boston. A rock-ribbed Republican, she left behind in the mansion a large collection of elephant statuettes, the oldest of which were believed to have been brought home by Captain Alden.[28]

The ship *William J. Rotch* was long-lived and successful. In November 1887, under Captain S. B. Gibbs, the *Rotch* returned to New York ten months, twenty-five days (including port time) after departing Philadelphia for Hiogo with case oil. During this notable feat of steady sailing she traveled 42,537 miles, or, twice the circumference of the globe.[29] After the sale of the remnants of the Besse fleet in 1900 the *Rotch* became the ship (later bark) *Helen A. Wyman*, of New York.[30]

In 1906 the *Wyman* earned $7,125 in demurrage, at $125 a day, from the German government while swinging at anchor in Lüderitz Bay, German Southwest Africa (now Namibia), with a cargo of hay. (Captain David Van Horn, a shrewd Mainer, having learned the high prices being charged at Lüderitz Bay for water and provisions, had sailed from the River Platte with extra supplies of both.)[31] Not long afterwards the *Wyman* was cut-down for a coal barge.

Captain David Van Horn, of the bark Helen A. Wyman, *ex-ship* William J. Rotch, *1906.* COURTESY OF ANDREW J. NESDALL.

1. Most of Frank's frequent reports of sightings of birds and sea creatures have been excised for brevity.

2. Rodman W. Paul, "The Wheat Trade between California and the United Kingdom," *Mississippi Valley Historical Review*, vol. XLV, no. 3, December 1958.

3. In the peak year of 1874, eighty-two ships and barks (including some barkentines) were built in Maine, and twenty-nine in Massachusetts.

4. *Bangor Industrial Journal*, 26 February 1886.

5. Captain William W. Bates, *American Marine* (Boston: Houghton, Mifflin, 1892), pp. 241–60. In 1889, American ships averaged 112.86 days to Cork, as compared with 131.32 for British, the second fastest fleet. Of 234 ships, 213 were sail; eleven of these were German, three were Italian, two, each, were Swedish and Norwegian. p. 269. From July 1, 1881, to July 1, 1885, of the larger fleets in the trade, the total American losses—"wrecked," "missing," "abandoned"—was less than 0.5 percent, while British iron losses exceeded three-quarters of 1 percent; p. 252. Half of the British losses went "missing," with all hands lost. Astonishingly, Bates listed no lives lost from American ships, as compared with 86 lost with British ships, p. 257.

6. The 4:00 to 8:00 P.M. watch was divided into two "dog watches" so that the nighttime duty hours would vary. On a happy ship, in good weather, the second dog watch, after supper, was often a time of socializing between the two watches.

7. Wider-beamed American ships tended to roll less heavily than did narrower British ships. California grain was shipped in bags carrying a hundred pounds to lessen the danger of its shifting. Heavy cargoes such as grain were generally divided in the hold, with one-third carried "above the beams" in the 'tween decks, slowing the period of the roll and decreasing the possibility that the hull would be strained or the spars rolled out of her, although the arc of the roll was thereby increased.

8. A fleet of tough little barques, manned by tough men, carried Welsh coal to Chile, returning to the great copper smelting center of Swansea with copper ore. The heavy ore was carried in the hold in raised timber compartments, thus raising the metacentric height. N. L. Thomas, "Swansea's Copper Ore Barques," *Sea Breezes*, no. 236, August 1965.

9. *India* was built in 1868 by and for the Pattens.

10. "Rattling down" means seizing on—or in this instance, overhauling—the ratlines, rope (or wood) rungs attached to the shrouds of the masts.

11. The *St. John* was built at Bath in 1870. American ships could be identified when hull down, beyond the horizon, by their characteristic lofty sail plan, which, compared to British ships in particular, appeared more tapered. Also, American cotton sails were lighter colored than flax sails favored by vessels of most other flags.

12. "Deals" were softwood planks or boards several inches thick. Many cargoes of deal timber disappeared into mine shafts, never to be seen again.

13. What might the steward, Mr. Delano's enemy, have fed poor Tobey?

14. To "wear ship" is to bring the ship to the other tack by going around before the wind. To bring the ship "about," by contrast, is to change tacks by going across, or into the wind.

15. *Big Bonanza* was built at Newburyport, Massachusetts, in 1875. In 1881 Captain Oliver Jones, of Newburyport—a fellow townsman of Captain Bray—had succeeded the *Big Bonanza*'s longtime master, Newburyporter Captain James Stanley, who had been washed overboard.

16. The *G. C. Trufant*, of London, was a wooden ship built at Newburyport, Massachusetts, in 1874. Her master, Captain Gamiel Thomas, was an American.

17. The Robinson Hotel was favored by American captains—indeed, a "daughter of the house" married Captain Gorham Knowles, the well-known master of the ship *South American*, and brother of Captain J. I. Knowles of the ill-fated *Wild Wave*.

18. Built at Thomaston, Maine, in 1876, the *Mills* was one of the largest American merchant ships then afloat. He first master was Captain Warren Mills, who was Captain Harvey Mills's son. A hard-luck ship, she was badly damaged by fire in her first year. In May 1882 she struck and sank the British copper ore barque *Eta* and nearly sank herself. Her owners bought her back at auction, but after finally setting out for New York she was nearly dismasted. In 1886, after departing Seattle, she sank in a heavy gale with but three survivors. Matthews, *American Merchant Ships*, Series I, pp. 145-49.

19. The ship *Willie Reed* was built at Waldoboro, Maine, in 1877; Captain Oscar Yates was from Bristol, Maine. The *Reed* had made the passage from San Francisco in 114 days. The ship *Great Admiral* was a notable vessel built at East Boston, Massachusetts, in 1869. The *Annie H. Smith* was a lofty, handsome ship built at Calais, Maine, in 1876.

20. Dublin was experiencing a wave of murders, which included those of a policeman and a juror.

21. For brevity, details of Frank's extensive theater-going, socializing, dating, and sight-seeing have been largely omitted.

22. The ship *Fiona*, of Glasgow, was built at Glasgow in 1878.

23. Demurrage was money owed to the ship by the shipper for delay of vessel beyond the "lay days" agreed to in the contract. Dublin grain merchants were notoriously slow in unloading a ship, in effect utilizing the ship as a sales warehouse.

24. Frank and Mr. Delano had been keeping company with Annie and Mary McCudden, daughters of a tailor who was patronized by ships' people.

25. The bark *Low Wood*, of St. John, New Brunswick, was built at Portland, New Brunswick, in 1878.

26. On departing Queenstown *Cephalonia* carried 1,055 passengers, 180 in the cabin, and 875 in steerage, the latter being mostly Swedes, Germans, and Irish.

27. The ship *Lucy A. Nickels* (she replaced a bark of that name) was built at Bangor, Maine, in 1875. A successful vessel, she sailed for over twenty years before being cut down for a barge in 1898. Captain Charles Nichols was from Searsport—Searsport has a "skinny million" Nickels and Nichols, and a good many of them were square-rigger captains. In 1885 about thirty Searsporters commanded full-rigged ships, or, nearly 10 percent of the full-riggers in the American marine. Confusion over the definition of the term "ship" led to the persistent and patently false claim—still very much alive—that 10 percent of the captains of the American merchant marine were from Searsport! Captain Charles Nichols was an outstanding shipmaster immortalized in *Under Sail* (New York: Harcourt, Brace,

1918), Felix Risenberg's wonderful account of his own first voyage as a sea struck young man aboard the magnificent Bath-built ship *A. J. Fuller* in 1897–98. Some account of Captain Nichols's adventures, including towing the becalmed *Lucy A. Nickels* away from a cannibal island in the Solomons with the ship's boat, are found in Matthews, *American Merchant Ships,* Series II, pp. 200–05.

28. Grandson Bruce Besse remembers visiting the mansion, especially on Thanksgivings. The first floor formal rooms were draped in purple velvet, and furnished with heavy mahogany. Breakfront cabinets were filled with booty from voyages, including scrimshaw and sea shells. An abundance of well-shined silver was on display. Portraits of ships hung on the walls. The house, somewhat lightened of its cargo, was sold by the estate to Frank's son, Harry. Harry Besse was a piece of work. Against Frank's wishes he left college to become a World War I ambulance driver in France. Frank was still so mad at Harry when Harry got home that he refused to pay for him to return to college. Undaunted, Harry set out on a stellar career that would lead to, among other accomplishments, the presidency of the Boston Stock Exchange.

29. *American Sentinel*, 24 Nov. 1887.

30. A good photo of the bark *Helen A. Wyman*, shorn of her mizzen yards and main skysail, is found in my book *Portrait of a Port, Boston 1852–1914*, p. 382.

31. Mark Hennesey Notes, Library, Maine Maritime Museum.

PART *Three*

CARLETON ALLEN

Chapter 13

Carleton Allen and Captain Walter Mallett

We Meet Carleton Allen, Our Next Young Seagoing Scribe, and Captain Walter Mallett and His Wife, "Aunt" Kate.

In 1979, at age ninety-nine, Carleton Allen recalled:

> WHEN I WAS A TEENAGER, I had two ambitions. One was to drive a fire engine, and the other was to go around Cape Horn. I was telling this to a neighbor and he said, "I can't help you with the first, but can help you with the second because my brother is a sea captain." To make a long story short, he arranged it. My guardian didn't want me to go. I think he would have liked to go himself, so I promised to keep a log of the journey, and I did.[1]

The Pittsburgh, Pennsylvania, neighbor was John P. Mallett, an industrial engineer originally from Maine.[2] His brother was Captain Walter M. Mallett. Young Allen had no idea how remarkably lucky he was—Walter Mallett, of the highest professional repute, was also among the most sociable of captains. He liked to have company in the cabin on long voyages, particularly on the rare occasions when he was not accompanied by his wife Kate. He and Kate had no children and took a special interest in the welfare of boys and young men aboard their ship. They became particularly fond of Carleton, and Walter would become for Carleton a most estimable father figure.

Carleton Allen was born at Holliston, Massachusetts, in 1880. His father died when he was two, his mother when he was eleven, after which Carleton went to live in Pittsburg with his brother Charley, who was fifteen years older. Little is known about Carleton's family's background although it is apparent from his sophisticated writing style and by the fact that he could afford to pay for his passage—not to mention that he wore a necktie at sea—that he had a good upbringing, was well educated, and was of some means.

Walter Mallett was born on a large and prosperous farm in Topsham, Maine, in 1859. Although young Walter stood to inherit the farm, in 1876 at age seventeen he elected to go to sea, instead, joining Captain William Besse's new Bath-built bark *Belle of Oregon*, as "boy."[3] Her master, Jacob Merriman, was Walter's brother-in-law.

Mallett sailed aboard Besse ships for as long as there were Besse ships to sail in. In 1884, while serving as first mate under Captain Merriman in the ship *Henry Failing*, Mallett commanded the *Failing* from San Francisco to Liverpool while Merriman took a vacation. Returning to San Francisco as first mate, he then took command of the Besse bark *William W. Crapo* for a voyage to Liverpool and to Philadelphia.

In 1886 Walter married Katherine Cox and was given his first ship of his own, the old ship *Syren*. He commanded *Syren* for two years before

The old clipper Syren *drying sails at New Bedford.*
COURTESY OF THE PEABODY-ESSEX MUSEUM.

Captain and Mrs. Walter M. Mallett, of the bark Guy C. Goss, *of Wareham, in Japan, likely in 1888.*
COURTESY OF THE MAINE MARITIME MUSEUM.

being promoted to the splendid bark *Guy C. Goss*. He remained aboard the *Goss* for thirteen years, until she was sold. Mallett then served as master of the fine four-masted steel bark *Hawaiian Isles* from 1901 until 1910. Between 1911 and 1917 Mallett had two stints in command of the famous steel four-masted bark *Dirigo*, and then he and Kate retired to Topsham.

Kate had made her honeymoon voyage across the Atlantic to France in the old *Syren* and subsequently remained home for only three of Walter's many voyages, rounding the Horn twenty-eight times—Walter's total was about forty. The daughter of a shipwright, "Aunt Kate" was a commanding presence in her own right. Regarding her husband's daily cigar, which she disapproved of, Kate claimed that she could have prevented him from starting the habit had she never let Walter sail without her.[4]

The "medium" clipper ship *Syren* had been built in 1851—when a "clipper" was definitely a clipper—at Medford, Massachusetts, a town then well known for its production of first-rate East Indiamen, packet ships, and clippers. Her builder was the famous John Taylor, her owners, the Salem East Indies shipping firm of Silsbee & Pickman. *Syren*'s sisters in the Medford Class of '51 included two extreme clipper ships, three medium clipper ships, eight other ships, three barks, a schooner, and two steamers.[5]

As a speedster, *Syren* was a disappointment in the California trade and, indeed, she was dogged by relatively slow passages all of her life. Apologists claimed that she wasn't really slow, but cursed by calms and head-winds.[6] In the late fifties *Syren* joined the fleet of Charles Brewer & Company, of Boston, the pioneer trader between Boston, New York, and Honolulu. She was mostly employed carrying out supplies for the whaling fleet, returning with whale oil and bone. In 1877 she sailed to the Arctic (by way of San Francisco) to load "whaleman's catch" for New Bedford, the first of several such voyages.

In 1879 Captain William Besse added *Syren* to his fleet, owning her in equal shares with Jonathan Bourne, Alden Besse, and Gerard Tobey. Under Besse's management *Syren* continued servicing the Pacific whaling fleet, although in Frank Besse's account we glimpsed her carrying Chinese passengers from Hong Kong to Victoria, B. C., followed by a cargo of "Oregon pine" spars for Bath.

In 1886 *Syren* became Captain Walter Mallett's first full-time command, and for a couple of years *Syren* tramped about the North and South Atlantic under Mallett while Besse sought a buyer for her. Letters from Besse to Mallett have an almost fatherly tone—complete with the occasional reprimand, usually involving the spending of money, Besse dispensed advice on many topics, including ship repair and care, on cargoes and trim, on freights, weather, passages, practices of ports, and how one might outwit the locals in a port. He never failed to extend his kindest regards to "Mrs. Mallett."

On August 23, 1886, Besse wrote ahead to Mallett, due at Havre (with his new bride), regarding a charter to load salt at Turk's Island for Boston:

> THE CHARTERER PUTS the salt on board but you will have to trim it. The worst job you will have is getting out your ballast. There is about 12 tons of iron in the run which you will leave there. You ought to put some dunnage down in the sharp of the floor to keep the salt clear of any water. You will have no trouble about water in the bilges. The trouble will be in the sharp of the floor. Don't put any salt in the ends of the ship. Keep it well up amidships. You will need at least one-third of the cargo between decks to help keep her easy.... I suppose you will take from 1,100 to 1,200 tons. Draft of water about 21½ feet. The only risk you will have at the islands is in case the wind should suddenly shift to the southwest.[7]

On January 29, 1886, Besse wrote to Mallett, due at Liverpool:[8]

> BUSINESS OF ALL KINDS is extremely poor. I believe there is not one wooden ship building today in any part of the United States. A bark could be built very cheap at Bath now, if there is to be any business for ships to do. Before you come home would like for you to find out

> how many iron sailing ships there are building in England now, and how much they charge a ton for a steel ship, say 1,500 tons register, with all outfits paid ready for sea. It might be well for you to see how much of a new bark you could get taken up in Liverpool by Ross, Skolfield, and others.[9]

On May 20, 1887, Besse wrote to Mallett, then loading hard pine lumber at Pensacola for Buenos Aires:

> I HAVE MADE ARRANGEMENTS to send your homeward stores from Boston in the bk. *J. D. Peters*.... You can manage to get the stores from Capt. Lane transferred from one ship to the other without duties, I think...you must keep this matter strictly private.... Capt. Lane may make a show of giving them to you or of selling them to you, as the case may require.... I will send you canvas to make a foresail....

On December 23, 1887, Besse wrote to Mallett, at Pensacola loading lumber for Washington, D.C., advising Mallett to forgo a pilot when entering Chesapeake Bay:

> I AM AN old pilot for the Chesapeake Bay. You need not be afraid to run into the Bay at night without a pilot if you can make Cape Henry Light. You can see the light 15 or 18 miles in clear weather. Get the light to bear West and run for it. You will have, when six or eight miles to the eastward of the light, six, seven, and eight fathoms....

In truth, it's likely Besse would not have been greatly upset if Mallett had broken *Syren*'s insured old back on a shoal. On February 28, 1888, Besse wrote Mallett at Washington, D.C.:

> THE BARK *GUY C. GOSS* is at Philadelphia loading oil for Japan. Expect she will be loaded about the 10th of March. I would like you to go in her, as Master, if you can get around in time. Telegraph me on receipt of this whether you wish to go in the *Goss* or not. What kind of a man is your mate and would you advise letting him take the *Syren*?... I have not decided what to do with the *Syren*. Would like to sell her. Write me what condition the ship is in, how are her sails, and does she make any water.

Besse obviously liked what he had seen in Walter Mallett. Although nine years old, the splendid, big *Guy C. Goss* was still in youthful form and a choice command. Mallett took her. The captain whom he relieved was none other than the redoubtable Captain Alfred Doane.

Mallet's replacement aboard *Syren* was one of his Topsham relatives, Captain Angier Merriman.[10] In April, loaded to the gills with coal, the old ship left Baltimore for San Francisco. When seventy-four days out she put into Rio de Janeiro in distress, said to be making water badly. Condemned after a survey, she was turned over to the underwriters and sold where she lay, doubtless to the relief of her owners—one wonders if Captain Merriman thought to treat the insurance surveyor.

Given *Syren*'s advanced age and her long history of structural damage—she had twice gone ashore in the Golden Gate—it would not have been surprising if she had indeed reached the end of her days. In fact, after receiving repairs and a new name and hail—*Margarita* of Buenos Aires—she would still be found in *Lloyd's Register* in 1920, surely the last clipper of her generation afloat. Slow and steady had won the race.

Walter Mallett's new command, the bark *Guy C. Goss,* had been launched by Goss & Sawyer on Thanksgiving Day, 1879. She was the one hundredth vessel launched by the firm. To mark the dual occasion a "jollification" was held, and each employee received a free holiday dinner. Painted Besse's favored bronze green, the big bark slid into the Kennebec

Captain and Mrs. Walter M. Mallett (at left) with an unidentified woman aboard the bark Guy. C. Goss. *The deck structure at left, called the pilothouse, or coach house, was a vestibule enclosing the forward companionway to the main cabin. Aft of the main cabin may be seen the wheelhouse, which sheltered the helm and was a feature common to large American square-riggers.*
CAPTAIN WALTER M. MALLETT. COURTESY OF CAPTAIN W. J. L. PARKER.

with a rush, parting a pair of four-inch lines with which the tug *Knickerbocker* attempted to stem her way. A near-sister to the bark *Gerard C. Tobey*, at 1,524 tons she was the largest bark-rigged vessel built in the United States up to that date.[11] Along with her builders and managing owner Besse, other owners included Alden Besse, Gerard C. Tobey and other Tobeys, New Bedford whaling merchants Jonathan Bourne and Thomas Knowles, and her master, Captain Abel Reynolds.

The *Goss*'s maiden voyage began with a passage from Philadelphia to Yokohama with case oil, thence to San Francisco (for grain) and Antwerp. Until 1892 all of her passages from the Atlantic Coast were to China or Japan, returning by way of San Francisco, or Columbia River or Puget Sound ports. From 1892 until 1901 she traded between Atlantic ports and the West Coast.

In November 1888 Captain Besse wrote Captain Mallett at Hiogo, Japan:

The bark Guy C. Goss *loading timber at misty Nainamo, British Columbia, in the 1890s. The heavy ramp leads to a stern port. The bark, like the forested background, was green.*
CAPTAIN WALTER M. MALLETT. COURTESY OF RICHARD P. MALLETT.

SUPPOSE YOU WILL be loaded about October 1st. This will be on the change of the monsoons and you will be liable to hurricanes anywhere in the China Sea. I should take the passage home around Cape Horn leaving Japan anytime before October 15th. After that I should take the passage down the China Sea. If you take the Cape Horn passage I should run over in about Lat. 38-40, and when you get across to Long. 130 W or thereabouts, then...bear off to the southward and get into the trades and come home on the California track as near as you can.... Notice the Mass. Humane Society...have awarded you and first mate each a silver medal also the crew bronze medals for saving the crew of sch. *Alice Montgomery* in March.[12]

Within a week of leaving port, headed east, the *Goss* was caught in a suddenly building typhoon and had her sails blown away before they could be properly furled. For six hours the bark was subjected to the full force of the typhoon. Thrown on her beam ends, she righted only when the rigging for the main and mizzen topmasts and fore topgallant masts was cut away. On November 3 she limped into San Francisco under a jury rig, forty-seven days out.[13] On November 12 Besse wrote Mallett:

YOUR TWO LETTERS at hand describing the typhoon, etc.... Think you must have had a pretty tough typhoon by your description. Don't suppose you could have got her before the wind. If you could perhaps might have done better. While on her beam ends though, it must have been impossible to have got her off before the wind.

On November 12 Besse wrote:

IT SEEMS TO ME you are losing considerable time. The ship's time is worth $75 a day. Should have started at once and taken the main yard and the other yard you had on deck and put some shears on end, hired some riggers, taken out mainmast with windlass or engine. I shipped your [14] sails today...also bag of twine, wax, and needles rolled up in sails.

On November 14, Besse wrote:

I WOULD KEEP the Chinese cook on board. They ship for the voyage and you put in in distress. Don't see why you should send him back.... Sails that were blown away do not go into general average, but all those that went with the spars that were cut away can be recovered.... I would avoid saying in the manifest that anything blew away. Would say, "I cut away the rigging to save the ship and spars and sails went overboard together."[14]

PS. Enclosed a rough plan of a spliced mast at the heel. The mast can be made as strong as new.

With the ending of the Chinese passenger trades and the squeezing out of American ships from the San Francisco grain trade, William Besse had pursued the niche trade of carrying West Coast timber to the East Coast.[15] On January 16, 1890, Besse wrote Mallett at Port Townsend, Washington, advising him how to load a cargo of timber and spars:

> YOU WILL NOT NEED less than 300 tons stone ballast under your spars, trimmed fore and aft.... Ship will need to be trimmed about 24 inches by the stern.... The main thing in stowing spars is to keep their ends clear of the ceiling and have them bear equally the whole length.... See the ship does not get knocked to pieces in handling the spars.... Capt. Hardy [of the bark *William W. Crapo*] paid his stevedore twenty-four hundred dollars to do all his work, take ship from Port Townsend, put her in loading berth, trim all ballast, unbend and bend sails...take ship back to Port Townsend, stow all the cargo, take in all necessary [dunnage] wood for same, secure deckload, take out and put in bow and stern ports and properly caulk them ready for sea. Stevedore to hire ship's engine and pay $10 a day for its use.... Draw on Mr. Failing First National Bank of Portland, for money to pay off your crew.... Better buy straight cedar blocks [for dunnage]. We can sell them here to split into shingles.

March 3, 1890, Besse wrote Mallett at Port Blakely, Washington:

> I WISH YOU HAD put on copper paint on the bare places on her bottom.... There is no trouble about laying a vessel ashore, cleaning her bottom, and putting on copper paint. I have been doing it for the last forty years. I consider little danger from worms low down on her bottom, at least for this passage. The worms do their work within 2 feet of the water line, wherever that may be.... Your bad copper will prevent her sailing some....

February 7, 1891, Besse wrote Mallett at Yokohama:

> SHALL LOOK FOR your arrival the last of March although I have not seen you spoken since the *Goss* sailed from New York. Notice the most of the ships had long passages down to the Equator. Have chartered the *Goss* to load tea at Yokohama for Tacoma; at the enormous freight of $2 a ton, per 40 cubic feet measurement on tea.... Suppose the *Goss* will require about 200 tons ballast under the tea. This amount will be about what she will require if she loads lumber on the Sound. You

must clean out your poop deck, and fill it full of tea. Put in a ton of tea wherever it is possible to do it.... This tea business is poor freight, but am in hopes to secure fair business from the Sound. You will need neither pilot or tugboat on the Sound until you get to Port Townsend. Hope you will send me a draft as soon as you can, as the ship is considerably in debt to me for her New York bills. Think it would be a good plan to get clear of part of your crew as soon as you arrive at Yokohama. When ready to sail, you can ship some Japs, and pay them less wages. They will do very well in the summertime, to run across to the Sound. They would also be more likely to remain by the ship on the Sound.[16]

On August 3, 1891, Besse wrote to Mallett at Port Blakely, Washington:

> THERE HAS BEEN a story going about the country telling how one of your Jap sailors fell overboard, was swallowed by a whale, and thrown on deck. Please write whether there is any truth in it.[17]

On January 21, 1894, Besse wrote Mallett, laid up at San Francisco since at least August:

> I CANNOT SEE MUCH profit in any of the business you name, think lumber to Chillie [*sic*] the best business.... It is rather early to go to that Russian port. If they would pay $10,000 it might do. Ask Capt. Knowles to try and give you a monthly charter to go up to Alaska in the Spring with fishermen's supplies & c[oal?] and stay there until the people and salmon are ready to return in the fall. There is no expense in this business. You would not need any crew as the fishermen would sail the ship up and down.

A charter for hard-to-spell Vladivostok was made—cargo unknown—and Besse wrote Mallett on February 20, 1894:

> IN REGARD TO YOUR passage to the Russian port, think I should shape my course direct for Hakodate and pass through the straits [Tsugaru Strait] direct to your port of destination. There is nothing in the way going through there and the only thing against you will be the easterly current. When you get up to the straits if the wind is to the westward keep just to the southward of the straits under the lee of the islands and you will avoid the current and wait for a slant to go through. I think the passage across in the trade winds and up through the Japan Sea would be two thousand miles further.

On February 27, 1894, Besse wrote regarding a possible return charter carrying sulfur from Japan:

SHOULD YOU LOAD a full cargo of brimstone at Hakodate you must then be particular about loading it; it should be stowed fore and aft, the whole length of the keelson; also a large amount in the 'tween decks. Have it built in the center at an angle of about 45 degrees into the wings, in the lower hold and 'tween decks; keep it clear of the wings and build it fore and aft to the upper deck, in order to make the vessel easy. It must be stowed fore and aft, the same as for nitrate or guano; that is, a whole cargo of heavy brimstone; there is a lighter kind, that is stowed in sacks.

On September 23, 1895, Besse scolded Captain Mallett, then at Port Townsend, Washington:

HAVE JUST RECEIVED San Francisco vouchers of the *Goss*.... Think your rigging work might have been done at sea; the blacksmith and ship chandlery bills appear large, the prices on same being 50 percent more than New York prices; am surprised the *Goss* took a pilot out as the ship was in ballast and summer season; this I consider as money poorly invested. Do not wish to be considered a growler but feel it my duty to remind you of these things as the owners are constantly after me looking for some sort of dividend...should not think it necessary to keep any crew by ship while loading...according to my experience, sailors' work in port amounts to nothing....

At sea the captain of a well-run ship, ideally, often had little to do. Captains' pastimes were many and varied. Walter Mallett's pastimes were making model yachts for his young nephews—Kate sewed the sails with tiny stitches—and reading.[18] Described by his nephew Richard Mallett as being "even-tempered, fair-minded, blessed with a sanguine disposition," Walter was as well a man of great natural and intellectual curiosity.[19] Among his favorite books were Plutarch's *Lives* and Gibbon's *Decline and Fall of the Roman Empire*. During their voyages together he and Kate religiously pursued regular and genuine courses of instruction.

Walter Mallett was a "gentleman captain," but of a different sort than that once typified by educated, upper-class Boston mariners. (Captain Frank Stone was in the old Boston tradition).[20] Walter absorbed his higher education not in college, but in the cabin.

Mallett, whose entire career was under sail, never lost a vessel or a cargo. In an era when crew problems plagued the American merchant marine—some captains had continual problems— Mallett appears not to have been much troubled. Indeed, Walter Mallett almost made it look easy. Historian and sailor Alan Villiers, referring to beleaguered, dead-ended British Cape Horn shipmasters at the turn of the century, wrote:

> NO MAN TAKES TO THE SEA life naturally.... The long—or too frequently short—life of deepwater seafaring was forced on them, or it was an escape. Having embarked on it and risen to command, they were caught.[21]

Alan Villiers never met Walter Mallett. But Captain Mallett is about to make the acquaintance of Carleton Allen, whom we have already met.

---

1. The *[Cleveland] Plain Dealer*, 9 Feb. 1979. In 1898 driving a fire engine drawn by fleet-footed Percherons was indeed a worthy aspiration as well.

2. John Purington Mallett was a graduate of Tufts Engineering School where he was captain of the baseball and football teams, second in academics, and, as proven by tests, the strongest man in the college. He spent part of his career with Westinghouse and advanced to major in the army in WWI.

3. *Brunswick Record*, 18 Aug. 1931. Walter's uncle, Elisha Mallett, master builder at Bath for Trufant & Drummond and later for the Sewalls, built over ninety ships.

4. Kate wrote, "A Captain's wife is not supposed to know anything about a ship beyond the cabin. She is simply a passenger. She often longs to have a finger in the pie, especially when there is a poor cook. But she must eat what is set before her and hold her peace." Anyone who knew imperious Kate might wonder if she was describing the ideal or what transpired. *Lewiston Journal Magazine*, 21 Jan. 1956. A mother, after watching the war of wills between Kate and an infant as to whether or not the child would taste some ice cream, was heard to remark: "Aunt Kate knows everything there is to know about children because she never had any!"

5. Hall Gleason, *Old Ships and Ship-Building Days of Medford* (West Medford, 1936), pp. 73–74.

6. Howe and Matthews, *American Clipper Ships*, pp. 653–59.

7. Library, Maine Maritime Museum. Somehow these letters escaped the fire which later consumed the Mallett homestead.

8. His instructions to keep the heavy salt out of the ends of the ship may reflect his concerns over the "hog" which is evident in an undated photo of the ship taken at New Bedford, likely under his ownership. (A ship was "hogged" when its ends drooped.) Putting some of the salt in the 'tween deck would slow her roll, easing the strain on hull and rigging.

9. Besse's interest in the cost of British-built tonnage was surely only by way of comparison, since such a vessel could not have been placed under the American flag. The bark he had in mind for "Ross, Skolfield" to invest in would have been Bath-built. Ross and Skolfield were the ship's Liverpool agents, and it was common practice for managing owners to recruit chandlers, brokers, sailmakers, and such to "take up" shares in new vessels in return for custom. Wherever American ships traded in large numbers there was likely to be an agent with ties to maritime New England—Captain Alfred Skolfield was from Brunswick, Maine, just across the Androscoggin River from Mallett's hometown of Topsham. See Erminie S., Reynolds and Kenneth R. Martin, *A Singleness of Purpose: The Skolfields and Their Ships* (Bath, ME: Bath Marine Museum, 1987), p. 201.

10. Children born in a foreign port were commonly named after it. Some recipients were subsequently more pleased with the location fate had chosen for them than were others!

11. The *Goss* sported main skysail and the double-topgallant yards characteristic of the Besse fleet. Sensibly, the mainmast and foremast were identical, as were topmasts and topgallant masts and yards (excepting the main yard).

12. The *Montgomery,* of Bath, was bound for Providence with coal when she got into trouble in a gale. Her captain later wrote: "We kept pumping until all but one man gave up and the mate gave out, he having been washed overboard twice and badly frozen. I was washed from the wheel but saved myself by catching a rope. Tuesday night will never be forgotten with its terrible seas. We could not keep the water down." And so on. On Thursday, March 16, with the decks awash and hope nearly gone, they spotted the *Goss*, which had departed from Philadelphia. The men were taken off by the *Goss*'s boat, commanded by the mate, in three dangerous trips, and were later landed at Pernambuco, Brazil. (Ships bound for either Cape Horn or the Cape of Good Hope sailed close to the bulge of Brazil.) Hennesey Notes.

13. *American Sentinal*, 18 Nov. 1888.

14. When a sacrifice has been made by the vessel to preserve property—in this case rigging was cut away to preserve the vessel and cargo—liability for the loss is shared by shippers through "general average."

15. This trade had its beginnings in 1876 when Besse's friend and shipbuilder Captain Guy C. Goss visited the Pacific Northwest with the idea of establishing a shipyard on Puget Sound. Recognizing the superiority of Oregon pine, i.e., Douglas fir, for certain purposes, Goss had the bark *William H. Besse* loaded with a cargo of masts, spars, decking, and knees. The *Besse* arrived at Bath in November 1877. William Avery Baker, *A Maritime History of Bath, Maine* (Bath, ME: Marine Research Society of Bath, 1973), p. 534.

16. This may not have been as ominous a suggestion as it may appear. Although some captains prided themselves on making life so unpleasant for a crew that was shipped at high American wages that the sailors would desert the ship and their pay, a captain could also pay off sailors who left the ship by mutual agreement. Sailors were very prone to desert in Puget Sound ports for the high wages paid ashore, and considerable "blood money" was demanded by shipping masters—"crimps"—for supplying replacements.

17. An example of dry Besse humor, no doubt. The suggestion that the *Goss* had had a Jonah on board was likely a reference to her very prolonged passage.

18. In 1899, aboard the *Goss*, Walter built a sloop 40 inches overall to be raced against a model yacht to be built by kinsman Captain Merriman—presumably Jacob, of the ship *Henry Failing*. Merriman, however, had a 5-footer built at Seattle. Walter, disappointed, had intended that Merriman build his yacht himself, and of similar length to Walter's. From a letter in the possession of Richard P. Mallett.

19. Richard P. Mallett, "An Education at Sea," *Down East* (Dec. 1979), p. 48.

20. In Boston's golden age of mercantile shipping it was said that no proper family was complete without a shipmaster in its ranks. Such "gentlemen captains"—unlike the typical merchant captain—were educated men who chose the sea over the counting house, the law office, or the pulpit. Captain Arthur Clark,

distinguished mariner and author—see *Some Merchants and Sea Captains of Old Boston* (Boston: State Street Trust Company, 1918), pp. 51–52—and Captain Richard Banfield, son of a Boston lawyer, and the fair-minded master of the wonderful bark *St. James*, were among the last of such gentlemen captains born to the role. Captain J. H. Drew, of Hallowell, Maine, also a writer, was among the self-educated gentlemen captains.

21. Alan Villiers, *The War with Cape Horn* (New York: Charles Scribner's, 1971), pp. xvii–iii.

Chapter 14

CARLETON'S WISH

Carleton Allen Joins the Bark Guy C. Goss *for a Cape Horn Passage to New York*

IN APRIL,1898 at Port Blakely, Puget Sound, Washington, Carleton B. Allen, aged eighteen and between high school and college, joined the bark *Guy C. Goss* of Wareham, Captain Walter Mallett, as a passenger.[1] (Mrs. Mallett had elected to remain ashore for this passage.) The *Goss* was bound around Cape Horn to New York with a cargo of spars. Carleton had left Pittsburg on March 12. Two days later, crossing the prairie aboard a train rapidly filling up with "Klondikers" headed for Alaska and the gold rush, he wrote:

> RUNNING IS GOOD, healthy exercise; especially when you have an end view like the end of a through-bound train, carrying all your worldly possessions and also your hair brush, leaving a station called Council Bluffs.
>
> MARCH 17TH. Wear my money in my stocking and my watch under my belt, for according to an old sailor's report Seattle is very dangerous now with the Klondike boom.
>
> MARCH 18TH. Take boat *Sarah M. Renton* for Port Blakely. Capt. at wharf to meet me. Had spotted another man…as the Capt.…so was surprised when he stepped up behind me…. [The ship is] larger than I expected. Wheelhouse and pilothouse.[2] Long poop and large forehouse…. I occupy stateroom off cabin on port side about ten feet aft of mizzen mast. Vessel loading spars which are being hewn on the beach nearby. Big saw mill nearby, over 500 ft. long.[3]
>
> MARCH 25TH. Spars are very pretty ones. Some 36 inches hewn square at butt and over 100 feet long.
>
> MARCH 26TH. In evening went with Capt. to Mr. Price's home. Mr. Price is the general utility man of Port Blakely—he is a postmaster,

telegrapher, musician, understands and practices the use of the telephone and unlimited other things.

MARCH 29TH. Get on all deck load. Almost ready.

MARCH 30TH. Tug *Wanderer* comes from Seattle at 6 P.M.... Second Mate, Mr. Siggins, is sleeping pretty good since his repeated visits to the hotel. Have Jap. cook, steward, carpenter, boy, and one sailor, besides Mr. Merriman, the first mate, the Capt., and myself aboard. 40 miles from Blakely to Townsend.[4]

MARCH 31ST. Arrived in Port Townsend...a small place which once had a boom, leaving it worse than ever, with a lot of buildings empty and unfinished. Advocate Harbor, N. S., is not in the same class as Townsend for slowness and dullness. There is a Custom House here [and] a pretty little Revenue cutter.... Secured six of crew, came aboard very drunk. The boardinghouse runners are about as heartless and as apt to cheating as any people I know of.[5]

APRIL 1ST. Two men brought off in morning, one with his head cut open by a blow from one of the runners and the other half sick, the latter a half-breed Indian. Later in the day another man is brought off with his mouth banged out of shape. In the evening a Chilean is brought off with a black eye and roaring drunk.

APRIL 2ND. Secured our last man, making 14 in all. This last man is older than the others and is a typical old salt.

APRIL 3RD. Tug came out at 10:30 p. m., started at 12.

The bark *Guy C. Goss*'s passage from Puget Sound to New York, via Cape Horn, began on April 4, and ended August 18, 1898. It took far longer than expected due to persistent easterly gales encountered in Cape Horn waters, where powerful westerlies usually prevailed. Indeed, while the *Goss* was at sea the Spanish American War was begun and ended.

APRIL 4TH. Are towed by tug *Wanderer* again.... Tug signals shortly for us to set all sail as we have a fair wind. Well the process is indescribable as are a great many things to-day. One must see and hear the sailors to appreciate this.... Capt. does up a packet of letters and hitches them to the end of hawser when tug leaves us. Don't feel seasick yet.

APRIL 8TH. Wind blowing a gale.... Ship rides easy as she is so light in the water. Heels over easily on account of deck load.... The noise of the wind and water on deck...the creaking of the woodwork in the cabin. The tables and all the furniture seem to have an affinity to the lee-side. Capt. occupied lee sofa during this unsettled weather, and has to dig himself out whenever he is called on deck. Can sleep in spite of noise and motion. Get about 12 hours a day. Very tired from my incessant labor.

APRIL 9TH. Caught my first "goonie." Second mate skinned him. Chopped up the carcass and gave it to the hens.... Stuffed head with oakum and 2nd mate made a pouch of one of the feet....[6] Played cribbage with Capt. during evening after an hour's walk on deck.

APRIL 10TH. First time I saw them tack with all sail on. Lots more trouble than on a schooner, but it was done pretty quickly though. The men sing and shout all the time they are pulling in braces, sheets, etc.

APRIL 11TH. Capt. and I played cribbage and euchre in the evening. Mr. Merriman, the mate, thinks we had a fair wind because the fish tackle for the anchors was taken down. We have two landsmen aboard. One an Indian, whose name is Kelly, and who isn't an Indian for his father was Irish. The other landsman is an Irishman.

The after cabin, or saloon, of the bark Guy. C. Goss. *The view is across the cabin, from port to starboard, looking aft. One of two sofas, or settees, is set into an alcove. The captain's cabin is glimpsed through the open door. The organ, at far right, is bolted to the after bulkhead. Obviously these photos were taken in port, with furniture in place and carpets rolled out.*
CAPTAIN WALTER M. MALLETT. COURTESY OF JAMES F. JUNG.

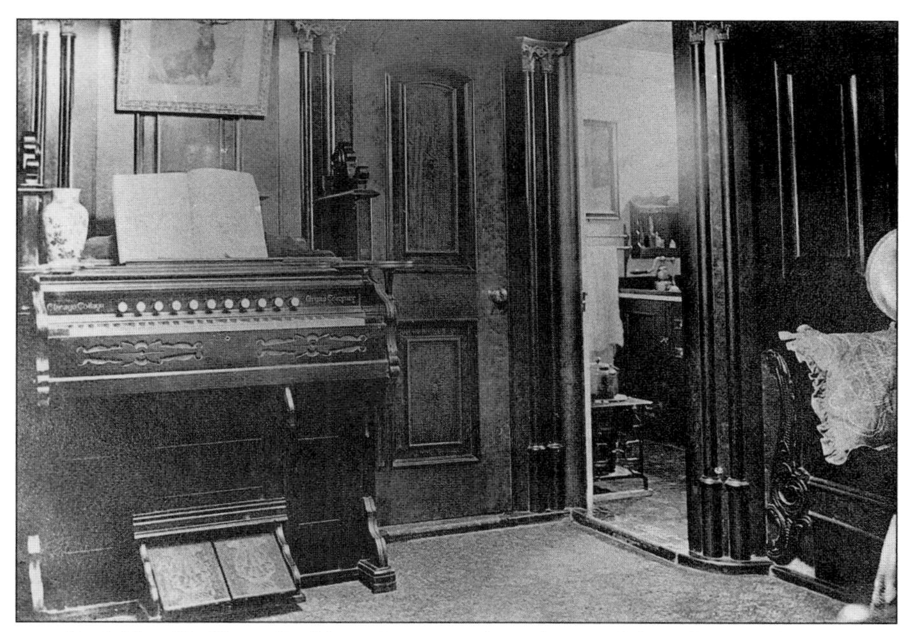

Bark Guy C. Goss. *Looking aft, to port, into the captain's bathroom. The door to the right of the parlor organ leads to stairs to the poop deck.*
CAPTAIN WALTER M. MALLETT. COURTESY OF JAMES F. JUNG.

Bark Guy C. Goss. *Looking forward and to starboard in the after cabin. The portrait is of Captain Guy C. Goss, himself. The doors on either side lead to the dining room in the forward cabin.*
CAPTAIN WALTER M. MALLETT. COURTESY OF JAMES F. JUNG.

APRIL 14TH. Made my first voyage to the end of the jibboom.... Made also my first trip up into the maintop. Vessel looks narrow, and the top is higher from up there than it is from down here. Put up the punching bag in the forward wheelhouse.[7] Capt. seems to like it by the way he hits it up...it is rather awkward punching, but after the bag gets its sea legs it will be all right, I guess.

APRIL 15TH. Beautiful day, fine, elegant, can't describe it and how beautiful the vessel's cutwater looks from the end of the jibboom. Capt. made a fish-trap for trolling.... There is a cord fastened in such a way that when a fish gets on, this cord is broken and an axle spins round on which are notches. A piece of springy wood is bent over these notches so that when the wheel goes round it makes a terrific clicking noise.

APRIL 18TH. Capt. cut my hair, and I cut his. Didn't know I could do so well. The most comfortable place aboard and doubtless the best suited to me is on top of the "booby hatch." I spend much of my time there.

APRIL 19TH. Helped the Capt. take the sun at noon. Capt. cut out some blocks of wood for boat hulls. He intends making three. I shall attempt a small one too.

APRIL 22ND. We are off Mexico now. No fish. New moon to-night. Looks fine in the clouds. Turned up, so Capt. says it will be a dry moon.

APRIL 23RD. Sailors have been employed overhauling sails and re-serving lifts and foot ropes for the last few days.

APRIL 24TH. The ship's boy got insolent and the second mate brought him aft to the Capt. Capt. sent him up on the skysail yard for awhile. The boy has been with the ship on the voyage out, and the Capt. has had trouble with him stealing, etc. The cook lost a clothes brush some days ago. Capt. called boy down and accused him of stealing the brush but boy denied it. Capt. searched his bunk and found the brush. He as yet has only given him a word thrashing. Boy seems to be penitent, but appearances are sometimes deceitful, and so are boys.... On the whole the Capt. says he has a better crew than coming out. There are certainly some good old salts among them, and the saltiest one of all is a man that was never aboard a ship before.... He has anchors all over his arms already. Some of the shanties they sing when hoisting away on the upper topsail or topgallant halyards are amusing, as well as rather weird at times.

APRIL 25TH. Capt. took some pictures, one of the first and second mates and myself, showing the deck aft of amidships, another of the main deck and deck load along with the forecastle head. Developed them in evening and they were first rate.

APRIL 26TH. Took my first trick at the wheel.... I could keep her within a quarter point of her course. Sighted a full-rigged ship.... I viewed her from the fore crosstrees.... I managed to blow my nose and tie my necktie while on the crosstrees. Now this wonderful feat may not seem wonderful, but, nevertheless, it is more difficult than a great many would think...we fired away, first with our ensign and number, then she answered with the British ensign and the name *Haddon Hall* from San Francisco. We...asked if anything decisive had happened and before we could add "with Spain," she answered, "No."

Bark Guy C. Goss. *Looking aft along the poop. At left we glimpse the sailmaker's bench. Second mate Siggins stands at center; First Mate Merriman sits on the booby hatch, which is lashed atop the lazarette hatch. Carelton Allen, wearing his necktie, sits atop the so-called pilothouse. The* Goss*'s long poop, extending nearly to the mainmast, was typical of Besse's ships. For those ships employed in the coolie trade the commodious lazarette beneath likely provided secure storage space for provisions.*
CAPTAIN WALTER M. MALLETT. COURTESY OF CAPTAIN W. J. L. PARKER.

Then we bid her good-bye; as we sailed two or three feet to her one, we drew away from her in great shape.

April 27th. The sun now rises and goes northward.... Heat and chain lightning by the wholesale...the amount of moisture in the air is astonishing.... She heels a trifle more than is comfortable on account of the wet sails.

April 29th. We have struck the portion of the Pacific known as the "Doldrums".... We are about opposite...[the Republic of] Columbia now.

May 2. Rained all night.... Capt. and I did the washing, viz. the Capt. did the washing and I did the heavy looking on.

May 3rd. Just a month to-night since we cleared Port Townsend. This sweet old dream, the only thing I remember as lively about the place is a certain little typewriter girl.... Breaking violin strings by the wholesale.

Bark Guy C. Goss. *Looking forward from the poop. The deckload of lumber has been stacked to the height of the poop, leaving a well around the mainmast and the pumps. The forward house housed the two sailors' fo'c's'le, the galley, the carpenter's shop, and so on. At far right we glimpse the sailmaker at his bench.*
Captain Walter M. Mallett. Courtesy of James F. Jung.

MAY 5TH. Tacked ship in a pelting rain.... Was of my first real use aboard tonight, by taking wheel when the whole watch was needed in a squall to brace around.... Got a good look at the moon from the crosstrees.

MAY 7TH. Cast my keel to-day and filed it. Capt. cast keel for his third boat too. One of the men lost his straw hat overboard...and a large shark came up and swallowed it.

MAY 8TH. I suppose we crossed the line sometime last night, but I didn't feel it when we did.

MAY 14TH. Was out on the end of the jibboom enjoying everything in general...when she took a plunge and put her knight heads under, thought I should have to telegraph in for my dinner or swim. Decked over my boat.... The men are doing the slop chest up brown in the tobacco line—40 pounds in the last three weeks. They are teaching each other draw poker. Good as any normal school to watch them.... Am becoming a sailor. Can do up a gasket on the main upper topgallant yard with a sea and breeze like today.

MAY 18TH. Rose at 3 bells and helped bending sails all day. Have had five hours at the wheel this last twenty-four hours.... Succeeded in getting up all the new square sails, thirteen in all, to-day.... Singing first shanty on the main lower topsail halyards. Pretty hot work.... My hands might be in better shape.[8]

MAY 19TH. Capt. and I printed forty-six pictures to-day. Took us nearly all day. Wish a thousand times I had gotten a camera.

MAY 21ST. I was at the wheel about six bells when the wind lightened up considerable then of a sudden it changed, taking her aback. Got the wheel up in time to get her off before we lost headway.

MAY 24TH. It is blowing half a gale of wind from the S.W. according to the Captain and two or three gales according to me.... Two men have been required at the wheel all day. I got several pretty smart duckings this morning when helping to shorten sail. But the sea has been grand and beautiful.... At about 5 bells this afternoon a four-masted bark was sighted off the lee bow about two points.

MAY 26TH. Heavy squall last night at 5 bells.... All hands to reef topsails.

MAY 27TH. A fire feels good. Hail today. The decks looked, after the squall, as if there had been a marriage aboard...we still occasionally roll our boomkin under.

MAY 28TH. Caught two albatrosses this morning. Second mate caught two albatrosses and two molymokes.... The sailors had a time skinning the birds and making pipe-stems, tobacco pouches, caps from the breast of the birds, and stuffing heads, etc.

MAY 29TH. Shipped three big seas this afternoon. Nobody hurt but lots wet. Saw some ice birds and Cape Horn pigeons.... One of the men is going to stuff an albatross. Each Sunday the Capt. and I wonder what the people at home are doing. He wants to see his better half and I want to see my better seven-eighths.

MAY 30TH. This morning the sea was mammoth, a regular Cape Horn sea, so the Capt. said.... Reefed the mainsail and set it at 8 bells this morning. Reefed the main topsail at 2 bells.... If there is anything prettier to the ear than a crowd of good singers, as we have aboard here, singing a "shanty" I would like to hear it. It has a sort of fascination to me. The songs are not difficult either in music or words but nevertheless they are pretty on a moonlight night like this. "Johnny's Gone to Hilo," "Whiskey," "Blow the Man Down," "Hoe the Cotton Down." "A Yankee Shipped Down from the River," and one or two others are favorites aboard.

JUNE 1ST. Caught four molymokes to-night and put them in the vacant pig pen on the main hatch. Intend putting a copper tag around their necks, with the ship's name, date, and the latitude.

JUNE 2ND. Ten days blow to-day and it is blowing too...we are under reefed topsail and mainsail now.... Put a tag on one of the molymokes this morning and let him go. Let others go later on. Been working all day on the brasswork for my boat, the Capt. has something like a hundred pieces for his three boats.

JUNE 3RD. My specialty lately has been rainbows. Saw a double moonlight rainbow to-night and wonderful of wonderful I saw the prismatic colors distinctly.

JUNE 4TH. Overcoats and gloves in June!... A beautiful night this, with enough light on deck from the moon to read a newspaper.

JUNE 5TH. The Second Mate caught a Cape hen this afternoon. A queer looking bird with a queerer beak. He saved the skin. The skull, feathers, and feet of a cape pigeon were found inside. However the bird swallowed the pigeon is beyond me.... Hear the Capt. tramping around on deck and will have to join him for the sake of a little exercise.

JUNE 6TH. We are carrying on a considerable taxidermists business under the forecastle head.

JUNE 7TH. Capt. says he never had such a siege going to the eastward down here.... Good night. Sleep tight, hear the Steward's bunk creaking, mine will pretty quickly.

JUNE 9TH. Still she blows from the eastward.... Lamp lit at 2:30 P.M. Sun does not rise until quite a while after breakfast, and then it gets 15 [degrees] high.... Capt. rigged his big boat. She is a beauty with all her brass work, etc.

JUNE 11TH. Blowing a heavy gale from E. N. E.... Things by this time have all been secured or have reached lee limits so we don't have much banging around.... If we were deep loaded we would roll fearfully in this heavy sea.... Capt. and I read *Puck's* and *Judge's* and hoped for a change of wind most all day.

JUNE 12TH. Same wind but more of it.... We made 60 miles good last week.

JUNE 13TH. Blowing very hard and a terrific sea running. The wind is shrieking through the rigging in great shape. Sighted a three-masted bark on the lee bow this morning.... She was loaded light and probably in the Australian wool trade.... Shipped a big sea just now.... Put out the binnacle lamp and filled the forward wheelhouse pretty well.

JUNE 14TH. Three weeks to-day since we had this blowy weather and twenty-two days since we steered [our desired] course.... Blowing a heavy gale according to the Capt. you can imagine what I call it.... The sea is tremendous and during the squall it was as well-covered with foam as a thirsty Dutchman's whiskers.

JUNE 15TH. Woof! Still she blows, and blows hard too.... Tremendous long, deep sea running, regular hills and valleys.... The sea is magnificent to look upon.

JUNE 16TH. It is curious how much superstition can be crammed into one sailor.

JUNE 17TH. There is no use in making sail with a head wind.... We would have been paid better to have hitched to a post nine days ago.... Dear knows how long this wind will continue. Capt. overhauled the ship's stores to-day. Have enough meat to last 108 days. May have to economize some.

JUNE 18TH. Pitching like a farmer, only more so.

JUNE 19TH. Whew! We are heading N. E. Northerly again and blowing great guns.... Capt. said he never did so much reefing and furling as he has done in the last four weeks, in all his experience. Capt. surprised me by trying another box of candy on the scene.

JUNE 20TH. If you want to sleep sound, just go out and have a pull at the topsail halyards just before turning in. Walked two or three hours to-day from the starboard anchor aft to the rail lashings on the poop.

JUNE 22ND. A mammoth flock of Cape pigeons around to-day.... The wheel has had the tackles on it and there has been no steering at all, only laying, most of the time. The Second Mate still persists that it is my fiddling and whistling that has caused this spell of head winds. I don't follow his reasoning. There must be fiddlers and whistlers aboard a good many vessels bound eastward in this region.

JUNE 24TH. This is the first time in thirty-four days, five weeks tomorrow, since we have had the yards off the backstays.... The moon seems unusually bright here owing to the clearness of the atmosphere.

JUNE 25TH. Have every rag on her except the two light staysails and the upper spanker.... All the tobacco has been sold from the slop chest.... Capt. says he will put off to another vessel if we get near enough to one, and get some tobacco. A Seaman's Library was put aboard when the vessel left New York last August and the Capt. didn't open it until yesterday. Found lots of new and nice books...the libraries generally consist of stale books.... Hens laying in great shape owing to the amount of chopped molymoke and albatross they get. Cats don't lay but they get lots of molymoke and albatross.

JUNE 26TH. Capt. says such fine weather down here is something remarkable. Had the rails off the table to-night for the first time since we left the Sound.... Only 540 miles from the Horn now.

JUNE 27TH. Wind blowing half a gale tonight.... We would feel this wind and sea in great shape if we were by the wind, but running before it we are as steady as a Fall River boat, and "as easy as an old shoe," as the Capt. says.

JUNE 28TH. I sighted a vessel this morning.... We outsailed her in great shape, although she was a full-rigged three-masted ship with every square sail set but the crossjack.... Her name was the *Argomene*, an iron vessel hailing from Liverpool.... She was carrying a bone in her teeth and was rolling pretty badly, although no deeper loaded than we, while we were as steady as could be.... The Capt. of the ship had his wife aboard, and she showed herself on deck to have a look at us. First person in skirts I have seen in three months.

JUNE 29TH. This morning at daybreak the Horn was sighted bearing N by W.... We have been having something I didn't expect, a dead calm off the Horn.... Wish we might stay along with [three full-rigged ships] so as to get a better sight at them or perhaps some news. They are Englishmen and we sail faster than they probably because their bottoms are covered with grass and barnacles.[9]

JUNE 30TH. Staaten Land [Argentina] in sight this morning..."the raggedest country ever built out of doors," according to the Captain.... We seem to be outsailing everything that comes along, and they are all coming our way.

JULY 1ST. This morning at 4 o'clock the foremost ship of yesterday's fleet was a point abaft the beam.... We have...an elegant suit of sails, all nearly new and white and all fit finely.

JULY 2ND. Capt. made me a present of a "fid" of his own workmanship and I tell you it is a dandy....[10] Capt. spent a whole day on it. It is made from wood that originally came from China. It came aboard in the shape of a capstan bar and was broken so Capt. used it for fids.... I consider myself more lucky every day in finding such a ship and such a Captain through whose kindness I can make a voyage and so add to my stock of knowledge of the world.

JULY 3RD. And to-morrow is the glorious Fourth.... Would give five dollars to be in good old Holliston just for to-night and to-morrow and perhaps to-morrow night. Wonder what the boys are up to?... With a person as kind as the Captain he would be a pretty bad egg if he couldn't raise a good time here. Then there is the Mate, Mr. Merriman, and the Second Mate, Mr. Siggins (a "Mick be name and a Mick be nature") both old sailors, typical old salts. Certain members of the crew are first-rate fellows, and some are comical, both in their looks and actions. One old man, Miller...is unlike British tars or in fact any other kind of sailor, he don't growl, and forty-five years at sea. There is Tom, the bosun...a thorough sailor and has had twenty-three years' practice. John, another good sailor, and Peterson like him, both Swedes. Charlie, Fred (the taxidermist), Chris (the lazy man), Jackson (the bloody Hinglishman), Scotty (the Chilean, or the man with the gift of gab), and Silvey (the Mexican with red whiskers, almost as large as mine), all these are young with the exception of Fred, who is about thirty-five and had served twenty-two years at sea.... The Second Mate decided that Kelly's mind needed cultivating and has set him to work learning the ropes and I believe if you were to sing out to him now to slacken the main brace, he would get hold of the main sheet or maybe the tiller ropes.... [Jack] came aboard with a gash in the top of his head inflicted by the boardinghouse runners when they were arguing with him that he wanted to ship for New York. Now he walks the deck smoking his pipe upside down and his Arctic cap down over his ears with the thermometer at 40 as if he were the only sailor. If he would only look aft once in a while he would see the only *other* sailor aboard. That's me.

JULY 4TH, 1898. HURRAY! for the GLORIOUS FOURTH! Blowing a gale and down to reefed topsails and whole mainsail.... Capt. got out some crackers he got in Japan several years ago and we each fired two bunches. Had as much sport as the law and state of the firecrackers would allow. Only one in about every five or ten would go off, but when it did we got a surprise. Gave the man at the wheel a surprise by shooting one through the binnacle.... Saw a mammoth school of porpoises to-day with lots of black fish in amongst them.... Whoof! how it blows! Expect the Mate won't sleep a wink for being expecting to be called to furl topsails and mainsail. It is a misfortune to be so nervous. Now I, such an old sailor, don't mind a little zephyr like this, while he has only been to sea forty-five years.

JULY 5TH. Every rag on her all day to-day.

JULY 6TH. Fine day.... At work on old set of sails so as to be ready to unbend the good ones soon.... Capt. goes to bed for the first time in seven or eight weeks to-night and I'll bet he enjoys it. He usually has to wake me, but I'll have to wake him in the morning, I guess.

JULY 7TH. Don't say we can't sail. Have been going it since this morning at a good ten knots and in the squalls a good eleven.... I took lee wheel this afternoon in one of the squalls and I tell you, it was all both of us could do to keep her off she was so stiff.... Capt. won't get a chance to go to bed to-night, I guess.... Capt. looked up some signals to-day preparatory to firing away at some outward-bound vessel, in order to find out if we will have to run the gauntlet or not of Spanish cruisers.

JULY 8TH. Another gale! We have had more wind during the passage than almost any other in the Capt.'s experience.... Every little while she sends some water on top of the house and it sounds as if several hundred belaying pins had been dropped there from off the skysail yard. Rolling pretty badly.... Mammoth flock of birds around today.... Goonies, molymokes, Cape hens, and Cape pigeons were numerous.

JULY 9TH. The sea is enormous, the largest we have seen yet and we are rolling very badly. It is a frequent occurrence to take in seas now with us even and what would it be with an iron ship?

JULY 10TH. The Mate treated the Capt. and I to an apple to-day...it tasted mighty good even if it was gray headed and wrinkled.... The sea has been enormous to-day. Long, regular old he rollers. 30 to 35 feet high.... Capt. and I stood on top of the after house and we could look up at them.... The Port watch had the morning watch below. At noon they came out all washed, cut, and shaven. They looked amazingly whiter.

JULY 11TH. Been at work on sails all day. Capt. cut my hair and the Mate's hair and trimmed his beard and I cut Capt.'s hair; also did some shoemaking and mending.

JULY 12TH. 100th day out.

JULY 16TH. Guess this will be the longest passage the Capt. ever made around the Horn either way. He made it in 101 days last year. We will be 101 days plus a month and a half or two months. But I am glad that it is spun out long, only so I get in in time. On the lookout for vessels both for the sake of news and tobacco. The men would rather do without one less meal a day than without tobacco.

JULY 17TH. About 3 bells this forenoon a sail was raised on the weather bow. It proved to be a French bark bound out east in ballast. She was a very small vessel, iron, very shapely.... We asked her, "Is there peace or war in the United States?" She answered, "I do not know." ...She had single topgallants and hemp sails through-out.... She had a short poop and a great lot of truck around decks. The short poop gave her a funny appearance.

JULY 20TH. Wonder of wonders! I saw the greatest sight of its kind to-day that I ever saw. Just after noon a school of whales came up from astern, they were big fellows, all of them. The first one we saw attracted the Capt.'s and my attention by making a big splash close astern.... He came up right under the quarter and blew not 20 feet off.... He was enormous!... After he blew his back kept coming over and over until you would think there was no end.... Soon after two others made quite a rumpus astern...[one] jumped *half his length* out of the water!

JULY 21ST. Land Ho! Trinidad on the lee bow, six miles, at one o'clock this morning. At daylight it was astern some 12 miles. Very rocky and mountainous, but beautiful.... Chronometers were nearly right.... The English [Brazilians] own it and trees have been planted there and animals put on. Commence to tar down the rigging to-morrow and to get everything into shipshape for getting into port.

JULY 23RD. WAR!... War, plain war, and that is all we know. It is only one word and has only three letters at that, but it sets one thinking and wondering what is taking or has taken, or is to take place.... We sighted a French bark at 8 bells this afternoon.... She looked mighty fine and so much like an American vessel, duck sails, that Capt. thought she was one till he saw the flag.... She signaled us telling her name, *Mac Mahone* from St. Nazaire, France. We answered with ours and then asked her, "Are they at peace or war in the United States?" Answer, "C.G.N." WAR!!!! Whoop la!! We looked at each other and grinned a ghastly grin.... We suppose, of course, it is with Spain.... We are within a few hundred miles of St. Roque and we may expect [Spanish cruisers] here if anywhere. We take in our sidelights here as a precaution, which, let us hope, will have been unnecessary.... The Capt. is, of course, anxious to get reported so that his wife won't worry. I don't suppose my folks will worry very deeply on my account and I am rather glad of it...although it would be kind of nice to receive the welcome when I returned.... The cause for war may be Cuba's independence, but I should fight to avenge the *Maine*.... Fight to-day between the boy, Herman, and Chris Johnson, an able-bodied seaman. The former licked and both nearly went overboard.

JULY 24TH. Yesterday was the seventh consecutive day we saw vessels, and eleven vessels in those seven days.

JULY 25TH. Three vessels today.... We signaled [a Nova Scotian barkentine] but he merely answered with his ensign. Evidently had no signals. He came near enough across our bows to read the longitude on the blackboard.

JULY 26TH. Nary a vessel all day. All are bound our way, now that we have passed the Cape. Then too we are steering out of the usual track so as to avoid any chance of meeting Spanish cruisers or privateers.

JULY 28TH. I enjoy every day and every hour of the day, but they go so fast I can't keep track of them.... Capt. and I have coffee and crackers with orange marmalade every morning at 4 bells. Great stuff.

JULY 29TH. We have been listening to the delightful melody of the paint scraper all day.... The hens have laid nearly 650 eggs since we have been out.

AUGUST 1ST. I should like...perhaps a pear, or a peach, or an apple, or a grape, or an apricot...with an ear of corn and several sliced tomatoes.... Still, I get fat on salt horse and pea soup.

AUGUST 3RD. Been painting ship aloft. Yards and masts.... Find by measurement that I...have expanded my chest five inches since I came aboard. Thirty-six is my present measurement, expanded. The Capt.'s is forty-two.

AUGUST 4TH. I took the sun for Mr. Merriman and had a good time finding her.... The sailors are mending their clothes and painting their "kisten" boxes.[11] Even the Capt. has one varnishing it.

AUGUST 10TH. Beautiful day.... I discovered a three-masted ship when aloft this morning.... She had single topgallants and skysail. She was not visible from deck until after breakfast. Could see her topsails by noon.... She is a big fellow...American, undoubtedly.

AUGUST 12TH. Our friend, the ship, was about four miles astern at daybreak, and at night fell about two ships' lengths aft the beam and about a quarter mile to starboard. He has the advantage of us in that he is larger and has two studding sails, fore topmast and lower and that he gets the puffs first and walks up until we get them. He is a wooden ship and a pretty one. Built at Bath, Maine.... Her Capt. is seventy-five years old.... He is the ship *Charmer*, about 1,750 tons....[12] He sailed on the 23rd of April from Frisco...and said that [the war] began on the 21st.

AUGUST 14TH. Our friend is still abeam.... Today we have drawn closer somewhat and have watched each other pretty closely so as not to lose any time in making sail. We, being to windward...he can watch our movements and tell what is coming.

AUGUST 16TH. The *Charmer* was a little forward the beam and not over a mile off this morning at daybreak.... We entered the Gulf Stream about noon to-day.... The men signed their slop accounts to-night. All sorts and conditions of handwriting from a cross to the steward's bold stroke. One man claims that he was put aboard against his will and that he didn't sign papers at Port Townsend. He also threatens to sue the Capt. for $30,000 for taking him against his will. He is a Scotchman and very sincere in his arguments and very swift with his tongue. The boys are getting ready to go ashore. One fellow had on a swallowtail coat to-night.

AUGUST 17TH. It is now only 85 miles to Sandy Hook Light Ship. Hurray!!... If we get in to-morrow, we will have made it from the Equator up in twenty days, the shortest time the Capt. has ever made it in.... [The *Charmer*] was barely visible at sunset in the haze. Who said we can't sail when we get a chance? She couldn't use her studding sails and we beat her grandly.... The reason we gained this morning was perhaps because the Capt. and I did the steering for the forenoon watch and kept her straighter than the *Charmer*'s helmsman. We had a bad helmsman from twelve to two and lost, and a good one from two to four (the old man, Miller), and I steered the first dog watch.... Got both anchors over to-day.... The sailors are all enjoying the drunk they expect to have to-morrow by this time. They are singing forward now.

AUGUST 18TH. Land Ho! Jersey Coast at dawn.... All sorts of craft around us during the night. At dawn the *Charmer* was about two miles astern having kept the wind longer than we. Tugs hove up alongside both of us at 8 bells and told us the news. War is over and we have beaten. HIP!!!... We thought the tug Capt. was bluffing us but the Pilot boarded off the Hook at noon and told us the same story.... The harbor was something new and bewildering after seeing so little of rapid motion for so long. Saw a big transatlantic liner take aboard her pilot, and a whole boatload of watermelons go overboard, a fresh air party on an old sidewheel steamer in tow of a tug, and a hundred other things. Our sails were all stowed by 6 bells this afternoon.... We let go our anchor off the statue at 8 bells this afternoon and the voyage was done.... Everything is flags and I am glad to see them. Capt. went off in a tug and came back in one of the little spit boxes so numerous here. He brought letters and we devoured them. I shall go ashore to-morrow.

AUGUST 19TH. I went and shopped. Paid my bet of a box of candy to the Capt.[13] Got a hat and did New York. My feet are pretty sore from the pavements. Came aboard at 2 bells to-night.

AUGUST 20TH. I took my dunnage ashore.... Before leaving the old hooker we dressed ship for the naval parade and she looked pretty

> fine I tell you.... Got my gear over to the Fall River boat, and off my mind. Saw the parade from the Washington Building at #1 Broadway. Right at the Battery. *Brooklyn*, *New York*, *Texas*, *Indiana*, *Iowa*, *Massachusetts*, and a host of yachts and such boats. The excursion boats were packed and all listed terribly...towards the ships. The *New York* fired a salute opposite the Battery with her bow guns. I sailed on the Fall River boat *Puritan* to-night and saw the last of the old hooker and the Captain. I am sorry that my story is done, but it is nevertheless, at least for now.

Despite Carleton Allen's effusive account of the well-ordered life at sea aboard the bark *Guy C. Goss*, Captain William Besse's career as a ship-owner was nearing a sad end. That story plays out in the Appendix, page 351.

---

1. In April 1889 Besse had replied to an inquiry from Mallett regarding taking a young man as passenger: " If you wish to take him and he will accept the regular ship fare, and no extras...you can take him for seventy-five cents a day...would like him to pay $100 before the ship sails...and the balance when he leaves the ship."

2. The term "pilothouse" was sometimes used for the vestibule leading to the forward companionway to the main cabin, although the more common term was "coach house."

3. In June 1892 the 1,673-ton Freeport, Maine, ship *Sintram* arrived at Boston from the Columbia River with a spar cargo of 394 pieces for H. Pigeon & Sons Co. The largest "stick" measured 170 feet long, 30 inches at the butt, 25 at the center, 15 at the top. Another was 130 feet. *Bangor Industrial Journal*, 10 June 1892.

4. Mr. Merriman was surely one of Captain Mallett's relatives.

5. Back in April 1890, when it had evidently been impossible or impractical to try to find a crew in the labor-starved Puget Sound lumber ports, Captain J. N. Knowles, the *Goss*'s San Francisco agent, instructed Captain Mallett regarding the advances and bonuses that had to be paid to a San Francisco shipping master. Mallett's crew was to be delivered from San Francisco to the *Goss* by the coastal steamer *Al-Ki* (built by Goss & Sawyer at Bath in 1884 for William Besse and others). Knowles wrote:

> The advances and bonus will have to be paid here as soon as the steamer leaves the wharf. Fletcher has made arrangements to send them up on *Al-Ki*, sailing tomorrow. The crew are all ready. Steamer will go alongside your vessel and deliver the men to you. The amount to be paid here will be

12 Sailors	Advance $35	Bonus $40	Pay $900
Carpenter	$35	$40	$75
Passage up 13 men	$10		$130
Total			$1,205

> I am asking you to reply promptly whether I should pay the money here, as you cannot get the men otherwise. Will you receipt us the amount of same or shall I draw on Capt. Besse for it?

Evidently the controlling reach of the notorious San Francisco shipping masters reached far beyond that port. The corrupt system of manning ships, involving the payment of advances for the men to settle up their inflated boardinghouse debts, with added extorted bonuses, or "blood money," long defied efforts at reform. Underlying the problem was the inability of sailors to keep out of the clutches of the "crimp" or sailor's boardinghouse or shipping master, who strove to keep the sailor in his debt. Indeed, given the riotous condition newly landed sailors characteristically assumed, only a crimp would have them. As Captain George Ginn of the bark *Coryphene* observed, "The life of the mariner is attractive only to men of a certain type of character, the predominant feature of which is thoughtlessness of the future." *New York Maritime Register*, 12 March 1884.

6. Many entries in Carleton's log, most of which have been deleted for brevity, were devoted to birds and also fish, both caught and uncaught. Goonies, sometimes known as "black-footed albatrosses," and other hook-billed seabirds—including most notably the Great Wandering Albatross, were caught with a "triangle." A triangle was fashioned from three sticks, or else by tacking a piece of tin with a triangular cutout to the end of a shingle-sized piece of board. Pieces of pork were seized along the apex of the triangle. The trap was tethered to a 100- to 200-foot line. Just as the swimming bird struck at the bait the line was jerked taut, catching the hook of the upper beak. Line, trap, and bird were hauled rapidly in without giving the bird an opportunity to spread its wings.

7. Presumably the forward room of the two-room house.

8. Old sails had been bent for the tropics; new, strong sails were now bent in preparation for heavy weather.

9. Wooden ships could be copper-sheathed; iron or steel ships could not be, due to the corrosive action of dissimilar metals. Anti-fouling coatings applied to metal ships were of limited efficacy.

10. A carrot-shaped (but smooth!) hardwood rigging tool used to open rope strands.

11. Sea chests.

12. *Charmer* was built at Bath in 1881. She was barged circa 1911. Captain Joseph Holmes was a native of Mystic, Connecticut, where he died at the age of ninety-six. Matthews, *American Merchant Ships,* Series I, p. 288.

13. The bet was over the identification of the rig of a distant vessel in the South Atlantic.

Chapter 15

A Roaring Forties Passage

Carleton Allen Joins Walter Mallett Aboard Hawaiian Isles.

AFTER LANDING AT New York aboard the bark *Guy C. Goss* in 1898, Carleton Allen traveled to Boston to take entrance exams for the Massachusetts Institute of Technology. In 1902 he graduated with a Bachelor of Science degree in Ocean Engineering. He did graduate work on the revolutionary Parsons-type steam turbine, which he helped to introduce to this country. In 1903 Allen was in Baltimore, involved with the installation of turbines in a power plant, when he was invited by Captain Mallett to spend Christmas aboard *Hawaiian Isles*, then discharging sugar at Brooklyn. Mallett coaxed Carleton to join the ship for its next voyage as third mate.[1]

In July 1901 Walter Mallett, then in Honolulu, had written to his brother Wilbert back in Maine of his new command, the steel four-masted bark *Hawaiian Isles*, of San Francisco:

> SHE IS A FINE SHIP and a very fine looking one. Her cabin accommodations are good and commodious but not very clean. In fact they were very dirty.... As soon as the coal is out there will be a marked improvement along that line as well as some others.
>
> I had quite a picnic with Capt. Rice.... He was more or less sober and didn't take kindly to being relieved. He...was on the verge of the DTs. I got him on board the vessel and kept him there until he was sober and doctored up so he could straighten out his accounts with my help. I had to do all the writing.... He was a physical giant and a man of enough natural ability if he could only let liquor alone....
>
> Honolulu is a very busy place and a very cosmopolitan one. All nations are represented and there are all shades of color nicely graded.... I have never seen so many American vessels in any port at the same time, and many are good-sized ones too.... I have not even unpacked all our things yet. Capt. Rice could have taken all his on a wheelbarrow.[2]

Hawaiian Isles was built by C. Connell & Co. at Glasgow, Scotland, in 1892, the last year (excepting war-skewed 1920) when the world's sail tonnage increased over the previous year's. About 70 percent of the sailing vessels launched in 1892 were British, including about seventy-five large square-riggers; all but one was built of steel. Most were four-masted barks. (Germany launched seventeen steel square-riggers. The only American square-riggers built were William Besse's *Olympic* and the Sewall's huge *Roanoke,* both of wood.)

Hawaiian Isles was built to the order of Captain Andrew Nelson, of San Francisco, a Swedish-born Sacramento River steamboat man who became a sailing ship owner.[3] Since foreign-built ships could not gain American registry, Nelson placed *Hawaiian Isles* and her sister, the *John Ena*, under the flag of the Hawaiian Republic.

In 1900, following annexation, certain ships, including these two, were allowed to come under the American flag. The bark was then sold to Welch & Company which, in association with the old Boston-rooted C. Brewer & Company—once owners of Walter Mallett's first command, *Syren*—ran the prosperous Planters' Line of sailing packets between San Francisco and the Hawaiian islands.[4]

Whaling first brought Americans to Hawaii; sugar kept them there. Welch and Brewer were both engaged in the sugar business. Leaving the islands with cargoes of sugar for the East Coast, returning by way of Australia, Walter and Kate Mallett would make three 'round-the-world voyages in *Hawaiian Isles*. In 1908 the Planters' Line fleet was sold to the Matson Navigation Company; in 1909 Matson disposed of the sailing fleet, and the Malletts temporarily moved home to Topsham.[5]

But in January 1904, in a throwback to a historic and storied trade then in its final years, *Hawaiian Isles* was lying at New York's historic South Street, loading a general cargo for Melbourne and Sydney. She would follow the same lonely route which young Frank Stone, in command of the bark *Jonathan Bourne*, had followed.

Once again, Carleton:

> HAVING BEEN INFLUENCED by a strong desire to see a bit of the world, I have again decided to take a voyage at sea.... I feel it will prove a very profitable experience in many ways as serving to widen my knowledge and experience, as well as my chest.
>
> FEB. 3RD, 1904. We sailed at about 10:30 this morning from Pier 12 East River in tow of the tugs *D. B. Dearborn* and *Baltic*. There was a strong N. W. wind blowing and the *Baltic* kept alongside to keep us straight.... Began to make sail about noon and it was a hard job with

Aboard four-masted bark Hawaiian Isles *lying at the Spreckles Sugar Refinery, Brooklyn, December 1903.*
CARLETON ALLEN. COURTESY OF JAMES F. JUNG.

the ropes full of ice. The tugs left us about 2 P.M. and the pilot was taken off by a row boat from the pilot boat *New York* shortly after. The pilot took a pocket full of final letters. The watches started about 6 o'clock.... The port watch consists of the following:

First Mate J. B. MonteithAge 30, Nova Scotia
Third Mate C. B. Allen23, Mass.
Crew:
John M. Graves 22, Maine
John Jansen "Fred" 22, Sweden
Chas. Anderson "Charlie" 25, Sweden
Gustav Westernen "Blondie" 21, Sweden
Ludwig Nelson "Norman" 18, Norway
Kristian Nelson "Nelson" 23, Denmark
Sima Patar "Sam" 23, Finland
Boy Jas. S. Scott "Jimmy" 16, Scotland
Starboard watch:
Second Mate Chas. Carey 44, New Jersey

Sailors aboard bark Hawaiian Isles *at the mizzen topgallant halyard.*
CARLETON ALLEN. COURTESY OF JAMES F. JUNG.

Crew:
Christian Anderson "Chris" 31, Sweden
Axle Anderson "Axle" 22, Sweden
Olaf Oleson "William" 18, Sweden
Antton Mannonen "Tony" 26, Finland
Swan Mansen "Swan" 23, Sweden
Paul Martens "Paul" 21, Germany
Karl Reiche "Karl" 21, Germany
Carpenter "Chip" 51, Sweden
"Sails" France
Steward "Ah Foo" Shanghai
Cook Geo. Lum 38, Honolulu
Boy Allan Howes "Allan" 17, Australia
It is not what can be called a good crew and they have been somewhat addicted to smelly water, which has gone to their heads somewhat.

FEB. 4TH. We have the dirt, snow, and ice mostly cleaned from the decks now, so things look a little better than they did.

Sailors aboard bark Hawaiian Isles.
CARLETON ALLEN. COURTESY OF JAMES F. JUNG.

FEB. 8TH. 270 miles. What a breeze! The best day's run the Captain has ever made in this ship.... The Captain appears to have aged considerably since six years ago when I was last with him, but he is the same old Captain in most respects with the genial geam in his eye.... The duties of Third Mate thus far have consisted chiefly in holding down the poop with the mate.

FEB. 9TH. Mrs. Mallett shows herself but little these days. Too little I think. I never saw a couple so congenial to each other as this one. Their opinions, ideas, and actions have become so molded along the same lines after so many years of constant contact and companionship, much closer than it would be ashore. They get a whole lot out of life few of us have found or will find, even if they do miss much by being at sea so much of the time. They are good readers—readers of good material—and are well informed on most subjects, for they remember and discuss what they read, having time to do what people ashore do not get the opportunity to do.

FEB. 10TH. The mate tells a story of how the Captain of a certain ship was washed through the after end of the after house with the two men at the wheel and down into the cabin and forward to the poop bulkhead. This happened in one of those zephyrs which occur off the River Platte.[6]

FEB. 11TH. The duties of third mate are not particularly difficult or laborious yet it is work I am not accustomed to do and it makes me tired. I think the getting accustomed to keeping watch is the hardest thing.[7]

FEB. 12TH. The mate tells a story of a Russian carpenter the Nova Scotia ship *Norwood* picked up in Australia, who came aboard with a set of tools which consisted of six pairs of sheep shears in a gunny sack. The man had a beard like an anarchist.... He was no carpenter...and in trying to impress certain rudiments of the trade into the anarchist's noodle the chief officer planed a bare spot on the back of his head.

Bark Hawaiian Isles, *February 5, 1904. One day out of New York.*
CARLETON ALLEN. COURTESY OF JAMES F. JUNG.

February 16, 1904, bark Hawaiian Isles. *View aloft from the bowsprit.*
Carleton Allen. Courtesy of James F. Jung.

FEB. 17TH. A spanking easterly breeze which seems like the trades.... Men at work making...sennett for chafing gear....[8] Mrs. Mallett was kind enough to make the mate and I some candy today for our coughs. Our coughs are perceptibly worse in Mrs. Mallett's hearing. We are carrying full sail and have just about all she will stagger under, too. We celebrate a full moon tonight.

Bow of the bark Hawaiian Isles, *February 16, 1904.*
CARLETON ALLEN. COURTESY OF JAMES F. JUNG.

FEB. 18TH. Mrs. Mallett and the Captain keep the mate and I supplied with candy, oranges, and apples.

FEB. 19TH. The second mate is fast losing the respect of the Captain, mate, and his men, inasmuch as he does not prove much of a sailor man. He is...short, wiry, and looks like a sailor with a variety of experiences not too elevating behind him. He consumes seven pounds of tobacco each watch and can swear in fourteen different languages, forward, backward, right- or left-handed.... The Captain showed me a trick or two in working Longitude today and the mate gave me some help also during the dog watch.

FEB. 22ND. This morning when we came on deck at 4 A.M. the emigrant Nelson in our watch reported, "Watch is aft sir" when all hands were not aft. Fred was asleep in his bunk and had to be pulled out by the mate.... Charlie and Nelson got into an argument about it and Charlie got a cut on the A.M....they received a lecture from the captain after breakfast.

FEB. 23RD. The mate, Mr. Monteith, is a man of action and of energy. He is a bright man who has not neglected his opportunities. His has been a hard school...but the present result is a first class man and a gentleman. He is a thorough sailor. He is treating me in the best way possible, apparently overlooking my ignorance but helping me to correct and learn.... I have received as an additional chore, the oversight of gear aloft.... There is a vast difference between the first and second mates.

MCH. 7TH. A full-rigged three-masted ship passed between us and the moon as we were coming about at 11 P.M.... The second mate is showing up about as poor a sailor as the third mate.... The sailmaker is a queer character—a bald-headed Frenchman..... The carpenter is about the plumb of this aggregation as far as eccentricities go...short, wiry, active...an unintelligible brogue and an expert with tobacco juice and snuff. He has prevailed upon me to take his "photo," as he calls it, and has rewarded me by making a bookcase. The cook, of Hawaiian extraction, is short, busy, and cheerful. Jimmy—bright, active, small for seventeen years, Scotch, son of captain of *Gerard C. Tobey* and will make a good sailor.... John Graves, who lives in the midship house, is a Topsham man and a "Down Easter" of the most aggravated type. He is full of expressions typical to Maine's rural regions..."Gee Whiz!" "Lickety Larrup," and "Swiggle," "gosh dinged," "gosh hang it," and plain "gosh."[9]

MCH. 9TH. Booming along with ideal weather for the trade winds. "Bed bugs are healthy—never saw one sick."

MCH. 11TH. The ship is still with us.

MCH. 12TH. Bending sails all day.... At daylight our friend, the ship, was some miles over on our port quarter, but during the forenoon we hauled gradually together.... She is the *Ainsdale* of Liverpool, 1,700 tons...from Hamburg—52 days out—and for Melbourne, too.... She then set the signal—"Let us keep together for mutual company or protection...." To this we answered, "All Right" and she set the signal, "The Captain is invited to come on board," and we answered, "Thank you, sometime."

MCH. 18TH. And a wonderful thing has happened...the third mate has been promoted to take the place of the second mate and will attempt to fill that place. I think it is pretty good—one month at sea and second mate of a four-masted bark. At this rate I will be captain in a few weeks more. It happened this way. Carey got worked up over his inability and came to the Captain this A.M. and asked him to be

"Signalizing," South Atlantic, bark Hawaiian Isles, *March 13, 1904.*
CARLETON ALLEN. COURTESY OF JAMES F. JUNG.

allowed to go into the forecastle, giving up the berth of second mate. The Captain said it would have been only a matter of a few days before he disrated the second mate anyway. Big Charlie becomes my boatswain. It will mean much work for Captain Mallett.... The watch isn't much—only two who are anything like sailors, Chris, and Antton of the shoved-in face.

MCH. 19TH. I have had to set five sails today and made no very serious mistakes. Have had but three and a half hours sleep out of the last twenty-eight hours.... Caught William sitting down on lookout last night and had to call down Paul several times, but it didn't seem to hurt his feelings much.... Captain claims the ex-second mate was perfectly harmless and perhaps weak in his garret.

MCH. 22ND. Found Paul asleep in the forecastle during his watch on deck last night.... They are a pretty tough crowd. There are only about three men I can trust in the watch. *Ainsdale* out of sight—fifteen days in company.

British ship Ainsdale, *South Atlantic, March 13, 1904.*
CARLETON ALLEN. COURTESY JAMES F. JUNG.

MCH. 23RD. My watch still continues to be decidedly bum, indolent, and deceitful.... The Bos'n is a hard character to handle. He is a regular old shellback with nearly all their faults and many of their good points.

MCH. 25TH. The gang did a better afternoon's work and I feel much encouraged.

MCH. 27TH. We made the island of Tristian da Cunha abeam at daylight.

MCH. 28TH. Paul and the Bos'n had a seance this morning and would have come to blows had not the second mate intervened his carcass. Came pretty near thumping Paul myself. He is German of about nineteen, short, chunky, and has a bad temper.... These moonlight nights are something grand and weird.

MCH. 29TH. More Paul. When I relieved at midnight, Paul came from the wheel and reported the course and started down the weather poop ladder. The mate objected and respectfully advised Paul to use the lee side, but Paul was not very rapid in bearing off in that direction, so the mate fetched him a good, hearty kick "between the house and the barn," and before Paul had fully recovered his surprise, he received a slap on the jaw that laid him flat. He disappeared to the main deck in short order, but as he was not rapid enough in getting forward, the mate took him by the trousers and back of the neck and waltzed him forward in short order.[10]

MCH. 31ST. A howling gale for the last 24 hours.... Our decks have been pretty full of water all day and it gives promise of a lively night. I know of no more beautiful or fascinating picture than a ship placed like this in a big sea with bright clear sunlight between the squalls, making everything sparkle and shine as if set with gems.

APRIL 1ST. Long Cape Horn rollers. The captain thinks they are the longest he has ever seen.... We calculate them as 1,000 to 1,200 feet long...and at *least* 40 feet deep. Some will reach 50 feet...the sea looks like a vast undulating prairie with its sweeping hills and valleys.

APRIL 3RD. *Man Overboard!* Last night it began to blow and how it blew!...the sea was terrific, due to the strong current which always runs here off the Cape.[11] This morning, just after 8 bells when I was at breakfast, she shipped a big sea and washed my bosun from the main deck. He was standing with some others of the watch at the foot of the port ladder and it washed him to port, then back to starboard under both poop ladders and over the rail. He had on oilskins and sank sooner than we would have been able to reach him, even if it had been possible to bring the ship around in that sea…the ship was making 11 knots at the time…. The same wave…took Jimmy from the galley door, carried him aft to the break of the poop, and forward again to the Number 3 hatch, where John was perched. John saw him coming, made a lunge for him, and dragged him out of the water onto the hatch…. During the night the sea was one mass of foam…. The moon showed through the hurrying clouds frequently, lighting up the weird scene, the like of which I have never seen before.

APR. 10TH. [The carpenter] says: "The reason the bosun was washed over was because he told so many lies." The carpenter himself is a close second.

APR. 13TH. At 4 bells this afternoon, just as I had turned in, I heard cries of "Man Overboard" and hurrying feet. I tumbled on deck and we got her about and back to the swimming man—the ex-second

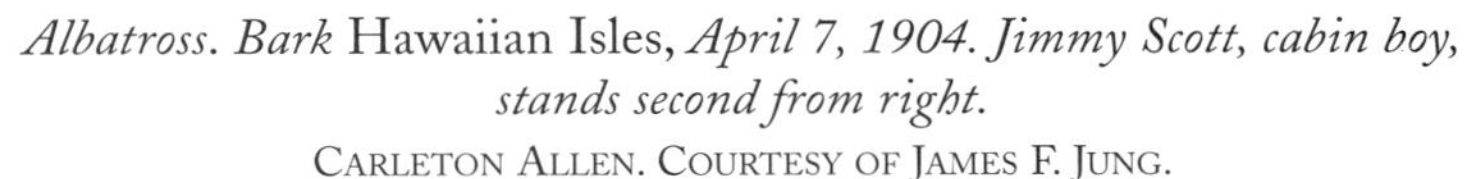

Albatross. Bark Hawaiian Isles, *April 7, 1904. Jimmy Scott, cabin boy, stands second from right.*
CARLETON ALLEN. COURTESY OF JAMES F. JUNG.

mate in less than eight minutes. A life buoy was thrown within a few feet of him when he went by the stern, a line from the forecastle head, and a line with a life buoy attached from amidships when we came back to him, but he deliberately ignored them all.... The life-buoy from amidships was within two good strokes, but he refused it—turning his back and letting the goonie pick at his bare toes and clothing. We tried to bring her about again, but she had lost headway and missed stays, and before we could wear around he was no longer to be seen.

APR. 16TH. A man can be nautical long before he can be a sailor. Now nine-tenths of these yachtsmen who own a 30-foot sloop and hire a man to sail her, are nautical and are blowing around more nautical terms than any sailor ever uses, but my experience is teaching me to become one of the old, tar-soaked, shell-backed, barnacled, and salt horse sailors of the practical type, who is not going to sea for the fun of it, but to get his grub. By this I do not wish to imply that I do not enjoy the voyage, for I do every minute.

Captain Walter Mallett, bark Hawaiian Isles, *at the standard compass, Indian Ocean, April 12, 1904. The compass stand, or binnacle, has been securely lashed against rogue waves. The standard compass was the compass of reference, and was, by its commanding location, used for taking bearings.*
CARLETON ALLEN. COURTESY OF JAMES F. JUNG.

Apr. 17th. Karl is laid up again with the rheumatism and had a bit of a loony spell this morning.

Apr. 18th. Another tragedy! Karl Reiche jumped overboard sometime during the night. Owing to his strange actions yesterday morning, we locked him into the hospital in the midships house yesterday, but he broke the lock of the door and disappeared, leaving his clothes and belongings.... The young fellow with his means and resources could have little to look forward to in life, laid up as he was with rheumatism.... Speaking concisely, it beats the Dutch! The bark we saw yesterday was about abeam this morning and we signaled her. She is the *Shandon*, London for Sydney, etc., ninety-two days out. My watch is certainly getting small.

Apr. 19th. The worst gale yet.

Apr. 20th. Terrific gale from the N. E.... I never saw anything like the way the ship looked this afternoon with the spoon drift flying over the waves sometimes as high as the foreyard. A wonderful, wild night.

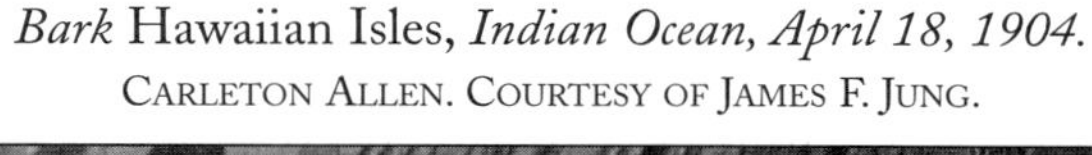

Bark Hawaiian Isles, *Indian Ocean, April 18, 1904.*
Carleton Allen. Courtesy of James F. Jung.

Apr. 21st. At 9:30 p.m.…all hands began to take in the rags until we had only three sails…about as soon as we got our sails in and furled, it began to breeze up from the S. W. and how it breezed!… We were making eleven knots with three sails set and two of these drawing…. This takes the plum for gales.

Apr. 22nd. A great day this. Gigantic sea running, but it is long as well as deep…. The waves carry us along bodily as if we were a chip on the surface of Lake Almonessen in a strong breeze…. Allan fell from the port main upper topsail yardarm this morning about daylight. I had sent him up to overhaul the gear, stop up the gaskets, and put in rovings and he turned sick at the rolling and let go. He caught on the outboard upper topsail lift and got back onto the yard, thereby saving his life, for he would have gone overboard.

Apr. 23rd. This gale has lasted for five days…. We have made 1,580 miles the past week and that is a fine record. The best week's work the captain ever made.

The Indian Ocean comes aboard Hawaiian Isles, *April 20, 1904.*
Carleton Allen. Courtesy of James F. Jung.

APR. 24TH. Last night during my second dog watch a hail squall struck us.... We could hear it hissing on the water long before it struck.... Inside of ten minutes it was blowing a howling gale and we were roaring along at 13 knots for a while.... Am willing to state under oath that [seas] were at least 60 feet deep.

APRIL. 29TH. Still more northerly gale and still our good record continues. We are close hauled and making southing but will soon get a slant so that we can make Cape Otway. We are now sailing across the mouth of the Great Australian Bight.

Bark Hawaiian Isles, *Indian Ocean, April 31, 1904. The view aft from the topgallant fo'c's'le deck. The cylindrical white object at left is the starboard running light; the lantern was lit and inserted below, under the shelter of the deck, and hoisted into place. For reasons not entirely clear, the shank of the anchor in the foreground has been encased in knotwork. A spare spar is lashed between the forward house and the fo'c's'le deck. A spare anchor, painted white, stands in place ahead of the bell. Note the foot of the triangular crojik (cross-jack) sail.*
CARLETON ALLEN. COURTESY OF JAMES F. JUNG.

MAY 3RD. In sight of land to the westward of Otway at daylight. At 11 A.M. we were abreast of the Cape and set our signals.... A three-masted bark, the Norwegian *Thora*...a three-masted British ship, the *Plenthesilia*...and another three-masted ship in shore which corresponds to the *Ainsdale*. She had lost her main yard. She had her ensign and number flying evidently for our benefit...it certainly is a wonderful coincidence that we should be out here together after two months of sailing. We first saw her off Cape St. Roque, South America.... The shore is high and well wooded generally with mountain peaks showing in the backwards.

MAY 4. Ninety-one days from New York to Melbourne.... Our tug... came alongside just after Mrs. Mallett had hauled in her third barracouta, at 10:30, and after some haggling we took her line. The pilot came off from the pilot boat *Victoria* just at this time and a wild scene of confusion only seen aboard ship when shortening sail for port, ensued.... All the afternoon we gazed at new sights and beautiful ones... and at last just at sunset the pilot muttered, "Let her go," and over went the anchor.... The customhouse officers plastered us all over with red tape and sealing wax. Nearly everything is dutiable and such a duty—50 to 75 percent. We can use none of our own stores while in port unless we pay this duty.

THIS ENDS THE VOYAGE. On the whole of it it can be called a prosperous one in spite of the three misfortunes which came with it. In all we have covered 15,158 miles in 91 days.... The *Fort George* was 107 days out and Captain Mallett is greatly elated.[12]

At the beginning of this same voyage, Captain Walter Mallett had written to his brother Wilbert, the distinguished principal of the Farmington (Maine) Normal School. Wilbert was addressed as "Bert" by a select few. Walter's first account was penned in the cabin of *Hawaiian Isles* on January 24, 1904:

DEAR BERT,
I left Topsham last Monday and got back into harness Tuesday. And the mate went home that night to take his exams for a master's certificate.

They have been loading the ship rapidly.... Have written Kate to start for N. Y. Tuesday so she will not be hurried about her sea shopping.

Our cargo consists of most everything in the way of merchandise. There will be 2,000 bbls, of rosin, cottonseed oil, lubricating oil, turpentine, churns, sewing machines, bathtubs, lamp chimneys, lamps, clothespins, roofing slate, hard pine, soft pine, hickory, walnut, and oak lumber, barbed wire, common wire, wooden butter dishes, tool handles, and I don't know how much else. The ship will be packed full, and will then not be down to her deep load marks, so we will be in better trim than on the passage home....

Walter then dove into politics and religion. He thought that William Jennings Bryan was as "crazy" in his politics as was the cult leader Frank Sandford in matters theological.[13]

At sea on February 21 Walter began a long letter (here severely excerpted) made up of installments:

OUR CREW ARE all young Scandinavians except three boys. We have the same carpenter we had last voyage, a good mechanic but a regular "crank." The steward is Chinese and smart as a whip. The cook is half Chinese and half Hawaiian. They are both small but seem to be able to do their work satisfactorily. The 2nd mate hails from New York; he seems honest and willing but I don't know much about his work. I like John Graves very much. He is smart and ambitious and will make a good officer. I shall take a great deal of pleasure in helping him along. Allan, the Australian boy, will give up the sea when we get to Melbourne but the other boy is as fat and contented as can be. He likes the sea life. I think I wrote you that his father was master of the *Gerard C. Tobey* now in this employ [Welch & Co.]. Carleton is as happy as can be. He stands watch with the mate and eats with us at the first table. He has a natural love for the sea and everything nautical appeals to him as it does to you. He is an entirely different character from Pierce Drew....[14]

Walter then listed their recent reading, including Fiske's *History of the United States*, Green's *History of the English People*, and the contents of a new Seaman's Friend Society library.

MARCH 13TH. Lat. 20 S Long. 34 W. 39 days at sea. Last Friday I disrated our 2nd mate and put him in the forecastle.... Carleton now has charge of the starboard watch and does first-rate. I promoted our best sailor to be boatswain and he stands watch with him. I will have to stand watch with them in real bad weather.... Just before supper a sea slapped up and threw about two quarts of water through the window into our room. It is surprising how much surface that much water will cover.

SAT. MARCH 26TH. Lat. 35.10 Long. 14.31 W. 53 days at sea. Our new team of officers are doing first-rate, and the old 2nd mate seems much happier in his present position than before.

APRIL 9TH. Lat. 43.10 S Long. 36 E. 66 days at sea. We had a sad accident last Sunday morning. Just after eight o'clock she shipped a heavy sea on deck which washed the boats'n overboard...there was nothing we could do but to keep on our course.... I have had two men fall from aloft and killed but never lost one overboard before. Wish you could see some of the albatross they have caught lately. They have measured several that have varied from 10ft. to 10ft. 9 in. from tip to tip of their wings.

APRIL 18TH. Lat. 42.53 S Long. 75.02 E. 75 days at sea. We have had rather hard luck with our crew for the last three weeks. Last Thursday, about 2 P.M., our disrated 2nd mate deliberately left his work and jumped overboard without any cause whatever as far as anybody on board knows.... One of the men said afterwards that the former 2nd mate said at breakfast time that he would never see Melbourne. He was an Irishman, forty-four years old.

Sometime last night another man jumped overboard, a young German about twenty years old.... Nobody knew anything about it until after daylight when Mr. Allen discovered he was not in the room. I hope this will be the end of this business. I have never had anything of the kind before.

MAY 1ST. Lat. 42.08 S Long. 136.20 E. 88 days out. We have had a fine run since I last wrote. Last week we had a succession of hard gales.... I wonder how long the *Fort George* was making the passage. The Capt. was determined to beat us this time and I shall not feel bad if he does, especially if we can do as well as the *Starbuck* did last year which was 95 days. Sewall's ship, *Dirigo*, was 124 days to Sydney last year.[15]

MELBOURNE, MAY 7TH. We arrived here last Wednesday P.M. after a passage of 91 days, which is the best time from N. Y. that has been made for some time. The *Fort George* was 107 days so we beat her three days more than we did coming home from Honolulu.... Suppose we will be in Sydney three weeks as we have 2,390 tons of cargo for there and only 2,042 tons for here.... The Capt. [of the *Ainsdale*] was on board this morning and seems to be a fine fellow. Is going to church with us tomorrow.

Kate joins in love and best wishes to you all.
Yours affectionately
W. M. Mallett

---

1. Some insurers frowned on the carriage of passengers aboard cargo ships, and as a result, passengers were signed on as crew members for nominal wages (to be promptly returned). When one was carried, a third mate was something of a supernumerary, neither fish nor fowl. As the third mate stood the first mate's watch, Mallett might have figured that his young first mate would enjoy Carleton's company.

2. My thanks to Richard P. Mallett—Wilbert Mallett's son—for use of this and other letters, and to his daughter, Anne Mallett, for transcribing them.

3. Iron clippers of the 1870s were followed by iron medium-clippers of the '80s and the big steel carriers of the '90s. Among this great fleet were ships noted for their unsurpassed beauty and others that clearly were not. Iron and steel ships were stronger than wooden vessels, and leaked less. They also proved much more dangerous for sailors, a result of narrow beam and deep lading which often kept their decks awash for weeks at a time. Although in the early years of the nineteenth-century British customs' measurements penalized beam, by the era of iron ships this was no longer the case. Aside from the old narrow-beam habit, there was concern that beamy metal ships would buckle. It was also felt that wide ships would roll too abruptly and would be slower, notwithstanding that beamy American ships—including many sailed under the British flag—had long proved both fears to be groundless. Keen price competition between builders in later years may also have continued the cheaper narrow model. See Hall, "Report on the Shipbuilding Industry," p. 200. With registered dimensions of 270 feet by 43.1 feet by 23.6 feet depth of hold, *Hawaiian Isles'* beam was on the broad side of the scale, and her single topgallants and three skysails may also have reflected American influence, via Captain Nelson, in her design.

4. Among the Welch fleet was the *Gerard C. Tobey,* formerly of the Besse fleet. Sold to Matson, she was resold to be barged in 1910.

5. Swedish-born Captain William Matson was backed by the wealthy Spreckles sugar-refining family. See Fred Stindt, *Matson's Century of Ships* (Kelseyville, 1991). Shorn of her skysail poles, *Hawaiian Isles* became the Alaska Packers Association *Star of Greenland*, a member of the great fleet of old sailers seasonally employed sailing from San Francisco to Alaska and back. In 1929 she was sold to the Rydbergska Stiftlelse, a Swedish charitable nautical school, for use as a training ship, and renamed *Abraham Rydberg*. Her 1930 124-day passage from San Francisco to Dublin was the last made by a square-rigger around the Horn carrying California grain. In the early 1940s, under the command of young Captain Oscar Malmberg, the bark became something of a celebrity while trading between American East Coast ports and Brazil. Sold in 1943, she became the Portuguese *Foz Do Douro*. In 1945 engines were installed, and her rig further reduced. She was scrapped in 1957. Lieut. (j.g.) John Lyman, "Fifty Years of Sail: The Bark *Abraham Rydberg*," *American Neptune*, vol. 2, p. 292. Lyman reported

that about 1900 a playful second mate aboard *Hawaiian Isles* named Murphy, during washdowns, hove water, wooden bucket and all, at the sailors to see if he could knock them down.

6. For zephyrs read pamperos, violent storms that make up on the Argentine pampas and come off the land with great suddenness.

7. Four hours on duty followed by four hours off duty, i.e., the duty hours of a ship with the crew divided into two watches.

8. Sennett, or sennett matting was woven from old rope. A large ship would have tons of it placed aloft during a long voyage, to be removed shortly before arriving home. Presumably worn chafing gear was then sold as "junk," for which there was a good market from papermakers and manufacturers of artificial leather.

9. Graves, having graduated from "boy," was being treated as an apprentice officer of sorts, and lived in the "halfdeck," not in the sailors' forecastle. Close contact with sailors was not thought desirable for boys or apprentices. Graves first went to sea in 1901 aboard the new Bath-built four-masted bark *William P. Frye*. When the *Frye* was towed to Hunter's Point, Queens, to load case oil for Shanghai, young Graves attempted, not entirely successfully, to keep a journal. The entry for Sunday, October 27, read: "Went over to N.Y. City, saw more than I ever saw in my life (Central Park)." Library, Maine Maritime Museum.

10. Shipboard etiquette required sailors on the sacred poop to keep to leeward.

11. This was the region where young William Besse, mate of *Western Belle*, was washed off the after house and lost.

12. *Fort George*, formerly a British ship built at Belfast in 1884, came under the American flag with the annexation of Hawaii. She and the *Hawaiian Isles* were both owned by Welch & Co. in 1904.

13. Sandford, one of the fathers of Pentecostalism, founded a commune called Shiloh in Durham, Maine. Sandford was imprisoned for manslaughter in 1911 following the deaths of six persons aboard the church's schooner *Coronet*, which had been inadequately provisioned for a transatlantic passage.

14. Pierce Drew was the son of Captain Edwin Drew, senior captain of the Welch fleet, and genial master of the bark *R. P. Rithet*. A native of Hallowell, Maine, he was the younger brother of Capt. John H. Drew, who wrote in the *Boston Journal* as "The Kennebecker." Young Drew had been a passenger aboard *Hawaiian Isles* on her passage to New York, and the Malletts had spent much time counseling him as to how best to make something of his life. They were concerned that he had unreasonably optimistic expectations of his natural abilities. Evidently they did not fully appreciate the value of family connections with the sugar business, in whose bosom he would pompously prosper.

15. The 2,025-ton ship *Tillie Starbuck*, built in 1883 at Chester, Pennsylvania, was the first large American iron sailing ship. The four-masted bark *Dirigo*, Walter's future command, built at Bath in 1894, was the first large American steel sailing ship.

Chapter 16

AUSTRALIA TO HAWAII

The Bark Hawaiian Isles *Loads Coal for a Pacific Voyage*

ON MAY 6, 1904, *Hawaiian Isles* was towed into Victoria Dock, Melbourne, described by Carleton as, "a magnificent affair, well built, well kept, and guarded by a collection of the most abominable regulations which could be invented." The cargo came out in very good order. Carleton judged the natives peculiar both in appearance—the males dressed in "any old meal sack," and favored beards and "long yellow-haired dogs, evidently a mixture of rat terrier and dried grass,"—and in language, of which the ship's company made "all manner of fun." Flies were numerous, large, and persistent. Railroads were "Hinglish to the last degree,"—Captain Mallett proclaimed the locomotives "spit boxes of the De Witt Clinton type." Carleton and Captain Mallett visited the four-masted bark *Clan Galbreath,* a fine vessel closely resembling *Hawaiian Isles;* the famous old four-masted ship *Lancing*, a converted steamer, under the Norwegian flag; and the American four-masted schooner *John E. Billings*, in drydock after striking Beagle Rock in Bass Strait.

MAY 12TH. Got the Captain interested in fox terriers with the result that the Mate, John, and I went up to the market this evening and purchased two—one for the Captain and one for me, for which we blew a "peound" apiece.

MAY 13TH. Lots of fox terriers. They...furnish sport for all hands. Mailed 52 letters of which I was the author of but half.

MAY 14TH. More fox terriers. A good investment they are already.

MAY 15TH. Nelson has deserted...and Paul, Blondie, and Allan have been paid off ... the vessel has been painted all around.... She looks pretty fine—by far the finest ship in port—a point some of our sailors would argue forcibly.... The carpenter was jagged and jugged Satur-

Skipper and Scamp, and First Mate Montieth aboard bark Hawaiian Isles.
CARLETON ALLEN. COURTESY OF JAMES F. JUNG.

Mate Montieth's room, May 26, 1904. Bark Hawaiian Isles.
CARLETON ALLEN. COURTESY OF JAMES F. JUNG.

day night and he leaves two "quid" in fines behind him. Fred and Norman amused themselves Saturday by throwing a lighterman's gear overboard and "now they're sorry they did it." Tony has had a night's rest in the place with the iron bars also. The cook came down in a "'ansom" tonight. A big team for such a small man...we have quite a lively time in the cabin now—a cat, two dogs [dubbed Skipper and Scamp], and two cockatoos.

On May 18 *Hawaiian Isles* departed Melbourne for Sydney, where the remainder of the cargo was to be discharged. The enjoyable passage along a mountainous, well-wooded coast included twenty-four hours averaging ten knots, while keeping pace with two steamers. At daylight, May 21, the tug *Champion* towed the bark to her anchorage in Double Bay, "the most beautiful inlet of the most beautiful harbor in the world." There Carleton rented a 22-foot sailboat—"no ballast and very light. She is what we would call crank, but here they use live ballast and light boats which can go."

MAY 25TH. Took a sail that was a sail. Got back with the boat half full of water, after beating up from Sow and Pigs Shoal.... Boat broke adrift shortly after dinner and it cost me 2 "bob" to get her back from an "Austrilian."

Bark Hawaiian Isles. *The carpenter in his shop.*
CARLETON ALLEN. COURTESY OF JAMES F. JUNG.

May 26th. Got up anchor at 11 A.M. in a pouring rain and towed to Dalgetty's new wharf. We are laying alongside the *Fort George*. She is a fine ship—what we can see of her through the rain.

May 27th. Didn't get "gone" on the crosseyed girl in the Consul's office, although Capt. M. and Capt Gove are touched (slightly). Offer them my sympathy for I know how it feels.

May 28th. *Rain*. Mrs. M. and I saw the *Marriage of the Kitty* at the Criterion.... Fats and chewing gum allowed by gentlemen and ladies. The stock inspector tried to take our dogs to quarantine, but the Captain literally *talked* him down. Captain is pretty good on the talk.

May 31st. Chris, Charles, Axle, Fred, Swan, Sam, and the carpenter paid off today. Chris and Charles were down for their dunnage in a hansom. They got into an argument with the half-fermented bos'n

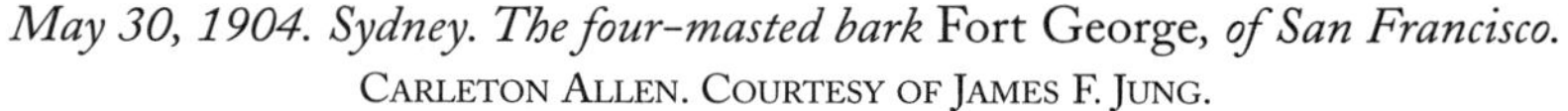

May 30, 1904. Sydney. The four-masted bark Fort George, *of San Francisco.*
CARLETON ALLEN. COURTESY OF JAMES F. JUNG.

about whether we were strict enough or not aboard the ship and the bos'n landed all fours on Charlie's chest...there was a rough and tumble and I got mixed up in it a bit but finally got them apart.

Carleton, sometimes with the Malletts and also other captains, took in the sights—including girls swimming in the surf at Manly in one-piece bathing suits. They were entertained in the home of a Captain Banks, whose large family included an entrancing daughter named Jessie. Fine times were had by all on various occasions and excursions—Carleton as well took an overnight rail trip to the mountain resort of Katoomba.

On June 17, with her hold cleared and shifting boards in place, *Hawaiian Isles* received coal "stiffening" from a collier for the short tow to Newcastle, to join a fleet of thirty or forty first-class sailing vessels waiting to load coal.[1] More trips were made back to alluring Sydney (and Jessie). On June 27 loading began—a hydraulic crane lifted the hopper cars bodily and dumped the two-ton contents directly into the hold.

June 6, 1904. Picnic at Middle Harbor, Sydney.
CARLETON ALLEN. COURTESY OF JAMES F. JUNG.

JUNE 29TH. Mrs. M. sick abed. We are nearly through loading and a mass of coal dust from one end to the other. An interesting character in the shape of a "Cullud" person is to be our stewardess up to Honolulu. Don't see where she is to sleep. I object to having her in my room and so does the Capt. and Mate, so I guess she will sleep in the storeroom. Mrs. M. is very sick and underwent an operation today.

JUNE 30TH. Finished loading our 3,372 tons of coal and towed out to the North Harbor buoy at noon. We have all but three of a full crew of fourteen men which will be our total before the mast to Honolulu.

JULY 1ST. Captain arrested for claims on Sydney cargo, one for £40 and one for £100. He is out on bail and will fight claims, which are visibly unjust. Mrs. M. is improving.

Shipping lying at Newcastle, N. S. W., May, 1904. The outboard vessel is the early iron four-masted barque Waterloo, *of Liverpool, built at Glasgow by Connell—* Hawaiian Isle*'s builder—in 1878.*

CARLETON ALLEN. COURTESY OF JAMES F. JUNG.

JULY 2ND. It looks as if we would get to sea tomorrow. Mrs. M. is much better. We have a nice little nurse (engaged unfortunately), Miss Grieves. Am helping Capt. a little with his business. Bos'n was discharged.

After two leisurely and enjoyable months in Australian ports, *Hawaiian Isles* finally departed Newcastle for Honolulu on July 3, 1904.[2]

JULY 10TH. We had an auction last night of the clothes and effects of four sailors—a cook who left in New York, Carl Reiche, Carey, and Charlie, the bos'n of last passage.[3] I officiated as auctioneer and we had a thrilling time. Got rid of the dunnage at good prices.

JULY 15TH. Mrs. Mallett up in the chart house for the first time today. School of porpoises under the bows.

JULY 17TH. A heavy sea running and we are rolling terribly [and the yards are] jammed up sharp on the backstays.[4] Taught "Skipper" to "jump" today. The pups are a whole circus about the decks and up to everything going.

JULY 18TH. Mrs. Mallett is much improved. Took a promenade on deck tonight [during the] dog watch for the first time.[5] Have seen very little of either Mrs. M. or the Capt. this passage. The Capt. is rarely on deck and leaves the handling of the ship almost entirely to the Mate and me.

JULY 19TH. Howling a strong northerly gale.... We are pitching into a sharp easterly sea and putting our topgallant forecastle under a great deal. When she pitches sharply at times she will bounce you clear off your feet as you stand aft on the poop.

JULY 21ST. I have just finished a pretty lively watch. A sudden shift of wind in a heavy squall accompanied by torrents of rain...at the climax the weather main tack pennant carried away and while we were getting the clew down off the mainstay again the wind jumped around with a bang from the North to a stiff S.W. breeze...one of the green ones came over. Clung onto the port poop ladder rail by both arms and legs. Loosened the screws. Don't know how I got there, but that's where I was when the smoke cleared away.

JULY 27TH. The Mate's opinion and my own have differed, as does our language, and there has been a coolness in the market at present. It will blow over shortly, however.

Bark Hawaiian Isles. *Aunt Kate with Scamp.*
CARLETON ALLEN. COURTESY OF JAMES F. JUNG.

JULY 28TH. Made an average of 11 knots from midnight until 8 A.M. All sail set and wind abeam. Didn't see Tahiti at daylight, as we expected, owing to rain squalls, but at noon it cleared and we could barely see it on the port beam.

JULY 30TH. Still booming along and skysails furled. At daylight we had two fierce squalls with torrents of rain. The second squall caught us aback and while Joe was putting the wheel up something snapped in the steering gear. We…found the rudder stock yoke pin on the port side was broken clear off. It was an old break…. Put tackles on the tiller and steered by them after that. It has taken five men to steer all day. We set to work to make a new pin out of a spare anchor shackle pin and it is proving to be a big job of forging. The machining will be a long job too, as we have but a chisel and file in place of a lathe.

AUG. 1ST. Last night at 9 o'clock we put the finishing touches to the steering gear and unshipped the tackles.

AUG. 3RD. Crossed the line last night.... This is my twenty-fourth birthday and I have been greatly favored from the Capt. and Mrs. M.... Am getting quite aged.

AUG. 7TH. Nearly dead calm all night and day.... This morning shortly after daylight Skipper had a fit and when coming out of it jumped overboard from the poop...the bos'n went out in a bowline just forward of the starboard main rigging and reached him in a few strokes.... Skipper had another fit this afternoon. Wish I knew what to do for him.

AUG. 10TH. Ted, Joe, and Bill are trying to kick up some kind of a row.... The starboard watch is getting their meat and food weighed out to them and they do not like it as well as the old fare they kicked against, but they are too ugly to ask for the old rations.[6] The port watch gets its food as usual.

AUG. 11TH. The ship is beginning to look fine about decks in her white paint and trimmings.

AUG. 12TH. An ideal day in every respect, bearing no comparison with anything I have ever seen, and that is saying a great deal. At daylight Hawaii was on port quarter and Maui on lee bow.

AUG. 13TH. Honolulu. Forty-two days actual sailing out of Newcastle. The recordbreaker of the year. The *Fort George* is here with a passage of 45 days...we have covered 6,655 miles at an average of 158.4 miles per day, or nearly 6.7 knots per hour.

At Honolulu Carleton, Captain and Mrs. Mallett, and Skipper and Scamp swam at Waikiki by moonlight. At a church fair Mrs. M. spent $1 on a cake, and another for Queen Lil's autograph; later, remorseful, she deplored the "utter deceitfulness and depravity of a church fair."[7] To see the volcano at Kilauea, Carleton boarded an interisland steamer, joining a jolly crowd of conventioning Republicans soon to be rendered into "poor seasick heaps of humanity." Along with Mr. Monteith, he admired the antics of native surf-boarders. Honolulu was an international town, with Chinese and Japanese influences predominating over American, English, German, Kanaka, and Portuguese.

SEPT. 20TH. Went to Chinese theatre tonight with John and it was about the most grotesque thing I have ever seen in the theatre line. The music is an abomination, and consists of about five pieces playing at the back of the stage, to which there is no curtain. The music twangs and thumps and hammers away while the actors are going through their antics and inhuman squeaks, which are supposed to be songs. It is a great farce yet does not produce a smile on the stolid faces of the audience.

Instead of loading sugar for New York, as expected, *Hawaiian Isles* was fixed to load sugar for San Francisco, then to return to load for New York.

Honolulu, August 1904. Bark Hawaiian Isles *lies at center. At left is the steel bark* R. P. Rithet, *of San Francisco, a Honolulu–San Francisco packet. In 1903 Pierce Drew, son of Captain Edwin Drew of the* Rithet, *a native of Hallowell, Maine, had sailed to Philadelphia aboard* Hawaiian Isles. *The four-masted schooner at right is the* Helene, *of Honolulu, built at Port Blakely, Washington. The square-rigger hidden beyond* Hawaiian Isles *is the bark* Kaiulani, *of San Francisco, built at Bath by the Sewalls in 1899.*

CARELTON ALLEN. COURTESY OF JAMES F. JUNG.

Carleton Allen, second mate of the bark Hawaiian Isles, *at Honolulu, 1904.*
CARLETON ALLEN. COURTESY OF JAMES F. JUNG.

Carlton decided to leave the ship at San Francisco and go home by steamer via the Isthmus of Panama.

The manning situation at Honolulu was volatile, with considerable tension between (white) union sailors and non-union sailors (including the locally despised Japanese).[8] Captain Mallett eventually shipped a union crew. Boarding sober, per contract, the sailors were a "husky lot," and could be trusted to "do what is told them and do it right."[9]

Sails were bent, the ship readied, and on October 5 the departure was made. The passage was uneventful until a "roaring howling" S. E. gale was met when approaching the California coast. When the thick weather cleared on the evening of October 30, Mendocino Light was seen close under the lee bow.[10] Sail was piled on, but the breeze had vanished, leaving a near-dead calm, with the rolling vessel being set in towards the shore with every wave.

OCTOBER 31ST. It is a rather unpleasant sensation to realize that you are gradually drifting in a dangerous direction without power to do a single thing to prevent it. The Captain spent a very trying night, and to all of us it has been a hard time. We have had a lot of pulling and hauling to do.... Scamp couldn't keep his footing on the bridge, even with his four feet, and slid off onto the hen coop. This is by far the ugliest sea I have ever encountered, and that is saying a good bit too, even though I am a fairly fresh saltwater sailor.

NOV. 1ST. Fair wind!... We got her down to topsails and foresail, for it was dirty weather.... She began to plunge into the sharp westerly sea, which still persisted and seemed to grow worse all the time. Blew out hawse pipe plugs and it was flooded underneath the topgallant forecastle in no time. The scuppers could not take care of it and she

View from the tug as bark Hawaiian Isles *departs Honolulu.*
CAPTAIN WALTER M. MALLETT,
COURTESY OF CAPTAIN W. J. L. PARKER.

rolled water over the chain pipe collars, down into the chain lockers. I took my watch up there and we had a big job plugging them up again, but we succeeded after many failures.

NOV. 2ND. At daylight we had a fine breeze.... At noon Point Reyes was abeam and at 4 o'clock the tug *Sea Rover* came alongside and after some argument and after the courses were hauled up, we took her hawser. It took about one hour and 30 minutes to take in and furl every one of the 25 sails and a good job the men did.... 'Frisco Harbor is a very good one...we can see very little [of the city] for there is a dense pall of smoke hiding much of it.

NOV. 3RD. A great day's work behind us and the crew gone. I never saw a crew work as these men have. This morning we unbent staysails, crossjack, mainsail, and spanker. At noon we got orders from Capt. M. to unbend all sails and at 1 P.M. we started in.... We had all the sails on deck, stowed below, gaskets made up, and the yards braced up by 4:45. The Capt. was much surprised.... The crew left just about 6 o'clock, after they had had their supper and a happy lot they were.

NOV. 5TH. Docked this morning at the Spreckles Sugar Refinery near Hunter's Point.... Today I sever my connection with this ship as an officer and I wonder if it is my last experience on salt water as a professional sailor.

The Malletts gave Carleton a gold seal ring; Carleton gave Mr. Monteith some pipes. On November 11 Carleton went to Los Angeles by train to visit relatives; returning to San Francisco he found that the Malletts had just learned of the destruction of their house back in Topsham, with all its accumulation of treasures from all over the world, by fire.[11]

THIS—MY LAST DAY of life on the *Hawaiian Isles*—was spent in arranging for my ticket to New York, packing, and generally getting ready. As the time approaches to leave, I am more than ever sorry.... I feel extremely grateful to the Capt. and the Mate for the forbearance and kindness they have shown in dealing with a greenhorn and landlubber and it seems hardly fair to leave the ship just as I am beginning to earn my salt. I am very much surprised that there has been so little friction between me—a mere "butterin" and the sailor men.

Carleton had booked passage aboard the thirty-year-old steamer *City of Panama*, which he described as having "oil lights and poor accommodations for first-class prices."[12] The twenty-eight first class passengers included old Klondikers; dope fiends (the ship's doctor was one); a retired drug drummer in search of health; a San Francisco saloon keeper; "two young ladies of doubtful details"; a Salvadoran general headed home to mount a revolution; a mining expert bound for Quito, Ecuador; a Vermont lady "with false teeth"; and "a dark horse not observed to smile or talk." The captain was "a kid-gloved sport," and the chief engineer, "a first class fellow and a lady killer."

The *City of Panama*, heavily laden and with a small tug in tow for a Guatemalan customer, made a leisurely three-week coasting trip with stops at Mexican, Guatemalan, and Salvadoran ports. At the Isthmus—the canal property had been obtained by the United States from French interests some months earlier—Carleton, the engineer, was most impressed by the vast amounts of abandoned French equipment rusting away. On December 13, on the Caribbean side, Carleton boarded the fine steamer *Seguranca* for a week's passage to New York.[13]

> DEC. 21ST. New York. Here at last. And cold!… About 40 below zero as we lay off quarantine this morning in my stateroom. Nearly froze…. New York appeared much the same as I headed for Charlie's office. Found all well…since leaving New York last February, let me state that I have covered 32,743 miles, or a little over 100 miles per day for 320 days…it is up to me to return to business. I am back where I started, but with a knowledge of the world with which I would not part for a fortune.

Carleton Allen never returned to sea, but would eventually head the marine department of the New York, New Haven, and Hartford Railroad. He later entered the insurance business in New Rochelle, New York, and served for twenty-five years as the president of a bank. He then moved to Ohio to be near family, dying in 1980 at age 100. A friendly and generous man, he never tired of telling people about his time spent as the second mate of a four-masted bark. To the end of his days he was called "Skipper."

Walter Mallet's next ship was the famous steel four-masted bark *Dirigo*, built and managed by the Sewalls of Bath, which Mallett first commanded from February 1911 to January 1912 and then again from October 1912 to 1917. As usual, Mallett mostly made it look easy.[14] Whereas Sewall ships in general, and certain Sewall captains in particular, were notorious for having crew problems, Mallett reported no such difficulties. Whereas other captains complained of being forced to take crews of hobos and riffraff—requiring the application of terror by the mates—Mallett reported his crews to be average or better. Of course, good, sober sailors avoided ships and masters with poor reputations, helping to create a vicious cycle aboard poor ships.

Interviewed aboard *Dirigo* in New York in January 1912, Kate, reflecting on the success of their marriage, stated:

The four-masted bark Dirigo. *Captain Mallett had her painted a light slate gray under his tenure and presumably was in command when this fine photograph was taken.*
COURTESY OF ANDREW NESDALL.

WE HAD ALL THE comforts of home and we never worried much. I think that our married life has been ideal.... On the long voyages we took together he seldom went out at night, and when he did I always knew where to find him.[15]

On the 112-day 1912 passage from San Francisco to New York the only mishaps suffered had been the loss of the cat overboard and the splitting of one sail, despite encountering a severe Atlantic Coast gale which had wrecked many vessels. Mallett had then spent two days jogging off New York bargaining with towboats for a cheap tow.[16]

Mallett's second stint in *Dirigo* was occasioned by the death, at Seattle, of Captain Omar Chapman from stomach cancer. Chapman had been nursed by Charmian London, who, with her famous husband Jack, a Japanese aide, and their dog, had been passengers.[17] From Chapman Mallet inherited an excellent mate, Fred Mortimer, who remained with him for the next three years.

Mallet was always proud of having taken *Dirigo* through the newly opened Panama Canal in 1915 on a case oil voyage from Philadelphia to the Japanese port of Shimonoseki, and equally annoyed that the four-masted bark *John Ena,* which transited a short time earlier, beat *Dirigo* for the honor of being the first big sailer to go through. During the course of this voyage *Dirigo* was sold. Mallett's final voyage began in October 1915 when he left Puget Sound with barley for Kalmar, Sweden. Intercepted by the Royal Navy in the North Sea in March 1916, *Dirigo* was impounded, taken to Fleetwood, England, and her cargo sold. When *Dirigo* was released the following February, Mallett, who had stayed aboard enjoying the English hospitality, brought *Dirigo* safely to New York, sailing through U-boat infested waters. On her next outward passage, *Dirigo,* under another master, was sunk by a U-boat off Eddystone Light. Barney Burnett, an AB aboard *Dirigo* on three of the last four passages Mallett made, wrote of Mallett:

HE WAS a gentlemanly skipper. Tall, clean-cut, with silvering grey hair and a well-trimmed Vandyke. Though he always spoke in an even tone of voice, and never, even in a crisis betrayed any excitement, his orders were always carried out exactly as he issued them...he had rounded the Horn so many times he was never able to remember how many.[18]

Mallett had maintained his citizenship at Topsham so that he could participate in local affairs during brief visits home. Retired, he threw himself into numerous civic activities, including terms as county commissioner and town clerk.[19] In 1919 he built a fine house on Elm Street to

Captain Walter M. Mallett, after his retirement.
COURTESY OF RICHARD P. MALLETT.

Richard P. Mallett, 2003, with a toy sailboat built for him by his uncle, Captain Walter Mallett, while aboard the bark Dirigo. *The sails were made by Aunt Kate.*
AUTHOR PHOTOGRAPH.

replace the home lost to fire in 1904. As always, Walter and Kate took a particular interest in working with young people. Mallett's death by stroke in August 1931 threw the community into gloom. The *Brunswick Record* reflected, "Nothing was outside his broad field of interest and few local activities were untouched by his active career." Kate lived to be ninety-five, dying about 1950.[20]

---

1. Shifting boards were temporary fore-and-aft partitions erected in the hold to prevent the movement of loose cargoes.

2. By contrast, a ship's turnaround nowadays is often but a matter of hours, and crew members may not ever get ashore over a six-month period. The biggest bulk carriers today have a carrying capacity equal to that of the entire fleet which *Hawaiian Isles* joined at Newcastle, with a crew about the same size as that of one sailing vessel. The 600 to 800 men required simply to man the fleet then lying at Newcastle explains why the Sailortowns of the world were lively places.

3. Carleton's watch now included a German bos'n, an Irishman, a Welshman, a Russian, an Englishman, a Scotsman, a Swede, and a sailmaker named Neil.

4. The bark, sailing hard on the wind, had her yards braced around as far as they would go.

5. The 4 to 6 and 6 to 8 P.M. watches, were so called because the watches were "dogged," thereby switching the two watches' hours. The 6 to 8 watch was often a social time in good weather.

6. Under American law, a scale of minimal required provisions was included in every article of agreement. Seamen had the option of accepting the fare provided, with the right at anytime to demand the proscribed scale of provisions. Dec. 21, 1898b (Sec.23), S. L. 30, p. 762 (R.S. 4612).

7. Queen Liliuokalani, after two attempts to restore native rights resulted in "revolutions" by whites, gave in to the inevitable and retired to enjoy her celebrity.

8. In 1906 Mallett shipped twelve green Japanese as sailors, led by a Japanese bosun, along with four "white" sailors for the passage from Kahului, Hawaii, to Philadelphia. In Cape Horn waters, he wrote his brother Wilbert: "Our Japs are improving all the time.... [They] do better than I expected in handling sail and they are learning English quite fast.... I wish you could see them as they look, rigged up for this cold weather. They are plucky little fellows." And later: "I wish you could see our Japs now. They have got as fat as cubs in the cool weather, and have appetites like pigs. We use a barrel of flour per week and other things in proportion. It is amazing how much they can stow away. They are certainly tough, hardy little fellows." Kate wrote a letter as well in which she noted, "I was very sorry to learn of Mrs. [William] Besse's death. I got a lovely long letter from her in Honolulu. She was a woman loved by all who knew her, one of the strong sweet women, the rare kind."

9. Two were Swedes, two were Scots, three were Finns, three were Germans, one was a Londoner, and one a Frenchman. A sailor's pay, under union contract, was $35 a month.

10. Strong currents, poor visibility, and a steep-to shore conspired to wreck many a San Francisco-bound ship on the Mendocino Coast.

11. Kate wrote Wilbert and Ella Mallett, "Your note of sympathy gave us comfort.... At first the news was overpowering but we rise to face the difficulties and losses as soldiers; it's the only way but it takes faith and lots of it.... I feel worst about the books because Walter read so many to me and in them are the dates of reading and where finished, which marks all the parts of the globe." She also noted, "Walter had the offer of a Pacific Mail steamer [command] at $200 per month. There was not money enough in it for him to think of it. It means a home on this coast and my being in it. We cleared about twenty-one hundred last year." Kate would not have been permitted to join Walter aboard a steamer. Doubtless the Malletts owned a "master's share" in the bark.

12. The steamer *City of Panama,* 1,400 tons, was built at Chester, Pennsylvania, in 1873.

13. The steamer *Sequranca,* 4,000 tons, was built at Chester, Pennsylvania, in 1890.

14. Mallett did make some long passages in *Dirigo*, which he laid to the ship's "affinity for light and head winds." Previously he had blamed her poor performance on her masters.

15 *Bath Times*, 25 Jan. 1912. The reporter was impressed by the fact that the newly arrived ship was "spick and span in every quarter."

16. Ibid., Jan. 23, 1912.

17. For insurance purposes, Jack London was signed on as third mate, Charmian as stewardess, and Yoshimatsu Nakata as cabin boy. Fare for the three of them was $1,000, their small wages being promptly returned to the ship's agent after they were paid off.

18. Claire Rankin, *The Tall Voyagers* (Los Angeles: Ward Ritchie Press, 1965), pp. 93–94. Theodore "Barney" Burnett was the sea struck grandson of a New York pilot who first went to sea under sail on *Astral.* In his "as told to" autobiography he described the food aboard the *Dirigo* on the outward case oil passage as being rank; a complaint by the crew to Mallett brought a weary promise to see what he could do, which evidently wasn't much. On the return passage in ballast, with a typhoon threatening, First Mate Fred Mortimer supervised the sending down of the skysail and royal yards, and the housing of the topgallant masts, a notable feat of seamanship. Burnett signed aboard again, and left a detailed account of the ship's arrest in the North Sea.

19. Topsham's Mallett Road is named for Walter's brother Edward, who got the family farm and was a long-serving first selectman. Mallett Hall at the University of Maine at Farmington is a memorial to Brother Bert.

20. A large reed pump organ now in the West Bowdoin (Maine) Baptist church reportedly had voyaged with the Mallets, presumably aboard *Dirigo.* Likely it had been installed in the cabin through the skylight, bereft of its tall, decorative pipes. The Mallets gave it to the Free Will Baptist Church of Topsham in 1916 and in 1917 it was hauled to West Bowdoin.

Part *Four*

Tod Swift

Chapter 17

Tod Swift Finds a Ship

Uncle Frank Arranges for Tod To Sail Aboard the Four-Masted Bark Astral, *Captain Jonathan W. Dunham.*

As Tod Swift approached his delayed graduation from Harvard in the spring of 1904 he had every intention of making his voyage in a square-rigger, per an agreement with his family. Agreement or no, his mother Sarah tried to dissuade him, citing danger to the scar left by an emergency appendectomy performed by his uncle, Dr. John Bullard. In April Tod testily retorted from Cambridge:

> Dear Mamma,
> I got your letter this morning in which you spoke about my not being able to go on a voyage.... I have often thought of that side of this question regarding scar left from operation.... Two years ago on the *Scout* I gave the scar a severe test for then I constantly had to exert all the power I had in various bad positions and no ruptures resulted.... I don't care for people's opinion as to whether they think it best or not. It is a case of doing what is most worthwhile to me. And if I should settle down now to a job I know I should not be satisfied. If I took a voyage first I might or might not be contented to settle down.

While young men of Tod's generation and class were the target audience of Teddy Roosevelt's advocacy of "the strenuous life," wherein a man "does not shrink from danger, from hardship, or from bitter toil," one should not underestimate the degree to which Tod's decision simply reflected Tod.

But there is boldness and there is foolhardiness, and only a fool would cast his fate to the tender mercies of the New York "crimps" who, even in the early 1900s, controlled the manning of ships. And there were a great many ships which even a seeker of the rawest adventure would have quickly regretted having signed aboard. Accordingly, Uncle Frank is believed to have approached Captain Smith, the New York port captain for Standard Oil and surely an old friend, to find Tod a suitable berth.

From his office at 26 Broadway decorated with ship portraits, Smith, a former English shipmaster, managed the American-flagged ships of the Standard Oil Company and the British-flagged ships of the subsidiary Anglo-American Oil Company, which constituted the most modern and best-equipped fleet of square-riggers under their respective flags. Even with these ships some captains were better choices to be entrusted with sea struck boys or young men than were others. Accordingly, Captain Smith found a berth for Tod aboard the American four-masted bark *Astral*, commanded by the well-respected Captain Jonathan W. Dunham. Although Tod would be signed aboard as an Ordinary Seaman, he would be housed apart from the common sailors, in a deck house located physically and symbolically between the cabin and the forecastle, and customarily occupied by petty officers, apprentices, and boys. *Astral* would be sailing in October 1904 from Philadelphia with case oil for Japan.

The first several years of the 1900s—*Astral* was built in 1901—with but a few exceptions, were the final years of commercial square-rigger construction. Within two decades—with the opening of the Panama Canal and the cataclysm of the First World War—square-rigged sail under any flag would be all but dead. Considering the speed of its demise, it is remarkable how large the doomed turn-of-the-century fleet was.[1] *Lloyd's Weekly Shipping Index* for September 7, 1905, listed well over 3,500 large and medium-sized sailing vessels, including 800 British, 550 Norwegian, 215 French, 250 German, 350 Italian (including many small vessels), 150 American, 52 Russian, and many Spanish, Portuguese, South American, Austro-Hungarian, Danish, Swedish, and a few Belgium vessels. Most of the British, French, German, and American vessels were of large size.[2] Many of the German, Norwegian, and Italian vessels were doubtless formerly British ships.

Most of the big square-riggers were employed trading around Cape Horn and the Cape of Good Hope. Given their great size and clumsiness, their proclivity to being swept by seas, the extreme penuriousness of owners, the small and often poor quality crews, and a dearth of good officers, conditions aboard these ships were, as a rule, more difficult and dangerous than those faced by previous generations of seafarers in those stormy high latitudes.[3] (By contrast, despite thousands of Cape Horn passages made by small, buoyant whalers, few, if any, were lost there.) Any similarities between life aboard a big cargo-carrying square-rigger of one hundred years past, and life aboard a modern "tall ship," are superficial at best.

Dirigo—Captain Walter Mallett's last command, it will be recalled—built at Bath, Maine, by Arthur Sewall and Company in 1894, was the first steel square-rigger built in the United States, and the first of eight similar four-masted barks built by this firm.[4] *Astral*, the fifth of the eight to be launched—along with sisters *Atlas* and *Acme*—was built for the Standard Oil Company.[5] Standard Oil likely ordered these ships, despite their greater cost, because the rest of their case oil fleet, being British-built and flagged, could not carry Hawaiian sugar to American ports.[6]

From 1823 to 1903 the Sewall family built and (mostly) managed over one hundred vessels.[7] In 1855 the original firm of Clark & Sewall was succeeded by E. & A. Sewall, comprised of founder William's sons Edward and Arthur. In 1879 Edward died as a result of an unexplained fall from a window of New York's Windsor Hotel, and the firm was reorganized as Arthur Sewall & Company, adding Edward's son Samuel, and Arthur's son William.

Whereas the more typical Maine shipbuilder/shipowner was a former sea captain, or else a practical shipwright risen up from the shavings, the Sewall scions apprenticed primarily in the counting-house. Their hands may have been soft, but not their heads for business.[8] Arthur Sewall, "the Senior," was a leading New England railroad executive, among other prominent roles. Politically an old-time Democrat, in 1896 he was the vice-presidential candidate on Populist William Jennings Bryan's ticket—strange bedfellows indeed, given the repeated appearances of Sewall ships in *The Red Record!*[9] Sewall lobbied against the admission of "free" foreign-built ships to American registry and for the annexation of Hawaii, in which cause his diplomat son Harold Marsh Sewall played a prominent role. (Political considerations regarding Hawaiian sugar and naval coal cargoes, along with possible Philippine trade protection, were key factors inspiring the construction of these ships.)

The Sewalls early understood economies of scale, having built a 1,000-plus-ton ship in 1841. In the early 1890s they built four very large ships—*Rappahannock, Shenandoah, Susquehanna*, and *Roanoke*—which demonstrated the limits of wooden construction.[10] The first steel ship to enter the fleet was the Scottish-built four-masted bark *Kenilworth*, which gained American registry by an act of Congress after undergoing substantial repairs. Although not without her problems, her performance convinced Arthur Sewall to convert to steel construction. The 3,005-ton *Dirigo*, designed by a Briton and of narrow British model, built of imported British steel by imported British shipwrights, was, in essence, a British four-masted bark topped off with Yankee skysails.

Dirigo very nearly capsized on her maiden voyage, but after her captain got used to her quirks he became fond of her. After Walter Mallett "took her" he wrote the Sewalls: "I like the ship very much. She sails well, steers well, and handles well in heavy weather or fine."[11]

The *Erskine M. Phelps, Arthur Sewall, Edward Sewall, Astral, Acme, William P. Frye*, and *Atlas* were enlarged from the *Dirigo* model simply by the addition of length amidships, not improving their stability or steering. The skysails of *Dirigo* and the *Phelps* were not repeated.[12] The great length of the yards of the later sisters may be attributed to the attempt to maintain sail area despite the short rig.[13]

The ships were no-nonsense bulk carriers, with midship sections that were almost rectangular. Only two—*Astral* was not one—were fitted with "Liverpool" houses, a lifesaving feature which broke the force of sailor-sweeping seas on the main deck.[14] Provided—as with any iron or steel ship—that they were not too badly fouled by marine growth, and given a fair gale, the Sewall four-masters made some impressive runs, but in general their passages were long—some even remarkably so.

Although the ships were bereft of any exterior decoration, the captain's quarters were palatial. (Mates' rooms, by contrast, were furnished as plainly as a monk's cell.) Most captains had to cough up a king's ransom for their required one-eighth share, far more than the Sewalls themselves retained in any one ship.[15]

Excepting the *Arthur Sewall*, which went missing in Cape Horn waters, the Sewall steel ships were long-lived. Despite myriad difficulties and dangers they delivered scores of cargoes in good order, if not without loss of life. Their captains, brought up in wooden ships that worked and leaked in heavy weather, marveled at the punishment which the steel ships took and frequently expressed pride in their mammoth commands.

Captain Jonathan W. Dunham, who would be the first master of the four-masted bark *Astral*, was a native of Barton, Digby County, Nova Scotia. Seagoing families of New England and the Maritime Provinces shared much in common; indeed, many Digby County people, in particular—very possibly including the Dunhams—were descended from American Tories.

New Brunswick and Nova Scotia deep-water shipping interests—centered at St. John and Yarmouth, respectively—boomed with the demise of the American fleet during, and for some years after, the American Civil War. By the late 1800s, however, the Provincial fleet suffered a severe decline and many maritime Maritimers emigrated to the "Boston states" of New England. There many worked in shipyards, fished, and went to sea in American ships, with a number, after becoming citizens, serving as mates and captains. Many such men had formed ties with Standard Oil when serving in Canadian ships employed in the North Atlantic "barrel" trade, carrying American crude oil to Europe, and a number were later employed in Standard Oil's own ships.[16]

Jonathan Dunham was born in 1853. The son of a sea captain, he became a licensed master mariner at age nineteen, receiving his first com-

Left top: Looking forward aboard the four-masted bark Erskine M. Phelps, *built by the Sewalls in 1898. Aside from having a taller rig, the* Phelps , *the fastest of the steel sisters, differed from* Astral *principally by measuring 20 feet shorter and of 292 tons less capacity.*
COURTESY OF MAINE MARITIME MUSEUM.

Left below: The main deck of the bark Erskine M. Phelps. *The catwalk provided a drier and safer route between houses when the deck was awash.*
COURTESY OF MAINE MARITIME MUSEUM.

mand, the brigantine *Halcyon*, at age twenty-one.[17] For over twenty years he commanded vessels belonging to W. Thompson & Company, of St. John, including the brigantine *Laura B*, and the barks *Young Eagle* and *Nocosia*. He then became the first and only master of Thompson's largest vessel, the 1,569-ton ship *Favonius*, built at St. John in 1883. Aboard *Favonius* he made four world voyages. In 1888 he received a gold medal for having saved the crew of the American schooner *George E. Young* fifteen minutes before she slid beneath the waves. *Favonius* burned off Pensacola in 1894 after being fired by her disgruntled carpenter.[18]

For several years after the loss of *Favonius* Dunham commanded steamers running between New York and Havana. When this service was interrupted by tonnage demands of the Boer War he returned to sail as master of the American ship *Paramita*, of Portland, Maine.[19] (At this point he had to have been a U.S. citizen.) During his second voyage, while at Cheefoo, China, the ship was sold to San Francisco owners. After delivering the ship to the West Coast, Dunham was employed in New York by a stevedoring firm.[20]

Dunham married Edith Ryno, a fellow Nova Scotian, and the couple had nine children with five, all girls, surviving. The family lived in Salem, Massachusetts.[21] On November 18, 1900, writing from New York, evidently while living aboard a ship as shipkeeper, Dunham wrote his youngest daughter, Lillian:[22]

> THANK YOU VERY MUCH for your kind wishes that I should be with you on Thanksgiving this year and I think by the present results I shall have the pleasure. Papa leaves next week for Bath, Maine, to take command of the largest steel sailing ship in the United States which certainly should please you all. I trust that you and Mildred may be able to be on board and play hide and go seek as I suppose you will find ample room for your games.... This is a beautiful day and I am alone except the number of visitors to look at the ship. We have two of the nicest dogs I ever saw. One is called a China chow

The cabin of the bark Erskine M. Phelps. Astral's *cabin would have been similar.*
COURTESY OF MAINE MARITIME MUSEUM.

Captain's bathroom. Bark Erskine M. Phelps.
COURTESY OF MAINE MARITIME MUSEUM.

Captain and Mrs. Jonathan Dunham.
COURTESY OF J. LEONARD BACHELDER.

dog, the other looks more like a fox and seems near as cute. They have both got to think as much of me as if I were their master and make such a time over me when I come on board but make a great barking noise if a stranger dares to venture on deck or near the cabin. We have a beautiful large United States ensign flying at the peak and at the ship's bow the most beautiful carved and gilded Eagle I ever saw, which means to say this ship is purely American and you know the captain is and votes for McKinley.

Astral's launching was indeed newsworthy:

THE FIRST SAILING SHIP to fly the American flag [in the] mighty fleet of vessels owned by the Standard Oil Company will be the four-masted steel ship *Astral*, which will be launched about one o'clock today.... The dimensions of the *Astral* are as follows: length, 332 feet; beam 45.3 feet; depth 26 feet; gross tonnage 3,206.47.... The *Astral* is built to carry 1,500,000 gallons of oil which is conveyed in cases containing 10 gallons each.... The forward deck house, 44 x 18 feet, accommodates the donkey boiler room with berth for engineer, in after end galley and cook's room forward and forward of this department the forecastle with bunks for 24 seamen. In the midships house is the messroom and four staterooms for petty officers, and the carpenter's shop and sail room in after end. The poop deck extends 44 feet in length, covering the commodious cabin finished in white and gold with hardwood floors.... On the starboard side is the captain's office and bed, fitted up with convenient lockers, desk, and a brass bedstead and private bathroom.... She will carry a complement of 35 men and will sail with oil to China and Japan, returning with hemp and sugar.... Captain Denham [*sic*], the commander, has been in town the past few days a guest at Mrs. Stover's on Front Street.[23] —*Bath Independent*, 8 Dec. 1900

AT THE LAUNCHING of the big four-masted steel ship *Astral* at Arthur Sewall & Co.'s yard Saturday the feature of the affair was the naming of the big craft by Miss Fanny Ruprecht, the fair, golden-haired daughter of Philip Ruprecht of New York, manager of the Standard Oil's foreign fleet.... While the vessel was shooting out into the stream the big port six-inch hawser attached from the ship to a tug snapped like a piece of twine but both anchors were dropped.... From starboard stern was a guiding hawser, fastened on shore, which turned the ship as she launched upstream. A crowd of 2,000 was present and was pleased with the superb slide the *Astral* made. —*Bath Independent,* 15 Dec. 1900

THE FOUR-MASTED steel ship *Astral* leaves for New York January 10. She will be brought to the depot wharf December 28 to load ballast. The royal yards will not be placed in position at present as the topmasts [*sic*] will have to be lowered for passing under Brooklyn Bridge. —*Bath Independent*, 22 Dec. 1900

LOOMING HIGH ABOVE the Shipping City the lofty masts of the mammoth four-masted steel ship *Astral* attract considerable attention to this magnificent specimen of maritime architecture.... The big vessel has been greatly admired since she has been taken from the yard of her builders to the Maine Central Railroad wharf where hustling crews are placing 800 tons of sand ballast aboard, about 600 tons of which have already been stored in the hold.... When the *Astral* reaches New York a telephone will furnish communications between forecastle deck forward and the poop deck aft. —*Bath Daily Times*, 3 Jan. 1901

THE STANDARD OIL CO.'S steamer *Maverick*...will arrive in the river this morning and tow the big ship *Astral* to New York leaving Sunday. A large crew was bending sails on the vessel yesterday and the work will be finished today. Capt. Dunham has made many friends during his stay in this city. Although he has carried oil for the Standard Oil Company for many years across the Atlantic, this is the first ship of the company's fleet that he has ever commanded. —*Bath Independent*, 5 Jan. 1901

HARRY DEMORE AND DON PREBLE, who went as boys on the big steel ship *Astral* to New York, arrived home Tuesday. DeMore went as cabin boy and Preble as apprentice and their intention, when they left this city, was to go to Japan with the craft. Reality on the *Astral* in commission, however, was no dream and when the boys reached New York they decided they had gone far enough. The entire crew was not invited into the cabin for games and recreation every evening and there were no four o'clock teas. On reaching New York all hands including the first mate said "So long" to the commander and after having difficulty in securing their pay, they sought at last the superintendent of the Standard Oil Co. who supplied them with money they had earned, and they departed for their homes. —*Bath Independent*, 16 Jan. 1901

SHIP *ASTRAL*, "probably the most modern sailing vessel afloat," as Thursday's *New York World* put it, hasn't enjoyed smooth sailing thus far since leaving Bath. Her mate and boys left in New York not wishing to make the voyage with Capt. Dunham. Sunday very heavily laden with oil the ship left New York for Shanghai and Wednesday off Rockaway Shoals there was a fight on board, the officers using

January 1901. The four-masted bark Astral, *at Bath, with tugs alongside, departing for New York. Being in ballast and with the Brooklyn Bridge yet to be contended with, her royal yards have not been crossed.*
COURTESY OF MAINE MARITIME MUSEUM.

> marlin spikes and drawing revolvers. Some blood was shed. The ship was helpless but safe at anchor and a mutiny was on. The reports are that the eight able-bodied sailors, learning that the sailors were inexperienced, rebelled —*The Bath Independent*, 9 Feb. 1901

The February 15 *Digby Weekly Courier* printed two versions of the mutiny story. According to the *New York Herald*'s version, twenty-six men had been signed aboard as able-bodied seamen, but when it was discovered, after dropping the tug, that all but eight were "stokers, beachcombers, and farmers," the eight ABs refused to do duty. Captain Dunham read them the law on mutiny to no avail. Dunham brought the ship back in, anchoring off Sandy Hook. Eventually, and with great difficulty due to gale conditions, three men were removed in irons by an armed crew from a revenue cutter. After they were replaced *Astral* departed.

The second version, from Dunham's adopted hometown newspaper, the *Salem Daily News* was based on a letter from Dunham in which he stated that shortly after being dropped by the tug a southeasterly snowstorm developed, and he decided to run back in, dropping both anchors. When the wind went into the northwest the anchor cables became fouled. The crew became frightened, and claimed that the topgallant masts had not been properly rigged.[24] Three men unwilling to continue were removed by marshals.

> CAPTAIN DUNHAM says there was not an angry word spoken and there was not the slightest trouble.... If the anchors could have been raised he would have proceeded but he was obliged to wait until the wind had subsided.... He sailed last evening with everybody on board satisfied and his friends wish him a prosperous voyage.

Several days previously the British four-masted ships *County of Kinross* and *County of Haddington* had departed New York with oil also for Shanghai, and the American ship *Helen A. Wyman*—formerly Besse's *William J. Rotch*—left from New York with oil for Chefoo, China. *Astral* arrived at Shanghai 128 days from Sandy Hook, the *Kinross*, in a very slow 161 days. The *Wyman* arrived at Chefoo in 144 days. The *Haddington* never arrived, disappearing with all hands.[25]

On *Astral*'s maiden voyage, Captain Dunham faithfully wrote to all five daughters and his wife, Edith. Youngest daughter Lillian, born in 1891, saved the letters she received (and a few others). Arriving at Shanghai—where Dunham dealt with the usual crew drunkeness and disobedience—he wrote Lillian:

I GOT YOUR LETTER and so pleased to hear from you. I am sending you a dollar bill in this and I put two dollars in Millie's. She will give you a half dollar which will make each one one dollar and a half.... The new steward has consumption bad and will have to leave, the boy is smart and will stay with me. He is a good cabin boy and looks after the cabin and all my clothes. I expect if you had come you would have been seasick. One of the passengers, the young man, was sick but the other was all right. I do not know how anyone could be sick in such a fine ship, she never rolls, just like a big house, and sails fast.... I am lonesome and homesick and tired of going to sea with such miserable officers and sailors. Wish I could be in Salem, work all day and come home at night. When you go to the Willows I hope you will have a nice time and see the Alabama Coons, and have a ride on the flying horses.... Tell Mamma the masts are all fixed so no one would ever know we struck the bridge. I don't think it will ever happen again, it was a sight for you all that you will not forget.[26]

Astral sailed on July 19 for San Francisco, arriving on August 30. During the passage a boy named Dole—very likely the cabin boy—the son of a minister, died. Below is an excerpt from the draft (in pencil) of Captain Dunham's letter to the boy's father:

I AM GREATLY PAINED to have to write you that your boy Richard died and was buried at sea in the North Pacific on our way from Shanghai to San Francisco.... Only about five days previous to his death he was taken with what seemed to be an acute case of diarrhea.... Several of the men after leaving Shanghai were taken similarly but we were able to pull them through. Your boy however seemed to waste away so suddenly and completely that I am inclined to believe that the final cause of his death was simple exhaustion.... The little fellow seemed not to suffer any pain or mental anguish and passed away as peacefully as if he had but just fallen asleep. We buried him at eight o'clock on Tuesday the 13th of August. The morning was a beautiful one. The ship was hove to and with the flag at half mast and all the crew in attendance on the poop deck his body was committed to the great deep, and his soul to his Maker who seemed to have unmistakenly called him home. The beautiful burial service of the Episcopal Church was read by one of our passengers.... Every respect was shown both by officers and men. His wasted body was clothed in a long nightdress of cotton and a pair of socks, a new undershirt, and a pair of white pants. It was then sewed in a clean, new cotton sail duck and weighted at the bottom most [with] heavy weights so that he went to his last rest as decently as it is possible to have a body when committed to the deep. It is a matter of profound sorrow to me that this should have been the outcome of his trip on the *Astral.*

To wife Edith, Dunham wrote:

THIS IS MY FIRST experience of burial at sea. I did everything I could for him but it was impossible, he was so sick from the first. He never was very strong, not like the other boys.... Hope I may never have the same thing again.

He wrote also of his pride in the fine appearance of the ship in San Francisco, and of finances and family matters:

SAILED IN THE HARBOR. This ship will tack and do anything that the others would.[27] She is a beauty.... There is a strike here and nothing doing.... Oh how I wish I could be home, I would look out for the lunch basket and not leave it on the car or anything else...*would do anything you wanted me to and be so good.* But it is better that I have employment. Colcord is paid, Williams is paid but I owe Mark Shaw for the chronometer $70.00....

To Lillian he wrote:

I AM PLEASED TO HEAR you have a little dog. You must learn not to be frightened of him.... All we can see where ever we look here is ships, the harbor is full of them waiting for the men to go to work.[28] It is a grand sight to anyone who likes to see ships. The *Astral* is the largest and she looks nice too and so many people come Sunday to see this ship. Last Sunday some lady asked Mr. Hoyt the passenger if we dined every day on board at sea.... I wish I could be with you but I must see lots of storms around Cape Horn first and probably get home in the cold winter when old Jack Frost is ready to bite.

Astral eventually loaded a cargo. Dunham wrote Lillian again:

I WONDER IF YOUR DOG catches rats. We have had none until now since we began the cargo of barley. The night watchman says he sees them on deck at night. I must get a cat and some traps, I am afraid to get a cat as I have two birds, two dear little Java sparrows. I got them the 11th last May at Anjer and I hear them now. I must go and feed them, they eat lots of rice.

Astral made New York after a 123-day passage. The major mishap occurred on the day she crossed the equator, a squall carrying away the fore-topgallant mast, breaking the fore royal yard. Six days later all had been repaired.

Astral's second voyage was with oil to Hong Kong, making a passage of 118 days, the fastest of any ship sailing at about that time. Dunham wrote Lillian:

> I HAD A PLEASANT VOYAGE, called at Tristan da Cunha Island, got sheep, geese, potatoes, eggs, and milk. And at Anjer got sweet potatoes, pumpkins, bananas, and coconuts. I beat the English ships after all.... I wish you could be here to go on shore with me and see all the nice China shops and all the pigtail Chinamen and have them haul you in a ricksha.... I am very sorry to hear that Eddie Dunham will never come to visit us again, how hard it must have been for him, trying to save his life in that storm....[29] I am saving all my soap money for you so that you and Mildred can get [a camera] and I guess I will have enough. I sold one box and will sell another on the way home....[30] I may go to Boston and if I do you can come to dinner some day and bring your wheel and ride on deck.... I will go to Java soon, the home of the sparrows...some will come on board the ship I expect and light on the ropes to rest themselves.

From Hong Kong *Astral* sailed to Surabaya, Java, to load sugar for Philadelphia. Dunham wrote Lillian:

> I AM ALMOST ROASTED and I expect it is freezing with you in Salem. It is getting near Christmas and I expect the shops are beginning to look nice. It is two years since I was home. Time has gone very quickly with me and I just wish I could peep in and see you all. I am quite tired of being away from home so much.... The *Astral* looks fine anchored here with her flags flying.... I have a very fine painting of the ship done at Hong Kong. I have lots of fine fruit here. I eat mangoes every morning before breakfast, and sometimes I eat quinces.... If I was home I could put some things on the Christmas tree but it will be just as good when it comes. Our sugar cargo is in baskets much larger than the soil[ed] clothes baskets and the same shape. It takes three baskets to a ton of 2,240 lbs, the cover is laced on with rattans, the sugar is dry and of fine quality, looks like sand. The holds of the ship are just newly painted light lead color and is so fine and clean, it is like a big storehouse. What a place between decks would be to ride a wheel. You will not hear from me from Anjer I go the other way past the east end of Java and probably out through Lombok Strait, but I want to hear from you at St. Helena.... We have had a lot of hawks on board coming from Hong Kong and they were

continually catching small birds, the sailors would kill as many of them as they could nighttimes, but could not kill them all. I had to keep my canary inside and then they tried to get through the window for him. The mate took one of his birds out on the hatch to give it some water, he somehow let it out of the cage, a hawk got it in a few seconds, ate the poor canary's head off, and threw the body on the deck. I wish I could have killed that hawk. Mine is all right and singing nicely, sometimes you would think he would hurt his little throat. My canary is Cantonese.

I am your loving papa J. W. Dunham,
sweet loaded ship *Astral*

Astral, her bottom foul and having lost her topgallant masts, made a very slow passage of 168 days to the Delaware Breakwater. Dunham wrote Lillian:

I HOPE THE SUGAR trust will want this sugar in Boston, what a nice time you could have. The first thing I would buy would be a book of railway tickets so we could...ride cheap and go often. The mate has a gramophone, plays all kinds of negro songs and recitations, it is great company at sea. *The song I like the best is yourself....* Got a good steward, he is very clean and a good cook, Chinaman with no pigtail, he cut it off to make himself look like Melika man. He was the cook going out to Hong Kong. He makes lots of nice things. I ask him sometimes what he has for supper, one night he said he had cheese Labbit, he meant welch rabbit [Welsh Rarebit], he often has lice and cully Fliday night. What a fine time the fish must have now while the ship is here, they get such a good breakfast, dinner, and supper off the bottom of the ship.

Astral discharged at Philadelphia, then towed to New York to have three new topgallant masts fitted. She then towed to Baltimore to load coal for San Francisco, arriving at San Francisco in January, 1904. Dunham wrote Lillian:

I HAD QUITE ENOUGH coal dust for a while I assure you.... My birdies sing whenever I come on board or go in the cabin. They know me when they hear me speak.... I see by the paper today that a storm is raging off Cape Cod, and many vessels are being lost.... I have met lots of friends here that I know and have not been so lonesome but will soon be on the ocean again where it is downright lonesome. I had a good crew coming out. I hope I may have as good going back, and I hope I may go to N. Y. then I can get home a while. Philadelphia is too far from home. Wish the ship could come to the Willows. What a nice time we would have.

Sailing to Honolulu, *Astral* loaded sugar for Philadelphia, departing in April. Before reaching Cape Horn she was pooped by a sea that broke in the wheelhouse door and flooded the cabin while breaking the skylight. She arrived after 133 days, having had crew troubles.[31] Dunham wrote Lillian from Philadelphia:

I DID WANT to get home [for] Edna's birthday the 18th. I had figured on this from out at sea and now I have to stay here until the ship is in the loading berth. If the ship loads here they say she will be a long time loading but one cannot depend on what they say at all times. I wish they would haul her up for a month. I want to go home and stay a while. I am tired of the sea and the miserable sailors we have to contend with. I wish you could see the [Negro] stevedores working in the sugar sending up the bags. We take out about twenty-three thousand bags in one day. I think the cargo will be all out tomorrow. A bag holds 125 pounds brown sugar. I have some in a bottle to show you.

Of the stevedores, Edith, who was visiting the ship, wrote home:

I WISH YOU COULD be here this morning to see and hear the crowd of [Negroes] on our deck at the small hatch close to the cabin. They are beginning to take sugar out of there this morning and I am sure you could not tell who was the boss, "Now Mr. Fisher, come on move you Charley Harris, does ye hear dat black Charley come on, come on now you black——" and all the comical language you could think of and see them pull out their gold watches to compare them when the whistle blew for seven.

With her sugar out, *Astral* was shifted to the Atlantic Refining Company's large Point Breeze facility to load case oil for Kobe. Dunham took a rare, brief, and well-deserved vacation at home.

---

1. These figures take no account of American schooners, many of which were as large or larger than most square-riggers, but which, while engaged in a number of deep-water trades, with but rare exceptions left voyages around Cape Horn or east of Good Hope to better-suited square-riggers. In 1904 the entire American fleet of square-riggers (including half-brigs, barkentines, and also whalers), as recorded in the *List of Merchant Vessels*, approached 300 vessels—twenty years previously there had been about 330 full-rigged ships, alone. Only about three

dozen American vessels were of iron or steel, most of these being British-built, having gained American registry by special acts of Congress.

2. Villiers, *The War with Cape Horn*, p. xviii.

3. Captain Fred Klebingat, who served in German and American ships and was once first mate in *Star of Poland*, ex-*Acme*, wrote in 1978: "Let me make some remarks on 'Wooden Ships and Iron Men'....Wooden ships were far better sea-boats than those steel tanks of later years. Their decks on the average were not up to the rails with icy water. In fact, those cabin doors...never would have been able to take what those of the steel ships had to take.... And even a fo'c's'le in a wooden ship, never mind how miserable it is, cannot look so cold and inhospitable as those of a later Limejuicer. Cold steel dripping with condensed perspiration and water sloshing about." (He did concede that pumping a wooden ship was another matter.) Courtesy of Andrew Nesdall. Conditions aboard French "bounty" ships, however, in certain respects constituted a very large exception to the rule. Between 1897 and 1902 a rise in shipping rates, combined with the French government's bounty program, resulted in the building of 212 new sailing vessels for the French fleet, most of between 2,500 and 4,000 tons. Since the bounty payments were based in part on gross tons—distance sailed also counted—vessels were fitted with large, commodious deck houses. French seamen had long benefited from pension systems, and French ships never wanted for French sailors—primarily Bretons. Alan Villiers and Henri Picard, *The Bounty Ships of France* (New York: Charles Scribner's Sons, 1972).

4. The only other large American-built metal merchant square-riggers had been the iron ships *Tillie E. Starbuck*, *T. F. Oakes*, and *Clarence S. Bement*, built on the Delaware, the first in 1883, and the latter two in 1884. The standard history of the Sewall steel ships is Mark W. Hennesey's *The Sewall Ships of Steel* (Augusta, ME: Kennebec Journal Press, 1937), which, while most useful, was subsidized by the family, and was not intended to hurt anyone's feelings.

5. *Astral* was immediately preceded by the three-masted bark *Kaiulani*, and was thus the sixth of nine steel Sewall square-riggers. An oil barge and the five-masted schooner *Kineo*, a disappointment, ended Sewall shipbuilding.

6. There was also a possibility that trade between the Philippines and the United States would be restricted to U.S.-flagged vessels. Standard Oil's British-flagged Anglo-American Oil Company fleet numbered twenty vessels, most of them four-masted barks, of which eight were purpose-built for the case oil business.

7. From 1869 to 1892 the construction of forty-six vessels was overseen for the Sewalls at their yard by master builder Elisha Mallett, Walter Mallett's uncle.

8. Or, on occasion, their hearts. At least some Sewall captains were charged not only board for their accompanying wife, but passage money as well.

9. The *Red Record*, published by a seaman's union, listed incidents of violence committed by ships' officers towards sailors. See Appendix. Among Sewall captains included in *The Red Record*, Edward's son, Captain "Ned" Sewall, was a thoroughly nasty piece of work, as was the sadistic Captain Joe Sewall, a nephew of Arthur's and Edward's.

10. Called "shipentines," the last three were four-masted barks. Blunt of model, very heavily rigged, yet constructed without stiffening metal hull strapping or fitted with any extra labor-saving appliances for their small, hard-pressed crews, the "Big Four" were big ships but were not advanced ships.

11. Letter dated 6 August 1911, in the Sewall Papers, Library, Maine Maritime Museum.

12. Letter from R. C. Viet, a Standard Oil manager, to the Sewalls, dated 8 May 1900: "...these vessels are intended mainly for loading [case oil] at Long Island City and that it is important that the masts of the vessels should admit of striking the top-gallant mast, in order to pass under the Brooklyn Bridge when light. We understand the height to be 133 feet, but assume that from the water the topmast, for safety, should not exceed over 130 feet." And on May 12: "We dislike very much to reduce the sail area even to this small extent, and...we prefer to leave the masts as originally designed by you, namely, 132 ft. from the light water-line." *Astral*'s shallow topgallant mast doublings were evidently the cause of the three dismastings of her topgallant masts. The height of the masts of the British-built oil carriers was also dictated by the Brooklyn Bridge. Sewall Collection. With topgallant masts in place, the height above the deck of the main trucks of *Astral*, *Acme*, and *Atlas* was 163 feet, 6 inches.

13. Fairburn, *Merchant Sail*, pp. 1611–15. "For ships lacking in beam and with the length of the lower yard 2.12 times the width of the ship, it is amazing that the uppermost [royal] yard should have been made 57 $\frac{1}{2}$ ft. long." By contrast, the earlier *Phelp*'s royal yard was but 43 feet. Fairburn, a Bath-born prodigy who was trained in naval architecture in Scotland, failed to persuade the Sewalls to build their steel ships wider, with more freeboard, and with water ballast tanks. He never forgave them for what he judged to be their penuriousness and also ignorance of naval architecture. Surely, however, the Sewalls deserved much credit for undertaking to build steel ships at all.

14. The lack of Plimsoll marks on American ships meant that the barks under Sewall management were often overloaded.

15. The total amount of Sewall ownership in the steel "Sewall Fleet" was $\frac{7}{64}$ in *Dirigo*, $\frac{8}{128}$ in the *Phelps*, $\frac{6}{128}$ in the *Arthur*, $\frac{7}{128}$ in the *Edward*, and $\frac{6}{128}$ in the *Frye*. Shrewdly, they risked little money of their own, profiting from building and managing the ships. They were happy to loan captains money to buy their shares, however. Fairburn, *Merchant Sail*, p. 1777.

16 Among many sailors a "Bluenose" ship was any ship with a Provincial captain or mate, whatever its flag. Among sailors, Bluenose ships were notorious for combining the poor food of a British "Limejuicer" with the harsh discipline of a Yankee "hellship."

17. Charles Dunham, Jonathan's father, a shipmaster and shipowner, died in 1907, worn down by the effects of yellow fever contracted during many years of West Indies trading. Charles's own shipmaster father had died of yellow fever in the West Indies when Charles was ten. Charles went to sea at age twelve and by age twenty-one commanded a schooner. He retired, due to his poor health, after eighteen years of command in the West Indies trade, never having lost a man, nor any vessel "through his fault." *Digby Weekly Courier*, 14 June 1907. Jonathan's Uncle James, also a shipmaster, lost all three of his sons, James, John, and Edward, to the sea. James and John were both lost at age nineteen. Edward was lost in 1902 while master of the fine British 2,200-ton four-masted bark *The Highfields*.

18. Before the ship departed Pensacola for Rio the carpenter, named Karson, had chopped off the ends of two fingers in hopes of being left ashore, but a local doctor deemed him able to proceed in the vessel. *Digby Weekly Courier*, 3 August 1894.

19. *Paramita*, a first-class ship of 1,879 tons, was the last ship built by the Soules, of Freeport, Maine.

20. Ardis B. Moore, "William Warner of Plympton, Nova Scotia and his Descendants," unpublished monograph (Oshawa, Ontario, 1993), p. 143.

21. The fifteen-room Dunham house is at 28 Linden St., formerly 2 Park Street.

22. All of the Dunham correspondence is courtesy of Mr. and Mrs. Leonard Bachelder.

23. A sailor would have been more impressed by the standard, bare-bones forecastles, the very heavy rig, the lack of brace or halyard winches, the dangerous open expanse of deck, and the lack of even a decorative fiddlehead to relieve her stark outward appearance. Some critics described the Sewall sisters as resembling a haystack with a broomstick jammed in it. Harold D. Huycke, "The American Four-Mast Bark *Star of Poland,* ex-*Acme,*" *American Neptune,* vol. 3, no. 4, p. 6.

24. Other reports indicated that the sailors thought the ship to be "crank," or top-heavy. The reference to the topgallant rigging is of interest, given *Astral's* subsequent dismastings.

25. Frank W. Thober, "American Oil Ships," *Nautical Research Journal*, vol. 8, no. 3., p. 72; Basil Lubbock, *The Last of the Windjammers*, vol 1 (Glasgow: Brown, Son & Ferguson, 1927), p. 236.

26. The reference to the ship's stability was surely in jest. The Willows was a Salem amusement park. Reference to the Alabama Coons, doubtless a minstrel act, is a reminder of the racial tenor of the times. Even with topgallant masts housed, the ship had struck the Brooklyn Bridge, with the family aboard.

27. In fact, a big four-masted bark was an easier vessel to tack than were the smaller three-masted ships Dunham was used to, since the greater length gave more leverage to spanker and foremast sails as the bark first headed up and then pivoted through the eye of the wind.

28. There was a stevedore strike.

29. Eddie Dunham, Jonathan's cousin, was master of the fine English four-masted bark *The Highfields*, lost when arriving at Cape Town. In bad and deteriorating weather, and with sails blown away, Dunham attempted to enter Table Bay. A German steamer anchored just outside the breakwater blocked the passage, and *The Highfields* fouled the steamer's cables and a collision followed, taking down the ship and twenty-three men. Basil Lubbock, *Last of the Windjammers*, vol. 2 (Glasgow: Brown, Son & Ferguson, 1929), p. 170. In 1899 Jonathan had visited with Eddie aboard his ship at New York.

30. Evidently Dunham was saving coupons from the soap he was selling from the slop chest. Selling "slops" was a traditional source of income for captains—although the Sewalls demanded a cut on their ships. By law merchant ships had to be provided with a slop chest containing outer and inner clothing, boots, tobacco, and blankets, to be marked up a maximum 10 percent. Waterfront stores in big ports specialized in selling captains cheap clothing for slop chests. Shrewd Yankee skippers, when off Cape Horn, were said to head further south than necessary to give slop chest sales of winter clothing a boost.

31. A sailor named Benton later sued the ship complaining that he was unjustly assaulted by the mate, and that the master refused to interfere on his behalf. The court found that the ship was not liable in an action of this kind. Undated, unidentified clipping from the Maine Maritime Museum Library.

Chapter 18

ASTRAL, OCTOBER–NOVEMBER 1904: OFF TO SEA

Tod Swift Joins Astral *and Sails Deep into the South Atlantic, Headed for Japan.*

ON OCTOBER 4, 1904, Mrs. Frederick Swift wrote to her son Tod, recently departed for Philadelphia and his long-sought berth as an Ordinary Seaman aboard the four-masted bark *Astral,* a square-rigger bound for a distant land.

> MY DARLING BOY—It is now just 4 P.M. and it does not seem possible that it is only ten hours since you and Fred went off.... I hope that you accomplished all you wanted to do, and that you did not buy yourself *too* hard a bed.[1] I have been thinking about you all day.... I hope you will never regret having gone, and I really do not *think* you *often* will, for you are too much of a sailor.

On October 5 she wrote him again:

> MY DEAREST TOD—This is the last letter I shall write you for a long time, and I will then try to obey your orders and send *one* letter to greet you on your arrival in Japan, with another to follow—but if you only have a decent Capt. and mate I do not believe by that time they will have any objection to your receiving letters, for they will have discovered that you are different from "ordinary seamen".... It is troubling Eliza that you have taken no *reading* matter, and I wish you had too, as well as pajamas and many other things. But when you reach Japan, if you find you ought to have had them and want them on your homeward voyage do not hesitate to draw on your L of C [letter of credit] dear, and supply yourself.... I shall begin tomorrow and try to have the N. Y. *Herald* every day and search the shipping columns for your sailing and further news of you.[2]

There are, of course, many things a mother cannot understand, such as why Tod did not want to be seen as educated, much less to be seen wearing pajamas! On October 5 Tod mailed a letter to his mother written on unfolded envelopes:

I AM AT THE P.O. and it is late so I can't buy paper but I bought all envelopers by mistake. So I will use one. Thanks for your two letters. I was very glad to get them. The ship is fine and so is the captain although I have not had occasion to say a word to him. The first mate is a German and I guess will turn out a good man; the 2nd mate is a small Englishman and I don't like him.[3] I live in a house with two Boatswains, the carpenter and sailmaker, the donkey engineman, and one apprentice and one ordinary seaman.[4] As long as we are tied to the dock we can't have a light or smoke on board so that is why I wrote at the P.O. The rigger came short handed so "Chips," "Sails," and I spent all day yesterday and half of today aloft bending sails with the rigger's men. So I am now quite used to being aloft. I am also tired and going back now to the vessel as we have to turn out at 5:30 A.M. We sail at 10 tomorrow morning for Kobe from there we go to Honolulu and get sugar and bring that home so I am going all the way round the world. The food is good now and I guess it will continue to be. I am stronger than the other boy and the donkey engineman so that I find they get most of the cleaning, sweeping, and dirty work. Send this letter to Helen to read I am too tired to write this all over again. Well I shall expect a long letter from you at Kobe and I shall send you my log besides writing.

Helen, unhappily married in Chicago, sent him a brief note telling him to stay well and to have a good time, and wishing she were going with him.

The opening entry in the log of the "ship" *Astral*, of New York, lying at the Atlantic Refining Company's dock, Point Breeze, Philadelphia, "From Philadelphia towards Kobe, Japan," reads:

FRIDAY 30TH SEPTEMBER. Myself, carpenter, and sailmaker came on board and went on duty.[5]

Traditionally the first mate—who was always called "the mate"—was the keeper of the log, and presumably he was "myself," even though Tod does not list him as being aboard on the 3rd.

SATURDAY, 1ST OCTOBER. Light westerly breeze and fine weather. Stevedores loading ship. Employed men from shore. Six men painting, eight men taking in stores, and one man sawing wood for the stevedores.[6] *In P.M. donkey man came on board. Ship carefully attended to.*

The opening entry in Tod's log reads:

October 1904. Bark Astral *at Point Breeze, Philadelphia, loading case oil at the Atlantic Refining Company.*
Courtesy of Maine Maritime Museum.

OCT. 3, 1904.[7] Joined the ship in the afternoon. She is at the dock at Point Breeze loading case oil. Aboard are the second mate, carpenter, sailmaker, and one sailor, a man named Monday.

OCT. 4TH. Turned out at 5:30 and cleaned up the ship till breakfast. All meals are ashore in a sort of shed in the refinery yard. No lights of any kind allowed on the ship. After breakfast, as the rigger was shorthanded, Sails, Chips, Monday, and I had to help bend sails. Aloft all day.

OCT. 5TH. Aloft bending sails all the morning. In the afternoon Monday, Sails, and I carried three tons of potatoes, turnips, etc., from the dock to a bin up under the fo'castle head. It almost killed all three of us, that job. Went up town after supper to write letters but was too tired to write much.

WEDNESDAY, OCTOBER 5TH. Light westerly breeze, later light southerly breeze and heavy rain. Crew employed taking in stores and getting ship ready for sea. Ship draft forward 22 feet, 9 inches; aft, 23 feet, 7 inches. 2 P.M. stevedores finished loading the ship. Total cargo on board 129,000 cases and 700 barrels. Night watchman. Ship carefully attended to.

OCT. 6TH. The rest of the crew came aboard at 3 A.M. They were shipped in New York and were put aboard here from a tug.[8] Nearly all of them drunk. At 5:30 we turned to and got the lines in ready to fall out into the stream. "We" being Monday, Chips, Sails, one boatswain, and me. First mate very drunk. Second mate half drunk. At 7 A.M. ship towed from dock. Two tugs. Monday and I at wheel till 10 o'clock then we were relieved and got some breakfast. Then up aloft to bend a brand new mainsail. Very heavy stiff No. 00 canvas. A NW gale blowing and cold. It was a heartbreaking job for we were very shorthanded. Most of the men still half drunk. I was at the wheel from 2 P.M. to 7 P.M. alone then got supper and turned in.

The crew had been divided into watches during the P.M. when I was at the wheel. I am in the port watch with the first mate and the little bosun. Port watch went below at 8 P.M. All hands called at 10 P.M. to make sail. Tugs left us at 10:30. We set foresail and three lower topsails and upper main topsail and two jibs. It was blowing a gale from the NW and the decks were full of water, soaking up to the waist. We had no chance to put on boots and oilskins. We were on deck till 4 A.M. very cold, perfectly wet, and tired. Mate still very drunk. About half the crew still drunk. Sort of a tough first night. We drive along before a gale with almost no lookout—that is, no one out on fo'castle head and you can't see ahead from the poop. There are a lot of boats' lights around us—fishermen, I suppose. I hope we don't run over any of them. Turned in at 4 A.M.

THURSDAY, OCTOBER 6TH. All this day light NE breeze and hazy. Crew came on board at 4 A.M. 8 A.M. pilot and towboat came to take ship to sea. Unmoored ship and towed down the river. 11 P.M. towboat and pilot left the ship. Set all possible sail. 12 midnight, Cape Henlopen Light bearing W by S about 12 miles from which I take my departure. Pumps, lookout, and lights carefully attended to.

OCT. 7TH. Turned out at 8 A.M. Went aloft and loosed the upper and lower main t'gans'ls. Everything set except royals. Decks all awash and knee-deep most of the time in the lee scuppers. Unbent the anchor cables and stowed the anchors. Big sea running. Turned in at noon. Got a bad cut on my right forefinger today.

OCT. 8TH. The wind has gone down and Gulf weed all around. The water is a very beautiful blue. Chips and I stowed the anchor davits. The slop chest opened and I got a cap and some matches. Washed down decks for the first time today. Yesterday we passed a four-masted Standard Oil bark with her jiggermast gone. She was the *Acme*, a sistership of our ship.[9] We are certainly kept working. If anyone is seen doing nothing he is cursed and given a job. All hands during their watches on deck were kept busy putting chafing gear on aloft. My finger very sore today. We are not allowed much water. About 1½ quarts per man per day and if the cook needs more we get less. We still have fresh meat but the cook is a bad one and the food is very badly cooked.

OCT. 9TH. SUNDAY. Finger still bad. Does not heal at all. Too much salt water and dirt. Rained hard all the morning and we filled up the donkey engine boiler by catching the water that ran off the top of the forward and amidships houses in tubs, etc. and pouring it in the top of the boiler. It cleared later and we did no work but trim sails. The air is hot and damp. Plum duff today but only half cooked, like dough, and half a dozen raisins in the whole thing. The steward gave Monday and me an apple each this morning.

The bosun of the starboard watch is a character. About sixty years old. He is a kind-hearted old duffer, which is more than can be said of the little bosun in our watch, who is a good sailor but, I suppose, because he is small he must act big, so is mean and noisy and always likes to use his authority. The crew as a whole are not bad. There is only one other besides myself who was born in America. That is Monday who comes from Missouri and is a queer sort. No brains and not a good sailor. The rest of the men are all sorts. Some fine men and fine sailors. Others poor sailors who have been on steamers only. Here is the list:

Captain J. W. Dunham	Nova Scotia
Mate Zube	Danzig
Second Mate Findley	England
Steward Charlie Marlo	Hong Kong
Cook Charlie (black)	British Guiana
Sails	Denmark
Chips	GermanyPort Watch
Bos'n Louis Stetson	England
John (black) Cape	Verde Islands
Charlie	Sweden
Anderson	Sweden
Nelson	Norway
Martin	Germany
Monday	U. S.
Chris	Denmark
Peter	Denmark
R. S.	U. S.
Kole	Holland
Walderman	Finland
Alf	Norway
Starboard Watch	
Bos'n Henry Smith	Germany
Fred	Norway
Sam	England
George	Sweden
Iceland	Iceland
Swan	Sweden
Mike	Austria
Albert	Finland
Hugo	Russia
Rabbit ?	
Dow ?	
Bill (black)	Honolulu

It looks like all the world and represents seventeen nations.

OCT. 10TH. While washing down this morning, at 5 o'clock, I spilled some water from one of my buckets down the leg of the bos'n's boot. Talk about a man exploding with wrath. It was dark and cold and I don't blame him much. But it was funny. Working putting chaffing gear aloft and in the afternoon watch we worked opening and stowing stores in the lazerette most of the watch. Strong north wind. Head E. Big sea running and every once in a while a big sea over the bulwarks. Tacked ship at midnight. Wind SE, head NNE.

OCT. 11TH. Spent most of our morning watch in lazerette handling stores. In the rice bin I saw many small black bugs running all through the rice. I wonder if they will taste sweet. Painting in afternoon.

OCT. 12TH. Stew for breakfast with a number of cockroaches. Big ones, too. In morning watch brought all the spare sails on deck. The mate is turning out to be a mean sort. He is a very good sailor though, which means we have much less work at the braces than the starboard watch. When the mate says belay, the yard is right and we don't have to go back to it. They say on Oct. 10th we were just west of Bermuda and that was why we tacked that night. This afternoon we took in the foresail. Beautiful calm day. Head N by E. Wind easterly. The mate cursing everybody today all day. Fine night at first but later it rained and the wind shifted entirely round the compass 360 degrees and we took in and set sail and hauled braces all night. Caught a bucket of rainwater.

OCT. 13TH. Oiled various chains and wire ropes. Taking them up from the hold and putting them down again. Hard work it was. Washed some clothes in the water I caught last night. Also did some needed sewing on my clothes. Strong SE wind. Head NE. Plum duff and beans for dinner. Hard work all right. You have work that is hard and you keep on the jump all the time. However I am in fine condition except for my finger which is still bad. Rained in the evening and none of us had time to put oilers on.

OCT. 14TH. Heading about E. On the wind, starboard tack. Mate had a real run-in with the bos'n today. Also the mate gave John and Anderson such a cursing that John got really mad, crazy mad, and started for the mate, but thought better of it. Both John and Anderson are fine sailors and take pride in doing their work well. John is a big, powerful Western Isle [Negro] and could beat up the mate easily.

During the evening the wind increased and at the end of the second dog watch all hands took in royals and staysails. During our watch below at 11 P.M. all hands were called to take in t'gans'ls and courses. Three of us had the devil's own time with the fore upper topsail—Charlie, Anderson, and myself. About 2 A.M. our watch took in the upper mizzen topsail and as only six of us went up it took us over an hour of hard fighting to subdue the darned sail. Altogether I spent 4 ½ hours aloft last night and every minute of that time was heavy work. It was raining and blowing a fierce gale. On deck the seas came over continually washing everyone again and again into the lee scuppers. I was lucky to be aloft so much of the time. We have certain sails that certain men always handle. For instance, I and John have the main royal and I alone have the mizzen topgallant staysail. The mizzen and main topgallant staysails are the same and are one-man sails. I think they are the meanest sails on the ship to tie up. Sometime I will write down how it is done.

FRIDAY, 14 OCTOBER. Comes in with fresh breeze and cloudy with light drizzly rain. 6 A.M. set light sails. Noon, fresh breeze, cloudy. Wind S, Dis. 194 Lat. by Obs. 35.14 Lon. by D.R. 63.33 W. 4 P.M. breeze freshening took in all royals, light staysails, jib topsail, gaff topsail and ringtail. 8 P.M. freshening and heavy rain. Took in upper topgallant sails. 10 P.M. moderate gale, heavy rain with lightning. Took in lower topgallant sails, crossjack, mainsail, jib, and spanker. Midnight same weather. George Bartolby AB in moving some barrels forepeak had small finger on left hand smashed. Captain dressed the finger. Pumps, lookout, and lights carefully attended to.

OCT. 15TH. Wind has hauled to NW and blowing a gale. Big sea running and washing across the decks continually. Martin and Anderson got washed into the lee scuppers and near drowned while we were scrubbing paint to windward. Rained all day and we scrubbed paint. Rained all night.

OCT. 16TH. SUNDAY. Fine day, strong W wind. Head East. Anyone on deck has to look sharp. Martin got washed into the lee scuppers again today and quite badly hurt. We quit work this morning at 7 o'clock. It is quite cold. At 5 p.m. passed a three-masted schooner heading about SE. Passed close to her. My finger is better. This afternoon, even if it was Sunday, I was kept at work aloft for an hour.

OCT. 17TH. Last night about 3:30 A.M. we passed a steamer. It looked like a big ship and was heading about W. The schooner we passed yesterday did not show her number. We gave her ours and perhaps will be reported. I am getting to know the ropes and where each one belays. I think in a week I can lay my hand on any one in the dark. There are hundreds. It is some time now since I have been cursed out by the mate. Sort of a lull in the storm. Others have been getting it. Today the captain asked the bos'n if he knew anything about me. The bos'n did not know and began asking me questions. He did not get far.

Last night the whole starboard watch while at the main brace were washed across the deck into the lee scuppers and two men were pretty badly hurt. That makes five men laid up. This ship is a bad one for washing and when we get down into really bad weather I guess we will really have some pretty tough times working on deck. Today head E by S on port tack on the wind with everything set and we are doing twelve knots.

OCT. 18TH. Head E by S wind North Hard day unbending heavy weather sails and bending light weather sails. Very hot today. All the men cursing the ship as a very wet ship and I guess it is true. They also cuss the ship as a bad one for hard work which I suppose is largely just sailors grumbling, for as I gather it all American ships are workhouses.

OCT. 19TH. Head E x S, wind NW, light and a hot day. Unbent the t'gans'l halyard pennants and bent new ones. Perfect night, bright moon. Warm and light wind.

OCT. 20TH. From 4 to 6 this morning we hauled braces and then the wind came out ahead about East. Heading South. Made mats [chafing gear] from 6 to 8 A.M. Water a very strong dark blue. Some flying fish around. We have had lime juice for several days now. One cup per man per day at dinner time. The food is all right but the cook is very bad. Everyone growls about it but what can you do. Came up to blow in P.M. and all during the night at intervals we were taking in sail. Blew away two jibs and one upper topsail. By morning we were under lower topsails and courses.

OCT. 21ST. We had an exciting time this morning. It was this way. John, Pete, Myself, Chris, Anderson, and the Bos'n were on the forecastle head bending a new jib. The ship dove and John and Chris were washed overboard. Pete had his head badly cut. Luckily the ship was practically hove to and we saved both of them by throwing rope to them. For the last two days I have had a very bad stomachache and the captain gave castor oil but I am not cured yet. Late this P.M. it began to blow and we shortened down to lower topsails. Our watch tied up the main and mizzen while the starboard watch was tying up the fore upper topsail. Blew a gale during the night and poured rain. Much thunder and lightning. It was a wild night on deck.

OCT. 22ND. Set upper topsails and lower t'gansails and some staysails. There is a big four-masted ship slowly overhauling us from the starboard quarter. She passed us at evening, and it was the *Falls of Garry* from New York to Australia loaded with case oil like us.[10] It rained during the night and we blew away a jib topsail.

OCT. 23RD. SUNDAY. Washed clothes and did some sewing. In the P.M. it rained. We sighted a ship to leeward probably the *Falls of Garry* again. The wind is about dead ahead for our course and we head NE by N. Tacked ship at midnight. It was a fine night but cold. It was the first night for some time that it has not rained some. The mate gets worse and worse cursing everyone all the time. The men don't like the captain but I think he is by far the best of the lot. I have nothing against him.

OCT. 24TH. Washed down decks and tarred down the rigging in the a.m. We turn to sharp at 5 A.M. although it is pitch dark but dark or no dark we start washing down at that time. And sometimes it is a cold wet job. Big excitement today. The mate was down in the lazerette after some rope and it was so dark he lit a match and somehow the match dropped down the center of a big coil of rope and soon a big fire was in progress and vast clouds of black smoke. Right down in the bottom of the ship. Great clouds of smoke coming out of the hatch. We rigged the wash deck gear and carried the water onto the poop. A slow job but after a fight we got the fire out. Not a nice feeling to be afire in the middle of the ocean and your ship loaded with 5,000 tons of kerosene. Speaking of oil. They only allow us one quart of kerosene a week for our lamp. Seems to me stingy.

MONDAY 24 OCTOBER. Wind E by N. Distance 80. Lat. by Obs., 34.42. Lon. by Obs. 42.38 W. Light breeze and fine clear weather. All sail set. P.M. Light breeze and fine weather. First part clear, later part cloudy. Employed repairing sail, etc. Pumps, lookout, and lights carefully attended to.

The mate evidently could think of no compelling reason to record the fact that he had almost set the entire ship afire.

OCT. 25TH. Good day. Wind fair and sheets slightly eased. Head E by S. Wind west of north. This morning while doing some work at the windward rail a sea came over and rolled me clean across into the lee scuppers. But by luck I was not hurt. Spent most of the day putting on chafing gear and making mats. No work to amount to anything could be done on deck on account of the big seas washing across. We made mats under the forecastle head. During the P.M. a very heavy swell came up and all through the night we were shipping water over both rails. First one then the other.

Oct. 26th. Last night I was sent to the wheel and steered for almost four hours straight. We have regular quartermasters so it does not often happen that any of the others get to the wheel. John and Nelson are the quartermasters in our watch. The sea on the quarter was so heavy that several times I was nearly thrown over the wheel.[11] Rained during the morning and we worked under the fo'castle head. Shipping too many seas to work on deck. I never have time to read and there are many books on board. In the afternoon it was hot with no wind and a tremendous sea. We rolled first one rail under then the other and often so far that a man standing on deck would slide right down unless he held on to something. The decks were all awash all day. Some rain during night. Rolling rails under all night.

Oct. 27th. Head SE by S. Wind light about NW. Set up turnbuckles on all backstays and bent an old mainsail in place of the new one. Also bent two jibs that have been off being patched. The mate was very mean all day.

Oct. 28th. Fine warm pleasant day. Every sail set. Head SE by S. Wind NE. The food question is a tough one. The food itself is not so bad but it is spoilt by the cooking. Today it was perhaps a little worse than usual and the bos'n took the breakfast aft for the captain to see. I don't think it will do any good. Making punch mats again today.

Oct. 29th. Fine day same as yesterday. Bent a fine weather cro'jack today. Made mats and shined brass. The starboard watch went aft with their breakfast this morning. Think there will be more trouble about food. Each man is on a whack now. Among other things we get one ounce of butter per day and it is given out every two weeks. We have no place to keep it and it is so terrible that no one tries to keep it for you just can't eat it. It comes out of a can about the size of a gallon can. A picture of a cow on the can but *no* maker's name. Both ends of every can are much bulged out. Lost my good old sheath knife today.[12]

Oct. 30th. Sunday. A day of rest? This day our watch was on deck from 4 to 8 A.M. and we were working all the four hours washing down and handling sails. Then in the P.M. watch a squall came and we were wet and working another four hours. We are supposed to be in Lat. 21 N now. Head SE by S wind aft. The talk is that if we go to Honolulu the captain will pay us off there. In the 2nd dog watch just to make us work a four-masted bark was sighted ahead with main yards aback. We supposed she was in trouble and wanted something.

So it was take in all fore and aft sails and lower royals and back the fore yards. It was then dark and we passed close to her but she gave no signal so we squared away again and set all sail. During the above maneuver it had been raining hard. It was a very warm rain.

OCT. 31ST. Fine day. Head SE by S. Wind NE. This day as usual is warm and clear with *very* blue water and small white cumulus clouds. Squalls are frequent with wind and much rain. Then clear off again. Just a nuisance for you get all wet and have to work hard handling sails. My back is somehow very lame and it is no joke for I have to work just the same whether it hurts or not. I guess I must have strained it.

November 1 found *Astral* in the southeast North Atlantic, northwest of the Cape Verde Islands off the bulge of West Africa, positioned so as to be able to clear the bulge of Brazil when sailing before the northeast trade winds.

TUESDAY, 1 NOVEMBER. Comes in with light variable breeze and fine weather. Wind NW. Dis. 80. Lat. by Obs. 22.3. N. Lon. by Obs. 29.30 W. P.M. light breeze. Hatches off. Employed variously. Pumps, lookout, and lights carefully attended to.

NOV. 1ST. This morning we sighted a steamer and we hoisted our number. She then changed her course and came over to us and we exchanged signals. She was a German tramp bound for South America and hailing from Hamburg. Today was a scorcher with almost no wind and that dead aft. Head SE by S. Bent fine weather upper fore topsail and did a good deal of painting. Food bad. Very bad, and we do not get what we should under the U. S. laws. But what can you do?[13] We caught two dolphins and two bluefish today.

NOV. 2ND. Very hot and calm. Spent most of the day painting. This calm gets tiresome. Cockroaches are everywhere, in your soup and coffee, etc., etc., and in your bunk and blankets. But I am now quite used to them.

NOV. 3RD. Hot and calm but what wind there is has shifted from NW to SW. Head SE by S. Passed a steamer last night. Also had a squall. Making mats and painting today. My back is still very sore. I had a shave last Sunday. It was the first one I had had. I have been aboard a month now. Time goes fast. Spent this afternoon on the fore royal yard with the mate putting on a [thrummed] punch mat.[14]

NOV. 4TH. Hot, calm. Head S by E. Close-hauled on port tack. Martin and the captain had a word contest this morning. I don't like the captain any too well and sometimes he acts mean, but Martin is a bad one. He is small and sly and looks for trouble. My back is worse today and is very painful.

NOV. 5TH. Fine day but hot. A gentle breeze just makes us move. Close-hauled on port tack. Head SxE. My back very painful and last night I could hardly get out of my bunk but after working a while it gets a little easier.

(At San Francisco on this day, Carleton Allen left *Hawaiian Isles.)*

NOV. 6TH. SUNDAY. Washed clothes this morning and slept in P.M. Fine day. We head about ESE close-hauled on port tack and are going about five knots. We are in Lat. 19N. Back a little better today but still painful. Bought some slop chest yesterday including a straw hat and knife and other things. This is our first day on our second month and we are only halfway to the line.

NOV. 7TH. Cloudy, damp, and hot. This morning about 6 o'clock we passed close to a tramp English steamer. We sent up our number and she answered. I could not quite read her name on her bow. If all the vessels we signal report us, those on shore will know pretty well where we are. Spent afternoon watch painting life boat. Back is still sore.

NOV. 8TH. Painting all day. I should like to brain the mate and so would all the rest of my watch. Heading S by E close-hauled on port tack and making about seven knots with everything set. Half the watch have been overhauling the shackles and turnbuckles in the rigging, chipping them and greasing and painting them. Food very bad today.

TUESDAY, 8 NOVEMBER. A.M. fresh breeze and cloudy. Course S by W. Wind SE by S. Lat. by Obs. 10.16. Lon. by D.R. 25.21 W. P.M. comes in with fresh breeze, cloudy. 6 P.M. to 10 P.M. heavy rain, squalls, plenty thunder and lightning. Took in all light sails. 12 midnight light breeze and cloudy. Employed repairing sails and slacking up starboard lower rigging and backstays, drawing chain plate bolts, cleaning them and setting rigging up again. Pumps, lookout, and lights carefully attended to.

NOV. 9TH. Squalls with lightning all night at intervals. Caught much rain water for washing. Lightning struck foremast and knocked the truck off. I was looking at it at the time. It was a fine sight but pretty close. Scrubbed paintwork all the morning with sand and canvas. The mate and bos'n have both been in a bad humor and we have been cussed more than usual today. It has been a hard day. Scrubbed paint with sand and canvas in P.M. also. Very hot, no wind. Decks too hot to go barefoot. In first dog watch passed a Spanish steamer very close going opposite way. Signaled her. She had many passengers, just could not read her name. Head S.

The ship's log made no mention of the lightning strike.

NOV. 10TH. Very hot. Head S. Made punch mat. Passed a four-masted bark this A.M. going same as us. Food bad. Starboard watch went aft about it last night. No result. Calm all day.

NOV. 11TH. Hot calm. Heading S. Two swallows came on board today. Captain says nearest land was the Cape Verde Islands. We must be about Lat. 13 N as I judge by the North Star.[15] Made mats again today. I made a punch mat which was fifteen feet long and one foot wide.

NOV. 12TH. Rain all day. Head about S and going about five knots. Sand and canvas all day.[16] Warm and wet all day.

NOV. 13TH. SUNDAY. Rain and variable squalls. Washed some clothes and spent much time aloft overhauling main buntlines to work off the bos'n's spite. Everyone is cross and hungry for we could not eat the breakfast. Most all my clothes are wet. Lucky it is warm weather. By the North Star we must be about 10 degrees North. Late in the day a good strong SE wind came and we boomed along with all sails set (thirty-one sails). Nowadays I am getting used to getting up at night and walking up and down steadily for four hours. The mate won't let me sit down at all and I have to stay between the mainmast and the poop and the trouble is he can see me from the poop.

NOV. 14TH. Beautiful day. Close-hauled on port tack heading SW and going five knots.

Last night we had a squall and blew away three staysails and two jibs. Monday and I went up to make the main royal fast and the yard was not down nor the buntlines up and we had a hard time. We have now got the good steady trades. Sand and canvas all day today. Just now the bos'n has a grudge against me and gives me all the hard jobs. In the night the mate called me up on the poop and told me to go to the wheel for three hours. It was the first time I had steered the ship on the wind and I found it very easy. But you have to keep her just right or the mate gives you thunder. I don't get the wheel except on special chances, for, as I have said we have regular quartermasters.

Afterwards the mate gave me a sandwich made of tongue and good bread made of fresh water. It tasted mighty good for we never get tongue, only salt meat for us crew. Also we don't get good bread for ours is made of saltwater and is sour most of the time and is like dough. We passed two ships in sight at one time in the P.M. Also we bent another mizzen upper topsail and two jibs and three staysails that were blown away last night. The North Star no longer can be seen. My back is better nowadays. I guess it is cold at home but we just swelter down here night and day. Good breeze and we head SW as usual and make about six knots. Close-hauled.

NOV. 15TH. Wind same. Fine day. After washing down it was sand and canvas till breakfast. Sand and canvas in the afternoon watch also. That finishes up the ship so no more sand and canvas for the present. Fine breeze. Head SW on port tack and go about ten knots. All sail set.

NOV. 16TH. Crossed the line last night. Fine day and good breeze. Head SW by S. Still on the wind. Spent all day scraping the deck. It is an easy but tiresome job. Hot day.

NOV. 17TH. Fine day. Good breeze. Last night the wind hauled some so now we can only head S and go about six knots. Painting aloft all day, sheet and halyard blocks, etc. Passed an English steamer and signalized her this morning. She was from the River Plate bound for Liverpool. We are now heading our course and going good. Quite a relief after head winds and calms. Forty days to the line and six weeks at sea today. The captain said today it would be a six-month voyage to Kobe. Food very bad today. Meat stew not fit to eat for the potatoes in it were rotten. The bread was extra sour. The bad food is beginning to tell on me.

NOV. 18TH. Fine day, good breeze. Head S and go about eight knots. Made a mat today. Bent another mizzen upper topsail in dog watch.

NOV. 19TH. Fine day same as yesterday. The captain says we are ten degrees S and going two hundred miles a day. Made mats and painted. Got cursed a lot today as I could not seem to do things right. More trouble over food and bos'n went aft again to the captain. We were refused bread and the cook refused to bake some hash the bos'n made. We want our whack of everything that we are entitled to. I wonder if we will get it.

NOV. 20TH. SUNDAY. A real day of rest. We did not touch a rope all day. Beautiful warm day. Did mending and washing and got my hair cut. Good breeze at sunset and absolutely no clouds and the colors were fine. I never saw the sun set in such a cloudless sky.

NOV. 21ST. I am pretty well tired out these days with the bad food which so often is so bad we just can't eat it and go hungry. Also little sleep and hard work. Oiled decks today. Also painted aloft. In the dog watch oiled my oilskins.

NOV. 22ND. Good day. Hot. Light wind. Painting waterways and bulwarks. I asked the mate for an old small barrel to cut off and make me a tub to catch water in and wash my clothes in. He got mad and cursed me all around. I don't know whether I shall get it or not.

NOV. 23RD. Rained all day and most of last night. My oilskins are not ready to use yet so I have been wet last night and today. Today all hands have been chipping the iron sides of the ship in the coal bunkers which are in the lower forepeak. It is a fearfully hot and dirty job and the air is very bad and very dusty. You can't see ten feet. Also it is hard work. Such is the life of the sailor. Up on deck to handle sail then get all soaked then down into the forepeak and get all dirty.

NOV. 24TH. Thanksgiving day I think. I suppose we give thanks because we are at present at work on the worst job we have had. Last night we went under the sun and today it is north of us. We are about Lat. 20 degrees South. Chipping iron in the forepeak all day. The forepeak has several decks and the coal bunkers are called the lower hold of the forepeak. Seven weeks at sea.

NOV. 25TH. Still chipping in the forepeak. Hard dirty work. Head SSE. Fine, warm day but we work by lantern light in air you can hardly breath on account of the dust and "Patent" paint fumes.

NOV. 26TH. Painting coal bunkers in forepeak using "Patent" paint. Eyes weep and smart so you can hardly work and when I came up I was as if drunk and was so dizzy I could hardly stand. Last night wind hauled and we are running SSE with square yards. About nine knots. We took in all fore and aft sails in our watch last night. Now work begins when the watch comes on deck at 4 A.M. and we knock off in the second dog watch about 7 P.M.

NOV. 27TH. SUNDAY. Wind strong and in the A.M. we head E with wind W and go 14 knots. In P.M. wind hauled about S and we go E nearly close-hauled. Take in royals. Blowing hard and raining and decks full of water. Plenty of work for a day of rest. Lat. 26S and it is getting cold. Nothing fit to eat. Too tired to write much though I have plenty I should like to put down. During night it was cold and rainy and wet. Much wind and many seas coming on board.

NOV. 28TH. Tacked ship at 8 A.M. and head SW. Bending bad weather sails all day. Bad food today.

NOV. 29TH. Blowing strong. Head SSE. Lat. 29S. Cold! Six of us were working to leeward of the foremast this a.m. and the to'gallant backstay parted at the band aloft and came down landing within a few feet of us. It was a close call for if that big wire had hit any of us we would never have known it. We then tied up the royals and outer jibs. Reeving new gear all day. We are nearly as far south as the Cape of Good Hope now and may get bad weather any time. I can't help thinking it was a remarkable piece of luck when that wire and collar came down among us and hit no one. Food still bad. Both bos'ns complain bitterly about the poor food and hard work on this ship. The bos'n in the starboard watch was once on the *Francis.*

NOV. 30TH. Rain and blow. Wind gradually working astern so in P.M. we had only square sails set and going about 15 knots. Spent A.M. handling sails, halyards, and braces and between times all hands making sennet under the fo'castle head. It's cold today and I think we are about Lat. 34S and head SE. Seas often are coming over bulwarks. I suppose we will have bad weather now till we get past Australia. I get more sleep now. Not that I am in the bunk longer but it is cold now and it is possible to sleep when I am turned in. I get an average of about six hours' sleep a day.

---

1. Sailors had to provide their own straw-filled mattress, or "donkey's breakfast." In most instances this was provided by the shipping master, who charged an inflated price for it against the advance paid by the captain against the sailor's wages.

2. Surely one purpose of this voyage was to break free of Mother Swift's apron strings, and a real sailor didn't receive a stack of mail from his mother. Not only would Tod not have wanted his shipmates to know that he had a letter of credit, but he did not want anyone—forward or aft—to know that he was keeping a journal, which accounts for its brief entries. An educated man, whether in a forecastle or a lumber camp, was invariably the object of scrutiny, speculation, and even suspicion.

3. Masters and mates in American ships were required to be American citizens, so they would have been naturalized.

4. *Astral*'s steam donkey engine was rarely if ever used at sea, and there is no further indication that she carried a donkeyman as a member of the crew. Often this office was filled by the carpenter.

5. HDC 115 Folder 326, Alaska Packers Association Collectcion, National Maritime Museum Library, San Francisco Maritime National Historic Park. *Astral*'s logs, and others from the Alaska Packers Association fleet, were rescued from a bonfire in the 1950s by Harold Huycke.

6. Case oil cargoes required large amounts of wooden dunnage to fair and shim the sides and floor of the hold.

7. On October 3 in Honolulu, Carleton Allen and Mr. Monteith swam in tropical seas by torchlight. Two days later *Hawaiian Isles* put to sea for San Francisco.

8. Very likely Captain Smith at Standard Oil had an arrangement with a particular shipping master who supplied Standard Oil ships with crews, whether at New York or Philadelphia. New York, in any event, was sailor central. A tug was the standard means of transporting a crew of drunks to the rail of the ship, even if the ship was lying at Philadelphia or Newport News. The coastal tug *Britannia* appears to have enjoyed a special relationship with both Standard Oil and the Sewalls.

9. Tod was misinformed. *Acme* was then lying at Hiogo, Japan, where, in December, Captain Lawrence fatally shot himself. She then was sailed to Hong Kong by her mate, a man named Amesbury. At Hong Kong Amesbury was given command of the sistership *Atlas*, whereupon he promptly fatally shot *himself.* Amesbury's death was a suicide; that of the 7-foot 2-inch Lawrence may have been one, also. Lawrence was a Mainer; Amesbury was likely one as well.

10. *Falls of Garry* was a member of the celebrated Glasgow Falls Line, which operated nine magnificent four-masted ships. The first, *Falls of Clyde*, is preserved at Honolulu.

11. Aboard the *Frye* the marks left by the boots of helmsmen thrown over the wheel were left on the overhead as a warning. Francis M. Cushing, *I Once Knew a Ship* (Bangor: Furbish-Roberts, 1963), p. 74. The "vicious" helm of *Atlas* killed a man on her maiden passage from Bath to New York. Harold Huycke, "Case Oil and Canned Salmon: *Star of Lapland,* ex-*Atlas,*"*American Neptune*, vol. xvi, p. 25.

12. Since 1866 it had been illegal—and still is—to *wear* a sheath knife on an American merchant vessel (R. S. 4608), the master being liable for a $50 fine for every instance where he did not "inform every person offering to ship himself of the provisions of this section, and to require his compliance therewith...." This measure was likely an attempt to reduce shipboard violence. On some ships the mates broke off the points of the sailors' knives at the outset of a voyage.

13. A precise scale of provisions, last updated in 1898, stipulated articles to be supplied, and amounts, per day of the week. About two dozen items were included, along with numerous allowable substitutes. At the outset of the passage it was customary for the captain to ask the crew if they wished to be fed strictly by scale or to accept the captain's "whack."

14. A type of woven sennit mat.

15. The actual position was 6°29' latitude, 24°53' longitude, or, about 400 miles south of Tod's estimate.

16. Sand and canvas, cheaper then sandpaper, were used to prepare surfaces for painting.

Chapter 19

Astral, December 1904–January 1905: Past the Cape, to the Islands

Astral *Sails From the South Atlantic into the Indian Ocean.*

DECEMBER 1 FOUND *ASTRAL* at 36°25' south latitude, 21°41' west longitude, nearing the South Atlantic midway way-point islands of Tristan da Cunha, located on the southern end of the Mid-Atlantic Ridge.

DEC. 1ST. 36 S 21 W. Cold, rainy, heavy sea and much wind. Head E with yards square. Made sennett under the fo'castle head most of the day. Last night the mate called me aft and sent the quartermaster forward and made me steer for 3½ hours. I was glad enough when eight bells went for the big following sea made her kick very badly. Everything on board is now thoroughly soaked, all of our clothes and most blankets. We often have to bail out the deck house for when a man goes in or out of the door a sea is apt to come in although the door sill is two feet high above the deck. Today we put in some time reeving new buntlines and gaskets.

DEC. 2ND. Rain cold and blowing. Took in royals, upper to'gansails, cro'jack, and mainsail. Head about E, wind N. Everything is wet including all my clothes. Seas are all over the deck. I had the wheel in the second dog watch and half of the middle watch last night. She kicked badly. The mate is talking of making me a quartermaster in place of John. I hope he does *not*! I got sworn at more than usual this morning. Today all hands in the interval between hauling braces work at sennet under the fo'castle head. I am making a thrummed punch mat for the anchor fluke as a chafer for the jib sheets. Speaking of jib sheets, pennants on the jib are three-quarter-inch chain. That gives an idea how heavy things are aboard this ship.

DEC. 3RD. Cold and raining and blowing. Worked most of the day under the fo'castle head. My rubber boots are worn out and I got a new pair out of the slop chest. We go along in great style nowadays, fourteen knots. Sighted land about dusk.

DEC. 4TH. SUNDAY. Hove-to last evening, and this morning we squared away and ran down to the three islands. They were what sounds like Tristra Dacua [Tristan da Cunha]. They are British and are 1,800 miles W. of Capetown. We hove-to again off the island that is inhabited and two boats came off to trade. The captain got sheep and ducks, both alive, and also potatoes and much else in return for biscuit, coffee, tobacco, oil, flour, etc., etc. They also did a lot of small trading among us men. I got a quart of milk for a cake of soap. Two penguin skins for a cap. An albatross skin for a shirt. Three albatross feet for tobacco pouches for a cake of soap. The bird skins I got are beautiful but I am afraid I will have trouble keeping them as I guess they are not well cured and I have to keep them in my bunk. The milk was great and I wanted more. I am all the time hungry nowadays.

There was a man who came off in one of the boats whose name was Egan. He was born on the island and is the son of a Captain Egan of New Bedford, master of a whaler (schooner) lost years ago on the island. There are sixty-seven people on the island, but only twelve grown men. The rest are women and children. The island is five miles in diameter. It is a mountain 7,640 feet high with no flat places on it.

DEC. 5TH. Very cold and clear. Head E with square yards. Putting on new braces today. Turned to at 4 A.M. and knocked off at 7 P.M. in the second dog watch. Hard day.

DEC. 6TH. Cloudy and cold and strong breeze. Head about E with yards square. Although we got lots of fresh meat from the Island we get so little of it. I am all the time hungry. I fill up on biscuits but even the biscuits are often poor. The name of the island is Tristan d'Acunha [*sic*].

DEC. 7TH. Rain—Cold—Blowing. Much hauling of braces. Some work under fo'castle head. Someone threw the draw bucket overboard and there was a terrible row when it was found there was no bucket to get water for washing down this morning. Another bucket is now being made and much larger. Food very bad again today. In P.M. a gale of wind came from NW and we took in everything but topsails. While at the fore brace a sea washed us *all* to leeward and I hurt my knee quite badly. When a sea comes aboard close at hand the first thing you know is that you are underwater and unless you had a good grip on something and were not in the direct path of the sea you go washing across the deck hitting everything hard. My knee is all swelled up.

DEC. 8TH. My knee very stiff and sore. Am hungry for we had nothing for supper we could eat but some very watery soup. Wind S. all sail set. Four knots. Cold and drizzle and all my clothes are wet.

DEC. 9TH. Gale of wind from NE and rain and cold. Last night at 8 P.M. we had all sail set and by midnight we had taken in everything but the topsails, foresail, and a couple of jibs and staysails and we are close-hauled. Much water on deck. You have to look out for yourself all the time on deck. Have not done much but trim and take in sail and stand by. In P.M. the wind hauled dead aft W and blew a living gale. We took in all sail but three lower topsails and foresail.

Decks full of water coming over both rails and deep up to your waist. It is no joke working on deck. I was washed while at the brace once and grabbed a rail stanchion. The weight of water landing on top of me crushed me down flat on the deck still hanging on to the stanchion. Then I was torn away and washed across to the lee scuppers where I hit another stanchion which I grabbed and managed to hang on to. When I came up I was near drowned. It seemed like ten minutes. This is only an example and is liable to happen at any moment in this weather. It does not pay to change your clothes although it is cold for you are immediately wet again. I talk of changing clothes but of course you can only do that on your watch below. You can't go into the fo'castle during your watch on deck. Martin and Anderson got hurt this P.M. They were washed to leeward.

DEC. 10TH. Heavy gale all last night. At 11:30 P.M. we called the other watch and took in upper topsails and at 2 A.M. they called us out to take in foresail and mizzen topsail. The wind hauled from aft and we braced her up sharp under fore, main, and mizzen topsails and fore top staysail. Very big sea washing clean over the ship. Even on the fore and aft bridge which runs from the poop to fo'castle head eight feet above the deck it was dangerous for at times amidships it was liable to wash you off the bridge in spite of holding onto the handrails. So you can picture what kind of a time we had down on deck working with buntlines and braces, etc. The mate from up on the bridge would sing out when a big sea was coming and all hands would take to the rigging. If you were caught on deck it was all your life was worth for you could not possibly hang on to anything through one of those washes. It was very exciting work. It was also very cold and wet.

Several men were hurt. The wind went down in the a.m. and we were gradually setting sail all day. Very cold. All my clothes wet and my bunk wet.

DEC. 11TH. SUNDAY. Fine day but cold. Tacked ship in A.M. Much work and little rest.

DEC. 12TH. Fine clear day with real sunshine. Overhauling rigging all day. Got most of my clothes dry. Now I am ready for more bad weather. I am pretty sore and lame in several places from being washed round. My left knee is bad and pains me and is swelled up. The food today somewhat better. Although one of the sheep was butchered we got none of it. They had it aft. Salt horse for us.

DEC. 13TH. Fine day. Head E as usual. Wind South. Bright sun and cold. All hands making sennet. I was at work on a mat. When the mate says anything to any of us and we answer him telling the truth he always calls you a liar and cusses you. He is continually calling all of us vile answers whenever he happens to meet a man.

DEC. 14TH. Off the Cape of Good Hope today. Lat. 40 S. Lon. 18 E. Three hundred miles to the south of the Cape. Beautiful bright clear day. Overhauling the halyards today. Almost absolutely smooth. Wind has hauled NW and we may expect rain.

DEC. 15TH. Beautiful warm calm day. Wind shifting all the time and so there was much handling of braces and fore and aft sheets and halyards. Wind started SW and ended same place. The ship has a strong list to port caused by "The Big Sea" that hove her down last week. It struck her that night about 8:15 P.M. I forgot to mention it. It went over the bridge and over the deck houses. All of us in our watch were scrambling up the rigging for our lives. We were near the mizzen rigging and went up that. One man, Bill the Kanaka of the starboard watch, was washed overboard that night but hung on to the loose end of a buntline and came back on the next wave. The sights you see in those times are deadly serious but very funny too.

DEC. 16TH. Still calm, warm, and pleasant but a big swell has come up and I guess the bad weather is not far off. Working in rigging today. The ship is now about ready for bad weather. We had better get the bad weather and have done with it, for though this calm is very nice and pleasant we don't get anywhere. Ten weeks at sea.

DEC. 17TH. Wind hauled last night to North and now we are having rain and a good breeze. All sail set. Food very bad today. Salt meat hardly cooked at all. Potatoes rotten and bread very sour. Yesterday we got our whacks of butter. I have mine and it is for a month. It is bad to start with and after you keep it a month in your bunk it is not eatable. Many birds around today. Albatross, Whale Birds, Cape Pigeon, and Petrel, also others at times. Heavy swell. Cleaning paint today, which is the usual rainy day work when there is not too much wind.[1]

DEC. 18TH. SUNDAY. Calm, warm. Wind astern. Nothing much done all day. Last night had rain and fog. The second sheep has been killed but we don't even get a taste of it.

DEC. 19TH. Cold and damp. Wind in a.m. strong gets lighter and keeps hauling back and forth from SW to NW and keeps us busy with braces and staysails. Making mats at odd times.

DEC. 20TH. Strong N wind and rain and cold. Made a fifteen-foot mat for topsail. More hungry than usual today. Food was worse. Last night was a cold one on deck for spray kept coming over.

DEC. 21ST. Cloudy, damp, and cold with rain squalls. Wind varying from North to South by way of West many times. Therefore much work at braces, etc. Heavy swell last night. All our watch was sitting on No. Three hatch at 8:30 smoking and talking when a big sea came over and washed us all into the lee scuppers. The hatch is 2 ½ feet above the deck. None of us had oilskins on and we were as wet as if we had fallen overboard. By good luck no one was hurt.

DEC. 22ND. Cold day. Made sennet. This A.M. the starboard watch refused duty and said they would not wash down at 4 A.M. unless they were given coffee first. Tomorrow our watch will do the same thing. But I guess we will get all the more work for doing it. The usual custom is to serve coffee at one bell which is rung at 4:45 then you have fifteen minutes to drink your coffee then turn to and wash down at 5 A.M. We had it that way at first. It is pitch dark at 4 A.M. Cold and rain last night.

DEC. 23RD. We are down to 45 degrees South or more and it is very cold. Blowing strong from SW. Everything set and going 14 knots. Much water on deck. Our watch refused duty this A.M. as to washing down at 4 A.M. with no coffee. We took in the royals and set them again between 7 A.M. and 8 A.M. The mate thought it was going to blow. Made sennet and mats between jobs today. Numerous cold rain squalls.

DEC. 24TH. Cold and wet and rain. Strong SW wind. All sails set. Seas coming aboard. In last twenty-four hours we made over 250 miles. Very fair. Making sennet. All my clothes wet and nothing will dry at all. The only way to dry your socks is to put your wet socks underneath your undershirt when you turn in.

DEC. 25TH. SUNDAY and CHRISTMAS. Lat. 45 degrees S and about Long. 50 E. Cold and blowing. No work during day but all last night and early this morning we were kept busy with the sails. It rained all the time and was cold work. To celebrate we had a mince ? pie for dinner.

DEC. 26TH. Holiday today. No work. Strong N wind. Go twelve knots. Fog and cold. Too cold to sit down on watch on deck. All sail and ship going good.

DEC. 27TH. Fine, warm, sunny day. Strong N wind. All sail. Dried my boots today. At work cleaning rust off wire ropes and making sennet. Food bad today. Cut my left forefinger badly yesterday, a two-inch cut. A large whale swam slowly alongside close-to last evening and made a great noise blowing. He was about one hundred feet from the ship.

DEC. 28TH. Clear, cold, and bright day. Cleaning and painting wire ropes. I should like to heave the bos'n over the side.

DEC. 29TH. Started to blow last night and we took in royals. Chris and I had considerable trouble with the mizzen. Took in to'gansails and remaining staysails today. A good deal of water on deck. All my clothes from socks to cap are soaked and none of them will dry in this weather except the ones you sleep in and they only partially. Cold day today and I guess tonight will be a tough one.

It certainly was a tough one for it blew up a gale about dark and at eight bells all hands took in cro'jack and mainsail and our watch the lower to'gans'ls. Big seas coming aboard all night and it blew hard, the wind continually hauling to West so we were at the braces all the time and we were consequently all washed round the deck time and again and wet through. Wind went down in A.M. and all sail was set.

DEC. 30TH. Fine warm calm day. Dried a few of my clothes. Overhauling ropes for stages and bending main and mizzen topgallant staysails, I am sorry to say, for they are mean to make fast. I think the worst of any of the sails and it is always my job to make fast the mizzen to'gal staysail. The stay comes down to the mast about twelve or fifteen feet above the top. The stay passes through the eye then down the after side of the mast to form a sort of jackstay. To make the sail fast you shin up the sail which will be blowing out to leeward then work down the sail passing the gasket round the sail and jackstay as you come. The sail is so big and bulky you can't reach round but throw the gasket through between mast and jackstay then reach round and grab it if you can. All this time riding the sail and nothing but sail to hold to. A gale of wind, ship jumping, rain and oilskins and rubber boots. And the mizzen to'gallant staysail is mine—I also have the main royal with one other man, but the royals are easy compared to the mizzen to'gallant staysails. And speaking of royal yards, ours on this ship are fifty-six feet long.[2] Only two men are allowed to go up to make a royal fast. Upper to'gans'ls have three men. And so it goes. It is a heavy ship to work.

DEC. 31ST. Good day. Calm and warm. Scraped paint on bulwarks. I should like to get a good square meal. This food is doing me up. Saw a big whale today.

January 1, 1905, found *Astral*—Tod's information (below) notwithstanding—at 39°55' south latitude, 85°26' east longitude, running her "easting down" in the Great Southern Ocean, about halfway between the Cape of Good Hope and Western Australia. After having passed the Cape of Good Hope the route selected to Japan depended on the season, the captain, and the handiness of the ship. Ships due to arrive in the summer, with the fair southwest monsoon, would head for the Strait of Sunda then head north into the South China Sea, and run to Chinese or Japanese ports. (Two big Anglo-American oil ships were lost in the Strait.)

From October to April, during the northeast (often, actually, north or northwest) monsoon, the South China Sea door was closed to anything short of a true clipper. Many of the big oil ships sailed south into the Great Southern Ocean, passing south and east of Australia and heading north through the islands of the South Pacific. This route had its own hazards—the Sewall's fine new ship *Rainier* was lost in 1883 on an uncharted reef while attempting to pass through the Marshall Islands. The big steel barks could take six months completing the 20,000-mile passage.

The third option was to pass through one of the island straits east of Sunda, then head north, generally through Makassar Strait and the Molucca Sea, and out to waters east of the Philippines. Some sailors recalled a passage through these waters as the highlight of their years at sea. This path led through a thousand miles of poorly charted waters rife with hidden reefs and natives with a shadowy history. Also, the winds did not always comply with their printed descriptions. This was the route chosen by Captain Bray of the *William J. Rotch* in 1881, and in 1905 by Captain Dunham with drastically different results.[3]

JAN. 1ST. SUNDAY. Fine day. Wind hauled from N to W and we took in all staysails, etc. We are 45 degrees S, 88 degrees E. I smashed the lamp chimney in our fo'castle today. There will be a proper row as I have an idea there are no more. Let us hope for the best, however.

JAN. 2ND. A HOLIDAY. After washing down very thoroughly we did no work for the rest of the day. Cold, foggy—wind right aft. To celebrate we had rice pudding made with molasses instead of milk. It was pretty bad.

JAN. 3RD. Cold day. Wind right aft. Big swell from aft. Chipped side of donkey engine room. We will shift our course soon, I hear, and I will be glad to get back to warm weather. They say we are [to be] going through the Spice Islands Passage.[4]

JAN. 4TH. Rain and cold. Two of us were scraping and painting the inside of the donkey engine room. The rest were holystoning the fore and aft bridge. That is where Dutch and I had the best of it. But none too good.

JAN. 5TH. Fine clear day. Finished chipping, scraping, and painting the engine room. Started today to bend fine weather sails. That is a good sign. Food was worse than usual today.

JAN. 6TH. Three months at sea. Rain last night and although in Lat. 37 degrees S it is still cold. Took in royals and staysails this morning. This P.M. while we were chipping and painting round the deck a squall came up and we took in upper to'gansails and mainsail and cro'jack. No oilskins. Result, soaked to the skin. It makes it bad, for nothing dries well these days.

JAN 7TH. This morning about 2 A.M. the wind dropped some and we set all sail. Fine day chipping and painting on deck. Last night seas came over her often. A bad night.

JAN. 8TH. SUNDAY. 34 S, 107 E. We are nearly opposite New Bedford. Seems odd. A fine, warm, bright day with very little work. Dried my clothes. Washed clothes. Mended clothes. Had a peaceful day. We head about NNE.

JAN. 9TH. Clear, calm, warm day. Bending fine weather sails all day. Hard, hot work for always Hurry Hurry Hurry.

JAN. 10TH. Tarring down. The food was bad today. I am getting thin and the other men show it too. The food just is not enough. For instance, this is what we had today.

Breakfast. Coffee (last night's tea grounds were in the bottom of the pot under the coffee. Half-cooked cornmeal mush.

Dinner. Lime juice. Potatoes (very rotten). Half-cooked salt meat.

Supper. Rice and bad curry.

It is a fine kind of food to do hard work on and our work is hard. We had bread besides but that was so sour and soggy that I could not eat much of any.

JAN. 11TH. Fine day head NNE. Lat. about 30 S. Tarring and painting in the rigging. A dirty job. Real summer weather now and I go barefoot. Only wear a pair of dungaree pants and thin shirt. Quite a change from the thick underclothes, woolen pants, and sweater.

JAN. 12TH. Strong SE wind. Scraping and painting. It has been a hard day for all of us as both the mate and bos'n have been on the rampage. This is the kind of day that puts murder in your heart.

JAN. 13TH. 21 S 112 E. Blowing fresh SE. Sand and canvas on capstan bars and other bright work. Too much wind to paint aloft. Bad food today as usual. Why note it down here when it is bad every day?

JAN. 14TH. We are only 100 miles off the NW coast of Australia. Painting aloft all day. Strong wind aft. Hot and sunny. I certainly would like a good square meal.

JAN. 15TH. SUNDAY. Hot day not much work. Too hot to sleep in watch below. I got into a proper row last night in my watch on deck by going to sleep and not being awake at one bell to wake the bos'n who was asleep himself. The mate then found the bos'n asleep and gave him hell. However, the bos'n is mad with me. The mate did not mind my being asleep.

JAN. 16TH. Very hot and calm. We are north of the sun now and ought to get to the straits this week. The deck is so hot the pitch in the seams bubbles up in great bubbles as big as my thumb. It is the hottest weather I ever saw.

JAN. 17TH. Chipping and painting outside the vessel on stagings. Very hot. Too hot to sleep or eat. The potatoes are almost gone, and from now on we in the crew get no more. All the rest go to the cabin. Almost calm today. Sleep is scarce now. It is too hot to sleep in our watch below in the daytime, and on our watch on deck at night they keep us on our feet now. Today for dinner we had salt meat, lime juice, and soggy pie. Fine food, especially when the meat is so little cooked it is like leather.

JAN. 18TH. Very hot. Today we got the anchors over and bent on the chain. Got a squall which blew away three topmast and two to'gallant staysails. We get so little water this hot weather that we drink it all and then I am always thirsty. This being thirsty is worse than being hungry.

JAN. 19TH. LAND IN SIGHT. We can just see land on the port bow. Very hot chipping and painting over the side on stages. It is terrible working on the sunny side against the hot plates of the ship. We have almost finished the top plate. A squall is coming up now astern and I hope it rains, for then I can get a bit of a wash. We are all in need of a wash.

JAN. 20TH. Very hot. We came up to an island last night and now are passing another which is 10,000 feet high. Very green with trees solid from the water to the mountain tops. Much rain in the dog watch yesterday and I got myself and some clothes washed. This heat is fierce and even at night one can hardly sleep. We are kept constantly at the braces and halyards day and night for one wind does not last, then shifts. During the day, between times at the braces and halyards, we go on the stages overside chipping and scraping. It is hard work and hot.

JAN. 21ST. Very hot. Chipping, scraping, and painting over the side. Bad squall last evening and we took to'gansails in and of course the royals. Tacked ship twice in our watch last night and once in our watch this morning and each time we did it alone without calling the starboard watch. The starboard watch never has tacked the ship without calling us out. Last night the captain caught the mate asleep in his watch on deck. Today the mate and I had words.

JAN. 22ND. SUNDAY. Hottest yet. I just sit quiet in the shade and the sweat runs off me. And when we work!!! Tack ship every eight or four or two hours as may be. We are beating back and forth between Timor Island and Flores Island. Islands all around and they are all covered with high mountains from five to twelve thousand feet high. With no level spots and the green trees growing all over them right up to the tops of the mountains. We are working slowly up to the Ombai Passage and are supposed to be going out through Molucca Strait.[5]

JAN. 23RD. Nearing the end of Timor Island and very close to one on our port which is I think Ombai Island. They are both very mountainous. Squalls all last night and continual work. It is infernally hot today and between the times of hauling braces we are at work on stages over the side in the blazing sun chipping and painting the outside of the ship. It is very calm but what wind there is is behind us.

JAN. 24TH. Hot as yesterday. Painting over the side on stages. Very light wind. Tack ship very often. We hardly get straightened out from the tacking and over the side on the stages before it is tack ship again. We are now entering the Banda Sea and have passed Timor and Kambling Islands.[6] We saw lights on several of these islands at night but saw no signs of life in the daylight. The men talk about an English ship some years ago which went ashore on one of these islands and the natives ate all the crew. Some story and it must have been long ago. Words with the mate again today.

JAN. 25TH. Squalls all last night and today. Scrubbing paint work round on deck today getting ready for painting. The mate worse than usual and the men are nearly crazy with him. Last night I was barefoot as usual and hit my toe on an eyebolt and cut the toe deeply. It is all-fired sore today. Rained hard all day and I wore just a pair of dungaree pants and was almost cool. I got two hours' sleep in the afternoon watch below.

JAN. 26TH. Bright and hot. Sand and canvas and sougy on paint work around deck.[7] We had enough to eat today. Yesterday was starvation day. It is hard work most of the time on our knees in the sun scrubbing paint. It was a fine night and I fell asleep on deck and by luck no one saw me.

JAN. 27TH. Hot—sand and canvas all day. Our drinking water supply in our tank in the forecastle is always almost gone and we have to be very careful with it. We are all thirsty most of the time. The mate and John had a big row and in the end the mate backed down before John hit him. The mate has been very meek since then but that will wear off.

JAN. 28TH. Yesterday P.M. we sighted land ahead. It was Bouro [Buru] Island. The wind was W and our head N and directly for the island. Must pass to the west of it so tack ship in the first dog watch and again at 4 A.M. this morning and again at noon today. We don't make much to windward. Sand and canvas all day. We begin painting Mon-

Sailing track chart for the Indian Archipelago for the north–east monsoon.
FINDLAY'S DIRECTORY, 1889.

(2) Page 1344
Tropic of Cancer
TAIWAN or FORMOSA
Amoy
Pescadores
Kelung Har.
Taiwan
Botel Tobago
Pratas
Bashee Channel
Bashee Is
Batan I.
Balintang Chan.
Babuyan Is
C. Bojeador
C. Engaño
NORTH
PACIFIC
OCEAN
PHILIPPINE ISLANDS
LUZON
Palana
Polillo
Macclesfield Bk
Scarborough Sh.
Catanduanes
Bernardino Strait
Mindoro
Samar
Surigao Is
Yap
Matelotas
Pelew Is
Babelthouap I.
Sequeiros
Rasa I.
Kendrick I.
Parece Vela
Helen Sh.
Palawan
Balabac
Samboangan
Sulu Archipel
Darvel B.
Kini Balu
Labuan
CELEBES SEA
Sangir
Siao
Menado
Banka
Morty
HALMAHERA or JILOLO
Ternate
Tidore
Salibabo
St Andrew Is
Pt Mariere
Helen Rf
St David Is
Equator
Mysory I.
Jobi
Geelvink Bay
NEW GUINEA
Dampier
Waygiou
Tomini Gulf
CELEBES
Tolo B.
Pitts Passage
Boero
Mysol
CERAM
Amboina
BANDA
BANDA SEA
Kei Is
Arru Is
Dourga Str.
Timor Laut
FLORIS SEA
Tokan Besi
Buton
Kabeina
Salayar
Wetta
Flores
Sumbawa
Lombok
Bali
Sandalwood I.
Savu
Rotti
Timor
ARAFURA SEA
C. Valsche
MAKASSAR
STR. of MAKASSAR
1370
1373
1374
1375
1376
1384
1385
R.H. LAURIE, 53, FLEET STREET, LONDON.

day. I wonder how long it will take to round the west end of Bouro Island if this west wind holds.

JAN. 29TH. SUNDAY. Good strong breeze and we are going good and have not tacked since noon yesterday. We head westerly and see no land. I don't know where Bouro Island is now. The starboard watch called us out in the middle of the afternoon watch to tack ship for rocks were sighted ahead. Two of them stuck up about fifty feet above water. No island in sight. We ran back all night. Strong breeze. Took in to'gallant staysails, etc., in our dog watch. Water coming on deck during night.[8]

JAN. 30TH. Tacked ship at 5:30 this morning (we don't call the other watch when we tack) for we sighted Bouro Island dead ahead. So here we are back again. We want to go north but the wind is now north so we go east or west. I was so tired last night I went to sleep in my watch on deck and I got into a mess of trouble. Was sent aloft to overhaul buntlines and clewlines which the bos'n broke the stops on so I could stop them up again. He kept me at it a couple of hours.[9]

The P.M. log entry for January 30 reads: *Hans* [looks like] *Honneker signed A.B.* [able-bodied seaman] *on 12 of Nov. incapable and useless. Reduced to O.S.* [ordinary seaman] *$15.*

JAN. 31ST. We had a big, bad squall last evening. Lasted three hours and we took in everything down to lower to'gansails. We are still close hauled and trying to round Bouro Island but can't do it. The fo'castle is now being painted so we are camping out in the sail locker on the sails. The captain spoke to me yesterday. It was the first time since the row over the food which was long ago. Several times the breakfast or dinner was carried aft to the break of the poop and he was called for to see it, then the man would throw it overboard and we would go without it rather than eat it. But it did no good.

---

1. Dust from the atmosphere and fiber particles from the rig accumulate about the deck and houses of a vessel even when far at sea. Of course, even if there was nothing to clean the men would be kept at it—permitting any idleness among sailors on watch during daylight hours, Sunday or extreme weather conditions excepted, was unthinkable.

2. 57 feet, 6 inches long, according to Thober and Fairburn.

3. In the early 1900s oil passages for Japan from May to November averaged over 160 days, while those made from December to April averaged about 135

days. Frank W. Thober, "American Oil Ships," *Nautical Research Journal*, vol. 2, no. 1, p. 7.

4. This was also called the Molucca Passage. The Spice Islands reference is a reminder that in centuries past Europeans desired the spices of the Far East more than gold. Some New England mariners of the early 1800s who sailed to these islands for spices became very wealthy. Salem, Massachusetts—Captain Dunham's hometown—had been the leading homeport of American spice traders.

5. Findlay's *Directory* describes Ombai Passage as being sixteen miles at the narrowest point, "apparently deep water throughout.... It is generally used by ships bound to China late in the [S.W.] monsoon." Findlay, *Directory*, p. 753.

6. Findlay included an 1844 report by a Lieutenant Hooft describing the hostile manner of the natives of Kambling Island, who "rolled large stones from the tops of the hills in order to impede the ascent along a steep path." Ibid., p. 754.

7. Sougy was soap-and-water solution.

8. One cannot truly appreciate the pressures on Captain Dunham who has had little but unseasonable headwinds, forcing him to tack his big bark through very poorly charted waters with no buoys, marks, or lights. To have run the ship aground would likely have been disastrous. By comparison, the sailors' complaints were very small potatoes. In October 1905, *Astral*'s sister *Acme*, under the command of another Nova Scotian, Captain Adelbert F. McKay, when entering the Strait of Sunda grounded and pounded heavily on an uncharted reef. Repairs at Singapore cost about $80,000. From the diary of Mrs. McKay, courtesy of Captain Harold Huycke. Captain McKay was an outstanding shipmaster; his record for fast passages made with *Acme* and the *Atlas* were the best of any of the Standard Oil captains. McKay switched to *Acme* from the *Atlas* at Hong Kong in December 1904, following Captain Stanley Amesbury's suicide. *Atlas*'s mate, John C. Amberman—another Nova Scotian—succeeded to command, and gave *Atlas* the reputation of a "Hell Ship," reportedly—according to sailors—tricing men up by the wrists, stinting on food, employing the cat-o'-nine tails, and taking pot-shots at a sailor. Thober, *NRJ*, vol. 9, nos. 5 & 6, p. 138, 140. *San Francisco Chronicle*, 17 July 1905, 22 July 1905. For a less lurid account, see Harold Huycke, "Case Oil and Canned Salmon," *American Neptune,* vol. xvi, no. 1.

9. This was a standard form of petty harassment of sailors by officers. Buntlines and clewlines, ropes that helped to gather the square sails to the yards, were "overhauled," or pulled up a bit, and then "stopped" aloft with rope yarns, by sailors, to prevent chafe on the sails. A sharp jerk on the lines would break the stops.

Chapter 20

Astral, February–March 1905: Passage End

Astral *Tacks Through Islands and Reefs, Into the Pacific, and on to Kobe.*

FEB. 1ST, 2ND, 3RD. Living in sail locker on top of the sails and no chance to write.

FEB. 4TH. Today we passed Bouro [Buru] Island after eight days of beating back and forth. We now go our course which is said to be for Molucca Passage. Good breeze. The mate is looking for trouble these days and he may get it if he drives some of the men too hard. Painting and scraping paint spots all the time now. This ship is gray outside and all white on deck, deck houses, inside of bulwarks, etc. Everything is either white paint or bright oiled wood. It means a lot of work. No chipping hammers are allowed on the houses or inside of the bulwarks. You rub down the old paint with pumice stone then red lead then white paint. Last evening in the dog watch our watch tacked ship *twice* all by ourselves without any rest on account of a rapid shift of wind. We are just between Bouro and Sula Besi Islands. Got two hours' sleep in my watch on deck last night and was not caught, which I call good luck.

FEB. 5TH. SUNDAY. Our side washed down and tacked twice all in one watch by ourselves. Then in the P.M. we tacked once and kept bracing and squaring the yards the whole time and in our dog watch we tacked four times without calling out the other side. It was a very hard day. No day of rest today. We are just off what they say is Gay's Island.

FEB. 6TH. Tacked three times before noon. I spend the between times scraping out a beef barrel to catch rainwater in with which to fill the tank. The others shined brass on pin rails. We have harder work and no better food nowadays but in spite of that I am getting fat and am in first-rate condition now. I don't see why, for the weather is so hot I get very little sleep and not much to eat and work night and day all the time. But it's so.

FEB. 7TH. Fine day, light head wind as usual. Tacked all last night and all today. We are in the midst of a lot of small islands and they are so near to us we can see the land all night. There seem to be hundreds of them and the captain says there are also many reefs and bars. We have had a fair current and head wind and make fifty to seventy miles a day. We are sixty miles to leeward of Gebi Island where we will heave to for the natives to come aboard for "changy for changy."

I holystoned the deck of the oil locker today; the others scraped paint spots off the deck. Food is bad. Since the potatoes gave out we often get oatmeal and yellow corn mush for breakfast. And in almost every plate you find big white worms about an inch long. However, one soon gets used to them, and in spite of the large amount of fresh meat in the mush I am always glad when I see it come out of the galley. For it is good food compared to the other things.

FEB. 8TH. Fine hot day. Head wind. Light work all day scraping paint spots off deck. Tacked ship several times. Gebi Island where we will have "changy for changy" is in sight. About forty-four miles dead to windward N by E. Too hot to sleep much. I don't believe we go through Molucca Passage but I don't know.

FEB. 9TH. Rain squalls all day. Hove to off Gebi Island and a boat is now coming out to us. We have been cool all night and today we have been wet the whole time. The natives came alongside and we got coconuts, pineapples, shells, sugar cane, nutmegs, etc., etc., in return for old clothes, bread, matches, tobacco, soap, etc. They left at dark.

FEB. 10TH. Another "changy for changy" boat coming off from Gilolo Island which is close to the NW of Gebi Island.[1] It was a sailboat. Sort of a lateen sail made of leaves and sewn together. The boat itself was made of wood and put together entirely without the use of nails. Some of the natives had straight hair and some curly. All were without clothes except for a belt. They stayed alongside all the morning and we got many coconuts and pineapples, nutmegs, pumpkins, bananas, shells, corn, sugar cane, also four parrots and some monkeys. These natives are a queer lot. We crossed the line this morning. Frequent rain squalls today.

FEB. 11TH. Tack ship every four hours day and night. We are about thirty miles north and to windward of Gebi Island. Chipping under the fo'castle head. Many squalls. Took in anchors and chains and stowed them.

FEB. 12TH. SUNDAY. Rain and blow all last night and we had about as close a call to shipwreck as I ever want to come. It had been raining and blowing hard and was very dark and a big sea was running. Our watch went below at the end of the middle watch. I was just getting in to my bunk when I heard, "Land ahead" "About ship" "All hands." The rain had stopped for a couple of minutes, it seems, and the lookout then saw we were right on top of an island. We tried to tack but she would not come so we had to wear ship. Before we got round we were right into the breakers, almost. It was not pleasant, for if we went ashore we might not be able to get to land for all the islands round here are very steep and rocky. However, we got clear. Squally and blowing and rain today.

Of course, nothing about this very close call appeared in the log. A miss is as good as a mile, and what the owners didn't know wouldn't hurt them!

ALL THIS DAY moderate breeze and part clear with passing heavy rain squalls. Tacked ship at 4 A.M. & 10 A.M. Pumps, lookout, and lights carefully attended to.

FEB. 13TH. 2 N 130 E. Last night in the middle watch we were taken aback in a squall and worked 2 1/2 hours before we got all straightened out again. Hard work too. Today still head winds—I think we have had head winds all the time, except for one afternoon since we passed Sandlewood Island on Jan. 20. We bent new main to'gals and royal for the old ones were torn and are to be patched. That was this morning. In the P.M. our watch tacked ship. I have eaten so many coconuts, etc., that I am having troubles inside me. Last night alone I made fast the gaff topsail, ringtail, and jigger topgallant staysail and Pete and I the mizzen royal. I was being punished for cussing the bos'n.

FEB. 14TH. Rain and wind squalls all last night. We had hard work all of our watch on deck. Today strong head winds and frequent rain squalls. Holystoned the deck. Good exercise for arms and back.

FEB. 15TH. Fine day and we set the royals this morning. I loosed the fore and mizzen. I had bare feet and my feet were very sore after loosing both sails and overhauling the buntlines, etc. I won't do that again with bare feet for a few days. Holystoned the decks all day. It is a hard job as the deck is very rough. We are twenty weeks at sea.

FEB. 16TH. Holystoned this A.M. and oiled forecastle head in P.M. Wind is very light but has come fair.

FEB. 17TH. Scraping deck under fo'castle head also painting bulwarks and houses and rails. Wind has hauled ahead again and we are by the wind. Oiled my oilskins again yesterday. Three of the parrots have gone. Two died and one flew overboard. The fourth is still with us but sick. The chicky bird (a small sort of chicken) still thrives. He goes round eating cockroaches and that is about all he eats, but he does not eat a lot of them.

FEB. 18TH. Warm bright day. Painting with a capital P all day. Last night Sam had $40.00 and all his papers stolen and we are not sure by whom.

FEB. 19TH. SUNDAY. Nothing to do but rest all day except "wash down." The day is hot and a light wind, head our course NE close-hauled since this morning. Today is the captain's 52nd birthday and we had chicken stew (only a little meat and that tough), canned peas, and raisins in our duff in honor of the day.

FEB. 20TH. No more holystoning!!! We oiled the main deck today. Also painting scuppers and waterways. Yesterday was a marvelous exception to the general run of Sundays for we did not touch a brace, halyard, or sheet all day. We caught two big sharks today. It ought to bring a breeze.

FEB. 21ST. Painting all day. In the morning watch we holystoned the fo'castle floor. The two mates had a fine row today.

FEB. 22ND. Tacked this A.M. Still head wind. It does not seem as if the head winds would stop. Painting on poop. Bent another mainsail today in P.M.

FEB. 23RD. Cleaning paint and shining brass. Rain squalls. The captain told me that after crossing the line near Gebi Island we recrossed and went as far south as 3 S then crossed again and we are now north of the line vainly struggling against head winds.

FEB. 24TH. Head wind. Tacked twice last night and twice so far today. Today we holystoned the poop and I guess it will take all day tomorrow, too, for we have to do it very carefully. The food is very bad today as usual.

FEB. 25TH. Strong head wind. Holystoning the poop. The bos'n laid up with a boil. All our watch are pleased about it. I got a good sleep in my watch on deck last night. Also I have caught some much needed water for washing. Saw the North Star last night for the first time. It seemed like meeting an old friend.

FEB. 26TH. SUNDAY. Tacked ship once last night and twice today. A clear warm day and I did much washing.

FEB. 27TH. Head wind. Tacked ship twice. Bending sails and oiling the poop. This was a hungry day.

FEB. 28TH. Tacked ship at noon. Bending sails all day. I had a row with the mate today. Makes me feel better to swear back at him but it gets me more hard work.

March 1, 1905 found *Astral* at 6°55' north latitude, 138°34' east longitude, or, east of Palau, in the Carolines.

MARCH 1ST. Washed paint work and tacked ship in our morning watch. In our P.M. watch we took the fore topsail lifts down on deck and overhauled them and sent them up again. Oiled the poop. Shined brass. Food bad and scarce today.

MARCH 2ND. Light head wind. Scraping bright work on grating and skylights.

MARCH 3RD. Light head wind. We have easy work these days for everything is ready for going into Kobe. All we do now is keep everything clean and bright and, of course, handle sails. Today I scraped out a beef barrel for a water barrel. Sam's valise and money were found in the chain locker today and Fred gave Iceland a pounding on the suspicion that he stole it. The food is very bad now. We get very poor mush for breakfast five days in the week, and one can't do much with only that for breakfast. For supper we get rice three days a week, and rice and tea is not a very substantial meal. The salt meat is never cooked enough, neither are the beans. Luckily the work is light. The starboard watch caught a dolphin yesterday and had it for supper. They said it was fine!!! Wish we could manage to get one.

MARCH 4TH. Light head winds. Cut my right forefinger badly on an axe today. Iceland after being beaten by Fred yesterday went at noon up to the fore upper topsail yard and has been there ever since, and it has been now twenty-six hours. He is afraid if he comes down, his watch (starboard) will give him a worse licking. Later in the day, after thirty-one hours, Iceland came down. He is a lowdown mean sort of man. Rained hard all night. Tacked ship four times during the night.

Strong head wind and all sail set. So much rain we did not wash down this morning.

(No entry for March 5th.)

MARCH 6TH. Strong head wind and rain squalls. In our forenoon watch I spent a cheerful four hours scraping the fore to'gallant and royal masts. There is a big head sea running and jumping to beat the band. I had to hang on by my teeth in the rigging and scrape that blooming mast all around. Not to mention a constant procession of rain squalls. In the P.M. we took in t'gallant staysails, royals, spanker, Jimmy Thompson, and Jimmy Green.[2] Rain and blowing all night. Big sea and much water on deck. Tacked twice. Once at midnight and once at 8 o'clock this morning.

MARCH 7TH. Rain and blowing. Same sails as last night. It blew up late in the day and a tremendous sea came up and we had a busy day. We made sennet and stood by and handled sails. Seas coming on deck heavily. Tacked ship at 4 A.M. after a hard night. Rain hard and blowing hard all night.

MARCH 8TH. Lat. 11 d. 17' N. Still blowing hard and a very heavy sea and much comes aboard. Made sennet and stood by. Today we made 33 miles north in 24 hours and yesterday 38 miles. That is slow when you have 25 degrees to go. Lon. 138 E.

MARCH 9TH. Wind died in night but a big sea is still running. Set all the kites in the forenoon watch. Made sennet and I started a punch mat for the fore topmast stay. We bent fore topmast staysail today. Calm and hot.

MARCH 10TH. FAIR WIND. Lifted the yards about a point last night and now we have a strong breeze and go 10 knots on the course N by E. Made sennet and finished my mat. All sail set today and some water on deck. The food was bad today, the pea soup was like raw peas and water. The captain called me aft today and told me we would pass over the Manila cable about midnight tonight and we are now between Manila and Guam.[3]

MARCH 11TH. The wind has hauled back some but we can head within a half point of the course. Scrubbing paint today.

MARCH 12TH. SUNDAY. Light wind and we just can't head our course. Had no work all day.

MARCH 13TH. Put my mat on the stay and made sennet and cleaned up the fore hold. Fine day. Light wind. Head about one point off course. This was another hungry day. The macaroni they put in our soup is so full of little black beetles that you can't get a piece ¼-inch long without getting several beetles. As for the pea soup, there are as many cockroaches in it as there are peas.

MARCH 14TH. Almost heading on course. Light wind. Made sennet and bent another foresail. I got a good sleep in my watch on deck last night. I slept all the four hours. But to get away with it you have to be lucky, for if you are found asleep it is trouble.

MARCH 15TH. Very calm. There has been a great deal of pumice stone floating all around and the captain told me it came from the Ladrone Islands. I spent the afternoon watch aloft with John putting in wire seizings and fairleads, etc. The mate got called down by Alf this noon. It was good. The doughboys in the stew this noon were actually good.

MARCH 16TH. Made sennet all day. 600 miles to Kobe. That does not sound like much and we shall surely be in next week. I wonder if the Japs and the Russians are still at war.

MARCH 17TH. The wind hauled completely around sunrise and it is now ahead. Kobe may be a month or more away although only 500 miles. Made sennet all day except when trimming sails. Chris is sick. Rats are everywhere nowadays.[4]

MARCH 18TH. Made sennet, washed paint, and cleaned brass. Light, fair wind. The mate and bos'n had a good row. The cook and all of us had a row. Someone caught the cook out on deck without his cleaver so he grabbed him. He, the cook, got a good licking and was a sorry sight afterwards. Each man of us came to him and took one swing at him, and of course, at the same time, the cook took a swing at each of us. But each of us only took one swing at him, even if we missed him. The night was cold and raining. The weather has turned cold now, and to us so long in hot weather it seems very cold, especially at night.

MARCH 19TH. Sunday. Fine day. Nothing much to do. We have 250 miles more to Kobe. Wind abeam.

MARCH 20TH. In the early morning it began to blow NE and blew hard all day. Making up a big sea. We shortened her down. During the day the wind worked round to SW. It rained hard and was cold all day. About 10 P.M. it cleared and came NW, and we set all sail.

MARCH 21ST. At 4 A.M. we shortened her down again and tacked ship. Wind NE cold and rain. Big sea. We are in the Japan Current, and a sea gets up very quickly. Much water on deck.

MARCH 22ND. The wind came up and blew a gale last night, and at 2 A.M. we took in everything but topsails and we had a hard, cold, wet night. At 8 A.M. we wore ship and now are hove to on the port tack. The land is somewhere close to leeward, but we have got no sights since Sunday, so the captain was scared to go any closer. Hence we "lay for topsails" and head SE. Many seas coming aboard. All my clothes are wet and the weather is cold. In the afternoon the wind came up. It blew a gale. Just after dark all hands took in the upper topsails. Then at midnight we took in the foresail and "lay for lower topsails."

MARCH 23RD. Wind howling and a tremendous sea running. All last night and all today, except, of course, when we were handling sails, we stood by on the poop. No one could well stay on the main deck. The wind kept up all day, and at 2 P.M. broke off two points and our watch alone wore ship. It was a tough job, for the decks were all awash with very big seas. After dark the wind hauled to SW and dropped, and we put all sail on her. And no sooner had everything set than the wind popped out of the NE and took us all aback. We clewed up the royals and got her straightened out, then braced her sharp on the wind. We then went below at 4 A.M.

MARCH 24TH. The other watch called us out at 6:30 A.M., and as I came on deck things were bad. The poor old ship was hard pressed. The other watch was wearing ship with almost no wind when it suddenly began to blow a hurricane from the NE. She had all except royals set and the watch belayed the braces and let go every halyard. The braces being loose, the yards swing badly and the ship was heeled over on her beam ends and sails were blowing away and great pieces of canvas sailing to leeward. The upper to'gans'ls got the worst licking. We made everything fast and went below for breakfast at nine o'clock. All day we lay with only the lower topsails set and we stood by all day on the poop. The wind and sea were wicked. The deck full of water. At midnight the wind dropped and we wore ship. But it was a tough job as big seas came over.

MARCH 25TH. Strong E wind. Set the upper topsails and spanker. In the afternoon we sighted the western side of the Ki Channel, which is the entrance to Kobe. All my clothes still wet. They have all been wet now for a whole week steady. Something dry would feel good, especially at night. In the second dog watch we wore ship and set the cro'-jack and mainsail. At midnight we took in all but topsails and foresail.

MARCH 26TH. SUNDAY. Blow and rain and cold all day, and we went course into the entrance but at dark we wore and stood off. At 10 P.M. a regular hurricane struck us and I really mean a hurricane. We called all hands and took in all but the main and fore lower topsails. We lay under these two small sails.

SUNDAY, 26 MARCH. 8 P.M. Muroto Point Light bearing N distance 10 miles. Found current set the ship NE 130 miles in 6 days. Wore ship at 6 P.M.... Pumps, lookout, and lights carefully attended to.

MARCH 27TH. The gale is something fierce, and we are buried under water. These great seas come at us and go right over the ship. No one can go onto the main deck at all. Time and time again it seemed as if the old vessel would not recover herself after being knocked down. Many on board thought this was the ship's finish, and at times I could not understand why and how she could straighten up. She lay so far over you could not stand on deck. This kept up all day. We stood by on the poop, though even that was badly washed at times. Our bunks are flooded.

MONDAY, 27 MARCH. 8 P.M....wore ship. 9:30 P.M. wind hauled to ENE blowing fresh & increasing to strong gale, took in all sail but fore & main lower topsails fore topmast & jigger staysail. 12 midnight strong gale & high sea...a high sea. Decks full of water all the time. Carried away fore topmast staysail..... Pumps, lookout, and lights carefully attended to.

MARCH 28TH. The wind went down somewhat in the night and this morning we set the mizzen lower topsail and spent the day repairing damages and getting ready for another gale. Of course, all my clothes are still wet and even my blankets are soaking wet and of course there is no way to dry anything. Towards night we sighted the entrance to the Ki Channel lighthouse. It was still blowing a gale and raining, but we stood in till about midnight then we hove-to.

MARCH 29TH. At 6 A.M. we squared in and the wind going down we set all sail and put for Kobe. Land close to us on both sides. It still rains. The hills and trees on top of the hills look just like those pictures on Japanese fans. You would know this was Japan even if you did not know where you were. Many fishing boats around. We anchored near Kobe about 10 miles from the oil works at about 10 P.M. Made fast all sail.

WEDNESDAY 29 MARCH. Comes in with moderate gale.... 9 A.M. pilot came on board. 12 noon passed Kama Point. 8 P.M. came to with starboard anchor in 8 fathoms of water. Kobe Light bearing N distance 1 ½ mile. Furled all sails & anchor watch for tonight. So ends this day of 36 hours to work civil time. Pumps, lookout, and lights carefully attended to.

MARCH 30TH. Set all sail and beat in to Kobe and anchored off the Standard Oil Co. warehouse at Yokoya at 5 P.M. Unbent all sails. Made them up and stowed them in the sail locker.

FRIDAY, 30 MARCH. All this day light and variable breeze and fine clear weather. 7 A.M. doctor paid his visit. 8:30 A.M. hove up anchor, set all sail and proceeded to discharging ground. 3:00 P.M. came to with starboard anchor in seven fathoms of water. 45 fathoms cable. Unbent all sails. Albert Winsel and Chris Crisjohnson laid up sick. Albert Hickman night watchman. Pumps, watch, and lights carefully attended to.

MARCH 31ST. Cleaning up the ship.[5]

---

1. Gilolo was the old Dutch name for Halmahera Island, the largest of the Molucca Islands. Gebi Island lay in the middle of Gilolo Passage, a doorway to the Pacific. Findlay notes that on adjacent Fow Island, "Spars fit for yards and masts abound on either shore." *Directory*, page 869.

2. A Jimmy Green was a fore-and-aft four-sided sail set along the bowsprit under the headsails—a clipper ship sail, surely of no earthly good on a 3,292-ton bark. What the Jimmy Thompson was is anyone's guess.

3. Clearly Captain Dunham now recognized that Tod was not an ordinary Ordinary Seaman if, indeed, he had ever been fooled.

4. Rats were traditional shipmates.

5. At 175 days, this would be *Astral*'s longest passage. The Sewall's wooden four-masted bark *Susquehanna*, which had sailed from New York a couple of weeks before *Astral*, was 180 days to Tsingtau, China, while the wooden ships *A. G. Ropes* and *S. P. Hitchcock*, both over twenty years old, were 150 and 149 days to Hong Kong.

Chapter 21

Kobe, April and Part of May: In Port

Astral's *Prolonged Stay in Kobe; Tod Suffers Guilt Trips By Mail.*

APRIL 1ST. Cleaning up the ship.

APRIL 2ND. SUNDAY. Liberty 12 hours. Had a good dinner. It was the first time ashore in six months less four days.

APRIL 3RD. Rain—only five hands of us to turn to. Sand and canvas over the side on stages, working on the plates we chipped and painted at sea.

APRIL 4TH. Still sand and canvas over side. Started cargo out. Seven men still ashore and half those aboard not fit for work.

Tod made no journal entries between April 4 and May 13. He later wrote:

> THE SHIP LAY AT ANCHOR off Yokoya from March 30 to May 18. The cargo was discharged by coolies into big lighters which had masts and sails and sailed themselves into the warehouse dock. They did not have to be rowed. Each watch got every other Sunday ashore. So each watch got three Sundays ashore. We took in 1,300 tons of sand ballast before we sailed. After discharging the cargo and before taking in ballast, we painted the entire inside of the hold. Sides, bottoms, etc., and the undersides of the decks. Then we oiled the 'tween decks. All the time we were at anchor we worked all day from 7 A.M. to 5 P.M. except Sundays. And we had all night in.[1]

Log entries indicate that discipline broke down in port—the usual pattern with the oil ships. Sailors went ashore without permission; sailors given permission to go ashore did not return for a day or so; sailors were brought on board by the police; sailors, upon returning from shore, were laid up "sick"; two were paid off; and so on.[2]

Despite Mother Swift's promise to send but one letter to Kobe, a veritable stack awaited Tod, followed by a flurry of new ones. Some excerpts:

> I WONDER HOW you will feel about mining when you get back, dear boy, do not let the sea wean you too far away from your profession, and remember what I told you, that you must go to work after this voyage or I should have to hide my head...do not...lose your heart to the sea—you must keep that for some nice girl some day.
>
> I AM AFRAID you will break the record of the bark *Johanna,* which was 210 days from Kobe to NY if you do not hurry. We did not bargain on such a slow old tub did we! The SO Co. told Fred she was just due a week ago, and might not be in for two or three weeks. You will have a strong dose of sailoring, Tod.... Helen has had a hard

Bark Astral *anchored at Kobe, April or May 1905, cargo discharged, topsides partially repainted after the long passage out.*
RODMAN SWIFT COLLECTION.

time for servants—a letter today says her new second girl is still with her and a cook coming today and she has a fine 25 y o nurse.

YOUR FATHER SAID he saw some fellow at the A. D. dinner...who had had a letter from Billy Hague from New Mexico, where he liked his job.... It still troubles your father that you are losing so much time and that Billy will be way ahead of you and be your boss.[3]

UNCLE FRANK STONE was at Milton A[cademy] last evening to speak to the boys and they said Francis felt quite nervous about it. Mr. Cobb had to ask him several times and beg and entreat before he consented. William says he said very little about himself or his experiences. He told how he and his mate walked off the end of a wharf somewhere and how he once was caught in a great storm with a big load of Chinamen and all his deck houses were swept away, but the rest was mostly about ships and boats in general and currents and winds, which Wm. thought was rather beyond the comprehension of most of the boys.

For Valentine's Day Sarah outdid herself:

TO MY LOVE

My Love is on the water,
A-sailing o'er the sea
In the Standard Oil ship *Astral,*
Bound for the port, Kobe.

He should have gone a-mining
in Grass Valley, months ago,
For he captured a "Cum Laude"
With his Degree, you know.

So he is really therefore,
A mining Engineer,
And to go to sea before the mast,
To some, must seem right queer.

But this is only for one voyage,
And when this voyage is o'er,
He's promised to return to work,
And to go to sea no more.

And why, my Love, he promises,
We may set our minds at rest;
He'll return to his Profession,
And he'll do his very best.

Sarah Rotch Swift, circa 1900.
RODMAN SWIFT COLLECTION.

For he must make a fortune,
And find a little wife,
Who will make for him a happy house,
And bring joy into his life.

Just now we are all waiting
Most anxiously, to see
The arrival of the *Astral*,
In that foreign port, Kobe.

The next port's Honolulu,
Where for sugar they must go,
And then HOME, all round old Cape Horn
My, how the winds will blow!!

And I trust by next November,
Philadelphia they will see,
And that my Love, life's dream fulfilled,
Contented then may be.

And that as a Mining Expert
In the future he may shine,
Is the dearest and sincerest wish
Of his loving "Valentine."

Tod's arrival telegram—"PANTOP," economical code for "arrived, all well"—and a follow-up letter, were received at New Bedford.

IT WAS GOOD to hear from you, dear boy, and we know you were well in spite of poor food and all. We shall look eagerly for your log and will make all due allowance for the grumbling, for things always seem worse at the moment.... We think you had better leave the ship by all means. It would be a terrible waste of time to stay these several months and do you no good in any way.

The arrival of Tod's log, however, created great consternation, and, throwing all pretense of economy to the winds, Mother Swift spent the princely sum of $44.37 to wire Tod:

SWIFT SHIP *ASTRAL* KOBE Get discharge now. Home or Grass Valley or Europe as you think best. Better see Japan. Will cable additional credit Monday care American consul Yokohama. Answer.

On May 12 Tod answered with "PREFER NOT," which was eventually understood to mean that he wished to stay by the ship. He followed up with a letter:

DEAR MAMMA, I got your cable last night and have come ashore today to send an answer. I said "prefer not" meaning that I don't want to leave the ship yet. If you really want me to come back you will cable me again.... The Capt. gave me liberty today to answer your cable and told me that he would discharge me if I wanted it.

We go to sea in a few days now and we are getting ready now, bending sail, overhauling rigging, etc. I think we shall probably go to Honolulu or Frisco.... It would only take us about two months to go to Frisco and then I can communicate with you easier. It must have cost you a fortune for that cable you sent. You need not think I am hard up for I still have $640.00 that has not been touched.... I am sending Father a postcard photo of the ship taken April 20 when we had just finished unloading...the sheds on shore to the right are the S. O. Co.'s warehouses.

On May 15 Tod's mother wrote her son:

SO WE INFER from your cable that you prefer to go to SF in the ship. That is all right, for I suppose you feel you ought to go to Grass

Tod Swift's postcard to his father, reading "The Astral *April 20 '05. Cargo out and ready for ballast. Off Yokoya."*
RODMAN SWIFT COLLECTION.

Valley, but I do feel very sorry you should not see something more than that awful old ship and the crowd on board.

On May 15 Tod wrote his mother:

I WORKED ALL DAY yesterday so the Capt. let me come ashore this morning. We sail tomorrow for San Francisco.... The more I think of it the surer I get that it must have been that blooming diary of mine that must have made you think I was having a horrible time and wanted to leave—Don't think that, however, for I am getting along all right and am in first-rate health so you need not worry. Japan is all right in its way but I don't know as I should want to travel round over it much. I am not very keen about the Japanese. I warned you beforehand that the diary would sound bad and you would not take it right. But when I get back I will explain why it is that I have had a good time. I write things down in the diary just as they happened and did not put sugar on them as I perhaps ought to have done.... We will have a peaceful voyage probably and there will be nothing to worry about, since we are only drawing 12 ft. we are way out of water and will have dry decks.

Meanwhile, Captain Dunham, keeping lonely bachelor's hall in *Astral*'s cabin—captains typically enjoyed little social contact aboard ship, particularly when the mate was a man they disliked. On Sunday, April 23, he wrote daughter Lillian:

> THIS IS A BEAUTIFUL SUNDAY and I am alone except for a few peddlers and half the sailors. I get very lonesome and homesick. I only had three letters yet, one from Effie, one from Edna, and one from Fannie. I don't know why nobody else writes to me.... We have another U.S. vessel here now, the *I. F. Chapman*.[4] The Capt. has his wife so I shall have some company.... I had a long passage and but could not help it a bit. Had head winds all the time. Was struck by lightning, too, the truck of the foremast the same as the bridge did at N. Y. when you were on board.
>
> I hope you have written me and that I shall soon get your letter. I miss the letters so much. I have not been on shore much yet. We are six miles from the town. Lighters come for the cargo. I stay on board and eat oranges. I don't know how many I have eaten. I seemed to want an orange more than anything when I was out at sea where there were none to get. I got some coconuts and bananas from a boat canoe off at the Spice Islands when I came through Gilolo Strait, and I got 680 nutmegs. If I get them home there will be enough to last some time.... I am tired all ready of looking at these Japs and hope soon to be going away.[5] The cargo is about half out.... God bless you all, Papa never goes to bed without praying for you all again even if it is for a short time
>
> Japan...is under the great war cloud. It looks like it very often when I go to the railway station and see the many poor fellows through the car windows...with their white suits and the red crosses on their arm.... I know you would like Japan for a while, seeing the different ways of doing things...the boats, the rickshaws, the little low houses, but the electric cars are up-to-date. The women are so small and the men too are small. All the biggest men are sent to the war. I asked one of the customhouse officers why he was not a soldier, he said he was one *inches* too small.[6]
>
> I have been cold all day but now we have an oil stove burning. I am looking for letters that you wrote I hope when you heard of my arrival. I did not get letters from anyone but Effie, Edna, and Fannie until last week I got a letter from Mamma, it seemed so good I read it a number of times over. When you take a photo of the house send me one and I will send you one of the ship. I expect to see them for sale, so many have been taken here....[7] I get very lonesome and homesick

and I wish I could come home and stay but this would not do except I could get something to do to earn a living and pay my board.... We had two eggs [on Easter] laid by our own hens, *Philadelphia hens.* Chickens are very scarce here. The Russian prisoners are eating up everything. The eggs all come from China by the steamboats, living is very high in Japan just now.

On April 30 he wrote:

YOUR NICE LETTER came last week and I was so pleased to hear from you. I am pleased to know you are better now. Mamma wrote me to Philadelphia about taking you to the doctor. I have been thinking about it so often during the voyage. I was not home to sit in the bed and read those true stories to you out of that truthful book I got for Mildred.... I have not seen any dogs yet. I understand they want $25 apiece for them. I will see what I can do next week about a dog

for you. Birds are cheap and I see some of those small hens like I have tried twice to get home. We have only a dozen hens now and our rooster crows every morning and sometimes evenings and the hens lay eggs. My dove crows anytime I ask him to and bows good morning to me as many times as I bow to him
I am your loving Papa, J. W. Dunham.

Lillian never spent the dollar enclosed with this letter.

---

1. The coolies passed the cases from person to person, some standing on staging rigged to the ship's side.

2. Dolman went off to complain to the consul and ended up in prison for a week, being returned to the ship just before it sailed on May 17. Refusing to work, he was placed in a spare room in the cabin, but returned to his duties the following day.

3. Father and son communicated through Sarah. Billy Hague, Tod's Harvard roommate, was the son of the prominent California mine owner who had offered Tod a job at Grass Valley, California.

4. The splendid and long-lived 2,038-ton, three-skysail-yard ship *I. F. Chapman,* of New York, Captain Charles S. Kendall, was built in 1882 at Bath, Maine. Her owner, for whom she was named, was one of the leading and most respected ship owners of his era, and a Maine native. Twenty years or so later, the tough, old *Chapman* was still in use as a coastal coal barge.

5. The term "Jap" did not carry the stigma it does at present, and was then freely used in the *Encyclopedia Britannica.*

6. In Korea, the war between Japan and Russia was then at its fiercest.

7. The Dunhams' Salem, Massachusetts, house had just been enlarged. Letter guilt-trips were a common refrain in Dunham family correspondence.

Chapter 22

Astral, May 13 to June 30, 1905: Back to Sea Again

Tod Sails His Final Passage, Kobe to San Francisco.

RETURNING TO HIS LOG, Tod wrote:

MAY 13, 1905. Still at anchor off Yokoya. Turned to at 6 A.M. and cleared all running rigging for bending sail. Cleared clewlines, sheets, etc. After breakfast started bending squaresails and at 4:30 P.M. had all the squaresails but mainsail and cro'jack bent. Knocked off and cleaned up the ship for Sunday. It was hard work today, but most of the work was aloft. No liberty or money for any of us except the mate. Only worked one port for ballast today. Used the donkey for hoisting up sail.

MAY 14TH. SUNDAY. Off Yokoya. The mate is ashore, so I must work all day tallying ballast. We are working through both [side] ports and the second mate and I are roped in to tally. It is a fine day, and I wanted to get an hour off to do some washing but could not so must now wait till we are at sea. We ought to get away Wednesday. Today is almost like summer, it is so warm. Quite a change. I tallied from 6 A.M. to 6:30 P.M. at the fore port and took in 206 tons of sand. The captain came down in the hold and saw me tallying and said he would give me a day off for working on Sunday. I wonder if he will.

MAY 16TH. All hands today discharging the dunnage into lighters to be taken ashore and sold. Our stores came today. A new O. S. came aboard today. He lives in Honolulu and came from the ship *I. F. Chapman*. Today also painted hatch coamings inside and fore and afters and underside of hatches. Fine warm day—and no wind. In P.M. all hands and numerous Jap men and women were carrying lumber and dumping it out the ports into lighters. A lot of fun was had by all hands. The Jap men and women were coolies from C. Nickle & Co., our stevedores.

MAY 17TH. Can't go today for no wind. In the A.M. we gave the hatches, etc., another coat of paint and took in the gangway and stowed it. Cleaned up the 'tween decks and put potatoes in a bin in the 'tween decks. Had steam up on the donkey all day in hopes of a chance to get out. All hands knocked off at noon from all work. We probably sail tonight if we get a breeze. However, we did not go for in the P.M. wind and rain came from SW dead head. It blew hard in the night.

MAY 18TH. All hands putting on chafing gear and washing paint-work. Wind in SW so we can't go. After dinner took port anchor in on forecastle head, then knocked off for the rest of the afternoon. Probably we sail tonight if we get a northerly wind. About 5 P.M. we got a NE wind and they called us out. I had had a good sleep. Loosed all sail and got underway. It was a fine, clear moonlight night, and we had a fine breeze. Our watch on deck at 8 P.M.

MAY 19TH. Hove to at 1 A.M. to drop the pilot, but no boat came off, and we remained hove to till 5 A.M., then we squared away and chased a fisherman and put the pilot aboard him. We then cleaned up the ship and took the starboard anchor inboard. Then breakfast. Painted out the coal locker in the lower forepeak and it was the same old fierce job with patent paint. Painted in 'tween decks. No wind in P.M. and hot. During the night we had variable winds and much bracing and squaring and tacked twice. I got an hour's sleep in the middle watch without being seen.

MAY 20TH. A fair wind came up about 4 A.M. and we went about 9 knots all day. In A.M. we did odd painting jobs on deck and in the hold (lower). Nowadays things go very smoothly on board and we are given our jobs and left quietly till we are done. That is, of course, if we do the work right. There is no unnecessary shouting and cursing. Life is easy. I wonder how it will be when we leave Frisco bound out again. I suffer it will be the same old cursing, swearing method. In the P.M. the wind came up and blew heavy from SW and we with all sail set made 16 knots. This kept up all night with rain. 15 and 16 knots. About midnight we took in royals and to'gal staysails. I had a bad time with the miz to'gal staysail.

MAY 21ST. SUNDAY. Gale of wind about SW going 6 knots and raining. The ship is light with 1,300 tons of sand ballast. When it blows she stands up to it and goes like hell. About 2 P.M. wind dropped and we set the royals again. Still raining at 4 P.M. I did much washing of clothes as there was a lot of fresh water coming down. From yesterday noon to today noon we did 350 miles. It rained all night and was a nasty night on deck.

MAY 22ND. Calm, hot, and rain. We cleaned paintwork with sand and canvas all A.M.; also scraped the deck. Also for an hour we walked round the windlass capstan to get it going easier, but it did not get to go easy, and it was a hard job. In the first dogwatch we walked round the windlass capstan again for two hours. It still goes just as hard. Rained during the night and variable winds and much bracing and squaring and very little wind.

MAY 23RD. A dull, rainy day and hot with little wind. Scrubbed paintwork on deck and painted some in the 'tween decks. Scraped the deck under the forecastle head. In P.M. it came up to blow from the SE and we had all we could stand with full sail. In first dogwatch took in the ringtail and gaff topsail. Looks like an uncomfortable night. During first watch we took in the to'gal and topmast staysails, three jibs, and royals, and upper to'gans'ls and cro'jack and mainsail. It blew and rained hard. My guess that it would be an uncomfortable night was right. In the last part of the middle and first part of the third watch we set all square sails again for a breeze directly astern WSW. It sure was a mean night.

MAY 24TH. Rain and blow. Scraping and holystoning the deck forward. Food very bad and starboard watch went aft with the breakfast. Rained all day and all night, and we had a good breeze on our quarter. During the day we saw a whale half a mile on the port beam and during our watch at night a large whale swam slowly along the starboard side very close-to and blew three times. It sounded like a steam engine blowing off. We could see him distinctly right alongside.

MAY 25TH. Not raining!!! But looks like it. Scrubbing paintwork with sand and canvas. In P.M. I cleaned out and holystoned the lamp locker. Others scrubbing paint on fo'castle head. Dried most of my clothes today although the sun did not come out. We are today 1,080 miles from Kobe. In our second dogwatch on deck the wind suddenly hauled from SW to NW and blew brisk. We made fast the spanker, gaff tops'l, ringtail, jigger staysail, three topmast staysails, and three jibs, and hauled up the mainsail and cro'jack. Some job for our watch (eleven men) for one dogwatch. We had a strong NW wind all night and it was cold.

MAY 26TH. Tarring down the rigging. A busy day indeed. Before we got her finished the tar ran out and then the mate was in a bad way. It will be a tough job holystoning the deck, for now in addition to pitch from the seams, it is covered with tar. It was a fine, clear night and we had the first watch and actually did not have to do any work, but it was so cold you could not sit down but must keep on the move all the time.

MAY 27TH. Good day but "awful" cold. Painting around deck and painted all four lower masts. In P.M. painting round deck. Also painted out lower forepeak, which is under the chain locker and is a dirty hole; it was a dirty job. Tomorrow is Sunday "Come day, go day, God and Sunday." And let it be a pleasant day with a steady wind. At about 6 P.M. wind hauled E and we tacked ship at 8 bells.

MAY 28TH. SUNDAY. Cold night and today is very cold, so you must keep on your feet and moving. There is no reading on deck today for if you sit down, you feel the cold. It was our forenoon watch today, and we took in royals, to'gal staysails, and Jim Thompson. It blew up strong and clouded over. We can head NE. In P.M. the other watch took in 'gansls and in the first dogwatch our watch took in spanker and topmast staysails and in the second dogwatch the other side called us out to make fast the cro'jack and mainsail. It blew hard all night with rain. The vessel certainly goes fine in ballast, for she is very stiff and when we take sail in we can walk to the buntlines instead of swimming. It was a bad night all night.[1]

MAY 29TH. At 4 A.M. we set the gans'ls again, then got the holystone out and started to holystone the main deck. The stones are very big and the deck is very bad. It takes a lot of pushing to get it clean at all. Hard on your knees and back. Your bunk feels mighty good at 8 bells. The night was raining, foggy, and cold.

MAY 30TH. Lat 42 N, Long 175 E. Rain, fog, and cold. Holystoning all day. There was been a thick fog for the last two days, and we keep a hand on the fo'castle head on lookout in daytime, too. A man is on lookout always at night. We have been blowing the foghorn night and day. Nasty weather. Rain during the night. The fog has been so thick that water drips from aloft just like rain. "Down on your knees and get at it" all day.

MAY 31ST. Wednesday. Rain and cold. Began holystoning at 5 A.M. and worked at it all day. Strong W wind, making good time. It is a cold, wet job on your knees. The captain told me he had been across here in December and had not had weather as cold as this. It blew strong and we were working all P.M. under the cro'jack and a gale of wind was thrown by the sail down on us. And talk about aching fingers and shivering all over. The work is hard enough to keep you warm most days, but today under that sail!!!

MAY 31ST. Again Wednesday. Blowing hard with rain squalls. Holystoning all day. It is just as cold and wet as yesterday. We crossed the 180th meridian at 4 P.M. yesterday, and today we are halfway to Frisco. Talk about cold weather. Rained during the night. It was an uncomfortable night.

JUNE 1ST. Rain and cold. Holystoning all day. Nice job that cold rainy night.[2]

JUNE 2ND. Cold but NOT RAINING. Holystoned all day. I had a row with the mate today because I refused to cut his tobacco up for him last night. We were on deck the first watch and the mate sung out for me to come aft. He said to go down to his room and keep warm and cut some tobacco for him. I told him I would not do it because I had done it once before and he had accused me of stealing some of the tobacco. I did cut some for him last week for he asked me to do so for a favor as he could not leave the deck and had none out with him. Then he accused me of stealing some. He can cut his own tobacco for I am not his servant. But he will get back at me somehow.

JUNE 3RD. Cold and raining. Holystoned as usual all day. These days the mate and bos'n seem to have lost their control over us. Almost every watch at night the mate and bos'n tell us to stay around No. 3 hatch, but we wander forward in short order and they both get mad but it makes no difference. Then they set us to bracing the yards and sweating them up, then someone starts a slow chantey and that makes them madder still. But they can and do get even in the daytime.

JUNE 4TH. SUNDAY. Long 162 W. Today for a change was a fine, sunny day with a steady wind. It was pretty cold, though. This is the first really sunny day we have had for some time. Spent most of my time sewing, mending my clothes. Also made a canvas bag for my tobacco. The wind being very light, we got much fun with the boobies with pieces of meat and string. The night was fine, but the wind hauled ahead in the second dogwatch. We deserved a good Sunday after an eight-day week with holystoning every day. The bos'n told me to cut his tobacco today and I refused. They must think I like the job. I get all I want cutting my own.

JUNE 5TH. Cold—Rain—Head wind. In the morning watch we holystoned the tops of the wheelhouse and charthouse, and in the P.M. we did the port side of the poop. It was a cold, nasty, wet day, and my oilskins leak all over, but I can't get a chance to oil them in this kind of weather. I hope we are now finished with holystoning, and I guess tomorrow we go over the sides on stagings with sand and canvas on the topsides. In the night it blew up strong with rain, and in the first watch we took in all staysails and royals and tacked ship.

JUNE 6TH. Cold—Cloudy—No Rain. Holystoned all day on gratings and on spots on the poop. It was cold today, and the night was cold. They say we have 1,400 miles to go to Frisco.

JUNE 7TH. Cold. At times we saw the sun. Fine breeze. Oiled the main deck, poop, fo'castle head, and 'tween decks. The night was foggy and it began to breeze up.

JUNE 8TH. Rain and cold. Took in to'gal staysails in the morning watch. All hands (mostly) making sennet. I painted the windlass. Two hands cleaning donkey room. It blows harder all the time and now we head E x N-½N, which is 1½ points off the course. In P.M. all hands made sennet. We had the first watch tonight and it poured rain all the time. We were at the braces, etc., continually bracing her up sharp on both sides in succession. A very wet night.

JUNE 9TH. Raining hard. In the morning watch we had a busy time setting sail and bracing, etc., and a pouring rain all the watch. Flying jib blew away. My oilskins and sou'wester are first-class sieves. Hence all my clothes are wet but thank goodness it is not so cold as it was. It rained all last night and we had light, squally variable winds which means plenty of bracing, etc. A miserable night.

JUNE 10TH. Rain all night and most of day. We made sennet under fo'castle head and stood by royal halyards most of day. The bos'n now is very peaceable and never says much of anything to me. A day or so ago we had a real row. Rained during the night and was cold. While I was working barefoot as usual today, I stubbed my toe on an eyebolt and it is so sore I can't get a shoe on and at night I had only a sock on it and the deck was wet as it was raining. The mate saw this and thought I would now cut him some tobacco and so make me back down on what I told him last week. But even if my toe is mashed and cold, I won't cut tobacco for him. He was pretty sore about it.

JUNE 11TH. SUNDAY. Beautiful day and no work. We are supposed to be about 1,000 miles from Frisco. The food nowadays is as bad as it has ever been and is often too bad to eat.

JUNE 12TH. Cloudy and we can't head our course. Painting bulwarks all day. We passed a three-masted schooner going west this A.M. and we overhauled and passed a four-masted schooner going same way as us. We licked the stuffing out of her. Got a fair dinner today, for it is pea soup day. Blew up strong at night and we took in gaff rascal, monkey tail, Jim Thompson, the royals, and to'gal and topmast staysails. It blew hard all night with occasional rain.

JUNE 13TH. Cloudy and blowing. Painted all day. This about finishes the painting. In our dogwatch we took in the upper gans'ls. It blew hard during the night. The bos'n is certainly a changed man towards me. I wish I had had it out with him before, but I did not realize there was no real stuff behind his blustering, sarcastic bellowing. He still works his stuff on the dutchmen.

JUNE 14TH. Blowing and cloudy. Painting around deck all day. The night was wet and breezy. Much "standing by."

JUNE 15TH. The same old dreary-looking weather, almost raining. Even so, we painted all day around the deck. The same old strong north wind blows, and we are about three points off our course now. We can't make anything to windward against such a wind and sea as we have now.

JUNE 16TH. The same old story. Cold, cloudy, and Scotch-misty, and a headwind. I painted in the lazerette; the rest making sennet under fo'castle head. At noon the wind had gone down a little and all hands set the gans'ls. The ship has bad luck. Frisco now bears N x W. For days we have always been two to four points to leeward of our course. As we go, the wind keeps hauling and in all we have headed up about eight points but always a couple of points off the course. We now can head N x E. With a good, fair wind, Frisco is within an easy two days' sail.

JUNE 17TH. During the night the wind dropped entirely and we are becalmed and rolling and banging and slatting around till you can hardly hear yourself think. It is a dark day and misting heavily, and we are cleaning paintwork, etc. We may get a fair wind after this. We set the royals in the P.M. and we got a very light SW wind, but we only go about 2 knots. It was calm all day and all night.

JUNE 18TH. SUNDAY. Fine and warm and also calm. We are right off Catalina Island, which is in plain sight. In the forenoon I spent the whole watch mending my clothes. Calm all day and night. Fine Sunday.

JUNE 19TH. Calm and hot. We are close to the coast, which appears about 20 miles off. It's a very high coast. Cleaned up the ship in general in the A.M. Most of the time we did not have steerageway. In P.M. watch we oiled the main deck, poop, and fo'castle head, and tacked twice and tacked a third time at 6 o'clock. We have a very light headwind and tack often. Tacked at midnight. They say the NW wind blows here all summer.

JUNE 20TH. Tacked at 6 A.M. A fine day but almost cold. A dead headwind as usual. In A.M. we stood offshore and lost sight of the coast. We kept on this tack all day. At night it turned cold again and blew strong. All sail set. Standing by. We still have many whales round. I understand they are no good only having 4 inches of blubber. We were less than 100 miles off Frisco but have now run off again. I bet if the captain had followed the great circle we would have been in Frisco days ago.[3] Actually, our course was east. That is, the compass course that we steered was east.

JUNE 21ST. Still the same old song. Cold and strong headwind. We are still standing offshore on the starboard tack. If we don't get in soon, George will be in a bad way, and if it takes us a month he may die first. We made sennet today under the fo'castle head. The food seems worse on this passage than it was from Philadelphia to Kobe. We get potatoes but they are soft and yellow and rotten, and we can hardly eat them they are so bad. If only we had no potatoes we would go back on substitutes such as rice, mush, etc., which one can eat, but they have their drawbacks such as worms and bugs in them. Our breakfasts consist of coffee and bread and slum-gullion, which is a stew of potatoes, water, and pieces of salt meat which are not fit to use in any other way. Most of the fellows don't touch it, but I do and I seem to get fat on it. The above does not sound bad when written down, but it really is poor stuff.

JUNE 22ND. Strong headwind. Still on starboard tack. We are now 500 miles offshore heading NW and the wind has hauled to NNE so Frisco is still dead to windward. The weather is cold. Today was a hungry one. For dinner we had freshwater soup and half-cooked salt beef and duff that not one single man could eat and the bread was so sour and doughlike we made it into balls and played ball with it. The wind broke off about 6 and we tacked ship and again about midnight; it headed us so we tacked again and are now again on the offshore tack. It was a wet night with a very heavy Scotch mist. We certainly have had a lot of this co-called Scotch mist.

JUNE 23RD. Blows strong with a very heavy Scotch mist wetting you through in no time. We are making rovings and sennet under the fo'-castle head between jobs. I was doing a job on the poop today and the captain got to talking about winds. He said the summer wind hereabouts are mostly northerly—so I yet can't see why he did not come the great circle course from Kobe. It was a wet night.

JUNE 24TH. Wet night and we tacked about 4 A.M. and are heading NE x N (compass). The mate did a very characteristic thing with our watch. We had the middle watch on deck and at 20 minutes to four he sings out, "Bout ship." So we brought her around, our watch alone, and we were just finishing at eight bells when the other watch came on deck, but we had to stay up till all the ropes were coiled down and everything shipshape. It took over half an hour. Now why could not he have let us go below at 8 bells, we having finished bringing the ship around, and let the other watch do the cleaning up. Always if the other watch tacks ship on their watch on deck, they call all hands to do the job. The mate always makes us tack ship alone. We have never called out the starboard watch to help us tack. Passed a bark heading SW. Misty, wet day. We mostly worked under the fo'castle head making rovings and sennet today. We are about 600 miles offshore. A wet night.

JUNE 25TH. SUNDAY. Last night was a wet one. By a slant of wind we now head within a point of our course, which is NNE magnetic. Talk about phosphorous—all the way from Kobe it has been very strong. They talk of it in the tropics but we did not see so much there as on this run from Kobe to Frisco. It beats anything I ever saw. You can see the wake for at least a quarter mile and at the stem it is bright enough to read headlines of a paper if you held it over the taffrail. This day was misty and wet. I washed clothes and did some sewing as we had little work to do while on deck. In the first dogwatch we tacked ship. It was our watch on deck and we did it alone as usual. It is some work for eleven men to tack this ship and takes us about two hours for the whole job, including taking in staysails and jibs and hauling up the mainsail and cro'jack. Then setting everything again and coiling everything down. The wind had hauled back to North. Tonight, however, we did not set the staysails again. We made them all fast. It has breezed up and is cloudy. Our watch tacked ship again at 8 o'clock P.M. and we are on the port tack.

JUNE 26TH. The wind has favored us so we can just head course. Frisco is 300 miles off. Made sennet today between jobs. The *Manchuria* passed us bound for Frisco. Towards night the wind breezed up and all night it blew strong. The Old Man, however, was so glad to be "going course" that he cracked on to beat the band and it was a case of "stand by the royal halyards" most of the night. We, however, carried sail all night except for two hours in the middle watch, then the to'gal staysails had to come in. As usual, I had the mizzen to'gal staysail and it was a mean job to tie it up. It rained hard all night.

JUNE 27TH. Rainy night and morning. Heading course with a fine strong NW breeze. Then at 7 bells in the morning watch, bang the wind went slap ahead and dropped and all the rest of the day we slatted round with a very light headwind. In the P.M. our watch got the anchors out. In the first dogwatch the wind suddenly came up strong NW and we are again booming along, going course. If this keeps up, we should make Frisco tomorrow. They say our next charter will be for England and then return in ballast to the U.S. I should like that. But I don't suppose anyone really knows.

JUNE 28TH. It blew strong during the night and it was "stand by the halyards" time and time again. At 3 bells of the middle watch we sighted the Farallon Islands Light and about 9 A.M. we got a pilot and soon after that the tug *Sea Queen*. We then unbent some sails. We anchored about noon off Frisco and in the P.M. we unbent and stowed in the locker all the rest of the sails. It was blowing a gale and to pick up and carry the tops'ls across was a fierce job. For to get one side across and over the truss was like trying to move a board fence. But it had to be done before we could lower away clear. We worked all three masts at once. I got some mail today. The mate got drunk. We still have sea food but tomorrow we get our fresh food for "in port."

COMES IN WITH moderate breeze & clear. 8 P.M. fresh WNW breeze & clear. 12 midnight same. 4:30 A.M. Pilot came on board. Very light breeze and fog. 10:30 A.M. took towboat. Noon came to with starboard anchor. 45 fathoms chain. Alcatraz Island Light bearing NNW. Lime Point Light bearing W by S $1/4$ S. P.M. Civil day employed unbending sails & getting ship ready for docking.[4] 8 P.M. set the anchor watch 2 men on deck. Wind strong S with fine clear weather. Pumps, watch, and light carefully attended to.

JUNE 29TH. Turned to early and cleared the ship up and stopped up all the running rigging. Took out the starboard anchor and crane that was bent and got up all the wires and hauling lines. Towed up to Filbert Street dock about noon. Then made her fast. "That will do boys" soon followed. We then knocked off and washed ourselves and shaved, etc. I forgot to say that yesterday all sorts of doctors boarded us but we were all OK. The *Atlas* a month ago was quarantined and the crew had to discharge her ballast. The ship is to be tied up here at Frisco for an indefinite time as no cargo is in sight, so all hands will be paid off tomorrow.

JUNE 30TH. We were paid off at 11 A.M., that is we went at 11 A.M. and waited till one o'clock, then they paid us off.

The last 250 miles to San Francisco had required about 1,200 miles of sailing.

With the rise of union influence in West Coast ports in the early 1900s, shipmasters were well advised to try to forestall any complaints by crew members to the shipping commissioner. Before they were paid off Dunham had a private chat with each man in which he said that if the men made no complaint about the food he would say nothing about the "mutiny"—the coffee incident back on December 22.

Tod toyed with the idea of remaining aboard for the Cape Horn passage to New York—possibly he was rattling the parental chains just a little. Sarah Swift wrote:

AS YOU SAY IT would make you *very* late in getting to mining to finish out the voyage and it would also be a terrible season to round the Horn and it would be *very* hard for me.... I should think nine months of cockroaches—worms—rats, etc., to say nothing of your companions and the mate and the boatswain would be enough. We did not think that you grumbled any too much.

In any event, Tod decided to leave the ship. On July 1 Captain Dunham wrote the following, which Tod rightly treasured ever after:

THIS IS TO CERTIFY that Rodman Swift has been in the ship *Astral* as Ord. Seaman, from the 1st October 1904 to July 1st, 1905. I have found him sober, honest, and attentive. I take pleasure in recommending him to any shipmaster requiring his services.

J. W. Dunham
Master, Am. Ship *Astral*

This is to certify that Rodman Swift has been on the Ship Astral as Ord Seaman, from the 1st Oct 1904 to July 1st 1905. I have found him sober honest and attentive I take pleasure in recommending him to any shipmaster requiring his services

J W Dunham
Master Am Ship "Astral"

San Francisco
July 2 1905

Several days after the crew was paid off Captain Dunham wrote to his daughter Lillian from San Francisco:

> I HAVE NO ONE but the steward and myself. A new mate is coming tomorrow, not a Dutchman.[5] I never want to see one again. This man says he belongs to Boston.

On July 21 he wrote:

> I GUESS I SHALL be here until the 10th of August if not longer. [In] N.Y. they would send me out too quick to see anyone or even talk a few minutes, never can get any time home. I have a fine cargo this time, a good assortment of wine and iron ballast.[6] I wanted to get you a dog in Japan, they charged $13 and even $30 for them. I have known some Captains to try to get them home and they died.... They are sending me lazy stevedores and every one wants something.

Astral departed August 6 for New York, making a prolonged and difficult passage of 147 days. Two sailors were lost from the bowsprit. At New York, when paying off, the crew complained that they had been without butter for fifty-nine days, having had to eat jam instead. Dunham offered to give each man an additional $1.25—the equivalent of five pounds of butter—apiece, which offer was heartily accepted. Each man then shook Dunham's hand and wished him a happy New Year.[7]

Astral's fifth voyage began with a 134-day passage with case oil from New York for Yokkaichi, Japan. She sailed in ballast to Honolulu where, having arrived just too late for a sugar charter, she rolled at anchor for a month.[8] Sailing to San Francisco, she loaded the first cargo of case oil to depart from that port and sailed to Yokkaichi in fifty-nine days. Wife Edith and daughter Effie joined *Astral* for the voyage. At Yokkaichi Effie wrote to Lillian:

My dear Lilla May,
We are well but Mama has worn a long face for the past few days and we have both shed some few tears when the American mail came and we found it had no letters from home and do not understand why you girls have not written more.... Papa is very fussy at times and it makes it hard for poor Mama. I don't care for him. I believe I know how to handle him better than she does. Well, I don't know as I should tell you anything like this but you are old enough to know that Papa does get pretty salty at times and yesterday was one of the times and the disappointment of not getting any letters was too much for her so she had a good cry. Now do write often to Honolulu even if there isn't any news do write something.... The mate discovered that I had a birthday last week so he went on shore this morning and brought a lovely piece of silk for a waist and a feather boa. I truly have much to be thankful for but sometimes I forget that and feel dissatisfied with my lot.... I don't think Papa means to take us anywhere. It was all talk about Kobe and Yokohama. All the way along he has said we would go and now I don't think he means to take us anywhere. Oh dear, such is life on the *Astral*.... I can't bear to think of the long sail home.... If you only knew what a dead place this is. As soon as we get on shore the crowd starts in and they follow us all the time. If we go in a store they crowd around the door and wait until we come out and that makes Papa cross if they get in the way and makes us uncomfortable so on a whole we think it is best to stay on board. I wish Mama and I could be allowed to go by ourselves. Now here I am scolding again. I would like a gold medal for scolding.

Edith wrote:

Effie and I go ashore very little, we had rather stay on board, the sights and smells are disgusting, the children, that is, the street urchins, never had a bath in their lives I am sure and little bits of tots, not more than six years, carry a heavy baby on their back.... You may tell Nino that Mama sees dogs but they are not nice clean little doggies who have a bath every week and go in their mother's pantry and eat cake but poor little sad looking dogs who are tied to a cart and have to pull and help their masters haul great loads. My heart aches for the poor little beasties.... We have thirty men on the outside of the ship pounding iron rust and they are making so much noise that I cannot hear myself write and Effie and I have to scream to hear each other and to add to the din the canary is singing as hard as he can.

On February 13 *Astral* sailed for Honolulu. Four days later, in a blow, the ballast shifted and had to be retrimmed. At Honolulu, on March 31, Captain Dunham wrote home:

> WE HAVE NO MATE, no 2nd mate, no one to come on board drunk and disturb us. We three sit at the table the same as at home. I will be sorry when I see the crowd come again with their dirty old tobacco smoke and talk.

Shortly before the ship sailed with sugar for Philadelphia, Effie wrote Lillian:

> THIS WILL BE THE last letter I will write from this port and I won't have much time in the next so don't look for one for it will be one grand rush and pack for we will very likely start at once and not wait for Papa. When the ship is nearing port I am going to open my trunk and stand off and throw things in just as fast as I can with a whoop and a jump and away I go. No one will see my heels for dust.

On April 13 *Astral* sailed from Honolulu with a cargo of sugar and a crew of twenty-four Japanese and Koreans, arousing the white sailors in the port, who claimed that Dunham was hoping that the Asians would be deported upon arrival at Philadelphia, and that he would not have to pay them. *Astral* arrived after 122 days, having had one man die from a fall from aloft.

Astral's sixth voyage, 1907–08, began with coal (doubtless under navy contract) from Newport News for Honolulu. While lying at Newport, Dunham wrote Lillian:

> I KNOW IT SEEMS hard to you going to school and studying hard, but I look back at my school days as the happiest of all days I ever spent and the time has gone so quickly since.... I know I am getting old now and wish I could have lived on shore more of my time, but such is the life of a seaman. I think Mama and Effie got enough of sea life for a while. So many people think it is a pleasure trip and think a captain has a fine time. I am tired of it long ago but can do nothing else, must go until I go to my long home that will last forever.

Despite losing (and replacing) the fore topgallant mast, *Astral* made a good outward passage of 125 days, beating sistership *Edward Sewall*, which had left the same day, by twenty-six days. At Hilo she loaded sugar for Philadelphia and made the slowest eastward passage (147 days) of seven American square-riggers that sailed at about the same time, including three of her sister Sewall-built barks.

Voyage number seven, 1908–10, began on September 30 with coal from Baltimore for San Francisco, but was interrupted several days later by a fierce hurricane. *Astral* took a tremendous beating, losing her topgallant masts and many sails. Proceeding towards New York under a jury rig and with a severe list, she was picked up by a Standard Oil tug also named *Astral* (Standard Oil Company vessels were named for products, in this instance Astral brand kerosene). Dunham wrote Lillian from New York:

I SURELY HAD A hard time of it and the ship shows it, looks like a wreck up aloft but all right on deck and in the cabins. I think I will get a few days home sometime before I go. I want to see you all again.... It will cost about $20,000 to put the rigging all right and get the ship to sea again. I am so far well treated by every one in the office, they know it was no fault of mine. I could not help the hurricane. Many vessels and many lives were lost.

Before departing on November 28, Dunham wrote daughter Mildred:

I HOPE I MAY get a fine run off the coast into fine warm weather. I do not like the cold.... When I was [home] I wished I could stay all winter but fear I shall never have such good luck. I understand by Capt. Smith that the Company thinks of having a fleet of tank sailing ships. In this case they would never be in port in China or the U.S. over one or two days at a time. I told him they would never get captains or officers to stay over one voyage, this would mean being at sea all the time.

Written to Lillian January 13, at 31°00' south latitude, 96°00' west longitude, off the coast of South America:

THIS IS YOUR BIRTHDAY, you are now eighteen. I hope you have a fine pleasant day.... We only have taken two fish in over the stern, one a bonita the other a swordfish, we had to put a bowline on the latter and take him in tail first. I ate a piece of it, the sailors had a great feast. I have been lonesome, no one to talk to except my bird. He is great company. I take him out and he is with me on the poop deck under the awning every fine day.... How well I remember eighteen years ago today I arrived at Valparaiso, Chile during the beginning of the Chile War. The time has gone so quickly.... My plant did not come again but another one came up in the same pot and looks fine for an out to sea plant. It relieves the eye after looking at the blue water to see something green growing, shall try to keep it warm off the Cape if I can.

Astral arrived at San Francisco after a long run of 159 days, having been 45 days doubling Cape Horn; however, her time was only a few days longer than the average of nineteen other ships making the voyage. On her return passage *Astral* carried wine, hemp, canned fruit, lumber, gun cotton, and scrap iron. Only two other ships accompanied her, one being William Besse's old *Henry Failing*, with lumber, returning to the East Coast to be cut down for a barge. *Astral* made a good passage, reaching Hatteras in 112 days before encountering a ten-day delay reaching New York due to a storm. On the passage a German ordinary seaman had either fallen or jumped overboard. First Mate Douglas told a New York *Sun* reporter that only five out of the crew of twenty-seven could steer or furl a sail, the rest being "boxcar sailors more at home on a brake beam than a topsail yard."[9]

Voyage number eight, in 1910, was *Astral*'s last passage under Standard Oil ownership, and Captain Dunham's last earthly passage. Mr. Douglas remained as mate. A firsthand account of this passage, as told by Barney Burnett—who later sailed with Walter Mallett on *Dirigo*— describes what happened.[10] On July 7, off Cape Horn at 55°00' south latitude, 80°00' west longitude, in a terrific storm, *Astral*'s topgallant masts once again carried away, leaving the ship disabled and with the fearsome Diego Ramirez Islands a lee shore. According to Burnett:

> CAPTAIN DUNHAM must have had cruel forbodings on this score, yet he moved amongst us men with outward assurance, speaking only to issue an order, and then in a voice of unshaken authority that admitted of no despair.

A heavy steel yard, falling, narrowly missed spearing through the main hatch and into a large quantity of gunpowder stowed directly beneath. By dint of heroic labors the ship was freed of the wreckage and jury rigged. *Astral* arrived at San Francisco on September 16—it had been another harsh season off the Horn, and, remarkably, her time of 154 days was about the average for the fleet.

Captain Dunham had been ill when leaving New York, and after the dismasting was confined to his berth, refusing to be put ashore at a South American port.[11] Edith, summoned to San Francisco, wrote home on November 22:

> JUST A LINE TO SAY that Papa is very bad. They telephoned me at the hotel before I had finished dressing that they wanted me. I don't think I ever got into my waist and skirt quicker.... I ran over here and found Papa looking brighter than he had for some time and his mind as clear as it ever was but one side the left is cold and perfectly help-

less. He cannot move even a finger, his arm and leg lie just useless. But it is not for many hours he will be with us. His voice is strong yet and he talks a great deal about dying, he told me this morning he could only last a few hours. I cannot write more now.

Paralysis suggests that he had suffered a stroke; family tradition had it that he actually died of appendicitis. Once "fat as a barrel," in 1909 Dunham had complained to Lillian that he had lost twenty-five pounds and was feeling sick all the time, blaming bad cooks and stewards for spoiling his stomach. Likely he died also of depression. A lengthy obituary in his hometown *Digby (Nova Scotia) Weekly Courier* concluded:

> CAPTAIN DUNHAM was very much opposed to intoxicating liquors and never used them or tobacco. He was noted for his kind disposition and his greatest pleasure in life was pleasing others…his success as a sea captain has been surpassed by few. His carefulness in carrying

Bark Astral *at Howard Street Wharf, San Francisco, September 18, 1910. Note missing mizzen top-gallant mast (left corner of plate is missing).*
COURTESY SAN FRANCISCO MARITIME NATIONAL HISTORICAL PARK.

on the business of his owners was a feature he took great pride in and his integrity in all matters was widely known.... His death is a great blow to his wife and family who always looked forward to a time when he would give up the sea and enjoy a well-earned vacation on land.[12]

Also in November 1910, *Astral* was sold to the Alaska Packers Association. Renamed *Star of Zealand* and clipped of her troublesome topgallant masts, she joined the great "Star" fleet of square-riggers employed in the Alaskan cannery business.[13] Laid up in the late 1920s, in 1935 she was sold for scrapping to Japan, making a final eighty-two-day passage to Yawata carrying salt and scrap metal.[14]

Lillian Dunham never married. Much loved by students (and their parents), she taught kindergarten in Salem for fifty years. She lived in the big fifteen-room Dunham family house until her death in the 1970s. Like her sisters she always revered her father's memory.

Tod Swift always described Captain Dunham as having been a superb seaman.

---

1. Although the ballast weighed much less than the cargo, it could be strategically placed to best effect. Aboard *Atlas* in 1903, Mrs. McKay, the captain's wife, wrote after leaving Yokohama: "Next day we had a strong breeze and nasty sea. Ship rolled terribly [evidently the roll was too quick]. She was too stiff. So the men had to go into the hold and build up the ballast and ease her. She acts much better now." With an increasing gale *Atlas* laid-to with bare poles. "Oh, didn't she roll! I was afraid all the dishes would get broken; if she had been loaded she would have been much steadier, but being light and her ballast not in good trim she rolled terribly." The Japanese sailmaker, fixing his skylight, lost his balance in a roll, hit his head, and died two days later.

2. On June 1 *Astral* was at 41°08' north latitude and 171°11' west longitude, mid-North Pacific Ocean.

3. Had *Astral* been a steamer Tod would have been correct, as a great circle course in these latitudes would have been about 265 miles shorter than the rhumb line. (Great circles are those whose planes pass through the center of the earth; a great circle course appears as an arc on a standard chart, as opposed to a straight rhumb line.) However, a sailing vessel's navigator must also play the odds of expected winds and currents, and at this season this passage was usually found to be best made with a modified great circle course which included mostly sailing on the rhumb line. *Ocean Passages for the World* (London: Hydrographer of the Navy, 1973), p. 218.

4. The logbook used aboard *Astral* in 1905 (unlike the book used in 1904) was set up in traditional astronomical time, with days beginning and ending at noon.

5. At sea a German was a "Dutchman"; a Dutchman was a "Hollander."

6. *Astral*'s cargo for New York consisted of 8,575 barrels of wine, 24,381 cases of salmon, 360 tons of scrap iron, and 1,531 barrels of asphaltum, whale oil, rails, and other items.

7. *Bath Daily Times*, 6 Jan. 1906.

8. She rolled so that Dunham wrote letters with a pencil rather than risk spilled ink.

9. *New York Sun*, 9 Feb. 1910. First mate Bob Douglas, from Portland, Maine, age fifty-five, had spent thirty-seven years at sea. He had once sailed from Hatteras to Sandy Hook in twenty-two hours in the old clipper *Mary Whitridge*. He was aboard the Boston clipper *Fearless*, carrying 450 coolies, when she made a splendid twenty-two-day passage from Hong Kong to Mauritius.

10. Rankin, *The Tall Voyagers*, pp. 29-32.

11. In his as-told-to account, Burnett made no mention of Dunham's illness.

12. *Digby Weekly Courier*, 2 December 1910.

13. Other steel Sewall-built ships purchased by the Alaska Packers included the smart little bark *Kaiulani*, renamed *Star of Finland*; *Acme*, renamed *Star of Poland*; *Atlas*, renamed *Star of Lapland*; and the *Edward Sewall*, renamed *Star of Shetland*. Harold D. Huycke, "The Great Star Fleet," *Yachting*, February and March, 1960, and "The American Four-Mast Bark *Star of Poland*, ex-*Acme*," *American Neptune*, vol. 8, no. 4.

14. Much of the information regarding these voyages is from Frank Thober, "American Oil Ships," Part 2, *Nautical Research Journal*, vol. 8, no. 3.

Chapter 23

An Engineer on Two Coasts

Tod Becomes an Engineer but Ends Up with a Small "Ship" of His Own.

AFTER SIGNING OFF *Astral* Tod returned home by train, to briefly bask in acclaim at Nonquitt before heading right back to California. Thanks to Tod's Harvard roommate Billy Hague—Billy's father, James D. Hague, was a fabulously successful California mine owner—Tod had been hired as a surveyor at Hague's famous North Star hardrock gold mine in Grass Valley.

The North Star was practically an educational institution for young engineers, thanks to the enlightened culture fostered by superintendent Arthur DeWint Foote, James Hague's brother-in-law. Foote, a Connecticut native, was a legendary Western civil engineer whose bold schemes, while enriching many others, would ultimately leave him nearly penniless. His New York Quaker wife "Molly"—Mary Hallock Foote—was a gifted, pioneering, and widely published illustrator and writer. In addition to Foote's vision, practicality, tenacity, and hardihood, he was honest and enjoyed good relations with the North Star's Cornish miners. The Footes' lives would later serve as the basis for Wallace Stegner's 1972 Pulitzer Prize-winning novel *Angle of Repose*.[1]

At the North Star Tod was smitten by the Footes' daughter, Elizabeth. As but one of a stable of potential suitors, Tod had to come up with a novel tactic. Telephoning the Foote home regularly on Sunday mornings, Tod would introduce himself and then become tongue-tied, leaving the gracious Mrs. Foote no recourse but to invite him up for a meal. Tod and Betty were married in June 1906, in a Quaker-style ceremony at Grass Valley. Molly wrote to a friend: "What a supreme mercy, that [Betty] took this boy, so nice to live with, so proud in big ways and so simple and unfretful in little ways."[2] The Swifts moved into separate quarters in the Footes' grand, year-old "arts and crafts"-style home.[3] The Swift's first child, Agnes, was born at Grass Valley in 1908.

Home is the sailor, home from the sea. Tod at Nonquitt, summer 1905.
RODMAN SWIFT COLLECTION.

The Rodman Swifts at Grass Valley.
RODMAN SWIFT COLLECTION.

Residence of the Superintendent, North Star Mine, Grass Valley, California.
RODMAN SWIFT COLLECTION.

In 1908 Mr. Foote became interested in developing a hydroelectric project in the rugged Sierra Nevada headwaters of the Yuba River. Although falling electric rates would end the project in 1910, beginning in July 1909 Tod spent a year directing a small party in the rugged mountain wilderness building trails and surveying the dam site and the pipeline route. Supplies were brought in by burro train. Charged with cutting miles of sight lines through brush and tree tops; building bridges over wild rivers; maintaining crew discipline; performing celestial positioning; lugging a twenty-five-pound transit up cliffs and down gullies; executing exacting calculations; contending with heat, cold, rain, and heavy snows; coexisting with scorpions, rattlesnakes, and bears; and occasionally hanging from cliffs with ropes, Tod's position was anything but a son-in-law's sinecure. Most of Tod's diary entries are a dry record of difficult work accomplished under rugged conditions, but one entry in particular is a poetical departure:

> LAST NIGHT ABOUT 9:30 a thunder squall came up from the South over Gold Ridge. It was a great sight. The moon almost full was shining bright on the approaching squall which came along like a huge fog bank, for the clouds were right down to the ground and a bright silver color. With very frequent, and brilliant but completely enveloped in the clouds, flashes. And the whole great silver mass came rolling down the mountainside which is covered with big trees. And with its con-

Fording the Yuba River, 1909.
RODMAN SWIFT COLLECTION.

tinuous internal flashes it was almost as light as day for the moon was very bright and it happened to be a clear sky over me.

Nevertheless, Tod was homesick for New England weather and for New England waters. In 1910 he accepted a position with the Submarine Signal Corporation of Boston. Returned to Massachusetts, the Swifts moved into a cottage in Hingham, and later would have a new house built in the same town.

Tod's new employer had been organized in 1901 to develop underwater signaling warning devices. In ten years' time shipboard receivers homed in on the sound of bells mounted underwater on lightships, near lighthouses, and on buoys. The company made great advances during World War I, becoming a world leader in underwater acoustical technology. By 1925 Submarine Signal was manufacturing "fathometers," acoustical sounding devices of revolutionary importance.[4]

Tod was hired as the superintendent of Submarine Signal's Boston testing division, a position he held throughout his tenure. Brief entries in a 1918 wartime notebook show him making frequent trips to ship and navy yards from Boston to Philadelphia attending to matters regarding the installation and operation of "Forbes logs," "receivers," and "oscillators." When in Boston, aside from working in the office, attending meetings, and visiting the factory, he spent many days on the water aboard test craft, including the *Rodman Swift*, a husky 19-ton, 42-foot motor vessel, "pairing microphones."[5] The winter of 1918 was a cold one:

Motor vessel Rodman Swift, *built at East Boston in 1918.*
RODMAN SWIFT COLLECTION.

FEB. 11. SW strong. 10 degrees. Took 5:50 train from Hingham. For micro job. Left T Wharf in *Marie* at 8 but *Magnolia*'s engine balked and could not ring bell. Spent most of day cutting, sawing, and breaking ice with a tug round the *Maggy*. Got her out at last and towed her to Commercial Wharf. She was in 20 inches of solid ice and being jammed very badly.

Due to a coal shortage, at home on Sundays he "said nothing and sawed firewood." On March 2 he saw Betty and "the girls"—in 1913 Sarah, known as "Sally," had joined the family—off to Grass Valley, and moved his "dunnage" to the city. On March 15 and March 20 he dined with Uncle Frank Stone, who was teaching navigation at MIT. On both occasions he noted discussion regarding the "plan of going to sea." What this plan might have been is a mystery, but the wartime demand for tonnage had ignited sail's last boom, and perhaps the two were considering the possibility of Uncle Frank—who could afford it—buying a ship.

Sally Swift recalls that some of this testing work required long hours spent in the bilges of ships, awaiting signals. During these times he whittled boat models for his girls. He also often came home with a host of ship-jumping fleas. Tod laid the cable for the first underwater "tripod" off Nahant—tripods were electrically operated bells—a not inconsiderable job of marine engineering.[6]

The Swifts built a new home atop an old granite steamboat wharf—and called it the Wharf House—in Hingham, a town which Tod had scouted from a nautical chart. Designed by Tod and Betty, the shingled, two-storied, pitch-roofed house, with a windbreak of a porch, was without frills within and without, yet contained all the essentials required for a Swift family habitat.

The first floor was dominated by a large combined living room and workshop extending across the water-side end. Boating paraphernalia hung from the ceiling, and later Tod's large rigged model of *Tyche*—we will soon learn of the schooner *Tyche*—sat on the mantel of the large, central-chimney fireplace. During the winter Tod overhauled rigging and boat gear while enjoying the family and other comforts of home. He even built a skiff for Agnes there. The kitchen adjoined the living room end of the space.

The house contained no rugs, curtains, or bright colors. The wood floors were periodically oiled. While it may be tempting to link this spare and open-spaced concept with the elegantly elemental "arts and craft" style of the Grass Valley house, or even with the shingled, summer arks of Nonquitt, Sally Swift remembers the Wharf House as simply a reflection of Tod and Betty's tastes. Betty's aversion to bright colors may have been a reflection of having grown up amidst the muted landscape of Idaho. For Tod, the Wharf House's rugged simplicity, and the lifestyle it permitted, was surely part of a lifelong rejection of the extravagance of the over-sized and over-filled houses of his New Bedford boyhood. The sparseness of the Wharf House interior was matched in the winter by a decidedly brisk temperature—Yankee Tod hated watching good money flow out a chimney.[7]

Along with their similarities, Tod and Betty also differed in fundamental ways, both respectfully tolerating the other. Whereas Tod was the busy builder and fixer, the habitual recorder of minutia in pocket notebooks, and the compulsive sailor, Betty was a contemplative reader and writer. She

The Wharf House, Hingham.
RODMAN SWIFT COLLECTION.

enjoyed small boats but became seasick in larger craft and did not cruise with the family, surely experiencing times of much loneliness as a result.

For Agnes and Sally the Wharf House was a home with a dash of adventure to it. The Swifts' watery realm included little Button Island, which Tod whimsically mapped in Swallows and Amazons style. At high tide, eight feet of water lapped the wharf and volleys of gale-driven spray sometimes lashed at the windows; at low tide the watery realm was transformed into a mile of mud—and very sticky mud, at that! Successful boating required paying keen attention to the tides.

The big catboat *Coyote*, the first family yacht, sat on the mud at low tide, and in the winter was hauled out on Button Island. The second yacht, the big and wholesome yawl *Tangent*, was kept elsewhere, but her ample tender *Black Boat* (later renamed *The Golden Hind*), and later, the girls' twin catboats, *Pusheen Gra*—believed to be Gaelic for "Pussy Dear"—and *Catasal*, sat out the winter on the wharf, hoisted there in ancient fashion by a tackle and sheers.

Agnes and Sal grew up in boats and maintained their own boats. Tod—called "Dear Man" by the girls—was to them the perfect father, even bravely holding the nails when the girls first tried their hand at hammering.[8] In Quaker tradition the girls were reared by reason and example and were early given responsibility. They were given all the encouragement to try new experiences that sons would have received.

The Swifts' ark of a yawl *Tangent*, able to seat a dozen people in her cockpit, was an excellent family cruiser. As the girls grew older, however, Tod wished to have a vessel which he could sail alone, and also one which bore his stamp. The result was the 27½-foot schooner *Tyche*, named for the Greek goddess of good fortune. *Tyche* represented the meeting of the fertile minds of three men—Tod, designer and promoter John Alden, and draftsman Sam Crocker who actually drew the plans.[9] *Tyche* was built in 1922 by Baker Yacht Basin of Quincy, Massachusetts. Framed in white oak, she was planked with cypress.

At 27½ feet, she was very small for a schooner. Both Alden and Crocker tried to persuade Tod to make her a sloop, which would have made her faster, but Tod wanted a schooner. He would be in no great hurry, and for

Agnes Swift at the helm of Golden Hind, *August, 1916.*
RODMAN SWIFT COLLECTION.

Tod aboard yawl Tangent.
RODMAN SWIFT COLLECTION.

Schooner Tyche.
COURTESY OF LLEWELLYN HOWLAND III.

October, 1914, off Boston Harbor, photographed from yawl Tangent. *A tug ranges alongside a four-masted schooner while the tug skipper dickers with the schooner captain over the price of a tow into the harbor.*
RODMAN SWIFT COLLECTION.

calms or foul tides he would have an engine. A schooner's sails would be small and easily handled. No reefing of the main would be required in a blow, as she could jog along or lie-to under foresail alone. And there was something else—Tod called her his "ship," and treated her as such.[10] No sloop could be considered a ship. *Tyche* was a small—yet not even the smallest—member of a back-to-the-schooner revolt led by Alden and New Bedford's William Hand, challenging the ill-shaped, long-overhang-designs resulting from racing-handicap rules. Appraising *Tyche*'s design, *Motor Boating* opined in the May 10, 1922, issue:

> AS WILL BE SEEN from the lines and body plan, the little auxiliary shows the characteristic features that Alden has proved desirable in his many successful schooners of larger size. It will be noticed that she has unusually hard bilges which will give her great initial stability....

> While broad, and a bit chunky for windward work, the lines are clean with a fairly fine entrance and easy run and for all-around sailing she should prove a desirable boat.
>
> Alden does not want to give the impression that he approves of the schooner rig for such a small vessel, where the greatest efficiency is desired...but the little boat was actually designed to go to sea.... She will lie-to and handle under her foresail just as the bigger vessels will do.... "On a boat of this size," says Alden, "I like all the ballast outside as the chief weights are relatively far higher than on a larger boat and, therefore, it is necessary...to have the center of gravity of the ballast correspondingly lower...."
>
> In spite of the fact that the little ship will not be as fast as many another boat of her length...she should not by any means be a poor sailer and it would be difficult to design a better all-around cruiser either for singlehanded work or for two persons. She should be able to keep the sea, even in severe weather and with her auxiliary motor, calm weather or intricate inside passages will have no terrors for her.

In fact, "schooner boats," many of them no bigger than "sloop boats," had long been used by New England fishermen. While not a "character boat" copy of a vernacular type, *Tyche* was unmistakably a New Englander. After several first-season alterations she proved to be a very satisfactory pocket packet, if never a speed merchant.[11]

---

1. Although Stegner incorporated some of Mary Foote's letters, and used the actual names of many supporting characters, the lives of the Footes—with their names changed—were fictionalized in certain important respects. Descendants were not amused. The most recent biography of Molly is *Mary Hallock Foote*, by Darlis A. Miller (Norman, OK: University of Oklahoma Press, 2002). Some of the notable chapters in Arthur Foote's wide-ranging career include participation in the draining of the Comstock Mines; surveying Golden Gate Park; serving as surveyor at the Homestake Mine; and working as superintendent of a mine at Leadville, Colorado. He surveyed and planned a 600,000-acre irrigation system in Idaho, but funding for the project ran out and it wasn't built for another twenty years. His reactivation and expansion of the moribund North Star produced an additional $30,000,000 worth of gold. *Memoir 345*, American Society of Civil Engineers. At Grass Valley today the spacious, innovative superintendent's home, the famous 30-foot Pelton wheel—once powered by water delivered via a pipeline with a "head" of 775 feet—and the massive foundations of the horse-frightening hard-rock stamping mills remain as landmarks of Foote's enterprise. It was along the Yukon that William Besse had made enough money to buy two Great Lakes schooners.

2. Miller, *Mary Hallock Foote*, p. 228. In addition to sharing their mothers' families' Quaker heritages, Tod and Betty also had in common the experience of dealing with alcoholic fathers. Betty always claimed that Captain Dunham's description of Tod as "sober, honest, and attentive" was what convinced her to marry him.

3. The house was designed by Foote and the soon-to-be-famous Julia Morgan, the architect of William Randolph Hearst's San Simeon Castle.

4. In 1910 the company obtained the services of the Canadian-born genius Reginald Fessenden, now recognized as perhaps the greatest pioneer wireless inventor, surpassing even Marconi. In response to the 1912 *Titanic* disaster, Fessenden devised an apparatus, based on the Fessenden oscillator, for warning ships of icebergs, and also for communication between submarines. When tested successfully on an iceberg in 1914, the serendipitous discovery that echoes were also returned from the ocean bottom marked a breakthrough technological advance. In 1940 Submarine Signal became a division of the Raytheon Corporation.

5. When installed in a ship, two independent sets of "microphones" (to provide for backup) were mounted, port and starboard, within the hull to receive signals from bells, and to transmit the sounds to independent earpieces located on the ship's bridge. Whichever side—as selected by a control—the sound was loudest on indicated the direction of the bell. Bells could be heard from three to five miles, although deep-draft vessels could sometimes pick them up at greater distances. The *Rodman Swift* was eventually sold into a new career as a fishing boat out of Gloucester, Fall River, and finally New Bedford, from whence she finally disappeared from records in the 1980s.

6. In May 1918 Tod engaged a sixteen-horse team to haul a seventeen-ton reel of wire from Cambridge to the South Boston waterfront. The first tripod installation, on Egg Island, terrified a well-digger miles inland, who heard a bell ringing. The well had been dug near a ledge which extended far offshore. H. J. Fay, *Submarine Signal Log* (Portsmouth: Raytheon Company, 1963), p. 10.

7. The cold bedroom policy did not extend to Tippy, the dog. In winter Tippy's substantial doghouse was entered through an extended vestibule hung with several weighted canvas flaps. The inner sanctum was heated by a light bulb connected to a switch in the Wharf House, and several hours before Tippy's bedtime, Tippy's bedroom was well warmed up.

8. As an infant Agnes insisted on calling Tod "Man," which she then appended to Betty's "Dear," and later insisted on Sally using it also.

9. Alden's stable of young draftsmen was a veritable *Who's Who* of future famous designers, including Sam Crocker.

10. *Tyche* was always wintered in wet storage, i.e., afloat, like a proper ship.

11. *Tyche* initially carried an excessive weather helm. To correct it, the foot and head of the mainsail were reduced by cutting one foot off the leech. Also, 1,200 pounds of lead were removed from her keel, and 600 pounds was placed inside and fairly far forward. For plans see Robert W. Carrick, *John G. Alden and His Yacht Designs* (Camden, ME: International Marine, 1983), p. 350; and Roger C. Taylor, "Little Alden Schooner," *Motor Boating*, 10 May 1922.

Chapter 24

IN THE WAKE OF *JAG*

Tod Swift Goes Cruising With Tyche.

INITIALLY MOORED in front of the Wharf House, where she settled into a mud berth at every low tide, *Tyche* was soon shifted to a mooring at South Dartmouth, Tod thereby returning to the waters he had cruised in his boyhood in *Jag*. *Tyche*, in a squeeze, could sleep four, but more often she slept one adult and two girls—and even more often, just Tod and Agnes, as horse-crazed Sally often stayed home with Betty.

When cruising, *Tyche* often rendezvoused with the *Anna*, Uncle Frank Stone's big Cape Cod catboat, usually meeting her at Hadley Harbor, Naushon Island. On these invariably merry occasions dinner was prepared and enjoyed aboard the commodious *Anna*, whose larder was well supplied with thick steaks. (Aboard *Tyche*, by contrast, most meals came out of a can.) Uncle Frank relaxed smoking and doing crossword puzzles.[1]

Tyche's 1927 cruise began in July (most began in August). Both Agnes—nicknamed "Tyke"—and Sally, were aboard. Tod wrote in *Tyche*'s log at Marion Harbor on July 29, 1927:

> TURNED OUT AT 6 and found NW and rain. Turned out at 6:30 and found SW and dirty looking. Got underway for Menemsha.[2] Breakfast underway, wind SW. Steamed for Quick's Hole then set sail and sailed to Menemsha. Found strong SW on Vineyard side of sound. Ran into the harbor and tied up in the usual place at about 12:30. Tyke went for a swim before lunch. We have a date to meet Uncle Frank here today but as yet (1:30 P.M.) no sign of the *Anna*. He was supposed to be in Edgartown last night.
>
> During the afternoon Frank Stetson came over from Mr. Hand's boat *Water Witch* then we went to call on them.[3] About 5:30 Uncle Frank showed up off the entrance and circled round not coming in but waiting for a great fat unwieldy N.Y. flounder dragger to come in first. The N.Y. ark was named *Fluke* and promptly stuck hard on the bar at the turn. Uncle Frank then came in and tied up just outside us. A small fisherman pulled the *Fluke* off and after a while he worked in

and anchored south of us. We all had supper on the *Anna.* Just as we were finishing a squall from the North hit us. Francis and I ran out four extra lines to shore.[4] The *Fluke* dragged down on top of the *Water Witch* which was at Ashley's mooring. The *Water Witch* ran her engine and put out an anchor but the *Fluke* pushed her down till her stern grounded, then the *Fluke* went down on top of the *Bonito* and shoved her ashore. A white sloop had in the meantime dragged clear up the creek somewhere. Presently *Fluke* grounded. Later the *Water Witch* came over and tied up outside the *Anna* and the *Bonita* got off and anchored in the middle of the harbor. During the evening many large fishermen came in. Much sand was blown aboard from the beach. Things quieted down at 10:30 and we turned in.

JULY 30TH. Turned out at 5:30. Calm. Uncle Frank went back to SD and by 7 all the strange fishermen had gone. We went out at 7:30.

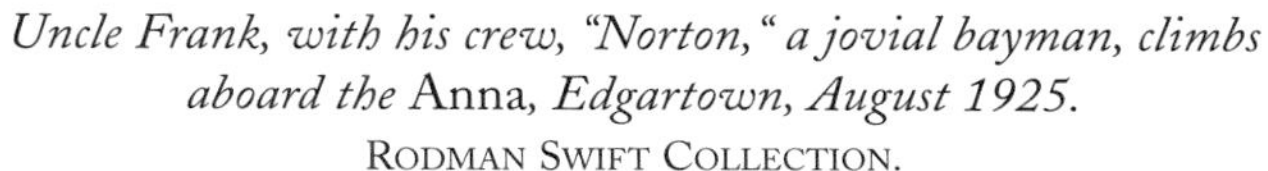
Uncle Frank, with his crew, "Norton," a jovial bayman, climbs aboard the Anna, *Edgartown, August 1925.*
RODMAN SWIFT COLLECTION.

Left: 1926. Tod, Sally, and Agnes aboard the miniature dory Tippy, *said to be so unstable as to be unstealable. Schooner* Tyche *in background.*
RODMAN SWIFT COLLECTION.

Right: Uncle Frank aboard catboat Anna. *Schooner* Tyche *astern.*
RODMAN SWIFT COLLECTION.

Stopped the engine outside and sailed across the sound, the wind North and tide running East. Tacked to East and went close to the *Selwyn Eddy* aground near Tarpaulin Cove.[5] Then to Tarpaulin Cove and anchored. Ashore for an hour. Tyke swam. Aboard for lunch. Then underway for Hadley's via Quick's. Tide to West in sound and wind SW. Beat fast down to Quick's. Ran down the islands and anchored in Hadley's about 7. Found many NBYC boats there.[6] On the No. pt. of Uncatena we saw a 30-ft. sloop up on the rocks. Probably the result of last night's squall. The *Kalinga* was in the harbor, mast gone, carried away off West Chop.

JULY 31ST. Turned out to find SE and rain. It rained till nearly noon. We then embarked in *Tippy* to row around Uncatena and to see the wreck.[7] When we got there the wreck had been removed. We landed and collected a great deal of firewood then rowed back and almost got caught by low water in the NW gutter. The wind now hauled to SW and rained.

Turned out and found SW and rain. It stopped soon and fog came in bunches. A and S went ashore and rode with Pauline Forbes. I up anchor and went for a sail in the bay. Stood NW for an hour and a half then back SE. It was thick much of the time. Anchored about 1:30. A and S came back. They had a fine ride and a swim. After lunch we went for a sail, beat down to Weepeckets, and it began to rain so we came back. It rained on and off all the evening, and most of the night.

Jumping ahead to August 7, we find *Tyche* back at Menemsha. The land mentioned below had been recently purchased by Tod:

TURNED OUT TO FIND no wind and hot. We all swam before lunch then at 2:30 we embarked in *Tippy* for our land. Fair tide up. Walked over and saw Mr. Rodman then back to the land and talked to Mr. Cooper about building a gate in the hole in the wall in Lot #8. At about 7:15 we started back to the *Tyche.* Fair tide. Late supper and turned in. Had a great day on the land but we all got sore heels.

AUGUST 8TH. Turned out at 6:30, light S. and fog. Ran out and as it was thick we anchored just West of the first fish net. At 10:30 it cleared up some and we ran across the sound and looked at the *Selwyn Eddy*. Her bow has been hauled out and she is on an even keel now. We then beat up the Sound to Quick's. Fair Tide. Big stew for lunch, anchored in Quick's about 2:15. Went ashore for half an hour on the beach. Then up anchor and sailed down the islands to Hadley's. Off Weepeckets it began to rain, wind SSE. It rained during the evening and night. Late in morning wind hauled SW and blew hard. In the evening before dark a sailor from the houseboat *Sally Jean V* brought us over a very ornate cake 12 x 20 x 3 thick covered with very fancy yellow frosting. He said the cake was too much for them. The address on it was Mr. Florenze Zeigfeld, Hotel Ritz, Boston. The cake was only half baked and too much for us too. Several boats in the harbor put out two anchors and one yawl dragged.

AUG. 9TH. Turned out and found SW rain. Sal and I put on oilskins and landed on Ram's Head for clams, walked all round it but got no clams. We then tried Nonamesset, same results. We then tried NW

Tippy *at Quick's Hole, Nashawena Island, one of the Elizabeth Islands, August 1929.*
RODMAN SWIFT COLLECTION.

gutter and got plenty. Back to the *Tyche* for lunch then steamed out to Weepeckets and anchored to fish. No bites so with great labor we got the anchor up and anchored East of Uncatena. Here we got eight scup and one flounder and several chogsheads.[8] Back to the harbor and cleaned them just before dark. Then supper and turned in. Everything had a strong smell of fish.

On the twelfth *Tyche* circumnavigated lonely No Mans Land Island:

OFF TO THE SE of the island we shut off the engine and sailed. Took noon sights and buried the cake at the No Mans Land Whistling Buoy.[9] We gave it a very proper burial. Then round the NW point and back up the east side to examine the harbor. Found it was a breakwater affair. The girls then swam and we started back for Menemsha. The wind was light and it was 4 o'clock before we rounded Gay Head. We saw the freight schooner *Alice Wentworth* go into the harbor just before we got there.[10] When we came in she was aground across-ways in the channel halfway up between the harbor entrance and Butler's place. We came in and tied up then rowed up and looked her over. A boat pulled on her and she swung round then after a bit went further along but grounded again and stuck for the present.

There was a catboat sailing around outside. She came from Fall River. Wind SW. Finally she got down her sail and one of the boys got into their skiff and they towed her in near the shore and anchored.

It seems they didn't know how to beat to windward. Later a fisherman towed them in and they tied up outside of us bow to stern. But they put their anchor down three times and are now in a poor position. The girls went ashore to post letters etc. Also to have a look at the schooner.

On the sixteenth *Tyche* was back at Marion where the crew visited boatbuilder Captain Jenny, who said that he and his brother would postpone their retirement to build Sal a catboat just like the one they had built for Agnes. By the twenty-first *Tyche* was back at Menemsha, joined by the *Anna*. The twenty-second was calm with fog, so all hands took Uncle Frank's power skiff and again visited the Swift land. *Tyche* and *Anna* then cruised in company to Vineyard Haven and Edgartown, then back through Quick's Hole in the fog and to South Dartmouth.[11] On August 26, Tod wrote:

> TURNED OUT AT 6 and found light NE and clear. Breakfast and shore-going clothes. Went ashore and started for Boston in "Julia" about 7:30.[12] We stopped at Mother's house and left Tyke and took aboard my rubber boots. Sal and I then went direct to Boston. Thus ends the cruise.

Unidentified four-masted schooner, photographed from schooner Tyche, *August 1931.*
RODMAN SWIFT COLLECTION.

Schooner Dorothy B *of New Bedford, photographed from schooner* Tyche *off Cuttyhunk Island, August 1923.*
Rodman Swift Collection.

Tod remained with Submarine Signal until 1931, by which time his job no longer included work on the water. Chafing at his confinement, he had for some time insisted on taking the full month of August as vacation, rather than the standard two weeks. Finally, at age fifty-one, with Agnes and Sally both out of school, he retired. He wrote in his journal:

> OFF
> July 24th. Left the Submarine Signal Co. for good this afternoon. I could stand it no longer.
>
> July 25th. Left Hingham at 9 a.m. with a good deal of gear bound for the *Tyche*. Betty is in California. Sal is in England and Tyke is in Maine. Mary [McGuire] stays at the house without pay—So it goes, not much money but free from all the mental strain of the SS. Went to Nonquitt and had lunch with Mother.... After lunch Helen took me over to the *Tyche*.

Tyche remained the apple of Tod's eye. They rode out the epic hurricane of '38 together on her two heavy fisherman's anchors in hard-hit Padanarum Harbor, South Dartmouth. Tod and *Tyche*, with Agnes, cruised Down East to Maine, and twice Tod sailed *Tyche* to Florida for the winter, shipping a second hand when sailing between the Chesapeake and New York. Heading once from Mystic to New York Harbor in a powerful blow, the buoyant little ship floated atop threatening following seas like the proverbial foam ball. Cast ashore at Menemsha in 1954 by Hurricane Carol, she narrowly missed hitting rocks on either side—afterwards, Tod shed tears of relief.

In 1932 the Swifts had taken in Betty's by then penniless parents, the Footes.[13] Shortly afterward, Betty's mother, Molly, wrote to a friend:

> WE ARE SETTLED now in our little snug harbor up-stairs, bedroom and sitting room in one, on the northwest corner of the house with a full view of the bay, of its shore lights at night when they seem to spring out of the darkness and the void, and of its cold pink mornings and its deep-colored sunsets on the edge of darkness.[14]

In 1933 Arthur Foote died. Molly died in 1938. Tragically, Betty Swift died in 1943. Tod had by then built a stone cottage on Martha's Vineyard,

The Stone Cabin, Menemsha Pond.
RODMAN SWIFT COLLECTION.

and after Betty's death he never again spent a night alone at the Wharf House. Until his own death in 1959—excepting four winters spent in Florida—Tod lived on Martha's Vineyard Island.

Roughly triangular, Martha's Vineyard Island is about eighteen miles by ten miles across its widest point. South of the barrier beaches lies the open Atlantic, interrupted only by lonely No Mans Land Island off the bold seamark of Gay Head's colorful clay cliffs. To the west and north lies Vineyard Sound. To the East, just below the horizon, lies the low, gray island of Nantucket.

When Tod bought his land in the 1920s, the Vineyard was a charmed place. Although the island economy was dependent on the summer resort business, most visitors were concentrated in the beehive of Oak Bluffs, first developed as a Methodist camp-meeting ground, leaving much of the land in farms. The natives included an assortment of farmers, fishermen, watermen, and old sailors and old whalers. Most were Yankees, along with "Western Island" Portuguese—Azoreans, first landed from whaleships—and Wampanoag Indians.

On the island's eastern apex was the sleepy old whaling port of Edgartown, its streets lined with gracious homes from its prosperous past. (The Vineyard in general, and Edgartown in particular, had been the home of many whalemen in general, and many whaling captains in particular.) Vineyard Haven, at the northern apex, was, in the 1920s, still an important haven for coastal shipping, with schooners gathered awaiting a "fair chance" of wind and tide to pass through Nantucket Sound.

Gay Head, "up island," at the island's western apex, was an Indian town. As elsewhere in the New World, the great majority of the Wampanoags, unprotected by natural immunities, had died from diseases contracted from early Europeans. The survivors, having converted to Christianity, never took up arms against the whites. Gay Headers became famous around the world for their prowess as whalers, particularly as harpooners.

Menemsha Bight, a gentle indentation on the Vineyard Sound shore east of Gay Head, was another important coaster anchorage. Along the shore of the Bight, between stone jetties, lay the scant village of Menemsha, a fisherman's outport, located on a tiny harbor alongside the channel, or "creek," to mile-square Menemsha Pond. On the shore of Menemsha Pond, Tod purchased forty acres of gently sloping pastureland, to which he added a smaller parcel composed of a confusion of Indian subdivisions. The seller was an Indian named Abraham L. (presumably Lincoln) Rodman.

Near the pond shore Tod had a single-room "stone cabin" built, the stones having been gathered up and piled in neat cairns by a local Indian with his ox team. An outstanding outhouse, built to government design, a handsome workshop, and a woodshed, all built of wood by Tod, followed.

Here Tod lived, without electricity or running water, and in great simplicity, for more than ten years. During the war, unable to sail in *Tyche*, Tod took up gardening with all the thoroughness and energy that characterized all of his endeavors. He found plenty of data to record in his unending chain of notebooks, including the dates that flowers blossomed and birds returned.

In the mid-1950s, after a heart attack and with his health failing, Tod followed the urgings of Agnes and Sally and moved into a new "wood cabin," fitted with electricity and running water. *Tyche* was moored in Quitsa Pond—Quitsa is sort of an annex to Menemsha Pond—and Tod slept nights aboard his faithful friend of a schooner.

Rodman Swift.
COURTESY OF LLEWELLYN HOWLAND III.

Tod's circle of Vineyard friends was not large, but the friendships he maintained—particularly with the fish dealer Donald Poole and his family, fisherman Robert Flanders and his wife Gladys, and retired actress and neighbor Margaret Webster—were very strong. Although never a gladhander, Tod was a genial host to any acquaintance stopping by, happy to sit and smoke and yarn in front of the stone cabin by the pond, while sipping some convivial rum. If some people came to view "Captain Swift" as a local character it was not due to any role-playing by Tod—Tod was the genuine article.[15]

When Tod's failing health prevented further extended coastal passages, he bought a no-nonsense power cruiser in Florida, which he named *Muskrat*. Never content with idleness, Tod went to work changing this and changing that until *Muskrat* was recast in his own unmistakable style.

Tod died in October of 1959. His death, well timed, was neatly accomplished. Having seen the *Tyche* put to bed for the winter at South Dartmouth, he had just returned to the island by steamer, picked up his mail, gotten into his car, and lit his pipe when he suffered a fatal heart attack. His friend Margaret Webster, upon hearing of Tod's passing, said that it seemed as though a piece of the Vineyard had broken off and been swallowed by the sea. His memorial service brought friends from across sound and bay, with one—Norman Fortier—arriving by small boat despite foul weather. Tod would have appreciated that.

Tod's greatest legacy was the example of a life lived well and simply and according to his own specifications. Ultimately reduced to essentials, it was uncommonly rich with satisfactions, chief among them being his voyage as a sailor aboard *Astral*. Whereas Tod's contemporaries from New Bedford's old elite more generally aspired to live their lives in the comfort and society into which they had been born, Tod never outgrew his beginnings as a sea struck boy.

Tod planned to stipulate in his will that *Tyche* be destroyed. As sensible Yankees, Agnes and Sally would accept Tod's death with equanimity, admiring his timing, and relieved that "Dear Man" would not end his active life as an invalid.[16] But they were not yet prepared to oversee *Tyche*'s end. In response to their pleas, Tod had agreed that *Tyche* might sail on for a while, provided that she never left the family. After several years the wisdom of Tod's directive became more evident, as it became obvious that the forty-year-old *Tyche* was wearing out and would require major repairs. And so it was that she was broken up by Tod's friend Waldo Howland, who had watched over her for so many winters.

1. Landlocked Hadley, surrounded by the Forbes family's island fiefdom, was a favorite anchorage. It's only drawback—from Tod's point of view—being tiresome visits from "The Gov," i.e., Cameron Forbes, former governor–general of the Philippines. Forbes held himself in very high regard, and Tod ducked below, hiding in the head if necessary, at first sight of his approach.

2. Menemsha is a village with a very small harbor, frequented mostly by fishing vessels, on the island of Martha's Vineyard.

3. *Water Witch*, built in 1926, was the first of New Bedford designer William Hand's famous motorsailer yachts.

4. Francis H. Stone, Jr.

5. The *Selwyn Eddy* was a 2,846-ton lake steamer, built in Michigan in 1893.

6. New Bedford Yacht Club. See Howland, *The New Bedford Yacht Club.*

7. *Tippy* was the well-named dwarf dory which served as *Tyche*'s tender and was small enough to stow on deck.

8. Chogsheads were also known as "ocean cunners." Once abundant, they no longer are.

9. Tod and the girls competed in celestial navigation, with positions scored from a buoy. Tod and Agnes had sextants, Sal had an antique quadrant.

10. The famous coasting schooner *Alice S. Wentworth* was then owned and skippered by the legendary Captain Zebulon Northrop Tilton, of Martha's Vineyard. In 1897–98 Zeb's older whaler brother George Fred—who we met in an earlier chapter—walked across Alaska in the winter to bring word to civilization about the frozen-in whaling fleet. Brother William had been a square-rigger chantyman.

11. The *Anna*, by this date, had acquired the geriatric rig of a marconi cat ketch in place of her original outsized gaff catboat mainsail. Uncle Frank, now seventy, was enjoying his thirty-fourth year of retirement. He would die in 1941 at age eighty-five.

12. "Julia," a Model T Ford, was the Swifts' first auto.

13. In 1913 Foote spent $50,000—all he had—to honor a commitment to build a road to the Tightener Mine. Unable by infirmity to personally stake out the route, Foote entrusted the job to a local surveyor who foolishly routed it along the face of a 600-foot cliff instead of a much less expensive route above.

14. Miller, *Mary Hallock Foote*, p. 265.

15. After Tod's death, Agnes and Sally were much amused to discover, stored in the Stone Cabin, bags of plastic measuring scoops from cans of Chock Full 'O Nuts coffee —Tod simply could not bear to throw out perfectly good scoops. An old friend was less amused when touched-up for petty cash—Tod, the frugal Yankee, having forgotten once again to have any money in his pocket.

16. Agnes made her career as the beloved librarian of famous Shady Hill School in Cambridge, Massachusetts. She spent many summers in Maine, teaching children to sail. Sally Swift, after a career with the Holstein Cattle Association in Brattleboro, Vermont, wrote *Centered Riding*. Both in person, and through her book, which is now a standard and a classic, she has taught countless people to ride, and to ride in harmony with their horses.

Appendix

Stray Bits Too Good to Cut

Fred Taylor's Wonderful Photographs

A Portfolio of Photographs Taken by Fred H. Taylor, a Schoolboy, Aboard the Four-Masted Barque Queen Margaret, *New York to Freemantle, 1905*

IN JUNE 1905, I graduated from Montclair [New Jersey] High School. Without my knowledge, my mother and father had determined that because of my light weight, it might be well to forego my pursuit of education for a year and send me on a voyage. They had thought that I might be put aboard a steamer and cross the Atlantic (possibly going to the Mediterranean) and then return refreshed to start my college years. However, before this idea had progressed too far, one of father's friends, learning about the proposed trip said," Why don't you send that boy aboard one of our sailing ships?" This friend of father's was stationed in New York for a line that had its main office in Glasgow, Scotland. He knew that I liked sailing and had a small boat which I enjoyed immensely in the summer when we were sailing on Long Island Sound. When this new idea was presented to me, the answer was quickly "Yes."
Fred H. Taylor

Fred selected a splendid ship—the British 2,144-ton steel four-masted barque *Queen Margaret* of Glasgow—with an exemplary master, Captain W. J. Scott. Slightly larger than *Hawaiian Isles*—both ships were built on Scotland's Clyde, the great center of iron and steel shipbuilding—*Queen Margaret* was likewise "clipper" rigged, Yankee-style, with three skysails over royals and single topgallants.[1] She proved to be one of the smartest and fastest carriers of the nineties. She was lost by going ashore in the English Channel in 1913.

Fred joined the barque, which was laden with case oil loaded at Brooklyn, late in September. She was bound first for Freemantle, Australia. Although a paying passenger, Fred, to circumvent regulations, was signed on as "ship's navigator." And in fact Captain Scott not only regularly employed him to mark the times of sights, but instructed him in navigation sufficiently so that before long Fred was able to work out longitudes. Possibly for his own amusement, Captain Scott also appointed Fred ship's doctor:

Sailors aboard the four-masted barque Queen Margaret *laying aloft to furl the crojik in a rainstorm, with bad weather threatening.*
FRED H. TAYLOR. COURTESY SMITHSONIAN INSTITUTION.

> He had given me a large book which described certain illnesses and what should be used for a cure. In turn, there was a large cabinet hanging from the wall in which there were twelve bottles...each having a number on it from one to twelve. When the captain and I were seated, the ailing sailors...would present themselves one at a time, explain their complaint, and I in turn would look through my doctor's book, endeavor to fit the complaint to some description, and then pick out a number. I would turn to the captain and tell him what I had in mind, and he always gave me the go-ahead.

Queen Margaret made an uneventful passage. A conservative navigator, Captain Scott steered well clear of all land—even Tristan da Cunha—until making landfall on the Australian coast on December 22, ninety-nine days out. Fred was sorry to see it. He returned on a steamer and never went to sea again, instead pursuing a successful career on Wall Street. Many years later he and grandson "Tad" Lhaman, searching in his attic, retrieved the delicate nitrate negatives of wonderful images made aboard *Queen Margaret*.

Left: Sailors "shifting," or, changing sails. Slatting calms being very harmful to canvas, the strong, good sails used in the North Atlantic were replaced by old sails as the equatorial latitudes were approached. Once the "doldrums" were passed, the good suit was bent on again in preparation for heavy weather in the South Atlantic.
FRED H. TAYLOR. COURTESY OF SMITHSONIAN INSTITUTION.

Below: Sailors furling the main upper-topsail. Barque Queen Margaret.
FRED H. TAYLOR. COURTESY OF SMITHSONIAN INSTITUTION.

Sea-struck Fred Taylor in the fore top of the barque Queen Margaret.
FRED H. TAYLOR. COURTESY OF SMITHSONIAN INSTITUTION.

At the fore truck. Boys, who were traditionally assigned to furl the skysails and royals, had to shinny up as best they could.
FRED H. TAYLOR. COURTESY OF SMITHSONIAN INSTITUTION.

Running her easting down, barque Queen Margaret *rolls her rail under.*
FRED H. TAYLOR. COURTESY OF SMITHSONIAN INSTITUTION.

Holystoning the poop with sand, water, and sandstone "prayer books," barque Queen Margaret.
FRED H. TAYLOR. COURTESY OF SMITHSONIAN INSTITUTION.

Preserved Fish, et al.

Some Other Outstanding New Bedford Mercantile Movers and Shakers.

THE SEAFARING DELANO FAMILY were early settlers of Fairhaven. Warren, Jr.—Franklin Roosevelt's grandfather—and brother Edward were partners, along with the Forbes brothers, in Russell & Company, the leading American trading firm at Canton. In the 1840s one Humphrey Hathaway Swift, while living at Canton with the Delanos, sent a cargo of tea worth $10,000, purchased on credit, to Brazil. His speculation paid off handsomely, and he continued trading with Brazil for more than fifty years, becoming an important power in Brazilian affairs.[2]

In the early 1800s New Bedford candle and whale oil merchant Cornelius Grinnell moved his business to New York; in 1815 he formed a partnership with his cousin, Preserved Fish, a New Bedford whaling captain, and the two founded the Swallowtail Line of Liverpool packets.[3] Grinnell's son Joseph became a member of the firm, while son Moses began his career working for William J. Rotch. Soon, desiring wider horizons, Moses shipped as supercargo on a vessel bound for Brazil. His subsequent speculation in a cargo of coffee for a European port proved most fortunate. Joseph, retiring to New Bedford due to ill health, became one of the Commonwealth's great men of the era and, among other accomplishments, founded New Bedford's textile industry.

Moses and brother Henry, along with brother-in-law Robert Minturn, eventually took the firm over, forming Grinnell, Minturn & Company. Grinnell, Minturn & Company—the Hathaways may have been the "Company"—became one of the great shipowning firms in an era of extraordinary maritime expansion. Operating packet lines to Liverpool and London, they owned some fifty ships employed in various trades, and played a large roll in the development of the port of New York.[4] (A Delano would also become a partner.) The Hathaways owned one-eighth of the firm's famous clipper *Flying Cloud*, whose master, Captain Josiah Perkins Cressy, had earlier distinguished himself while commanding the Hathaway's old ship *Oneida*.

The Grinnells' enterprise and success in New York, while outstanding, was but part of an invasion by shrewd New England Yankees, particularly from southern New England, and who led the development of the Port of New York, and the great city it fostered. A New York merchant recalled:

> TAKE FOR INSTANCE such a firm as Grinnell, Minturn & Co. In their counting room they have New York boys and New England boys. Moses H. Grinnell comes down in the morning and says to

> John, a New York boy—"Charley [*sic*], take my overcoat up to my house on Fifth Avenue." Mr. Charley takes the coat, mutters something about "I'm not an errand boy. I came here to learn business," and moves reluctantly. Mr. Grinnell sees it, and at the same time, one of his New England clerks says, "I'll take it up." "That is right. Do so," says Mr. G., and to himself he says, "that boy is smart, will work," and gives him plenty to do. He gets promoted—gets the confidence of the chief clerk and employers, and eventually gets into the firm as partner. It's so all over the city.[5]

It should also be noted that the southern New England coastline and navigable river valleys lying west of the barrier of Cape Cod fell naturally within the commercial sway of New York. Indeed, New Bedford has been called New York's Down East.

Dubious Distinction

A Bucko Mate Aboard the Francis.

THE LEGAL STATUS OF sailors aboard ship, as evolved from ancient times, was comparable to that of soldiers under a short enlistment, with their rights severely limited. Great authority was granted to masters, and, by extension, his subordinates, the mates. However necessary this arrangement might have been in the grand scheme of commerce, it was also a situation ripe for exploitation and abuse. Power, indeed, corrupts. Mistreatment of sailors, as defined by the law, was technically illegal, but relatively few mates or captains were ever convicted of doing so.[6] The difficulty of producing sailor witnesses for a trial—particularly if the alleged offenses were reported in a foreign port—made successful prosecution difficult.

Nor, of course, were sailors viewed as being reliable or unbiased witnesses, particularly in light of the way that too many carried on in port. Also, the forecastle often enough served as a social safety valve, a convenient refuge for the desperate, the dangerous, and the deranged. Many a ship was burned or its hull bored by departing malcontents. And surely many a bucko mate found himself being helped over the rail on a dark night at sea.[7]

In the 1890s San Francisco, a port long synonymous with the exploitation of seamen, became center of reform efforts. Unhappy with the response of the press to tales of brutality aboard arriving ships, the San Francisco-based National Seaman's Union of America published a pamphlet, *The Red Record,* containing brief accounts of alleged outrages, including the following:

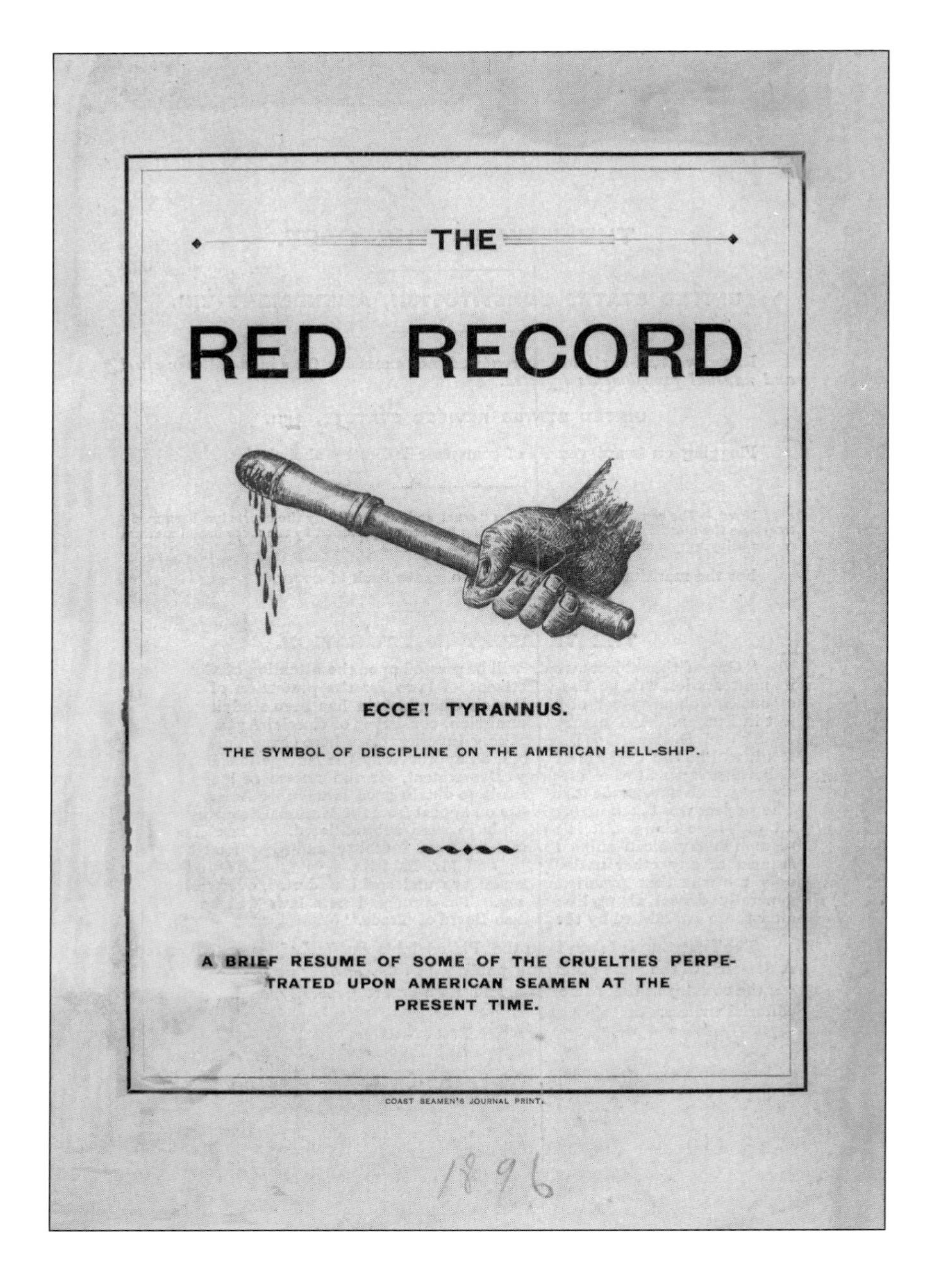
THE

RED RECORD

ECCE! TYRANNUS.

THE SYMBOL OF DISCIPLINE ON THE AMERICAN HELL-SHIP.

A BRIEF RESUME OF SOME OF THE CRUELTIES PERPETRATED UPON AMERICAN SEAMEN AT THE PRESENT TIME.

COAST SEAMEN'S JOURNAL PRINT.

1896

Francis, Captain Doan [*sic*], arrived in San Francisco, October 1893. First-Mate R. Crocker (late of *Commodore T. H. Allen* and *Tam O'Shanter*) accused of gross brutality to the crew. Seamen bore marks on their persons when they complained to the Commissioner. Crocker arrested and admitted to bail. Crew compelled to go to sea in the meantime. Case dismissed for lack of evidence.[8]

Standing six-foot three, and weighing 260 pounds, Mr. Crocker was truly a piece of work. When serving as first mate aboard the ship *Tam O'Shanter*, of Freeport, Maine, under the notorious Captain Thomas Peabody, Crocker was accused of having bitten off portions of sailor Harry Hill's left palm, taken a mouthful of flesh from Hill's left arm, and bitten Hill's left nostril off as far as the bridge of the nose.[9]

When serving as second mate aboard the ship *Commodore T. H. Allen*, of Richmond, Maine, Crocker was accused of knocking down the black cook with a belaying pin for having allowed the watch to warm themselves in the galley. Crocker then allegedly tried to gouge the fallen man's eyes out. The *Allen*'s Captain Robert Merriman was notorious as well, as was his son, Robert, Jr., first mate, who reportedly kicked the cook while he was down. Captain Merriman reportedly then made the cook wipe up his blood. After an 1894 voyage the Merrimans were accused of having beaten up a man together, the father using his fists while the son wielded a rope's end.

Likely Crocker, Peabody, the Merrimans, and others of their ilk were, to varying degrees, psychopaths. Doane clearly was not. To cast the best possible light on the situation, perhaps Captain Doane, with the *Francis* ready to sail, badly needed a mate—by the 1890s capable square-rig mates were becoming scarce—and believed that he could keep the bucko on a tight leash. And indeed, there were no claims that Crocker bit anyone aboard the *Frances!* It is also likely that he was a marked man, drawing complaints even when on good behavior.

A former sailor's account regarding an 1886 incident aboard Besse's bark *Belle of Oregon*, Captain Edwin Matthews (of New Bedford), from New York to Saigon with case oil, depicted what was likely a more typical means of enforcing discipline aboard a Besse ship:

> WE HAD THE USUAL troubles so far as rows on board are concerned and as the food was quite poor.... Later on, when nearing China, the crew again became disaffected and practically refused duty. We were all then called to the mainmast where the mate, with note book, made entries of the confab that followed, and the boy members of the crew were put to work shining up the hand-cuffs.[10]

Captain Frost's Careless Adventure

An Incident in the
Chinese Passenger Trade.

OPIUM, TO WHICH MANY Chinese were addicted, was a legal substance in the United States and widely used as a sedative, in patent medicines, and for making laudanum and morphia. Whereas the duty on medicinal opium—as used by whites—was forty cents a pound, opium prepared for smoking—as used by the Chinese—was $6 per pound. Every ship entering San Francisco from Hong Kong was presumed to have had opium hidden aboard it.[11]

Under federal law, one quarter of the value of seized opium was awarded to the seizing officers, unless the seizure was made as a direct result of information provided by an informer, in which case the informer received the reward. In July 1873 seven Inspectors of Customs at San Francisco petitioned to be awarded their shares of 96 ½ pounds of opium discovered aboard the bark *Alden Besse* hidden in a bread locker, in the steward's room, in the "kitchen," in the pantry, in a storeroom, and in a boat hanging on the port davits.[12] The opium was not listed in the manifest, had not been invoiced, and was not accompanied by a consular certificate. It was the property of the master, Captain Frost.[13]

On June 5, 1873, the *Besse*, just arrived from Hong Kong and anchored in the stream, was immediately put under close customs guard. The following day the passengers and baggage were searched, resulting in several seizures. The previous year Agent Leaman had found 450 pounds of opium in a locker under Captain Frost's bunk, and, on June 10, when the bark came to the dock, this locker was found to contain 4,000 cigars and fifty-three pounds of tobacco.

> THIS SAME LEAMAN...had a conversation with the said Captain, who after expressing his alarm at the result which would probably follow the thorough and systematic search which was being made, said to him, "Officer, I have 100 pounds of opium. Can't you get it off for me? Can't you take it off in your pockets? I will go and put it into the steward's room, or pantry, or bread locker." Leaman informed the other officers in charge of this conversation, who thereupon...seized the opium....[14]

Previously, when the passengers were being searched, a Mr. C. A. Morrill, Special Agent, had boarded the vessel and requested that the captain's room not be searched, "alleging the sickness of the captain's child." The petition was occasioned by the claim, filed by Special Agent Morrill, that he had been informed that the *Besse* would have contraband on board belonging to the captain, and that he had asked the surveyor of customs to seize the opium, "as he was very anxious to secure it for his informant's benefit, whose name he refused to divulge."

The surveyor, however, found in favor of the seizing officers, being "of the opinion that the suggestions of Mr. Morrill were of no assistance in making the seizure." To wit:

> THOSE NIGHT INSPECTORS who were detailed to search the *Alden Besse* had no reason to suppose they were engaged in a scramble with the honorable office of Special Agent of the Treasury, when they saw that estimable claimant looming up in the gang-way, while they were at work seeking to discover frauds on the Customs Revenue; or when he disappeared so suddenly over the vessel's side, that he was disappointed, and was hastening to their superior Officer to lodge verbal information, which intended to forestall any discovery by them, and to appropriate their prerequisites.

Captain Frost was promptly replaced by Captain William H. Besse himself, and the bark quickly departed or Nanaimo, British Columbia, to load coal for Hong Kong. Subsequent masters under Besse's management evidently included Captain Cyrus Noyes and his younger brother Allen, both of whom we met at Hong Kong.

The Fall of the House of Besse

The Demise of
Captain William Besse's Fleet and Fortune.

DESPITE CARLETON ALLEN'S effusive account of the well-ordered life at sea aboard the bark *Guy C. Goss*, Captain William Besse's career as a ship-owner was nearing a sad end. The 1890s had been challenging years for Captain Besse. Although the novel bark *Olympic* of 1892, designed for the spar trade, performed well, she would be the last ship built for the fleet, rather than the lead ship of a new fleet. In 1894 or '95, not long after a refit at Bath, *Western Belle* was sold to be cut-down as a coal barge.[15] In 1895 the bark *William W. Crapo*, loaded with nitrates, burned in a Chilean port. In 1897 the shapely bark *George S. Homer* went missing after departing Philadelphia with case oil. *Belle of Oregon* and *Francis* both went under other management.[16]

By 1898, Besse, age seventy, adapting to the times, had for several years been engaged as well in the East Coast barge business, operating the Belle

Line. His son Walter had followed his father into the shipping business, becoming the junior partner of the New York firm of Sherwood & Besse. War with Spain ignited a boom in coastal shipping rates and Walter was made general manager of the Atlantic Transportation Company, evidently a hastily hove-together financial construct intended either to take advantage of the shipping boom, or, possibly, of its investors. The ATC's board of directors included the wealthy New Jersey wire prince, F. W. Roebling, and New York toiletries king Gilbert Colgate.[17]

In any event, Walter strove to assemble a large fleet of barges and steamers in a hurry to fulfill a contract between the ATC and the Chesapeake & Ohio Rail to deliver 4,000,000 tons of coal yearly from Newport News to northeast ports. Father William's Belle Line was folded into the fleet.[18]

Seeking still more tonnage in, Walter looked to the Great Lakes, where his father's career as a ship owner had begun back in the 1850s with the purchase of two "Laker" schooners brought to saltwater. The recent advent of Rockefeller's steel steamers on the Lakes had depressed the value of wooden tonnage, and in October word surfaced of the ATC's plan to charter a large fleet of Lakers for transfer to the coast. One report listed thirty-nine schooners and seven schooner-barges inducted into the fleet, while another reported the acquisition of seven steamers. Each newly recruited vessel, when passing Ogdensburg, New York, was to receive a coat of black paint with its name painted in large white letters, so that its

Captain William H. Besse.

progress to the sea could be reported by lighthouse keepers. The news "created consternation among the other coast shipping men, who say that the business will be ruined...."[19]

> THE VESSELS BEGAN leaving the lakes October 1st and the last of them will be gone by November 15th. Some will pass down the lower locks of the St. Lawrence river, but some will have to run the rapids, as they are too long for the locks. (*The Door County Advocate*, 8 Oct. 1898.)

How many vessels actually made it to saltwater is not known, but the loss of several that did, and of several other ATC barges, in the terrible *Portland* Gale of November 26 precipitated the rapid collapse of the scheme, possibly through an inability to obtain further insurance, espe-

Bark Western Belle *at Bath in 1892 after undergoing an overhaul. Her sheer is so fair that historians have mistaken her for new, despite her reduced rig.*
WILSON F. KLIPPEL. COURTESY OF MRS. CHARLES E. HEWITT.

cially on the Lakers.[20] Early in January of 1899 it was reported that the "affairs of the company are becoming complicated," as its tugs, steamers, and barges—the latter including the old *Belle of Oregon*—were seized all along the coast.[21]

The day following William Besse's death in April, 1900—a death surely advanced by the hopeless mess—Walter declared bankruptcy, claiming $239,727 in liabilities and assets of but $3,500.[22] Captain William Besse's estate totaled but $17,000, with outstanding notes from Walter Besse, and Sherwood & Besse amounting to $46,000.[23] Walter also owed money to the owners of several of the square-riggers in Besse's old fleet.

William Besse's obituary described him as having been a "typical ship owner of the old school...a sturdy champion of American built vessels [who] regretted the fact that first-class American sailing ships are nearly all swept from the ocean." He had served New Bedford as an alderman, and had been a prominent member of the Trinatarian church.[24]

That William Besse, against all odds, had kept his house flag flying from the main trucks of even several fine wooden ships in the opening year of the twentieth century is perhaps his best eulogy.[25]

A Jury Rudder

Replacing and improving the Guy C. Goss's *rudder.*

On March 7, 1900, the bark *Guy C. Goss*, Captain Walter Mallett, loaded with Puget Sound timber, was running before a westerly gale one day after passing Cape Horn. As Mrs. Mallett later wrote:

> We were at dinner when the bark suddenly came up into the wind, almost aback. A dreadful flapping of sails. Captain soon found the ship did not answer the helm, and on looking over the stern found the rudder braces torn away from the rudder post. The thumping at rudder head was dreadful. Captain tried to see if anything could be done in way of repairs, but found it hopeless. So sawed rudder head off and let rudder sink, which it immediately proceeded to do.

There was, of course, plenty of suitable timber at hand for constructing a jury rudder. There were good reasons why a copy of the old rudder, with a full-length rudder post, would not have answered. Hanging such a rudder required intact gudgeons, material for pintles, and flat water, none of which obtained. Instead, the type built included a false sternpost, the head of which was inserted in the rudder well, and which was held against the actual sternpost by means of cleats and chain guys. The rudder's aft-facing tiller was steered by tackles hung from timber boomkins. The assembly was constructed, and installed without difficulty, over eight days. The *Goss* then completed a very creditable passage of 117 days from Cape

Above and Below: Jury rudder of the bark Guy. C. Goss. *1900.*
CAPTAIN WALTER M. MALLETT, COURTESY OF CAPTAIN W. J. L. PARKER.

Flattery to the Delaware Capes.

Mallet had long been convinced that the *Goss*'s rudder—and those of other ships—was too big, causing the bark to steer hard when sailing off the wind in following seas. Indeed, twisted rudder heads were perhaps the most notable weakness of the latter-day American wooden square-riggers, and were very likely the cause of some ships' having gone missing. Mallet took advantage of this opportunity to test his theory, making the new rudder fifteen, rather than twenty feet, long. The replacement proved much superior to its predecessor, and the new permanent rudder was built to the new dimensions. Captain Mallet, describing the jury rudder to the bark's new San Francisco owners, wrote:

> IT WAS A GREATER SUCCESS than I anticipated; we could handle the vessel very well and carry all square sails crossing the trades. We went through two gales with it. It steered us a distance of about 6,500 miles, which we made in 72 days.[26]

But that did not quit finish the story. Admiralty lawyers, a very litigious tribe, kept busy filing and defending against "general average" suits, concerned with the sharing of expenses associated with the voluntary sacrifice of part of the ship or cargo for the preservation of the whole. In 1902 the owners of the *Goss* sued the Keystone Yellow Pine Co., the owners of the cargo concerning the value of the old rudder which was cast adrift, and the extra wages paid to he crew during the time that the new rudder was built and hung. The judge found the rudder to have had no value, but decided that the expense of the extra wages should be shared.[27]

---

1. Her rig very likely reflected the tastes of her first master, Captain D. F. Faulkner, a Nova Scotian. (On Fred's passage First Mate Cotton was also a Nova Scotian.) The 1886 English-built iron ship *Bangalore* was rigged Yankee-fashion to suit her captain, Ray Congdon, a native of Rhode Island. Hawaiian Isles, of course, was built for an American owner.

2. Captain William L. Hawes, *New Bedford in [the] China Trade*, New Bedford, 1940, n.p.

3. Contrary to the delightful legend, Preserved Fish was not discovered as an infant floating in a box marked as such.

4. Robert Greenhalgh Albion, *The Rise of the Port of New York* (Yew York: Charles Scribner's Sons, 1939), p. 247; also Hawes.

5. Albion, *Rise of the Port of New York,* pp. 244–45.

6. R.S. 5347. 1835. Masters and officers of American vessels were forbidden, "without justifiable cause" to beat, wound, imprison, withhold "suitable food ," or inflict "cruel and unusual punishment" upon crew members. Of course one could

sail a three-decker through the loopholes provided. Flogging was abolished as a legal form of corporal punishment in 1850. See Walter Macarthur, *The Seaman's Contract*, San Francisco, 1919.

7. Nor, of course, was violence found only at sea. Far from it. The nation was but a generation removed from slavery and the Civil War. In the West, Indian wars raged. In the South, outrages against blacks were not only common but were beyond the reach of federal intervention. Big-city police dispensed justice with a club, as did private railroad "bulls." And conditions in many other lands were no better, if not far worse.

8. *The Red Record*, San Francisco, 1896, p. 16. There was no mention of the *Francis* incident in the *Examiner*, although it did list the ship's general cargo from New York, which included piano stools, books and games, bathtubs, oilcloth, harness hames, candy, tricycles, stoves, egg coal, glassware, clothespins, sheep churns, horseshoes, steel rails, copy presses, and scores of other items, including two whaleboats. *San Francisco Examiner*, 14 Oct. 1893. The October 19 *Examiner*, however, carried a story about the celebrated Bath-built and owned "shipentine" *Shenandoah*, under the famous Captain Jim Murphy, also recently arrived from New York. According to reports to the press by two passengers, the crew was primarily composed of boys, old men, and idiots. The food was so bad that the men stole grease "slush" to eat. When a boy fell into the sea from aloft Murphy made no attempt to rescue him, although the boy was seen struggling on the surface for "fifteen" minutes, and that Murphy "made ten times more fuss the next day over the loss of a fish from his line." In fairness, Murphy maintained that high seas and wind made any rescue attempt impossible, which was usually the case aboard a large ship in a gale. The claim that the boy could be seen for fifteen minutes was surely an exaggeration. Murphy complained to the Sewalls, the ship's managing owners, about the bad salt beef shipped on that passage; he was known for feeding his sailors well.

9. In 1876, on his first voyage in command aboard the bark *C. O. Whitmore*, Peabody had the second mate, hands bound, placed astride the sharp keel of an upturned boat, evidently causing a gangrenous groin infection. The disrated officer was later confined and starved in the lazarette, where he died. The sailors claimed that the second mate had been punished for refusing to brutalize the men. Peabody claimed that the man was insubordinate, and had died from a venereal disease. After a celebrated trial a Boston judge found Peabody not guilty. *Boston Journal*, 15 March 1879 and 21, 23 April 1879. Frederick C. Matthews, in *American Merchant Ships*, Series II (Salem, MA: Marine Research Society, 1931), p. 328, described Peabody as: "A strict disciplinarian, he was not well regarded by his crews." That same year he wrote privately: "I was a freight clerk on the [steamer] *Sheridan* when Capt. Peabody was master and got well acquainted with him...he was a hard loser in arguments. He was a gentleman with the passengers...but had a very hard name with seafaring people. His record is very bad. He came nearly being lynched at Hong Kong after the arrival of the *C. O. Whitmore*.... I have seen doings on the *Sheridan* that caused me to wonder how he had managed not to put her ashore before he did." Letter to Capt. P. A. McDonald, 27 Dec. 1931. Courtesy of Andrew Nesdall.

10. Frederick C. Matthews, *American Merchant Ships*, Series I (Salem, MA:

Marine Research Society, 1930), p. 46. For an account of the author's experience aboard *Belle of Oregon,* see William B. Sturtevant, "A Boy's First Day at Sea—1880," *American Neptune,* vol 1, no. 1, p. 58.

11. L. De Colange, *The American Dictionary of Commerce* (Boston, 1881), p. 832. Aboard the Pacific Mail Line steamers a large iron box, fireproof, almost airtight, and capable of holding several opium smokers, was located in the center of the forecastle deck.

12. The first vessel built for Captain William H. Besse's fleet, the *Alden Besse,* featured superior construction, modern appliances, and a fine finish. She was framed with pasture white oak, fitted with extra hanging and lodging knees, had very large breasthooks and diagonal pointers, was fastened with copper and treenails, and was thoroughly salted. She spent most of her long life in the Pacific, for a period serving as a training ship for the Japanese navy. In 1879 her hail changed from Wareham to Portland, Oregon, although she remained under Besse's management until 1887. She was employed in the Honolulu–West Coast trade, then laid up as a coal hulk in San Pedro, where a visiting Japanese admiral was said to have been moved to tears by the sight of her fallen state. Refitted in 1909, in 1915 she joined Hollywood's movie fleet for a final fling under sail. She disappeared from the *List of Merchant Vessels* in 1920. *Bath Daily Times*, 31 March 1871; *Wareham Courier*, 23 March 1916; Mark Hennesey Notes, Library, Maine Maritime Museum.

13. Frost is not identified in the petition. Shipmasters received but a small salary—perhaps $20 a month—to be supplemented by dividends on their shares in the ship (which income might go towards paying off the loan for the shares), and by a 5 percent primage on gross receipts. Captains customarily also had a stake in the ship's slop chest, selling cheap clothing and other personal items marked up to the sailors. Many engaged in a variety of kickback schemes. And then there was also the old practice of individual "adventures," or speculations, legal or nor.

14. *Application of Seizing Officers J. B. Leaman, L. M. Manzer, John H. Tennant, E. J. Levy, Geo. W. Towle, Jr., George Rodden, and W. W. Wilson, for Share of 96 1/2 Pounds of Opium Seized on American Bark* Alden Besse, San Francisco, Surveyor's Office, 29 July 1873, p. 6.

15. *Western Belle*'s buyers were Garfield & Proctor, of New Bedford, despite Besse's continued listing as owner in the *Record of Ameri*can *and Foreign Shipping*. Beginning in the 1880s many American ships and barks were cut down into barges, to be operated in competition with the schooner fleet primarily in the coal trade. The usual method of "barging" a ship included removing her main deck bulwarks, reducing the rig to a stump schooner rig. (Sails were set in response to whistle signals from the tug, and both added propulsion and steadied the barge.) "Ship barges" were popular with their three-man crews, who enjoyed the ample comforts of the luxurious cabins. *Western Belle* retained her official registration number as an ocean-going sailing vessel, albeit as a schooner. Regarding *Western Belle*'s conversion, an unidentified 1904 New Bedford clipping noted: "[*Western Belle*] is now spending the evening of her life as a dirty, grimy coal barge.... It is a consolation to know that the lady who used to be the guiding star of the aristocratic clipper ship is no longer forced to associate with the plebeian coal barge. When the vessel was transformed the figurehead was removed." For some years

the Belle resided in a Marblehead, Massachusetts, seaside figurehead garden. Today she is at the Peabody-Essex Museum in Salem, Massachusetts.

16. *Belle of Oregon* went under the management of her long-time master, Captain Edwin Mathews, who bought a substantial part of her. The *Francis*, of course, went under the management of Captain Frank Stone.

17. New York *Maritime Register*, 5 Oct. 1898.

18. Although William's name was not mentioned in news stories about the ATC, he was evidently involved in the company's affairs. A suit brought against William's widow in 1904 by the Burlee Dry Dock Co., of Staten Island, resulted from a dispute over an 1898 contract between Besse and Burlee regarding the purchase by Besse of certain vessels for which Besse agreed to pay Burlee $65,750 by means of drafts amounting to $20,000 and the remainder in ATC stock. One ATC note for $10,750 having become worthless, Burlee sued to be compensated from Besse's estate. The suit was rejected. *Burlee Dry Dock Co. v. Besse,* Circuit Court of Appeals, First Circuit. 13 May 1904. No. 525. *The Federal Reporter*, Vol. 130. My thanks to Captain Doug Lee, who puts himself to sleep reading cases from *The Federal Reporter.*

19. *Industrial Journal*, 4 Nov. 1898.

20. Named after the Boston-to-Portland steamer *Portland*, which was lost with all 176 persons aboard, this late-season hurricane caused the loss of over one hundred vessels from New York to Maine.

21. *New York Maritime Register*, 11 Jan. 1899.

22. New York *Times*, 11 April 1900.

23. My thanks to Bob Birely, first-rate courthouse snoop.

24. *Evening Standard*, 10 and 11 April 1900.

25. In 1900 the ship *William J. Rotch* became the ship *Helen A. Wyman* of New York, the bark *Gerard C. Tobey* was sold into the profitable Hawaii –San Francisco trade, and the ship *Henry Failing* was sold into the Pacific lumber trade. The *Goss* had been sold to San Francisco owners involved in the Alaskan salmon fishery in 1900 before Besse's death. For the next twenty years she sailed north in the spring with Chinese cannery workers and supplies, returning at season's end with workers and canned salmon. In 1925 the *Goss* delivered a cargo of lumber from Vancouver to New Zealand, where she was libeled and sold for a small sum. After forty-seven years of hard service (yet with her sheerline still looking remarkably fair) the *Goss* was beached for conversion into a stone crushing plant. John Sharps, the son of the plant manager, and who, as a young boy, lived with his family in the cabin, recalled sixty-five years later: "Life 'aboard ship,' for a small boy, was just wonderful with many interesting places to play. At times I would look up at the mastheads and if the clouds were moving, I would imagine the ship was sailing.... The Master's quarters, although showing signs of age, were beautiful. The saloon, I think, was paneled with birds-eye maple...the Master's sleeping cabin [had a] massive four-poster bed.... Port and starboard in the saloon there were red plush velvet sofas set into alcoves. Above each of these were two small frosted-glass windows with, I think, delicate floral patterns etched in.... On the for'd bulkhead there was a cabinet with a marble top and a brass rail which my mother kept polished." In 1935 the old ship was destroyed by fire, possibly the result of arson. *The (Maine Maritime Museum) Rhumb Line*, Dec. 2001.

26. Lincoln Colcord, "A Jury Rudder for the Bark Guy C. Goss," *American*

Neptune, vol. 2, p. 65.

27. *The Federal Reporter*, vol. 117, Oct.–Nov. 1902, p. 287. In 1898 Besse sued the owners of a cargo aboard *Belle of Oregon* for a portion of his expenses when he traveled to San Francisco after the bark, on a passage from Oregon to New York, put in after being damaged by a hurricane. It is interesting that although the cargo of salmon, wool, and barley was valued at $133,518.69, the ship was valued at but $7,270.68, and the "freight" was $4,154.30. Besse received partial satisfaction. *The Federal Reporter*, vol. 85, April-May 1898, pp. 677–78. My thanks to Captain Doug Lee.

Index

THE MARTHA'S VINEYARD HISTORICAL SOCIETY was founded in 1923 to preserve and present the heritage and history of the island. This is accomplished through exhibits, educational programs for students of all ages, a research library and genealogy program, an Oral History Center, various publications, and by actively caring for and adding to its collections. *Sea Struck* was inspired by Tod Swift's journal, which is in its collections.

THE NEW BEFORD WHALING MUSEUM is the world's foremost museum devoted to the historic interaction of humans with whales worldwide. The museum explores the history of whaling and the rich cultures—and conservation issues—it inspired. Located in the world's greatest whaling port, the museum brings to life the whaling era and history of the local area through exhibits, publications, and programs.